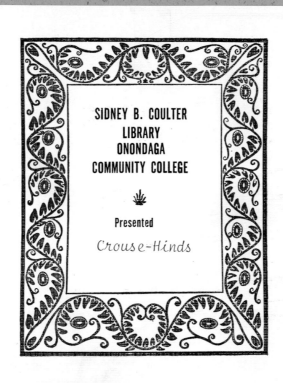

COOPER INDUSTRIES

The first Cooper cupola blower, obviously a one-horsepower operation.

COOPER INDUSTRIES

1833-1983

David Neal Keller

Ohio University Press
Athens, Ohio. London

Cooper Industries, 1833-1983, was
commissioned and funded by Cooper
Industries in observance of its
one hundred and fiftieth anniversary

Table of Contents

Acknowledgments

No history can be written without the support of many persons. In this instance, they numbered in the hundreds, ranging from approximately eighty who provided in-depth interviews to those who took a moment to explain a job or answer a question.

President Robert Cizik and other corporate officers took whatever time was necessary for interviews, and not one suggested limits on my investigative research. Senior Vice President Alan E. Riedel also personally contacted many retired employees to pave the way for my interviews. In each instance, I was made to feel comfortable in probing for explanations that would add significance to the story.

Thomas W. Campbell, Cooper vice president, and members of his public affairs staff were particularly helpful in coordinating the effort and checking information from time to time. Diane Erbstoesser assisted in locating and gathering photographs and in other ways providing regular liaison with corporate headquarters. Carl Mueller not only helped find information, but also remained unruffled by my frequent telephone interruptions of his primary work. The same is true of Marge Warden, Ellen Myers, Pat Mottram, and public affairs secretaries. Rita Kelly, Richard Hanlon, and John Lichty went far beyond the call of duty as coordinators for Cooper Energy Services, Crouse-Hinds, and Kirsch, respectively.

One pleasant, additional benefit of preparing the history was that some of the men and women I interviewed became good friends. Among those persons was Charles Cooper, grandson of one of the founding brothers (Elias) and son of former president, Charles Gray Cooper. After welcoming me into his home, spending many hours in conversation, and showing me a wealth of documents he had compiled before and after his retirement, "Charlie" continued his help through regular correspondence, but died before the book was completed. Beyond the information he contributed, the pride he expressed in Cooper Industries and his former colleagues was a great inspiration to someone attempting to capture the spirit, as well as the anatomy, of a company. Others who made similar efforts to assist in the research were former presidents Eugene Miller and Lawrence Williams, Charles Reagle, Ralph Boyer, Lloyd Lanphere, Michael Pollock, Stanley Johnson, Jr., and Paul Nicholson.

In singling out those persons I do not mean to detract from many others who helped through interviews, the loan of materials, and in other ways. Among them were Royal Anderson, Lewis Barnard, Jr., Leonard Bloomquist, Louis Bollo, Russell Burgett, Jack Castor, Mason Cocroft, William Crooks, Roland Doeden, Len Dwors, Leroy Fegley, Bill Fetters, Edwin Fithian, Dennis Gallogly, Hewitt Gehres, William Gilchrist, Gene Grove, Isabel Harrington, Ted Helsel, Harold Johnson, Stanley Johnson, Sr., Robert Jones, Anthony Kanda, Thomas Kraner, George Monroe, Fayette Plumb II, Dorothy Porter, Robert Rafferty, Joe Rega, Clarence Schwabel, Donald Steele, Harold Stevens, Arch Warden, Carl Weller, and Marshall Winkle.

To all these persons, and to my wife, Marian, who assisted in many ways throughout the project, I am most appreciative.

Introduction

In researching a corporate lineage, there is an initial tendency to dwell on the beginning years. The pioneering spirit of a man who balanced all his personal assets and energies on the thin thread of a frontier manufacturing enterprise amidst an agricultural society has a high degree of intrigue. And history is mercifully forgetful of the thousands who lost the gamble. When we glance back over a century and a half, we see mainly the survivors. Their stories become legends of success. A complex, successful industrial corporation exists today because a few daring men with courage and foresight clenched their fists, set their jaws, and plunged into new enterprises.

It is exciting and true. Founders deserve to be heroes. But a fascination with days gone by creates misconceptions. The greatest of these is a feeling that pioneering is a spirit of the past. Another is the premise that an initial step into the unknown is the most critical move that will be made.

Industry flourishes and suffers in cycles. Heavy industry is one of the most cyclical of all. As research for this book deepened, it became apparent that Cooper Industries can look back on so many venturous efforts that the only frustration is realizing it will be impossible to name all the persons involved. And that is too bad, because this is a story about people. Together, these people have met a never-ending series of apparent crises with new ideas, new products, and new financial structures. Some problems seemed so ominous they could have scuttled companies now included in the corporation.

But many persons were determined that their groups would survive. Even when it is possible to identify the specific inventor of a new engine or the creator of a new design, there is no determining exactly how many associates at the machines and in the offices contributed important thoughts to a project. The development of a new market could be attributed to a carefully planned management study of business trends or to the observation of a single salesman. Always there has been a need to project thinking into a *new* unknown future while meeting current situations. Even when total energy was being thrust into winning World War II, someone had to peer into a peacetime economy that would follow.

Each day's event is really just a passing scene in a continuous historic epic. Yet, each is vital to its time. And in reality, each is vital to the future, to some degree. The companies now included in Cooper Industries, Inc., came together at different periods of history because in each instance it was right for the times. Together they reflect not only the story of Cooper, but also the story of American free enterprise. This adds greatly to the value, as well as the interest, of a Cooper history.

As the story unfolds, it becomes evident that pioneering spirit does not die, it just changes form. It remains the key to industrial progress as much today as when Charles and Elias Cooper decided in 1833 to invest all they could borrow in a small Ohio foundry.

David Neal Keller

1

Plows and Troughs

The course of history is a phenomenon that defies all rational concepts of navigation. There are few reliable stars on which mankind can establish a fix. So we wander. And in our wanderings, we accuse ourselves of failing to recognize previously discovered waters. Perhaps that is true. But attempts to turn back have rarely, if ever, been successful. Waters change. The choice is between resisting or reacting.

History has been charted by those who react positively. Some call them adventurers, gamblers, and in a sense those are apt descriptions. Knowledge and skillful planning can improve the odds, but there is no sure thing.

Yet, history's reactors are not thrill seekers leaping into the darkness simply because they know not what is there. Rather, they respond to situations with positive forward movement. They recognize need as opportunity and view a problem as something that can be solved. They are the first travelers willing to change course, and when their decisions prove to be correct, they are considered lucky to have been in the right place at the right time.

Rare indeed is the person or nation or company that has never blundered. So history is a zigzag course. Happily so. If it were predictable, success would become humdrum. There would be no human decision, only acceptance. Fortunately, this is not likely to occur.

There have been many reactors whose individual and group contributions now merge into Cooper Industries, Inc. Some examples are amazingly similar, even though separated widely by time and distance. Coincidence, however, is a less than adequate explanation. More apparent is the common thread that has tied companies now included in Cooper Industries with America's social and industrial progress.

Americans in 1833 were moving west at a rate of more than five hundred per day, primarily because recently completed canal systems provided both passage to cheap land and feasible means of transporting agricultural products back to Eastern markets. The far western state of Ohio moved swiftly from seventeenth to third in population and already was threatening the South's dominance in agriculture. Men of imagination expected the infant railroad to expand westward from its eastern birthplace before many years.

Charles and Elias Cooper were native Ohioans. Their parents, Carey and Elizabeth Cooper, had emigrated from Butler County, Pennsylvania, to Knox County in central Ohio in 1808. Except for service as a captain in the War of 1812, Carey Cooper was a typical frontier farmer. He and his wife had nine children who helped on the farm, except when attending school three months each winter. The family lived on a farm south of Mt. Vernon, where Charles was born January 2, 1811, and Elias on March 26, 1813. They then moved in 1818 to another farm north of town.

After Carey Cooper died in 1831, Charles and his younger brother Elias moved to the Hamline Farm near Zanesville, Ohio, now part of that city. There, the two young men made a meager living digging and hauling coal. In little more than two years, Charles Cooper decided that the coal business in 1833 in Zanesville, Ohio, was not the best combination of time and place for an ambitious, recently married entrepreneur. Many years later he recalled a day that changed his life and created the first chapter in the story of Cooper Industries:

> The coal trade was followed with small success until the fall of 1833, and that summer I think I spent some of the bluest days of my life. One day while sitting on the hill overlooking the town, with the blues as seldom I have had, I saw the smoke curling up from the Old David Foundry. They used, as all foundries did then, an oven or air furnace for smelting, with raw coal for fuel — hence the smoke. I was soon upon my feet and made directly for that concern, and I have never had "foundry" out of my mind since. We commenced immediately to make arrangements for building one. I sold one of my three horses for $50 and took one Brown's note payable in coal for that amount delivered at Zanesville. I sold that note to Cose & Co., paper mill men, and their note for same payable in paper at wholesale. This note I took to Granville, Licking County, and traded to P.A. Taylor & Co., blast furnace men, for the bottom and staves for our first cupola to melt iron in.

With financing completed, Charles, his wife Almeda, and brother Elias, packed all their belongings on two wagons and returned to Mt. Vernon.

In 1833, Mt. Vernon, Ohio, was a collection of brick and frame houses, taverns, a bank, drugstore, cobbler shop, general store, newspaper office, tree lined public square, and slightly more than five hundred residents. Located on the pristine banks of Owl Creek, it had been named by a nostalgic early settler from the Potomac. Charles and Elias Cooper had chosen a site on Sandusky Road in the northwestern corner of the town for their foundry, appropriately named the Mt. Vernon Iron Works. In

the years ahead it would become better known by a series of proprietorship designations that would change with frequent alterations in ownership.

The first such name was C. & E. Cooper. As owners, Charles and Elias
also constituted the entire work force, with the exception of one horse.
Harnessed to a system of wooden shafts and gears, the beast walked a
repetitious circle, generating enough literal horsepower to blow air into the cupola. The brothers carried iron, cleaned ladles, and charged
the furnace by hand, producing from five hundred to seven hundred
pounds of castings in an afternoon. Their first advertisement announced, "C. & E. Cooper inform the citizens of Knox County & the
public generally, that they have lately established and have now in successful blast, an iron foundry."

Cooper claims were modest, but they set a precedent of identifying
specific needs of the times. Among their most popular products were
plows, hog troughs, maple syrup kettles, stoves, sorghum grinders, mill
irons, and wagon boxes. Furthermore, they assured the newspaper reading public that "prices will always be found as low as at Zanesville, or at
any other foundry."

America continued to be primarily an agrarian society, particularly in
the new West, but mechanization was beginning to accelerate change.
McCormick's reaper, invented the same year C. & E. Cooper poured its
first casting, was considered the harbinger of a new agricultural era. Development of iron smelting in the rich anthracite coal country of Pennsylvania in 1836 preluded an age of steel. And in the fall of 1836, C. & E.
Cooper replaced its horse with a small steam engine. "It was a 6-inch
bore and 24-inch stroke set on 6-inch timbers," wrote Charles Cooper.
"The shaft was cast-iron with a flange on the crank end. On this a cast-
iron crank was bolted and keyed. The pin was cast solid on the crank and
filed up a little. It never saw a lathe. The boiler was an 18-foot by 36-inch
plain cylinder."

The company also installed a cast iron blowing cylinder and switched
fuel from charcoal to coke, which the owners made themselves in an old
beehive oven. Production soon tripled. Business was good for C. & E.
Cooper and for all America. A boom-time expansion prompted easy
borrowing and heavy investments, with young western states leading the
way. But the fledgling foundry soon was to gain its first of many experiences with economic cycles. Purchasing power that had been flowing
generously through paper money collapsed suddenly in 1837 when
President Andrew Jackson issued the "Specie Circular," making payment for purchase of public land receivable only in gold and silver. Western banks, with no "hard money" to lend, went out of business. Construction ceased. Factories throughout the country closed their doors.
To make matters worse, the nation suffered a severe crop failure.

C. & E. Cooper barely weathered the Panic of 1837 and a dismal business year that followed. Struggling to buy iron, and with almost no opportunity to borrow money, the brothers kept their business alive only through hard work, personal economizing, and extending credit on faith in the future. In 1839 the economy began to recover. By 1842 the company was producing and selling carding machines and special power machinery, as well as its previous line of plows and hollow-ware. To meet growing demands, it expanded the foundry and created a two-story machine shop. Faced with a crisis, Charles and Elias Cooper had reacted positively and survived, gaining new strength from their effort. Although they could not have realized it at the time, their baptism in problem solving had set a pattern for the company's future.

The Cooper brothers did not consider themselves innovators. They simply were striving to manufacture basic farm implements better and less expensively than competitors. Yet, they represented a breed of young industrialists scattered throughout the twenty-six states who were igniting an American movement unparalleled in history, surpassing even the heralded industrial revolution that had been taking place in Europe for nearly a century.

As an underdeveloped nation, America had patterned its industrialization after England. The steam engine, considered by many as the single most important contribution to the machine age, gave birth to locomotives and soon was adapted for use in the metals and pottery industries, in the blast furnaces and mines, and on ships. Improvement in both quality and quantity of iron production brought new uses for that essential metal, including construction of iron sea-going vessels, startling the majority of persons who assumed such a metal could not be made to float. Textile mills, sprouting like wild flowers on the New England countryside, replaced hand looms with spinning machinery run at first by water power, then increasingly by steam. All of those developments came from England; some of the few important American inventions, including the cotton gin, metal and woodworking machines, and the concept of interchangeable parts that ultimately led to mass-production capabilities, were attributed to the genius of Eli Whitney.

Interestingly, this great surge of industrial output had brought a wealth of improved raw materials and manufacturing methods, but almost no new end products. An unknown writer observed that a family in the mid-nineteenth century actually could purchase few, if any, consumer items that were not available one hundred years earlier. The only differences were in quality. A family could have a nicer house, more affordable machine-made clothing and dishware, a fancier buggy, and a stronger plow, but nothing that greatly altered its life style. Men like Ford, Edison, Bell, and DeForest soon would bring that change, but not until their predecessors further refined the material and social foundations necessary for such innovation.

Nowhere were those foundations being set faster than in the United States. Efforts of ambitious American entrepreneurs, many of them recent immigrants, were receiving global attention, much of which was reflected in a celebrated two-volume work entitled *De la Democratie en Amerique (Democracy in America)*, written by a French aristocrat, Alexis de Tocqueville, following a yearlong journey through the United States in the early 1830s.

Tocqueville thought the American spirit was expressed well by Joel Roberts Poinsett, former ambassador to Mexico, a member of the South Carolina Legislature, and Secretary of War in 1837. Poinsett told the French visitor, "The American has a quality which, on sea as on land, makes him singularly apt to succeed and make money. He is very civilized, and he is thrown in a society which is just beginning and where the industries have not yet had the time to class themselves in a hard and fast way. It follows that with us every man knows a little of everything, has since childhood been habituated to doing a little of all. There is a phrase constantly in our mouths at the sight of an obstacle, and it's a phrase that portrays us perfectly: 'I will try.'"

Summarizing ideas that came from his observations and discussions, Tocqueville wrote in his notebook, "Political liberty is a food that is hard to digest. Only the most robust constitutions can support it. But when it comes to pass, be it even with other institutions, it gives the whole social body a vigour and energy that surprise even those who were expecting the most of it."

Many years later, in 1982, writer Richard Reeves would duplicate Tocqueville's journey, comparing his own experiences with those of the Frenchman in a book, *American Journey*. The material would also provide the basis of a Public Broadcasting Service television documentary sponsored by a company known by then as Cooper Industries, Inc., in its sesquicentennial year of 1983.

The pace of American enterprise was not hampered by centuries of traditions that forced European counterparts to glance toward the past while taking each step forward. As a result, a certain brashness characterized American business leaders. Still, it could hardly be attributed to birthplace, since the flow of immigrants had produced a social mixture unlike any the world had ever known. There was no denying a wide discrepancy in wealth. Yet, with the exception of slavery, America was relatively classless in comparison with other nations, so a man with an idea went out and tried to transform it into making a living for himself and his family. In the 1840s, men like the Cooper brothers started out by being both managers and working force.

America's greatest assets, of course, were the size and contents of its land. Free enterprise was fed by discoveries of resource wealths beyond imagination, and speculators fanned out across the country to develop them. Not everyone approved of this free-wheeling style of government.

Charles Carroll, last surviving signer of the Declaration of Independence and one of the richest men in America, had told Alexis de Tocqueville, "A mere Democracy is but a mob. The government of England is the only one that suits us. If we get along with ours, it's because each year we can push our innovators into the West."

Many industrial adventurers would have disputed that claim. As manufacturing grew, its geographic boundaries expanding like an inflating balloon, a large number of new firms still were established by "unknowns" who chose to stay in the East. In New Jersey, a young immigrant named Jacob Wiss began making shears and scissors (1848), confident he could buck the firmly established cutlery masters of Europe. A few years later, native-born William Nicholson found a new way to manufacture files and opened a business in Rhode Island (1864). Fayette R. Plumb bought half-interest in a fledgling Philadelphia company manufacturing hammers and axes (1870), then bought out his partner.

Manufacturers of products more directly related to natural resources were indeed springing up farther to the west. But the attraction was less the "push" described by Charles Carroll, than the "pull" of fertile fields and underground treasures. Lewis Bliss followed the call of oil to leave New York and begin manufacturing Ajax drilling engines near Titusville, Pennsylvania (1877). Scottish immigrant Robert W. Gardner opened a machine shop and foundry on an Illinois bank of the Mississippi River (1859), producing a governor to control the speed of steam engines. E.T. Lufkin learned how to make a board and log measuring rule better than others being used in the lumber industry, and went into business at Cleveland, Ohio (1869). Young Patrick J. Shouvlin started a machine shop operation at Springfield, Ohio (1889), repairing and later manufacturing engines for oil fields. Physician Edwin J. Fithian left his profession to manufacture friction clutches and cylinders for Pennsylvania oil-drilling engines (1898). With electricity at last promising to become a factor in power transmission, following more than a century of experimentation, Huntington B. Crouse and Jesse L. Hinds pooled their meager resources to gamble on manufacturing products that could be used in that new marketplace (1897).

Paths established by all these men would someday merge with those of the Coopers, in an age when exploding technologies would require perspectives totally incomprehensible to even the most visionary among them. There is no evidence that any of the men met. Yet, they shared what industrial counselor C.E. Knoeppel offered as the three essentials for success in that era: the vision to conceive, the willingness to work, and the patience to wait. "You may add several factors to that formula, but you cannot have any less," Knoeppel told a gathering of engineers in Cleveland.

Rapid expansion of the population and development of natural resources combined to shape America's emerging industrial society into a complex factory system. Managers no longer could keep pace by running machines themselves, nor could they finance the tools of expansion on which their businesses relied. General corporation laws were refined to limit liability and spread ownership, with a few industries chartered in 1860. At the turn of the century, two-thirds of all manufacturing in the country was done by corporations. The greatest migration of recent times, which brought nearly thirty-five million Europeans to the United States, swelled the population to seventy-six million, second only to Russia among Occidental nations. A tremendous growth of farms not only assured an abundant food supply, but also supported industrial expansion by providing markets and locations. Jonathan Hughes of Northwestern University later explained, "The successful filling up of the American continent with farms multiplied the number of potential industrial locations where residentiary industries of all kinds could supply the agricultural export base."

Transportation grew accordingly, spreading the marketing potential of infant farms. Where industrialization previously had concentrated on new ways of doing old things, the inventors now added new consumer commodities. Families could communicate by telephone, listen to gramophones, take photographs, and sometimes replace the horse and buggy with an automobile. Employment in manufacturing rose from 1.8 million in 1869 to 6.3 million in 1909. Basic industrial output surpassed that of Great Britain, and was approaching the total of the entire European continent.

Two British investigators who wrote jointly in the early 1900s said, "The machine age, which has reached its high development in America, has brought the greatest advancement in freedom and civilization." A German economist wrote that the United States had become the foremost nation of the world, "because of economic supremacy based on high wages and industrial development."

The speed of change at times boggled minds. Irving S. Paull, president of the Carpet Manufacturers of America, recalled an incident in 1909 when he gave a lecture on distribution. After listening for half an hour, one manufacturer asked, "What do you mean by distribution?" Paull explained that he referred to the physical movement of materials from the manufacturer into the marketplace where it could be purchased by consumers. "Hell," his listener replied, "you mean selling and shipping — two evils that necessarily attend manufacturing."

Writing in *The New Democracy*, Walter E. Weyl observed that "When we try to visualize the statistics of our American railroads, the mind sinks exhausted under the effort." He wrote also of the futility of comprehending the nation's wealth. "A billion dollars exceeds the fortune of any individual since the world began," he wrote. "It is like a light year or some other convenient but unimaginable astronomical term. Yet, in 1904 our total national wealth was estimated by the census authorities at 107 of these billions of dollars." That figure was 12 percent of the national budget for the single year of 1982.

What may have been incomprehensible in the early 1900s soon became ordinary, with the introduction of assembly lines and rapid development of new energy resources. Transportation progressed from land and sea to air and space, communications from print to radio to television and a variety of related media. Industrial mechanization accelerated, as the application of science replaced trial and error methods of research, then spurted to an even more rapid pace with the injection of computerization. Management became a science of its own, keyed as much to financing and forecasting as to operations. The pace of energy development and distribution created periodic fears of depletion, but continued to provide the underpinning for all areas of the nation's progress. (America's 1867 purchasing price of $7,200,000 for Alaska — scorned by critics as "Seward's Folly" — was approximately equal to the cost for three of the twenty-four Cooper jet gas turbine pumping units placed on the Alaskan pipeline when it was built in the 1970s.)

Reports on the impending death of individual enterprises were invalidated by men like Carl E. Weller, who started a company because he wasn't satisfied with his radio repair tools. Charles W. Kirsch, a Wisconsin farm boy, launched a manufacturing business by improving the curtain rod. Karl Peterson emigrated from Sweden and organized the Crescent Tool Company just in time to serve the automobile industry, whose assembly line techniques also provided the opportunity for Julius Keller to produce precision tools and instruments. Walter Martin and Elmer Decker parlayed knowledge gained in the oil fields into a company producing weight indicators for drilling rigs. Small groups of men organized Pennsylvania Pump and Compressor Company and Xcelite Company in the East. W.H. Leonard formed the Denver Rock Drill Manufacturing Company in the West, and inventor Roland Doeden started a small company manufacturing pneumatic finishing tools near Hicksville, Ohio. Other individuals or groups organized companies with names like Funk, Mayhew, Cycloblower, Apex, Drill Carrier, Demco, Hollis, and Advanced Controls. All those companies would prosper on their own, then become part of Cooper Industries.

True, as the corporate system continued to expand, the flow of innovation came increasingly from group efforts. Economist Tom Burns, who studied trends through the mid-twentieth century, concluded, "There is a constant grouping and regrouping of resources available to the development of new products and processes in terms of design teams or project groups, product engineers or production engineering departments. There is a perpetual analysis and reanalysis of organization charts and decision-making systems. All these efforts time and time again are reduced to a search for 'the right man.' The right man, I suggest, is no more or less than the classic traditional figure of the entrepreneur, who is as essential a figure within the system of the large corporation as he was in the old systems of technology and business out of which what we know as modern industries were born."

Continuing growth was intrinsic to the corporate system, just as it was to the owner-operator of the nineteenth century. Investing profits in the improvement of operations was essential to meeting competition successfully, which mushroomed with communications and transportation to encompass the world. One major difference between the owner-operator of the 1800s and the corporate manager a century later was that the latter had hundreds or thousands of other owners and operators depending on the wisdom of his decisions.

Labor developed also from circumstances that had at times approximated servitude, to an organizational framework similar to that of the corporation itself.

Machinery evolved to semiautomatic, automatic, and robotic equipment. But the need for individual hand tools in no way submerged in the backwash of the technological thrust, and would, in fact, represent an important element in Cooper Industries' diversified manufacturing posture of the 1980s. The company's early relationship with energy markets likewise would remain an important thread throughout its development into a worldwide, multibillion dollar corporation.

The roots of many separate enterprises would grow into a single entity, each important to the corporation they formed. But circumstances would be such that the company would continue to bear the name of the young Mt. Vernon owners whose main concern in the petulant 1840s was to carve a small nitch in America's exciting industrial revolution.

2

War and Revolution

As the nineteenth century approached its mid-point, two strong forces could be felt in America. Charles Cooper was involved in both.

Political differences on seemingly unrelated issues exploded into debates over freedom versus slavery. A new spark was kindled by the opening of each new frontier territory, with proslavery Democrats and opposing Whigs battling for power in Washington. Without realizing it, Americans were choosing up sides for a bloody contest. But political bickering did not deter the steam-powered march of the industrial revolution. Railroads, factories, sawmills, improved farm machinery, steamboats, and textile mills turned the economic cycle steadily into another boom. Ambitious Americans were caught up in the excitement of new products, jobs, and transportation. It was a stabilizing influence against the rumblings of conflict over slavery. Yet, a thinking person had difficulty setting aside his conscience.

Charles Cooper aggressively opposed slavery. His views were not shared by the majority of voters in the overwhelmingly Democratic district where he lived, but he was not a man to be intimidated by obstacles. His vigorous campaign influence was considered the decisive factor in the 1844 election to Congress of an antislavery Whig candidate from Mt. Vernon. Ten years later, when the Whig party collapsed under pressure from leaders of an even stronger antislavery group who called themselves Republicans, he became an active member of the new party.

Although Charles and Elias Cooper maintained equal partnerships in their growing enterprise, there appears to be no question as to leadership. Charles guided the company into the industrial mainstream of the times, manufacturing steam engines and machinery for agricultural, textile, and lumber markets of the 1840s.

C. & E. Cooper had forecast correctly the potential of steam power. Its products meshed precisely with the churning gears of economic expansion. They also assisted in the Mexican War effort of 1846–48, providing slide-valve steam engines and special war-related power machinery for the border campaigns of General Zachary Taylor. At the height of the

An early Cooper portable steam engine supplies power for drilling a well at a nineteenth-century rice farm.

war, the general became a popular hero, earning the nickname of "Old Rough and Ready" Taylor, after leading outnumbered troops to victory in an area not far from the location that would become the home of C. & E. Cooper's descendant company 120 years later.

But in the midst of success, tragedy ended the original partnership. Elias contracted "Painter's Colic," a form of lead poisoning from paint, and died in 1848, leaving a wife and two children, one a future president of the company. A year later, Charles accepted into partnership a creative engineer named T.L. Clark. His judgment was confirmed quickly when the new partner designed flour and grain mills that became important new company products. The firm was known as Cooper & Clark for three years. Then John Cooper, a younger brother of the cofounders, purchased an interest and the name was changed slightly to Coopers & Clark.

Charles Cooper was by then an established community leader. As a native son, he worked toward progress of his town as well as his company. A strict father, he had six children, one with his first wife and five with his second wife, Isabel, whom he married in 1846. In business, his handshake was considered a contract. He encouraged employees to purchase their own homes, and exhorted all eligible citizens to exercise the right to vote, even though most of them were Democrats. There was but one deviation in his pursuit of individual rights — an equally strong disbelief in the right to drink. Charles Cooper was a dedicated prohibitionist.

Like many towns, Mt. Vernon received a surge of new vitality with the arrival of the railroad. Few events in history can match the excitement that swept through a community when the last section of track was spiked into place and the first engine chugged into view. With completion of the Sandusky, Mansfield, and Newark Railroad on January 5, 1851, Mt. Vernon and Cooper had a modern link with widespread commerce. Both profited greatly. Cooper's immediate benefit was from improved transportation. Production of its first steam-powered compressor for iron blast furnaces in 1852 opened doors to the emerging steel industry. Many of these sturdy Cooper "blowing engines" were shipped by rail to Ohio's Hanging Rock District, where furnaces, sixty feet high, were chiseled out of solid rock in the sides of cliffs or constructed of heavy stone masonry. Some continued to operate for well over half a century.

But an even more direct association with the railroad came the following year. In 1853, the company (with its name changed to C. & J. Cooper after the retirement of Mr. Clark) built a wood-burning locomotive, the first manufactured west of the Allegheny Mountains. Soon Cooper locomotives were plying the Sandusky, Mansfield, and Newark Railways, later to become part of the B & O system.

Taking part in one of history's greatest transportation epics seemed plausible for a company manufacturing steam engines. This time, however, the company's economic divining rod had pointed to a dry well. More specifically, the railroad claimed it could not pay its bill. Finally, C. & J. Cooper was forced to issue script, in lieu of money, to employees. Local merchants accepted the script for food and merchandise, banking on Charles Cooper to do something that would solve their mutual problem. The action he finally took became a legend remembered through the years with slight variations but enough documentation to maintain its basic truth. Some persons say the irrepressible industrialist walked to the train station. Others say he chased a locomotive on horseback, catching up with it at the station. All agree that he chained the wheels of a locomotive to the track, padlocked it securely, and stood guard until he collected the long overdue payment.

Unfortunately, the incident was not an isolated echo of one railroad's problems. Heavy losses suffered by all U.S. railroads combined with other business failures to bring about the Panic of 1857. For the second time in two decades, Cooper clung to a thin thread of survival, recovering just as the country was splitting apart.

During the Civil War, Charles Cooper became known as an activist for another kind of railroad. He was reported to have helped a large number of slaves make the lonely underground railroad journey to freedom. Meanwhile, Cooper wood-burning steam locomotives and steam-powered blowing machines for charcoal iron-blast furnaces were among the products that enabled an industrialized North to outlast an agricultural South. Like most supporters of the Union cause, however, the Cooper leader was interested not in being a victor, but in preserving a nation. His political interests never waned. In 1868 he ran for Congress and was defeated by General George W. Morgan, although he ran well ahead of his ticket in a district that continued to be dominated by the opposing Democratic Party.

As one who rarely abandoned a cause, Charles Cooper was no less inclined to relinquish authority in his company, maintaining general supervision into his early eighties. Nevertheless, he was wise in selecting key men in the post-Civil War period of expansion.

"Our Southern Border (Cincinnati) was menaced by the enemies of our Union. David Tod, Governor of Ohio, called on the Minute Men of the State and the Squirrel Hunters came by the thousands to the rescue. You, Charles Gray Cooper, were one of them and this is your honorable discharge."

Before enlisting in the Union army, from which he received a Squirrel Hunters Discharge, Charles Gray Cooper, son of Elias, had enrolled in Oberlin College, Ohio. There he met a book and stationery store bookkeeper named Frank L. Fairchild. As the friendship grew, the young student urged his older friend to visit the C. & J. Cooper Company in Mt. Vernon. Then he suggested to his Uncle Charles that an outstanding man from Oberlin might be persuaded to leave his book store for an industrial career. It was a successful finesse. Frank Fairchild joined Cooper in 1865, the year the war ended. Just three years later he was taken into active partnership and the firm's name received another alteration, becoming C. & J. Cooper & Company. It was changed again the following year to C. & G. Cooper & Company when John Cooper sold his interest to become head of another manufacturing company and Charles Gray Cooper, who attended Rennsselaer Institute after the war, became a partner. At the same time, a Civil War hero and son-in-law of Elias Cooper also became a partner. His name was Colonel George Rogers.

The time was right for a strengthening of management. On the East Coast, a man named George H. Corliss had invented a device reputed to be the most important engine development in the decades since James Watt introduced the slide-valve steam engine. The Corliss engine, with its patented oscillating valve, was so efficient that the inventor often agreed to sell it under an arrangement whereby the savings from the first two years' fuel coal would be its total price.

Cooper was determined to become the first Corliss engine producer in the West. To reach such an ambitious goal, the partnership chose a direct route. It hired an engineer closely associated with development of the product at the Corliss Works, Julius C. Debes, luring him west with a 16 percent interest in the partnership. In 1869, Cooper built and sold its first Corliss engines, destined to highlight another manufacturing era. Julius Debes became chief engineer, then a partner, extending his genius into many new products before passing his engineering baton to a son, James H. Debes, who continued the legacy.

It is difficult to visualize the size of the Corliss engine. Some had pistons seven feet in diameter. The flywheel alone weighed more than an entire locomotive produced fifteen years earlier. One engine filled an entire factory building.

The Corliss valve permitted full bursts of pressure and steady speeds, both assets to power plants, textile and rolling mills that were among Cooper's major customers.

A Cooper grandchild later recalled having seen the engines at work in textile mills. "They were absolutely beautiful, with heavy rope drives extending from one floor to another," he said. "I've never been able to imagine how in the world they could build engines of that size and get them into plants. They had no traveling cranes in those days. They had to do everything with jacks and crowbars and rollers. Yet, my father told me they moved those huge castings around just like it was an everyday routine. It seemed phenomenal to me then, and it still does."

Forty years after the product was introduced, a prospective customer asked one Cooper salesman, "What is the life of your Corliss engine?" "We don't know," came the reply. "The first ones are still running."

One famous Corliss engine, built by Cooper, was sold to the National Cash Register Company in Dayton. The 210-ton giant was shipped in several sections by railroad, then hauled through city streets on special wagons. As many as five teams of horses were required to pull each section, the spectacle attracting more public attention than had the arrival of the city's first locomotive in 1851. Not only did the engine provide power for manufacturing, it also heated the NCR factory with its exhaust steam. After operating continuously for almost fifty years without a single failure, it was placed in retirement at Dayton's Carillon Park, where it remains today. At the time it was replaced by a turbo-generator, the venerable old Corliss was still running at full power.

But emergence of the Corliss did not overshadow manufacture of Cooper's conventional slide-valve steam engines immediately. In the 1870s, new Debes' designs also updated standard lines for farms, saw mills, cotton gins, grist mills, and as one Cooper man described, "anything that takes a revolving shaft." Usually the company produced more than just the engine. It built the entire saw mill or grist mill.

In addition to the stationary engines, there were portable models that could be pulled by horses into fields or woodlands, on wagons when the ground was hard, on skids when it was soft. Then in 1875 there appeared a modern new piece of farm machinery, the Cooper traction en-

This Corliss engine tandem operated almost continuously for 50 years at the National Cash Register Company plant in Dayton, without a failure. Man at the far right is one of the company's best known field erection men, Sam Clark, who supervised jobs throughout the country for many years.

gine. It applied power from the Debes-developed steam engine to the vehicle's own wheels. The transfer of power was made possible by a special bevel gear attachment invented and patented by Colonel Rogers.

Although it was referred to as a traction engine for many years, Cooper had produced America's first farm tractor. The company's advertisements showed a competitor's horse-drawn vehicle bogged down in mud, the farmer vainly kicking the stranded animals, while a Cooper traction engine puffed merrily by. Charles Cooper was so proud of the accomplishment that he had a painting of the new traction engine done by a lithographer named Courier. The lithograph, as well as drawings used in advertisements of the time, reveal a curious sidelight to the traction engine story. Although the vehicle was self-propelled, it was led by two horses attached to a tongue similar to that of a wagon and steered by a driver sitting on a seat atop the boiler. With previous experience in steam-driven mobility limited to vehicles that ran on rails, no one in the company had thought about inventing a device that would turn the traction engine's wheels.

One of the company's early portable steam engines, manufactured in 1870, was purchased from a Missouri farmer in 1954 and returned to Mt. Vernon, where it is maintained by the company.

An early Cooper traction engine and Cooper separator provide the machinery for this Ohio threshing scene in 1886. It was owned by J.R. "Jap" Watson, R.D. 2, Centerburg, Ohio.

The first self-propelled tractor in America was manufactured by Cooper in 1875. This painting was lost for more than half a century, before being discovered during building renovation in 1950. The horses were used only for steering.

Within a short time, many companies were building and selling traction engines. Cooper's own production leaped to five hundred in 1880. But even with competition sparking rapid engineering advancements, no one eliminated horse steering. Finally, in 1883, the Cooper traction engine took to the field with its own power *and* its own steering. All that was necessary was a steering wheel and a simple shaft-chain arrangement. Yet, no one in the country had thought of it in eight years. The delay caused some apparent damage to engineering pride. Records fail to mention the steering invention. The new traction engine simply appeared. The Courier Lithograph, meanwhile, disappeared until it was located among some storeroom rubble in a Mt. Vernon office in 1950. No one seemed willing in the era of steam to explain how American inventors overlooked what would seem to be the obvious. It remains a missing page in the annals of industrial history.

Cooper built nearly five thousand traction engines during a fifteen-year span and received royalties on its patented engine drive from other manufacturers. Despite such success, however, a decision was made to discontinue the product. Ironically, the reason was the company's farm-land location. Farmers could not afford to pay cash for traction engines, and small Ohio banks were unable to meet credit requirements. By contrast, competing farm implement manufacturers in Chicago arranged for large banking houses there to finance purchases by holding credit papers over long periods of time. Consequently, they captured the market. So the Corliss engine, sold to large mills and manufacturing plants with adequate purchasing power, became the principal product of C. & G. Cooper & Company. It remained so through the turn of the century.

3

New Energy Resources

The Charles Cooper hilltop home, with its long white stables at one side and a fence surrounding the entire property, was a colorful example of nineteenth-century architecture. It was in keeping with the owner's life-long business commitment that this luxurious home overlooked the factory. (The property later became a company parking lot.) But the proximity eventually caused a degree of consternation for colleagues. As he approached his mid-80s, the Cooper managing partner at last began to feel comfortable in delegating authority to other partners, who by then included his only son, also named Charles. But some changes were difficult to reconcile in semiretirement. The elder Cooper no longer adhered to his accustomed full work schedule. Yet, each day he arose at dawn and walked briskly to the company office, arriving just as the early morning mail was delivered. Going quickly through letters, he extracted all checks, put them in his pocket, and returned home before other partners got to the office. It took a persuasive son-to-father talk to evoke a shift in fiscal responsibilities.

The days of out-of-pocket financing were fading into the past. Political issues of the day concerned silver coinage, tariff bills, and business excise taxes, although a tax on incomes, passed in 1893, was declared unconstitutional by the U.S. Supreme Court.

In 1895, The C. & G. Cooper Company was incorporated. After sixty-three years of existence, the firm had its first president, Frank L. Fairchild. Charles Gray Cooper, who was always called "C.G.," became secretary. Another firm partner, Desault B. Kirk, was named treasurer. Charles F. Cooper, son of the retiring managing partner, had died a year earlier at the age of thirty-six.

President Fairchild had gained wide respect as a salesman of Cooper-Corliss engines, particularly through the textile mill regions of New England. Tall and muscular, with the easygoing mannerisms that reflected spirit and congeniality, he drew attention whenever he traveled. Hotel managers looked forward to his visits, and customers admitted that his personal charm somehow convinced them they needed new power

19

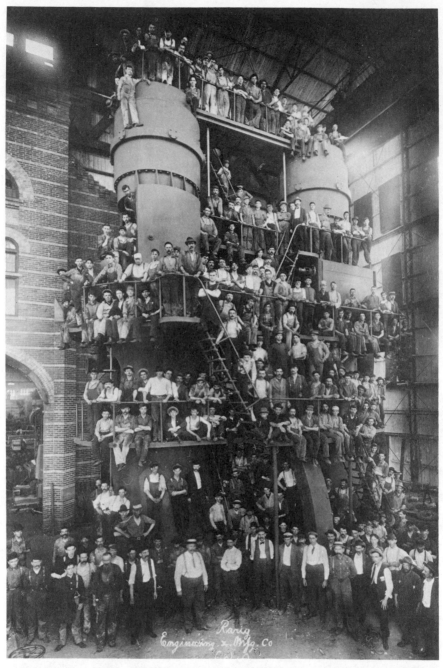

Blowing engine, made in Mt. Vernon, had to be taken to a plant in Columbus for assembly, because of its height. This crew of more than 200 Cooper employees did the job in 1907. Later, a building extension in Mt. Vernon made it possible to assemble the giant engines there.

This photo taken in 1903, shows only half of a Cooper horizontal Corliss compound steam engine, one of the largest ever built. It went to the Carnegie Steel Company's Duquesne Works.

Mt. Vernon foundry workers pose in front of the plant in 1902.

An erection crew, headed by Sam Clark, poses with an engine installed for generation of electricity on a trolley line in 1906.

equipment, even in the days of difficult financing. His reputation for maintaining an even temperament under trying conditions was well established. A colleague recalled one New York meeting in which a prospective customer interviewed representatives of several competing engine manufacturers at the same time. During the conversation, a competitor insulted the Cooper engine in vicious terms. In the uneasy silence that followed, Frank Fairchild became rigid, gripping the arms of his chair with powerful hands. His eyes flashed indignation. His face and bald head, set in a frame of closely trimmed side and chin whiskers, turned red. Everyone in the room could sense his momentary inward struggle. Then slowly the color receded from his face, his eyes lost their fire, his body relaxed, and he brushed aside the attack with a few quiet words. He also got the contract.

Conversation was one of the president's great loves. Speaking with friends seemed to make indelible impressions on his memory. When encountering an acquaintance, he often would resume a previous conversation after an interlude of several months. One Mt. Vernon merchant observed that "Everything seemed to look brighter after F.L. walked up the street." Selling was so much a part of Frank Fairchild's being that he continued to serve as sales manager during his seventeen-year presidency.

After the incorporation, Charles Cooper did not remain active in company management. But his continued community involvement included presidency of the Knox National Bank. That in itself linked him, albeit indirectly, with business affairs of the corporation. The 1890s were not thriving industrial years. Money was scarce. C. & G. Cooper often used a customer purchase order to borrow money from the bank so that it could build an engine. When the product was sold, the bank loan was repaid.

So the company moved into the twentieth century, limping slightly from blows of the earlier general business down-cycle, yet optimistic about an apparent economic recovery that helped President McKinley get re-elected in 1900. When Charles Cooper died on February 7, 1901, at the age of ninety, the company he and his brother had founded was tuned once again to the quickening tempo of new energy development. This time the beat emanated from beneath the ground.

Natural gas was anything but new. The Chinese had piped it through hollow bamboo poles before the birth of Christ. In America, the first gas well was drilled at Fredonia, New York, in 1821. That discovery touched off such frantic development that the *Scientific American* reported on January 7, 1893, "There is hardly a doubt that the natural gas supply is generally approaching extinction, and it will soon cease to be an important factor among the fuels of the country." But by 1900, gas was being discovered in widespread new fields and shipped more than 100 miles through pipelines. At the same time, an entire oil industry was developing from Colonel Ed Drake's 1859 discovery of a magic fountain near Titusville, Pennsylvania. Coal apparently existed in inexhaustible quantities. Engineers like Nikola Tesla and George Westinghouse were demonstrating the value of electricity as a means of power transmission.

Steam clearly was being challenged as the king of energy. C. & G. Cooper Company faced a critical decision. Several paths into the industrial future offered enticement, but none held a guarantee of safe passage. Convincing argument could in fact support the status quo. Cooper's giant steam engines were beginning to appear in America's modern new industries. Packard Motor Car Company and Victor Talking Machines were among its good customers. Moreover, the nation's emergence as a world power, fostered by its victory in the Spanish American War, enhanced world trade. Cooper products were being shipped abroad. Obviously, King Corliss was far from dead. But steam power itself was undergoing a dramatic change. Steam turbines, growing rapidly in size and efficiency, seemed destined to dethrone the reciprocating Corliss engines. At the same time, large engines fueled by natural gas were proving successful in the mushrooming steel industry and held promise for the compression stage of pipeline transmission.

Company officers narrowed alternatives to a final showdown between conversion to the manufacture of steam turbines versus gradual change

This building was the main office of C. & G. Cooper & Company in the early twentieth century.

to natural gas internal combustion engines. Then they selected the latter. One of the men instrumental in the decision was Cooper's young assistant secretary-treasurer, Beatty B. Williams, son-in-law of President Fairchild, who argued that development of steam turbines competitive with Westinghouse and Allis Chalmers represented too great a drain on company resources.

Since no one in the company was familiar with gas engines, a thorough investigation was conducted in the United States and abroad. Rather than accept an established concept, however, Cooper decided to combine the best engineering features of several engines into one of its own design. A German-born gas engine designer, Martin A. Thiel, was hired to mastermind the job.

In June of 1909, the company's first gas engine-compressor combination was installed on a short Manufacturers Light and Heat Company pipeline in West Virginia. A complicated 20′ x 42′ horizontal two-cylinder, double-acting machine, it had such slow action that a salesman, Fletcher Devin, later described it by saying its piston "goes out today and comes back tomorrow." Nevertheless, it provided long, faithful service and initiated an even longer close relationship between Cooper and pipeline transmission.

As before, the company's product transition was gradual. James Debes, who had succeeded his father as chief engineer in 1898, remained in charge of steam engine design. Martin Thiel confined activities to gas engines. The two engineering geniuses were contrasts in personality. Debes spoke softly and slowly, showing no variation in emotion until badgered to an extremely high boiling point, at which time he exploded with anger. Thiel always spoke in harsh, staccato phrases obviously not selected to cement friendships. But they survived equal billing and both were held in high esteem by colleagues.

During the phase-in period of the gas engine, the company was headed by C.G. Cooper, who became president when Frank Fairchild died of appendicitis in 1912. A small man with penetrating eyes and quick movements, "C.G." let no one doubt his feelings. In his opinion, failure to express honest feelings was akin to lying. Employees and clients knew they could depend on his word, because no one would disguise truth with such bluntness. A favorite story concerned the feisty president's visit to one procrastinating client. Without shaking hands or engaging in preliminary solicitation, C.G. blurted, "Do you want to buy a steam engine?" The other man replied that he did not want one at that time. "All right, then you can go to hell," said C.G., leaving the room as abruptly as he had entered.

A newspaperman later suggested that "if C.G. had been appointed ambassador to some foreign court, it is safe to say history would have had another war spread on its bloody pages. C.G.'s unrestricted candor would have started one." Still, associates agreed that the brusqueness rarely was abrasive. There was something refreshing about dealing with a man who always said exactly what he was thinking, whether or not you liked what you heard. Employees learned to find countermeasures that could substitute for futile disagreement.

One such instance was long remembered by Fred H. Thomas, a top salesman who later became vice president and sales manager.

An up-swinging business cycle in 1913 found Cooper enjoying good sales in both steam and gas engines. Leaving the office one day, briefcase in hand, Salesman Thomas was stopped by President Cooper, who asked, "Thomas, where are you off to now?"

"To Pittsburgh, sir. I know of a good prospect up there."

The president shook his head. "Put that briefcase back and don't go. We already have enough business."

Thomas complied without protest. But the next time he went on a sales trip, he lowered his briefcase out the window by a cord.

Fred Thomas played a major role in the sales shift to gas engines, and for many years thereafter. One president said that Thomas made a religion of business. "He never knew what he was being paid and he never cared. All he wanted to do was get business for the men and women out in that plant. He just dedicated his life to success of the company."

American industry, riding a crest of resource development and ambitious enterprise, received further boosts in the years just preceding World War I. A Federal Reserve System, adopted in 1913, set the foundation for unified banking, sorely needed in the nation's economic expansion. One year later, the first steamship passed through the Panama Canal, culminating an historic ten-year construction project to strengthen international trade and military defense. Entry into foreign markets was becoming substantial, tripling in dollar volume since the turn of the century. But an even greater acceleration of commerce was felt within the country as power transmission spread into a nationwide network.

When Europe went to war in 1914, America was urged to put some of its growing industrial muscle behind the Allied effort. Cooper's response postponed its impending transformation from steam to gas. Both types of engines, as well as machining expertise for unrelated products, were needed in the war effort.

The first desperate Allied call was for large caliber shells. In reply, Cooper set up a munitions department and soon was producing one thousand three-inch steel shells a day, using special purpose lathes, grinders, and cutting machines also manufactured by the company. When the U.S. declared war on Germany in April of 1917, total company production was placed at the disposal of the Government. By that time, the country's production of raw steel approached forty-two million tons annually. High capacity presses to forge large guns, shells, and other war materials, however, were in short supply. Since such presses required workmanship similar to that used in producing steam and gas engines, Cooper was called on to help meet the emergency. During the war, the company built fifty high-speed steam-hydraulic forging presses, ranging from one thousand to fifteen hundred ton capacity, for government arsenals, munitions plants, and shipyards. Sixty-nine giant gas engines and compressors, produced under government priorities, were installed in pipeline pumping stations to speed delivery of fuel to war industries. Triple expansion marine engines, built by Cooper for the Emergency Fleet Corporation, became part of the government's vast shipbuilding program. Casings were produced for turbines that powered destroyers attempting to subdue the devastating German U-Boat fleet.

Emergency war requirements also helped justify a Cooper experiment initiated several years earlier. In 1910, the company had created its first subsidiary, the Chapman Engineering Company, to manufacture mechanical gas producers and floating agitators. Key to the process was a "producer arm," invented by Will Chapman, an Oberlin College classmate of B.B. Williams. Steel plants, strapped for fuel, were able to increase output of furnaces and decrease consumption of coal by using the Chapman gas producers and floating agitators, which recovered small quantities of producer gas from the burning coal. A second subsidiary, the Chapman-Stein Company, was organized to produce furnace air re-cuperators and metallurgical reheating surfaces, through a reciprocal li-cense agreement with Fours-Stein of France. These enabled a furnace to heat incoming air with outgoing gas. Both subsidiaries were located in a section of Cooper's two-story brick office building.

After the armistice on November 11, 1918, C. & G. Cooper peered into the peacetime future. One thing was certain. The old Corliss en-gine, already staggered by competition from steam turbines, would soon be replaced completely by the gas-powered upstart. It was faltering rap-idly under the strain of two insurmountable handicaps: natural gas en-gines developed much higher thermal efficiency, and in pipeline trans-mission, gas engine fuel was available right at the point of use. The long Corliss reign came to an end in 1920, when Cooper shipped its last steam engine to Japan.

Like most suppliers of energy, gas production companies were poised for postwar expansion. Cooper was anxious to move with them. To do so, however, it recognized a need to modernize its major product, the horizontal natural gas engine, and to plan new programs of manage-ment and sales.

During the interim year of 1919, devoted almost entirely to a wind-down of war production, the Cooper presidency was held by former treasurer Desault B. Kirk, with C.G. Cooper moving to chairman. Friends of President Kirk knew him as a highly intelligent man who could read both Latin and Greek. Bankers knew him as being so meticu-lous with company funds that "he could account for any penny at any time," yet so careless with his personal bank account that he frequently had to rush in with funds after being notified of being overdrawn. And for several years, most notably 1908–1912, startled strangers thought they knew him as another Ohioan. Large of body and mustache, he was an astonishing "double," both in face and physique, for U.S. President William Howard Taft.

With the spillover from war's false prosperity ended, Cooper in 1920 launched its long-range program. To lead the charge, directors elected Beatty B. Williams president, elevating him from the position of vice president and general manager that he held during the war years.

Although he had married the boss's daughter, few in the company at-tributed the new president's rise to family connections. Highly intelli-gent, hard-driving and totally dedicated to the company's success, Beatty Williams represented the uncommon breed of leader, able to juggle seemingly infinite responsibilities without showing signs of strain. Even when he took his work home with him — which was most evenings — his wife, Amy, and their only child, Lawrence, did not feel neglected. Dis-cussing company events was a dinner ritual. To young Lawrence, it was fascinating to be taken behind the scenes of a growing industry. His own ambition to pursue a strong interest in YMCA work did not detract from

Lawrence's enjoyment of what he referred to as "the great debates of industry." One recurring story that made a particular impression on him was the 1908 decision to follow the path of gas engine production when the way to steam turbine conversion appeared blocked by better capitalized competition. It was considered a lifesaving move for the company, and Lawrence had heard about it since he was six years old. (Many years later, that memory would return with a sudden realization of history being repeated.)

Hewitt A. Gehres, a former employee who had left the company for another wartime position, returned to understudy Martin Thiel, by then in failing health, and soon stepped into the position of chief engineer. His initial assignment was to update the Cooper gas engine.

One of the plant foremen, later to become plant superintendent, became associated with the Cooper effort quite by accident. A Russian, Peter Letz, had been assigned to represent his country as an inspector on the Cooper production of shells shipped to that nation during the war. Before he could return home, the Bolshevik Revolution exploded. With sympathies well established on the losing side of the conflict, Inspector Letz decided to stay in Mt. Vernon and became Foreman Letz.

An aggressive sales effort became the responsibility of Fred Thomas, who by then was reputed to know nearly every leader in the natural gas production industry. And that market was where Cooper visualized its immediate future. Under the direction of "Hew" Gehres, engine-compressor redesigning gave birth to a new family of products, ranging from 80 to 1,000 horsepower.

Boom towns were springing up from cornfields, mountains, and plains with periodic discoveries of natural gas and oil. Natural gas became increasingly important in the manufacture of steel and glass, and in the infant petrochemical industry. Compressor stations were being constructed near supply sources to propel gas through pipelines to distant consumers. Installation of huge four-cycle Cooper engines and compressors was no routine task in the early 1920s. Field engineers returned with disquieting reports. During one West Virginia installation, an engine-compressor was unloaded in sections at a siding and hauled across a shallow part of the Elk River on skids. Things went well until one heavy frame became mired in the river bottom. Before it could be pried loose, the river rose to cover it. Much later the frame was retrieved and moved to the compressor station site.

Field service engineers, usually referred to as "erection men," were hardy individualists who learned how to live and work in what they affectionately referred to as "the boondocks." Pipelines were routed through some of the most remote areas of West Virginia, Louisiana, Arkansas, Oklahoma, and Texas, and it was not unusual for erection men to spend three months getting equipment assembled and started. Ordinarily, they hired local laborers to help. Finding places to live and eat in wilderness

The C. & G. Cooper band, started with a few members practicing in the foundry in 1917, grew to this size by 1921. It performed during lunch periods at the factory and in concerts, parades, picnics, and in greeting visiting dignitaries at the train station. Some employees purchased instruments and learned to play them specifically to join the band. This photo was taken in front of the Cooper family home.

locales could be difficult. Top erection men like Charles King, Frank Fishner, Charles Bumpas, and A.B. "Uncle Ben" Paulson usually had to search for farmhouses or cabins where they could receive temporary room and board. All insisted they learned to subsist on sow belly and beans. On one job, Charlie King stayed in the attic of an old house. His only access was by ladder to the single window in his quarters. Corn squeezings helped ease the pain of lonely nights there, he said.

Frank Fishner, noted for his lively sense of humor, told of a dilapidated backwoods "eating place" that he refused to call a restaurant. The food was bad and the surroundings were worse. After forcing down one meal there, he pointed to the counter and told the waiter, "I'll take a piece of that raisin pie." According to Fishner, the waiter swished his hand over the pie, scaring off a dozen flies. "It ain't raisin pie," the man said. "It's custard." Field engineers and their stories were legendary. The group had a camaraderie admired by other employees, and rugged as their lives could be at times, many young plant apprentices set their sights on becoming "erection men."

In just a few years, Cooper became the nation's recognized leader in pipeline compression engines. It was not unusual to have exclusive sales along an entire nationwide line. In the plant, new engines stretched the entire length of the assembly plant, positioned as close together as possible to permit adequate working room. Orders often backed up for months. In the winter, spectators sometimes gathered outside the plant to watch Cooper employees manning large crowbars, inching skids holding 1,000-hp engines down Sandusky Street to the railroad siding.

Smaller two-cylinder engines in the 80 to 170 hp range were used in natural gas fields to extract gasoline as it came from the well. In large fields, such as those being discovered in the American Southwest, as many as forty engines would be set in a long line, powering compression for gasoline extraction. But Cooper did not dominate small engine production for gasoline extraction. That distinction went to a competitor, the Bessemer Gas Engine Company of Grove City, Pennsylvania, whose future would soon be linked to that of Cooper.

4

Bessemer

The Bessemer Gas Engine Company had not planned to become a part of America's natural gasoline industry. The opportunity simply appeared in 1905, and the Grove City company was sufficiently alert to recognize it. After a wobbly start in the late nineteenth century, motor cars burst upon the transportation scene with a force that rebounded through myriad industries. Gasoline was transformed from a waste product to a treasured commodity. Demand exceeded the supply available from refinery distillation of crude oil.

Many oil wells in Pennsylvania already had declined to small production. But natural gas escaping from the casingheads was rich in gasoline. Engineers noticed that when their hands were held in the natural gas flow, they became covered with precipitated gasoline. Several enterprising men logically decided that gasoline could be extracted from natural gas through compression. Among them was a retired New York preacher named William Mayburg, who purchased a gas engine from Bessemer. Through a casual inquiry, the company discovered that Mayburg was using the engine to compress casinghead natural gas and recover the valuable gasoline. Foreseeing a possible new market, Bessemer studied the idea carefully for several years. Then in 1910, it hired Frank Peterson to devote exclusive attention to production of engines for the budding industry. Ingersoll-Rand Company became a pioneer in furnishing the accompanying compressors. Fifteen years later, with the natural gasoline industry spread to every important gas and oil field in the country, a publication of the American Chemical Society acknowledged the Bessemer Gas Engine Company's major role in establishing it on a firm commercial basis. The society estimated that 90 percent of the engines used in the compression method of gasoline extraction were installed by Bessemer.

Early detection of opportunity for innovation in the nation's oil fields, however, was not new to Bessemer. It was, in fact, the way the company came into being. And the original idea came not from an engineer, but from a physician. It approaches understatement to suggest that Dr.

Dr. E.J. Fithian, founder of
the Bessemer Gas Engine
Company.

Edwin J. Fithian was a man of varied interest. Born July 1, 1863, at
Portersville, Pennsylvania, just sixty miles south of the point where oil
had been discovered four years earlier, he grew up to be a physician, inventor, businessman, humanitarian, politician, and uncompromising
prohibitionist. Nothing in his youth suggested that oil production would
have an influence on his life, even though he lived in several small towns
amidst the oil fields of western Pennsylvania. His father, a cabinetmaker,
switched to the retail furniture business when machine-made products
threatened his trade. Young Edwin learned enough carpentry to work
his way through Grove City College and West Penn Medical College, receiving his M.D. degree in 1892. Married that same year, he established a
medical practice in Portersville, then moved a year later to the nearby village of Harmony.

Many oil wells at that time were pumped with steam engines. Unfortunately, production was beginning to fall to a point where the cost of
pumping appeared increasingly prohibitive. Old boilers, rusting out
from excessively hard water in that region, needed to be replaced. A
large water supply was required and steam had to be maintained steadily, even though pumping had become sporadic. Meanwhile, natural gas
byproducts escaped uselessly into the air.

Several small oil producers were among Dr. Fithian's patients. Being
"always of a mechanical term of mind," as he described himself, the phy-

sician became highly motivated to solve more than just the health ailments of these men who claimed they would be forced out of business. Why couldn't the escaping gas replace steam to power pumps? The question seemed too obvious to be overlooked, but no one was doing much about it in that area.

Dr. Fithian's interest in mechanics already had prompted him to join one patient, George Willets, and his brother, Reuben Willets, in developing an internal combustion engine. In 1897 he purchased the Willets brothers' interest for nine hundred dollars, hired them to continue working for wages, then sold their share to lumberman H. W. Bentle. After several months of experimentation, a 10-hp model was completed and tested. Turned down on an attempted sale to the Oil Well Supply Company, Dr. Fithian lost no confidence in his product. He was impatient to move decisively toward manufacturing oil well pumping engines before someone else captured his intended market. First, however, he was forced to repurchase the interest owned by Bentle, who was too discouraged to further pursue the venture.

Needing a new partner with mechanical expertise, the persistent Harmony physician contacted a successful machine shop operator, John Carruthers, who was experimenting with a similar engine in the nearby town of Callery Junction. It was a fortunate choice. E.J. Fithian was an idea man — John Carruthers could turn ideas into productive creations. In analyzing the plight of oil well drillers, they decided that most could not afford to abandon their steam engines, inefficient as they were, and purchase new gas engines. Perhaps an intermediate step would be more plausible. Dr. Fithian had pondered the idea of replacing steam engine cylinders with those that could be powered by escaping gas. John Carruthers liked the suggestion, but such a changeover necessitated a friction clutch, and there was no such creature on the market. So they decided to make the clutch themselves.

In 1898, the Carruthers-Fithian Clutch Company was formed. After inspecting several possible locations, the partners agreed on the small town of Grove City, population four hundred, where Dr. Fithian had attended undergraduate college. The choice admittedly was expedited when Dr. Fithian's brother-in-law, Dr. L.B. Monroe, a Grove City dentist, promoted a citizens' fund drive that enticed the promising company with property containing the abandoned J.C. Brandon's Tile Works. Carruthers supervised conversion of the building into a manufacturing shop, while Dr. Fithian phased out his medical practice. Both then moved to Grove City.

The company's original name has led to much debate over which came first, the cylinder or the clutch. Early records give no conclusive evidence, but the answer is of value only to collectors of trivia. Regardless of which was developed first, the Carruthers-Fithian two-cycle gas cylinder and friction clutch — which adjusted automatically to load changes —

were sold in tandem. For $125, an oil producer could remove a steam engine's cylinder and replace it with a 10-hp gas cylinder-clutch combination. A 15-hp outfit cost $175. Two men could complete the conversion in one day.

Acceptance of what became known among oil men as the "half-breed" was so immediate that in its first year of operation the company was unable to meet the demands of its first major customer, South Penn Oil Company. For three years, South Penn purchased all it could get from the fledgling company and paid royalties to manufacture additional "half-breeds" in its own shop at Allegheny, placing them on more than ten thousand well-pumping units in Pennsylvania and West Virginia. The Carruthers-Fithian "automatic short shaft gas engine friction clutch" evolved into a varied series of styles and sizes, transmitting from 5 to 1,000 horsepower, for sale to gas engine builders and users.

Meanwhile, the company itself took a natural step into gas engine manufacturing, fulfilling a plan both partners had nurtured independently before they met. This created the obvious need for a new company name. Weighing possibilities, the men decided to capitalize on the prestige of a railroad serving Grove City and a renowned steel-making process. In 1899, the Bessemer Gas Engine Company was incorporated, with John Carruthers president and E.J. Fithian treasurer. Arthur J. Hull and John "Jack" McCune, Jr., former machine shop associates of Carruthers, soon joined the corporation, becoming vice president and secretary, respectively. The Carruthers-Fithian Clutch Company continued for several years as a separate entity in name only. There was no operational separation of the two organizations.

Beginning with a two-cycle 5-hp natural gas engine, Bessemer enlarged its line steadily. In 1900 its first enclosed-case engine was introduced at the Pan American Exposition in Buffalo, announcing its entry into power fields outside the oil production industry. The original building expanded into a complex. The company added design and manufacture of vertical pumps for municipal plants, roller pumping power equipment, an oil well pumping jack, and a small gas-kero engine, with varying degrees of success. Some products were developed, then abandoned when attention was drawn to something more interesting. The direct gas engine driven compressor, pioneer of casinghead gasoline production, was a success from its inception. On the other hand, a vertical gas engine was brought to final development, then scrapped without a single sale.

Despite experiments in diverse fields, Bessemer Gas Engine Company continued to find its greatest success where it had started — anticipating and answering needs of oil producers. That is the business the company knew best, and the one in which it excelled. John Carruthers had a special talent for simplifying complicated mechanical equipment, something greatly appreciated by oilfield customers. Dr. Fithian, although never claiming engineering knowledge, was no amateur at a drafting table, and his creative ideas remained evident in the chain of product revisions. One distinct market advantage was gained with the single-acting characteristic of the crankshaft; nearly all others received a single impulse for every two revolutions.

Although it often was undersold, the company emphasized that it built its products heavier and stronger than necessary to prevent costly oil production shutdowns, and proclaimed proudly in all its advertising, "You buy the BEST when you buy the BESSEMER."

It appeared highly improbable that the two men who together molded Bessemer's configuration could exist as a team. Their personalities seemed incompatible. Yet, they rarely argued, and it was well known that neither would tolerate an unkind word about the other. One colleague rationalized that their opposite polarities must have accounted for their close association.

Employees described John Carruthers with the single word "tough." And he looked the part. A stocky man of medium height, with iron gray hair and mustache, the Bessemer president spent most of his time in the factory shops. Work was a compulsion for him. He could not accept its being less than the same for everyone else. It was said that no one ever forgot his first workday encounter with Carruthers. Michael C. Pollock, who rose to a top management position with the company, always remembered the exact conversation when he joined Bessemer on the erecting floor.

"Now, young man," the president barked in tones that nearly shook the walls, "we get to work here at seven in the morning, and when I say seven, I mean five minutes before seven, not after." Pollock's part of the conversation was restricted to a shaky "Yes, sir."

Nothing could have been more futile than attempting to fool President Carruthers. At 7:00 a.m. he was already at work in the factory. If any employee was missing, his time card was removed immediately from the rack. The offender was required to see his foreman before it could be replaced. By 7:30, Carruthers completed his first round of the shops, checking the work of every employee. By making a similar round in the late afternoon, he determined whether each had done a reasonable day's work. This amazing feat continued even when the work force numbered well into the hundreds. He was so knowledgeable about individual performances that he made personal evaluations for pay raises, consulting foremen only as a matter of protocol and overruling their recommendations at will. One employee explained that "he just decided how much you were worth and paid you that amount, period."

Reprimands were made in rough, salty terms, profanity constituting a sizeable portion of the president's vocabulary. A degree of fear was inevitable, but it rarely developed into animosity, primarily because Carruthers's demands were balanced by an instinctive impulse to assist employees. Walking through the shops, always dressed in a light-colored suit employees secretly referred to as his ice cream uniform, he would pause to help replace a belt, hold a tool, push, lift, shovel, or brace. Throughout the plant, as well as the industry, he was regarded as a mastermind of machinery. He held several patents and his designs were found in all Bessemer products. But many of those designs were never recorded on paper. It was not uncommon for Carruthers to walk out into the plant, a piece of chalk in hand, and sketch his ideas on the floor. Machinists followed the chalked directions as the president supervised, making adjustments when necessary. Several excellent developments in engines were thus recorded only temporarily on the Bessemer machine shop floor.

Nothing was unimportant enough to escape the president's involvement. An example was the teenage experience of a long-time employee, Ted Helsel, who later became Service Department supervisor. "I joined the company at the age of thirteen, fibbing a little about my age to get the job. On my first day, someone gave me a bucket of water, a cake of Bon Ami, some rags, and sent me up three stacks of ladders with another boy to wash the skylight on what we called the 'big shop.' Well, after a while, we leaned back to do a little loafing. But we made the mistake of leaning against the skylight and 'Old Johnny' saw us from below. Well, he came charging up through all those ladders and across that roof and really gave us a going over. We could hardly believe our eyes. That was a lot of climbing, and he was the company president, wearing a white suit. He sure didn't want anything to get out of hand."

While President Carruthers was occupied in the factory, Treasurer Fithian headed administrative activities in the office. An observer would have been hard pressed to determine which of the two men was chief executive officer. Neither worried about making such a distinction. Tall and lean with a carriage that somehow commanded respect, Dr. Fithian was held in awe by employees and most other citizens of Grove City. No one addressed him by any name other than Dr. Fithian. Even behind his back, he was referred to as "the doctor," although his medical practice was reduced to personally handling all first aid services for employees. At times he confessed that a reluctance to witness human suffering helped him decide to abandon the practice of medicine. Yet, that was a minor fact. More important was an irresistible drive to try new ideas. Industry provided the optimum outlet for his hyperactive mind. He had to put each dream to the test. There simply was no other way. Even the rapid acceleration of Bessemer operations could not keep pace with his fountain of inspiration, so he dabbled in various business sidelines as well.

Dr. Fithian's inventiveness was reflected in his home that, over a period of time, became a self-contained estate. Water from drilled wells was stored in a huge stand-pipe located in the woods, maintaining a pressurized supply to the entire property, including a swimming pool and a greenhouse. A gas well produced fuel to heat buildings and run a generator that provided electricity. The house itself featured a brick construction with air-pocketed walls giving the effect of air conditioning.

Regardless of circumstances, Dr. Fithian never appeared to waver from total control of his dignity. Neither did he compromise certain attitudes known by every man, woman, and child in his community and later by those in many other areas of Pennsylvania. The doctor could not abide drinking, smoking, or swearing. He also opposed dancing and playing cards.

Religion, although extremely important to him, was not the sole basis for such feelings. He was angered by seeing families go hungry while the breadwinners drank, smoked, and gambled. In addition, he carried the influence of a strong prohibitionist father who had seen a close friend nearly killed by a man in a drunken stupor. It was said that Dr. Fithian hated alcoholics as a group, but was sympathetic to individual drunks. He literally picked them out of gutters and tried to set them straight.

Dr. Fithian's imposing demeanor was seldom interpreted as stuffiness. Voters elected him mayor, and when he subsequently shut down all Sunday business, including filling stations and drug stores, there were only scattered grumblings that "you can't even get an aspirin tablet, and hardly a newspaper" on the Sabbath. "Most of us called the town 'Grave City' in those days, and wondered when the mayor would put a fence around it," recalled Louis Copits, a draftsman with the company for forty-three years. (After the merger of Cooper and Bessemer, Copits moved to Mt. Vernon, where he made layouts of diesel engines on a 6' x 6' vertical drafting board, then organized training programs for apprentice draftsmen.)

Employment at the Bessemer Gas Engine Company in the first three decades of the twentieth century was a family affair. Grove City was described as a "single industry town." Sons joined fathers, brothers, and uncles at jobs in the foundry and shops, often beginning as apprentices after completing grade school. Loyalty and long service were taken for granted.

Some out-of-towners did get jobs. Young Angus M. Winder moved to Grove City and joined Bessemer in 1908 at a salary of eleven dollars for a 54-hour week. "I told everyone I went to Harvard, because I did go there and walk across the campus one day," he said, "but the truth was I never even went to high school."

Winder, always known as "Sam," progressed to the position of production manager at a time when inventory records existed only in men's heads. Throughout the factory, each man was concerned just with his specific task. Many credited Sam with performing the near miracle of seeing that components of each engine somehow appeared together on the erecting floor. At the same time, Purchasing Agent R.E. English made sure such raw materials as pig iron arrived on time and nothing was wasted in the plant. Tall, stately, and extremely reserved, he toured working areas like a military leader inspecting troops, turning out unnecessary lights, checking for air leaks in hoses, and noticing any sign of material waste. Employees called him the economic watch dog. Dr. Fithian's younger brother, Fred, was sales manager, working almost exclusively through branch offices that sprouted in the wake of each new oil strike. Several became full distribution centers with sales, service, and warehousing of engine parts, as independent discoveries blossomed into large-scale Texas and Oklahoma oil fields. A company executive described the sales force as "a conglomeration of good men who went their individual ways, without much coordination, but all 'brought home the bacon.'"

Plant facilities in Grove City kept pace, as multiton cranes and milling machines expedited production of increasingly larger engines for drilling, as well as pumping. The company also developed a line of oil engines that progressed through improvement stages near the beginning of World War I. Those engines, which burned both crude and fuel oils, had many uses but were most popular for industrial power, irrigation, cotton ginning and mining. One important selling point, emphasized in marketing booklets, was "Where coal and wood are costly, oil is cheap, abundant, and easily transported." At the mammoth 1915 Panama Pacific International Exposition in San Francisco, a battery of Bessemer oil engines alternated with the Expo power plant in supplying current for the entire grounds.

Bessemer continued to operate family style. By pooling individual orders, the company purchased coal, potatoes, corn, and fruit in carload lots, selling them at cost to employees and their families. Each Christmas, the group purchase was extended to candy and nuts.

But labor strife, gathering momentum across the nation, reached Grove City. On the afternoon of March 6, 1916, Dr. Fithian returned from a short trip to face a mob of angry foundry strikers outside the plant. Adversity did not ruffle the doctor's pride. When a strike leader threatened to smash him in the face, Dr. Fithian replied, "It is your privilege to do so if you think it best." As he turned his head, Dr. Fithian was assaulted and severely beaten. Across the street, part of the mob had spotted "Old Johnny" Carruthers, and rushed to bloody his face as well. As Fred Fithian attempted to help his brother from the scene, the doctor said, "I would like to find my hat first." Someone handed him the hat and he went on to the foundry to drive frightened nonstriking workers to their homes. Then he returned to dress his own face, scalp and body wounds. Carruthers, meanwhile, was rescued by Jack McCune.

Bessemer's business was not affected noticeably by the early years of World War I. America's entry into the conflict, however, created a surge in the company's production. Twenty-four Bessemer oil engines were built and installed in army camps to power electric lighting and water systems. Forty-two others furnished power to machine shops and small arsenals behind the American lines in France. The company was gearing up for production of gun forgings and other war machinery when the Armistice was signed. But there was very little wartime interruption of the steady growth that was being plotted for the future.

Postwar plans called for broadening research and development that had established leadership in gasoline extraction into improvement of overall company products for oil fields, small gas pumping stations, booster stations, and industrial service. Results were seen in such products as the Bessemer Type Ten Compressor, a streamlined two-cycle machine that company engineers considered their major achievement of 1922. The following year, Bessemer introduced two types of four-cycle engines, one for oilfield pumping, the other a compressor unit for pipeline transmission. With the latter, it entered a competitive field dominated by C. & G. Cooper Company.

But the product that was to have the most profound effect on Bessemer's future was the diesel engine. Dr. Fithian was thoroughly convinced that demands for a cheaper fuel pointed toward the diesel. He was determined to be in the forefront of its development. That decision, coupled with the death of John Carruthers and subsequent events of the mid-1920s, set Bessemer heading toward an eventual merger with Cooper.

Dr. Fithian greatly admired a diesel engine manufactured by Atlas Imperial of California, through a license from Atlas of Sweden. After intensive study and extensive negotiation, he purchased one of the engines and obtained a license to build a Bessemer version. Because the move placed a heavy financial burden on the company, however, it found less than unanimous approval among the doctor's colleagues.

When President Carruthers died, Dr. Fithian succeeded him in office. A short time later he became involved in an unusual transaction with the late president's two sons.

Glen and Henry ("Bud") Carruthers both worked at Bessemer. After their father's death, they inherited most of his considerable financial share of the company. And although they maintained a mutual friendship with Dr. Fithian, they did not agree with his plans, particularly regarding heavy investment in diesel engine development. Specifically, they proposed that the doctor either sell them his interest or that he buy theirs. An agreement was reached that each party — the brothers acting jointly as one and the doctor as the other — would submit a sealed bid. The higher bid would constitute purchase. Charles E. Reagle, son-in-law of Dr. Fithian and at that time a diesel salesman for the company, was involved closely in the transaction. He recalled that no animosity was displayed and the Carruthers brothers in fact asked him, "Will you come with us and be in charge of diesel sales if we buy your father-in-law's stock?"

Reagle never had to make the decision. "The Carruthers bid was a good one, but Dr. Fithian managed to be a little bit higher," he explained later. "Everyone parted friends and we proceeded at full speed into diesels."

Progress was sporadic. Stories of success were punctuated with such temporary interruptions as crankcase explosions knocking out doors and windows of the plant. In one test, Engineer George Monroe (whose father had led the public drive to bring the beginning company to Grove City in 1898) was poised to fire a newly developed yacht engine. Excitement was high, because the yacht owner's chief engineer was on hand, wearing a cap bearing the vessel's identification. It was a moment the young engineer would not soon forget. He threw the throttle, heard a loud "varoooooom," and watched the room fill with flying objects, including one new yachting cap. Incredibly, no one was hurt, and research went back to the drawing boards.

With such problems solved by the late 1920s, diesel production moved into a new building. The Atlas original was refined into totally new Bessemer stationary and marine diesels ranging from 40 to 1500 horsepower and sold throughout the world.

Diesel design engineering was headed by Harold Shepherd, who had joined the company shortly after the Atlas license was obtained. Only the man's genius kept him with Bessemer. His dedication to drinking, swearing, and carousing, obviously abrasive to Dr. Fithian, became nearly intolerable by his insistence on flaunting it in front of the president. To further annoy the doctor, Shepherd liked to leave his job in mid-afternoon, saddle a horse, and ride back and forth past the main plant office. Employees considered it a strange method of proving one's value, yet it was no secret that Shepherd was indispensable at a time when top diesel designers were in extremely short supply. Somehow, the company president managed to remain silent. But few doubted the substance of his muffled thoughts.

On a basis of total product lines, an overlap was evolving between the Bessemer Gas Engine Company and C. & G. Cooper Company. But with major strengths in separate areas, they were not fierce competitors. Cooper produced diesels through what it described as "Americanizing" the famous Maschinenfabrik-Augsburg-Nurnburg (M.A.N.) product of Germany, birthplace of the diesel engine. But it trailed Bessemer's diesel development just as it did in production of gasoline extraction units.

Whereas Bessemer had produced oil pumping engines for nearly all of its company life, Cooper was just entering that arena. Conversely, Cooper was a world leader in large natural gas engines for mainline compressor stations, a market barely penetrated by Bessemer. A salesman at the time astutely assessed reputations of the two companies:

"Odds are favorable," he said, "that at most oil fields you will find natural gasoline being extracted by Bessemer engine-compressors and natural gas transported through pipelines by Cooper engine-compressors."

Observation from today's vantage provides another interesting comparison within the two companies — a striking similarity between the two principal founders, Charles Cooper and Dr. E.J. Fithian. Both men were active prohibitionists and community leaders. Each died within a month and a half of his ninetieth birthday. They shared a fearless compulsion to pursue innumerable quests. And both were unsuccessful candidates for high political positions.

Dr. Fithian ran for both governor and senator on the Prohibition Party ticket. The futility of representing a minor party in no way diminished his determination to stage a vigorous campaign. And it was characteristic that for his campaign he designed what many persons claimed to be the nation's first motor home. Using the elongated frame of a motor truck, candidate Fithian and a Grove City mechanic named Ed Black constructed a special bus for the campaign trail. The interior, designed by the doctor, featured cut velvet upholstery, built-in storage cabinets, a Pullman seat, table, icebox, lavatory, pure silk window shades, and copper window screens. Large bunk beds slept four persons comfortably. Powered by a Winton engine, the vehicle had a rear platform resembling that of a railroad coach, from which he spoke to voters across the state of Pennsylvania. Many years later, the campaign bus was purchased by opera star James Melton, who traveled to Grove City to claim his prize.

5

An Historic Merger

United States energy consumption was growing rapidly in 1928. Manufacturing enjoyed boom conditions. New foreign markets were being tapped. Corporations were growing in size and diversification, often through acquisition. In keeping with the trend, C. & G. Cooper, on October 1, purchased the manufacturing division of Hope Engineering Company, located only a mile from its own factory complex, thereby adding vertical gas engines to a line that had been predominantly horizontal in design. Then it turned attention to a more ambitious undertaking — joining forces with the Bessemer Gas Engine Company. August Belmont & Company of New York had informed Cooper that Bessemer's heavy financial commitment pointed toward the feasibility of such a move.

Records and memories fail to pinpoint the precise steps that led to a merger of Cooper and Bessemer. But no one doubted that the initiative came from Mt. Vernon and few disputed the major circumstances involved. Cooper needed additional production facilities to meet a growing demand for large natural gas engine compressor units. Bessemer, having stretched its fiscal capabilities in extensive diesel development, was hard pressed for new capital to continue the effort. Cooper also was interested in promoting diesel engine development for marine, as well as stationary and transportation, services. The companies were drawing closer to designing parallel product lines. Both could gain efficiency by combining research, engineering, and sales.

By 1929, Cooper had thirty-three buildings and 765 employees. Bessemer had twenty-nine buildings, including one of the world's largest industrial-plant foundries, and 1,180 employees. Average earnings over the previous three years were almost identical for the two organizations.

After negotiating through the winter months, the companies agreed to merger terms. An amendment to the Cooper Articles of Incorporation was filed with the secretary of state of Ohio, and on April 4, 1929, The Cooper-Bessemer Corporation came into being. Soon afterward it was listed on the American Stock Exchange. The merger made

The first Bessemer Atlas diesel engine shown here opened a new business for the Grove City Company.

Cooper-Bessemer the largest builder of gas engines and compressors in America.

Heading the list of officers was President and General Manager, Beatty B. Williams. President of Cooper since 1920, he had directed bargaining activities leading to the merger. Dr. E.J. Fithian, then sixty-six years old, was elected chairman of the board, remaining in Grove City, although principal corporate offices were in Mt. Vernon. Other executive officers named at the first official meeting of the new corporation were Zenno E. Taylor, secretary and head of production; Fred H. Thomas, vice president of sales; Michael C. Pollock, vice president and assistant secretary; Charles M. Reagle, vice president; Norman L. Daney, treasurer and comptroller; and Hewitt A. Gehres, vice president in charge of engineering.

Reassignments were made within the sales, engineering, and service groups, and some resignations were tendered, but the general tenor of the consolidation was well described in a letter from Vice President Thomas to established customers:

"The same faces will greet you as before and we just want you to know that the new company is really a change in name only, with enlarged facilities for better filling your engine and compressor needs. That you will feel as much at home with our new name as you did with our old one is the wish of your same good friends in the Cooper family."

One notable change came as little surprise to Grove City employees. It was reported that one of Dr. Fithian's questions during negotiations concerned the qualifications of Cooper's chief engineer. He was told correctly that Hewitt Gehres was one of the most capable design engineers in the business and had received professional acclaim throughout the industry. Satisfied with that assessment, Dr. Fithian fulfilled a desire of long standing. He fired his design engineer and unrelenting antagonist, Harold Shepherd, even before the merger was consummated.

As an epilogue to that incident, it should be noted that Shepherd promptly went to Mt. Vernon and successfully applied for a job with Gehres. However, the change in location apparently did little to alter his personality. He was dropped from the roster a few months later.

The rapid pace of technology put engineering in an industrial life-or-death position at that time. A company could be wiped out by sudden obsolescence, or saved by a single engineering breakthrough of its own. Combining engineering talents from both former companies, Cooper-Bessemer pushed to settle quickly on its most competitive product development under Gehres and an exceptional staff that included Bruno Thiel (son of the gas engine expert, Martin Thiel), Ralph L. Boyer, Monroe Bovard, Ralph Schlosser, and Edmund Frederick. The group decided immediately to drop the M.A.N. diesel design in favor of the more advanced Bessemer product. Other overlapping was eliminated with the better product prevailing in each instance, and all engineering effort put into its further development. The new Cooper-Bessemer line included (1) gas engine drive compressor units, (2) stationary and marine diesel engines, and (3) gas engines in the 25 to 250 horsepower range.

A steady flow of supervisory personnel between the two plant complexes was evident as Cooper-Bessemer blended into a single organization. But in the shops, change was nearly imperceptible. With strong tradition behind them, most employees still considered their groups autonomous. The ease of transition at executive levels was enhanced greatly by the personality of Cooper-Bessemer's president.

"The first time I met B.B. Williams was in the summer of 1929 when he came to Grove City to meet with supervisors," recalled Dennis L. Gallogly, who began his career as an engineer on the test floor at Bessemer and eventually rose to chief engineer for the combined company. "A sizable group of us gathered at the Penn Grove Hotel, where B.B. shook hands all around, asking names and all about our families. Two months later he came back, and he knew each of us by name. That was unbelievable to me, but he could do it. As I got to know the man, I discovered that he would meet an employee's wife on the street and ask her how her children were doing in school — usually referring to them by name. When it came to people, he had a computer memory."

Nearly everyone in the company and the communities called President Williams by his initials, "B.B." A sincere interest in civic affairs and a low handicap in golf helped establish his popularity among the citizens of Mt. Vernon. A proponent of developing community projects through private funds, he had been instrumental in the construction of a YMCA building for the city. Many years later he was to lead the drive for a new YMCA structure and a public library in the city he loved. B. B. always rested for half an hour after lunch, claiming that it invigorated him. He liked to walk through the plants frequently. When a newspaper reporter would appear at his office for an interview, the president would suggest, "Let's go out in the sunshine," and the reporter would find himself striding briskly through the Cooper-Bessemer grounds, taking notes on the move. Walking provided enjoyment and relaxation for the president, and he did it with a distinctive swing of his lanky body. R. Edwin Moore, a Mt. Vernon friend who left the city and later became president of Bell & Gossett Company of Chicago, liked to tell about an experience in New York City. Standing in the Roosevelt Hotel lobby, he was looking at some men walking across the mezzanine. Although he could see them only from the waist down, he suddenly said to a companion, "Why, there goes B.B. Williams. I haven't seen him for ten years." The companion laughed at Moore's assumption, but it proved to be correct and the two old friends enjoyed an evening of reminiscence. Later, Moore became an outside director of Cooper-Bessemer.

President Williams was always concerned that what he termed "an aloofness" could develop between offices and shops. He held conferences in which employees from the shops could air their views, and he set up a night school where any employee could enroll in production and management courses.

The highly cyclical aspect of heavy machinery manufacturing necessitated frequent layoffs, and B.B. Williams suffered when any employee was temporarily out of work. One specific incident on a cold December afternoon punctured his sensitivity in that respect. Walking across the public square in Mt. Vernon, he stopped to chat with a worker who had been laid off when the sales chart skidded to a low dip. With the man was his small son, who obviously did not recognize the company president. Since Christmas was just a few days away, President Williams asked the little boy if he was looking forward to the holiday. "No," the child replied. "B.B. killed Santa Claus."

The encounter left an indelible scar on the president's memory. Not only was it personally distressing, it somehow epitomized the frustration that overwhelmed the entire nation just a few months after the merger of Cooper and Bessemer.

Women employees pose outside main office in 1929.

It is not uncommon for carefully drawn plans based on meticulous studies of business trends to be shattered suddenly by unforeseen events. The boom of the 1920s, nurtured by heavy securities speculation, provided few apparent signs of collapse. Throughout the nation, business and industry moved forward optimistically.

After the Cooper-Bessemer merger, sales flourished on both fronts. In Mt. Vernon, production at the "Cooper" and "Hope" plants went to day and night shifts, but the demand for natural gas engines and compressors still created a huge backlog of unfilled orders. Among the company's successes at Grove City was a continuation of the leadership Bessemer had gained in diesel marine engines. No engine builder in the world could match it in powering vessels on the high seas and inland waterways. C-B engines, most of them still bearing the name of Bessemer, were helping revolutionize the fishing industry. Sun Oil Company had an entire fleet of C-B powered tankers. Canada's enormous dredge, the *Primrose*, largest in the world, had just completed a change from steam power equipment to a 1500-hp Cooper-Bessemer diesel engine. Grove City engineers had demonstrated successful development of diesel power for canal bulk carriers on the freighter *Grainmotor*, which had astonished skeptics with a remarkable performance on her maiden voyage. A 250' steel cargo carrier, the *Georgian*, had not performed to expectations

The *Helene*, owned by Charles Sorensen of the Ford Motor Company, was one of many yachts powered by Bessemer engines in the late 1920s. This 105-foot craft had a 170 horsepower direct reversible diesel engine.

since being launched in Scotland in 1912. On the Great Lakes she had won the nickname "Black Sheep" because of a consistently unsatisfactory and unprofitable performance. In a last desperate effort to make the ship pay, owners had changed to a Bessemer direct drive engine. The profitable results surpassed fondest expectations.

There were many similar stories. Some of the most interesting concerned luxury yachts on which the world's wealthiest families had formerly sailed, but now dieseled, the Seven Seas.

J.P. Morgan had made the memorable observation that "If you have to ask the price of such a yacht, you can't afford it." Howard Hughes owned a C-B powered yacht. So did Julius Fleischmann, Edsel Ford, Alfred Dupont, and D.C. Whitney. The *Savarona,* largest diesel yacht afloat and powered by two 1500-hp C-B engines, was so luxurious that passengers said they felt they were guests in a mansion by the sea. J.A. McDonald, president of Henry J. Gielow, Inc., leading designer of yachts, described the ultimate in commodious commuting when he reported that "Business and professional men who spend their working hours in lower Manhattan Island are experiencing the pleasure of motoring to and from business in private yachts." This means of transportation up and down the Hudson and East rivers and Long Island Sound, he added, "has so many advantages that it is sure to increase rapidly in popularity."

Since nearly all the shops were being built or converted on America's East Coast, the continuing upward business trend called for opening a Cooper-Bessemer sales office in New York City. Appropriate arrangements were made to have the new sales office located in the same building with Gielow. It was a logical move; Gielow designs specified C-B engines.

Charles M. Reagle, Cooper-Bessemer vice president in charge of diesel sales, and George Monroe, an engineer-salesman, took the train to New York City to open the office at 25 West 43rd Street. They arrived on Wednesday, October 23, 1929. That evening, the two men strolled toward Times Square. As they approached the Times Building they looked up at the famous moving lights that spelled out the news of the day. The words they saw were "Stock Market Crashes." The incident "was not an encouraging welcome to Gotham," said Reagle.

The New York office would survive the Great Depression that followed "Black Wednesday," but it would not be on the strength of yacht construction. Fortunes disappeared overnight in the nationwide panic. In one month, $30 billion in the market value of listed stocks was wiped out. Two years later, the figure had jumped to $75 billion. Banks closed. The index of industrial production dropped to an all-time low. With one slash of the economic sword, prosperous families lost all means of support.

The momentum of committed orders carried Cooper-Bessemer through the business quake for nearly a year. Marketing of diesel engines for fishing boats, developed for many years through the individual efforts of super-salesman Larry McEwen, continued after nearly everything else failed. But as Wall Street came tumbling down, there was no avenue for industrial escape. In a period of six months, Cooper-Bessemer common stock plunged from sixty dollars to one dollar per share.

As months passed, the United States realized it was in the grip of the worst economic disaster in its history. Factories closed, leaving millions of workers unemployed. Foreclosures on small businesses became commonplace. Many farmers had to revive the barter system, exchanging food for supplies and services.

Author Joe Alex Morris, in his book, *What a Year*, considered 1929 a year of transition. "It led out of the roaring, raucous, hell-raising, materialistic and individualistic postwar period and pointed toward an era of tremendous social change," he wrote. "People later would speak of 'before 1929' or 'after 1929' as Noah's children may have spoken of the days before and after the flood."

Construction on long distance pipelines and in American shipyards diminished to a near stop, shutting off the two major markets for Cooper-Bessemer products. Annual sales dropped more than 90 percent to $909,000 in 1931, and approximately half of that amount was for repair parts. Cooper-Bessemer, along with other industries, was forced into long layoffs and temporary shutdowns in various areas of its plants. Workers were often called to work for just a few hours to produce replacement parts for small orders. Mt. Vernon operations were closed completely for several months. Members of the sales force, with salaries sliced in half, fought desperately competitive battles with representatives of other companies for any business that surfaced. Stockholder dividends were discontinued indefinitely.

Throughout industry, previous plans for growth and development melted into the single goal of survival. Critics of the U.S. capitalistic system loudly predicted its demise, failing to mention that the Great Depression was worldwide. But Americans managed to retain a national optimism, even while singing "Brother, Can You Spare a Dime."

Determined to avoid stagnation, Cooper-Bessemer demonstrated its own confidence in 1931 by introducing two new four-cycle engines, one a natural gas unit, the other a diesel.

During the ordeal President Williams maintained an outward enthusiasm, assuring employees that the company would pull through. He encouraged engineers to continue the search for new designs that would strengthen Cooper-Bessemer's competitive position, and talked forcefully about the future. It was difficult for colleagues to determine his inner feelings, but there were occasional signs. Stanley E. Johnson, Sr., then assistant sales manager, remembered one that involved Fred Hudgins, who was named head of sales in 1932, following the untimely death of Fred H. Thomas.

"The company had gone for several months without a single sale, when Sales Manager Hudgins came in from Tulsa with an order for forty pumping engines," Johnson said. "That was a fantastic order anytime, a miracle in 1933. Well, Fred took the order in and showed it to B.B. Williams. He told me that tears came to the president's eyes and rolled down his cheeks. Fred left the room, and when he went back later, B.B. was bent forward at his desk, with the tears still flowing."

Although it still operated at a loss, Cooper-Bessemer proudly celebrated its 100th anniversary in 1933, announcing that it was "preparing for the next one hundred years." On the eve of its celebration, the company mailed beautiful calendars depicting its history to customers in the oil, gas, and railroad industries. The calendars contained illustrations of such historic products as the first Cooper cupola for making iron castings, the slide-valve steam engine that had been its principal product of the 1850s, a wood-burning locomotive, Cooper Corliss engines furnishing power for early Packard Motor Car Company plants, several sizes of diesel oil engines used "for every possible service on land and sea," and both horizontal and vertical Cooper-Bessemer gas engines in sizes from 10 to 1600 horsepower.

The *Grove City Reporter-Herald* quoted President Williams as expressing optimism in the company "starting on its second century with renewed enthusiasm and the hope that the first hundred years are the hardest." More specifically, he said, "While business continues at a low ebb, and is likely to continue to do so since business recovery now awaits political action, which is always slow and at present unusually so, we are doing many things in all departments which will help us to hold our own in the months and years ahead. At present, through the operation of Share-the-Work, we have over four hundred people on our payroll."

With the scramble for solvency affecting nearly every corner of American business and industry, federal programs proliferated in the New Deal administration. One of the most notable was the National Industrial Recovery Act, offering a set of codes to revive industry and reduce unemployment. (Later, the NIRA was declared unconstitutional by the U.S. Supreme Court.) It became apparent that the federal government would be increasing regulations and influencing product sales for many years to come. Consequently, Cooper-Bessemer, at the insistence of Charles Reagle, decided to open an office in Washington, D.C., where it could maintain direct contact with federal activities. The move proved beneficial not only during the remainder of the depression, but also in the war effort that was to follow.

Chosen for the Washington position was a young sales engineer named Charles Cooper. Grandson of cofounder Elias Cooper and son of former president C.G. Cooper, he was the last member of the family to be associated with the company.

As an undergraduate at Yale University, Cooper had worked summers and holidays on the erecting floor of the Mt. Vernon factory. After graduating in 1926, he became a field engineer for the company's first subsidiaries, Chapman-Stein Co. and Chapman Engineering Co. In 1929, he was assigned to develop a venturi-type combustion port for Chapman-Stein's recuperative furnaces and soaking pits. Under his supervision, the development was added to existing installations at Gary, Indiana, and Weirton, West Virginia, greatly improving Chapman-Stein's position in serving the steel industry. The subsidiaries were sold to the Surface Combustion Co. of Toledo in 1930. The following year, Cooper became a Cooper-Bessemer sales engineer, working out of the New York City office.

Charles Cooper's geniality and optimism were well suited to the needs of such trying times. He often pointed out that the depression contained an important benefit for Cooper-Bessemer. It prevented new would-be competitors from entering the gas engine compression field. Several had studied the company's success in the late 1920s, with an eye to joining the competition which already included Ingersoll Rand, Worthington, and Dresser Clark. The depression, understandably, stopped them.

Recovery would be a slow process. Success was being measured not in profit, but in loss decreases. The company probed for engineering breakthroughs that could increase its share of the depressed market and establish sales in totally new fields. Meanwhile, it continued to depend greatly on providing service and parts to existing installations. Customers without sufficient funds to purchase new equipment concentrated on keeping old machinery in good repair.

As company representative in the nation's capital, Charles Cooper was often questioned about Cooper-Bessemer's precarious balance on the depression's tottering financial structure. His favorite answer was, "Don't worry. Our company is like a cat. It always is able to land on its feet."

Two accomplishments were instrumental in reestablishing the company's footing in the dismal 1930s. One revived memories of another era when a Cooper steam engine helped pioneer the railroad industry. This time inducement focused on the growing notion that diesels were destined to supplant steam-powered railroad engines. Cooper-Bessemer, convinced that the metamorphosis was about to take place, hastened to develop a diesel locomotive engine for the emerging market.

Early attempts to sell diesel engines to General Electric Company, builder of a few small switchyard locomotives, were fruitless. Finally, however, G.E. agreed to a single purchase. Bolstered by that breakthrough, C-B intensified efforts in both sales and engineering. To make such sales at that time, diesel engine manufacturers had to get orders for complete locomotives. Cooper-Bessemer obtained five such orders, all for small connecting railways, constructed the engines, and purchased all other parts from G.E. From the New York sales office, which had dwindled to a one-man operation, Charles Reagle broke the "Class One Railway" barrier with five more locomotive sales to the New Haven Railroad. Later he convinced Henry Ford to purchase a series of C-B diesels for streamlined locomotives designed to match the styling of 1937 Ford automobiles.

While the company's reentry into the railroad market was underway, a diesel innovation announced in Switzerland was destined to have the second impact on Cooper-Bessemer's recovery.

Reading a European technical publication, Ralph Boyer, C-B assistant chief engineer, was attracted to a small notice stating that Dr. Alfred J. Buchi had patented a system of supercharging a diesel engine with its own exhaust. Intrigued, Boyer discussed the invention with Engineering

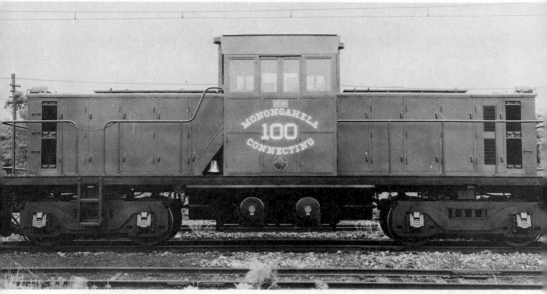

Sales of diesel engines for switching locomotives built by General Electric in the mid-1930s began a relationship that lasted many years. This "double-ender" was built in 1936.

Three generations of chief engineers are represented here. From left are Hewitt A. Gehres, James E. Debes, and Ralph L. Boyer.

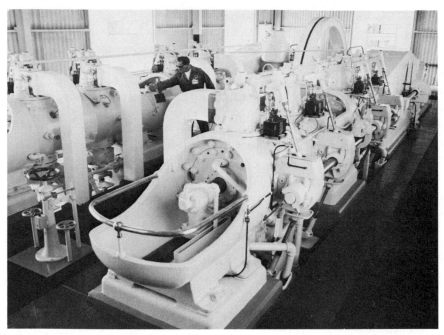

El Paso Natural Gas Company's first compressor transmission station went on line in the 1930s, utilizing Cooper-Bessemer Type 19 engine compressors.

Vice President Hewitt Gehres, then wrote to Dr. Buchi for more details. The response was immediate and beyond expectations. The Swiss inventor appeared without notice at Mt. Vernon carrying designs for his "turbocharger." None had yet been built commercially in the United States.

A license agreement was made with Dr. Buchi and within a few months Cooper-Bessemer produced the first turbocharged diesel engine in the United States. Overnight, horsepower ratings of the company's marine and stationary diesel engines were increased by 50 percent. Turbocharging spread through the diesel engine industry, but Cooper-Bessemer had established an early lead. Several years later, the company added turbocharging to many of its locomotive engines, bringing together two key elements of its return to solvency.

The C-B design principle was copied by other companies for a variety of uses, including all diesel truck engines. It also formed the base for decades of extensive experimentation and improvement within the company. William R. Crooks, a design engineer who joined the company during development of turbocharging, many years later increased its efficiency and output tremendously with his invention of a "turbo-cooler".

Locomotive engine production proved to have lasting value also. With diesels firmly established in the field toward the end of the depression, engine manufacturers no longer had to sell entire locomotives to market their products. They were able to sell directly to locomotive manufacturers converting to diesels or just entering that area. Among the latter was General Electric, which launched a full-scale locomotive production program, purchasing engines from Cooper-Bessemer.

But new designs of the '30s were not confined to diesels. The company became aware also of dangers in gas engine complacency. Complaints on the large horizontal pipeline engine-compressors were rare. They were dependable and efficient, proven leaders in a drastically diminished market. A highly accepted product in a depressed marketplace with almost no funds for development would appear to be ingredients of a safe status quo business posture. There was one aspect of the product, however, that could be vulnerable. The engine was massive. As many as seven flat cars were needed to ship its parts to a customer's site, where three months were required to erect it.

In California, a competitor had introduced a much smaller oilfield engine-compressor built with vertical "V" cylinders and a horizontal compressor, all in one unit. Tested and assembled at the manufacturer's plant, it was delivered on a single car for immediate installation. The 300-hp unit, used primarily in gathering stations, had less than a third of the power Cooper-Bessemer engines generated for pipeline transmission. But what if a similar idea could be applied to 1,000-hp engines? Cooper-Bessemer engineers believed it could be done. Certainly they could ill afford to let a competitor beat them to such a discovery. When a proposal to develop the idea was presented to management, the only question was, "How soon can we get it done?"

Market studies and even cost estimates were passed over for the sake of expediency, as work proceeded with haste and secrecy. The year was 1937. Added incentive was provided by the first noticeable pipeline construction splurge of the decade. In little more than a year, a 1,000-hp V-type engine-compressor was designed, built, factory tested, shipped intact (with the exception of compressor cylinders), and put to work on a pipeline. The effect was revolutionary. Suddenly all large horizontal natural gas engines that Cooper-Bessemer and competitors had perfected over the years faced obsolesence.

Just as suddenly, the upward swing of America's economy hit another snag and lapsed into a disheartening spin. Cooper-Bessemer sales, which had grown slowly but steadily for two years, were cut in half. The Mt. Vernon plant closed for more than a month in the summer of 1938, with operations consolidated in Grove City. Despite its engineering heroics, the company was forced once again to shake off a serious setback and gather strength to mount a fresh advance.

Such was the nature of the Great Depression. During the disastrous '30s, Cooper-Bessemer had improved products and entered new markets. It had negotiated an exclusive license for the Meehanite process of making high-test alloy iron castings. The process, imported from England, produced engine castings of uniform hardness and increased tensile strength almost 40 percent, bridging an existing gap between cast iron and steel. Yet, the company faced day-to-day crises over which it had little control. Long-range benefits would justify decisions made in the Depression years. But at the time, visualizing them was difficult. The company barely survived the depression. Close observers agreed it was only the determination of B.B. Williams that rallied others to keep it alive. Without that extraordinary will to survive, it would have gone under.

Business accelerated upward after the 1938 plunge. However, it was not until the company went on a wartime production schedule in 1941 that sales surpassed their predepression level.

> Our hats are off to the foundry men;
> Their efforts have won us the Maritime "M".
> Let's boost production without any yaps;
> We'll divide the Pacific with the Japs.
> By hustling up with never a stop,
> We'll give them the bottom, while we take the top.

America's patriotic fervor during World War II was reflected in this poem written by John Blair, representative speaker for Cooper-Bessemer employees at a December 18, 1942, ceremony in Grove City. The elaborate occasion itself, with employees assembled in front of a decorated platform, exemplified a nation's emotional immersion in the war effort. Rear Admiral Howard L. Vickery was on hand to present the Maritime "M" award "for outstanding achievement in producing diesel engines, steam cylinder castings, and other vital engine parts for cargo vessels and Liberty Ships of the United States fleets." Proceedings were carried over leased wires to a loud speaker in Mt. Vernon's pattern shop, where employees from that plant gathered to share in the recognition.

Like many other American companies, Cooper-Bessemer had been transformed into an official "defense industry" plant by the country's united response to the December 7, 1941, attack on Pearl Harbor by Japan. The shift from civilian to military production was hailed as the most comprehensive conversion in world history. Labor was mobilized in a manner similar to armed forces conscription. Twenty-seven million workers were "frozen" in war jobs by a federal War Manpower Commission. A War Production Board was given authority to mobilize the na-

Board of Directors in 1939. From left, front row, E.J. Fithian, W.C. Heath, F.C. Van Cleef, and John Gavin. Second row, W.A. Ackerman, C.B. Jahnke, Z.E. Taylor, T.F. Hudgins, B.B. Williams. Third row, H.A. Gehres, J.H. Anderson, M.C. Pollock. C.M. Reagle was not present for photograph.

tion's resources for a total war effort. Essential materials were controlled by a Board of Economic Warfare, and price ceilings were set by an Office of Price Administration. Other regulations were established by an Office of Defense Transportation, a War Shipping Administration, and a National Defense Mediation Board.

The familiar American "junk yards" that had blossomed as ugly symbols of a broken economy disappeared as the nation moved to salvage every available source of raw materials. Rationing of tires began less than three weeks after the Pearl Harbor attack, and it was soon extended to fuel, food, and even shoes. Military production, only 2 percent of the national output in 1939, jumped to 40 percent. The surprisingly low prewar figure, at a time when the conflict in Europe was already underway, was attributed to a combination of struggling out of the depression's depths, and strong public sentiment toward isolationism. But the country could not remain insulated from global hostility. In 1940, federal appropriations had increased for defense and minimal aid to Britain.

Cooper-Bessemer had sold engines to various military sectors for several years, although not in large quantities. The experience and reputation gained from those sales put the company in a high priority position with the Maritime Commission and the Navy. Motivated by German mine devastation of Allied shipping, the Navy decided to construct a fleet of minesweepers. Lieutenant Commander Hyman G. Rickover (later an admiral of nuclear submarine fame) headed the project and enlisted the aid of Cooper-Bessemer because of its known ability to manufacture strong engines.

C-B engines with steel foundations were soon built and sent to Annapolis, Maryland, where the Navy proposed to determine if they could withstand the shock of a mine explosion. A special test was set up with an enormous steel pendulum delivering a simulated mine blast to the underside of each engine. All of the engines passed the severe test, and in the years that followed, the company supplied them for nearly all Navy minesweepers.

Charles Cooper, who coordinated company projects with the Defense Department, had another reason to remember the minesweeper project. At one point during contract negotiations, he was seated in Rickover's office, nervously looking at his watch. Noticing the distraction, Rickover asked him the reason. Cooper replied that he had an airline ticket to Columbus, Ohio, and flight time was getting dangerously close. Without hesitation, Rickover telephoned an aide to cancel the reservation, smilingly explaining that the discussion wasn't close to completion. Cooper never regretted his host's brash action. The airplane he missed crashed shortly after take-off, killing all passengers.

Early in the war, foundry activities appeared to contradict the overall acceleration of company output. While total production sped toward six times its prewar pace, both foundries remained starved for casting orders. The paradox was created by Navy requirements for engines made of welded steel, eliminating the need for castings. So as most of the company stretched resources to meet unprecedented requirements, Lawrence F. Williams, son of the president and the assistant secretary of the corporation, began a personal search for foundry business. Associated with the company since 1926, he had become extremely interested in foundry development and metallurgical research. Traveling largely east of the Mississippi River, Williams met discouragement for months. "All I did was call on people, day after day, wherever I saw a smoke stack," he said. "I would just go in cold and see if they could use iron castings. We were regarded as a company of machinery builders, not foundry men, even though I knew we could produce complicated castings as well or better than anyone else."

In Hamilton, Ohio, Williams joined other industrial representatives meeting with a government group planning construction of engines for emergency cargo EC-2 vessels called Liberty Ships. When discussion progressed to division of responsibilities, he asked, "What part of such an engine is apt to pose the most difficult casting problems?" The answer was, "The power cylinder." Williams answered, "Fine. Cooper-Bessemer will take that." During the remainder of the war, Liberty Ship power cylinders were cast successfully by C-B. Other foundry business also emerged for machine tools and for parts used in heavy earth-moving equipment geared to the war effort.

Anticipated administrative changes were altered unexpectedly amidst the company's changeover to war production. Charles B. Jahnke was elected president in 1940, with B.B. Williams moving to chairman of the board, succeeding Dr. E.J. Fithian, who retired. A year later, President Jahnke died suddenly from a heart attack, and Williams returned to the presidency. An experienced industrial executive, Gordon Lefebvre, was brought to the company from General Motors as vice president and general manager.

With its products easily adaptable to critical military and support needs, the company became a major supplier of diesel engines for troop and cargo ships, battleships, cruisers, subchasers, aircraft carriers, tugs, rescue and patrol boats. Production of locomotive engines was increased substantially.

America boosted annual synthetic rubber production from 2,000 tons in 1939 to a phenomenal 930,000 tons, making up for its loss of imported natural rubber. Cooper-Bessemer natural gas engines powered many of the new processing plants. Other C-B gas engines and compressors were in demand for the country's mushrooming production of alloys and light metals, high octane aircraft fuel, and synthetic ammonia for munitions. They were vital to refineries, chemical plants, shipyards, and such energy transportation projects as the thirty-eight hundred miles of "Big Inch" and "Little Inch" pipelines constructed by the government to carry petroleum to the East Coast.

The change to war manufacturing was so sudden that it posed initial money problems. To finance production for a $25 million contract with the Navy, Charles Cooper and Company Treasurer James Brown had to work out a plan with the Pentagon to provide advance financing. Without it, they couldn't even meet the payroll. Such problems were not unique with Cooper-Bessemer, however. The U.S. government financed five-sixths of new plant construction through a hastily structured Defense Plants Corporation.

Patriotism dominated American thought. A total of 12,466,000 men and women entered the armed forces through enlistments and a draft system affecting males between the ages of eighteen and thirty-eight. Workers in key production jobs hesitated to accept deferments, despite exhortations from Washington that "the war will be won on the production line as well as the battle line." More than twelve hundred young

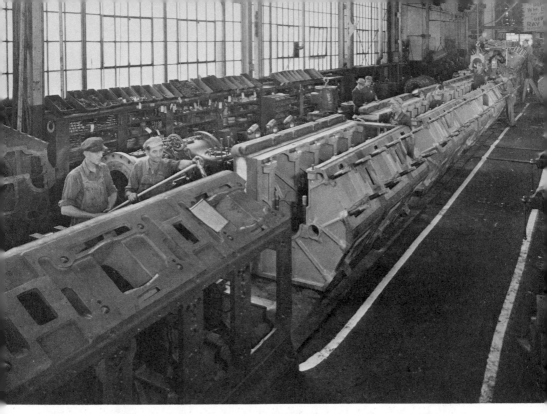

The Mt. Vernon assembly line hits a capacity pace to assist with the war effort in 1944.

men, many of whom could have received draft exemptions, left Cooper-Bessemer for military service. Fourteen were killed in action.

Women joined the work force, operating machines and carrying out other jobs previously reserved for men, as employment swelled to 4,337 on shift schedules permitting round-the-clock operations. A few women had held similar jobs in World War I, but the large scale of female factory employment was new, and somewhat startling to the men. Referring to women machinists filling positions in Cooper-Bessemer shops, a news writer noted that "It is amazing how quickly they have adapted themselves to an entirely new line of work, and how well they are doing the job."

Ambitious production goals were set for every order, with enthusiasm fanned by employee slogans, among them, "Good ole Yankee hustle will deflate the Axis muscle" and "Help the boys in khaki knock the japs wacky." One notable cartoon pictured C-B employees squeezing Adolf Hitler's head in a huge nut cracker. The caption read, "C-B production soldiers are helping to crack this nut."

Gordon Lefebvre was elected president and general manager of the corporation in 1943. B.B. Williams returned to the chairmanship. The new president was a natural leader. Personable and energetic, he liked to walk through Mt. Vernon and Grove City plant complexes in shirt sleeves and vest, regardless of weather. A career background in engineering and high level management with General Motors (including head of the Pontiac Division) and the American Locomotive Company had instilled in him a knowledge of engine manufacturing, and great confidence in dealing with other persons. A tough negotiator, he could be extremely persuasive. On one occasion, President Lefebvre was asked to help convince a Navy representative that Cooper-Bessemer could produce an emergency generating unit capable of going on line in ten seconds. Charles Reagle was set to conclude a multimillion dollar sale, if he could clear one last hurdle in the form of a skeptical Naval engineer. The man refused to take "a salesman's word" that his company could manufacture the special unit for emergency shipboard service. At Reagle's request, President Lefebvre went to Washington for a confrontation. "Gordon looked that fellow and all his assistants right straight in the eyes, one man at a time," Reagle recalled. "Then he said, 'Gentlemen, there isn't anyone in the world who can build those generators as well as we can. I will inspect them personally.' That's all it took. We got the contract." The president was described accurately by one colleague as "a hell raiser away from work, but an inspiring straw boss on the job." The Economic Defense Board recruited his services on the Joint War Production Committee coordinating production of war materials in the U.S. and Canada.

In 1943, net sales jumped to $43 million, more than tripling the all-time record of 1941. Sales to other nations, carried out for many years without formal departmental structure, were drawn together when Vice President Michael Pollock moved to New York City and established an international sales office. Quarters were shared with the domestic sales office on West 43rd Street.

Cooper-Bessemer's expanded war production also added an international flavor to the manufacturing plants. British, as well as U.S., inspection teams were frequent visitors. Fifteen engineering offices and electricians from the British Merchant Navy spent several months with Cooper-Bessemer, observing diesel engine construction and operation in preparation for handling C-B diesel-powered craft in war zone salvage work. The company shared in the Lend Lease program, retooling and converting several Mt. Vernon machines to produce twenty-four diesels for the Russian government. The Soviets later duplicated that order. Two gold stars were added to the original Maritime Commission award. The coveted Army-Navy "E" for outstanding production achievement was presented in another celebration, this one attended by Rear Admiral Thomas B. Richey. Victory flags were won for employee purchases of war bonds and workers continued to muster patriotic perseverance with new slogans such as "Speed up production and watch the Rising Sun go down" and "An engine on the floor never won a war."

Although the company had sold both diesel and gas engines in the western United States for two decades, World War II broadened its position there. Nearly half of the marine diesel engines produced for war use went to shipyards in San Diego, Los Angeles, San Francisco, Tacoma, Seattle, and other Pacific port cities. Robert Jones, a Pacific Coast service department representative since 1937, coordinated that segment of sales and service. "The country just had to get it all together in a hurry to fight that war," Jones said. "The government explained what it needed, and all kinds of industries told what they could do. Then the government sorted out jobs according to our capabilities, and, by God, it all fit."

German capitulation became inevitable under the final 1945 offensive squeeze by American, British, and Russian troops. The formal end of war in Europe came on V-E Day, May 8, 1945, with the unconditional surrender of Germany. Victory in the Pacific, V-J Day, followed on August 14, 1945, when the Japanese accepted Allied terms.

In the jubilation that followed, the return of G.I. Joe was enough to sustain the blissful mood of a nation in need of rest and rehabilitation. But for American industry, realism set in early. Abrupt cancellations of war contracts forced another sudden conversion, this time, thankfully, to peacetime production.

Cooper-Bessemer anticipated few serious conversion problems. Its diesels, gas engines, compressors and foundry products, which played wartime roles on land and sea and in government and industrial service, seemed applicable to peacetime needs. With the heavy majority of its war effort concentrated on diesel engines for the Navy, however, its principal business line — compressors — had been overshadowed. Still, some research had continued through the war years, and a few new developments were ready for product expansion. Among them was an alteration that permitted changing from gas to oil fuel while an engine was operating, and achieving an efficiency never before reached by practical engines of any type.

President Lefebvre reported that the company's postwar opportunity lay "in the constant improvement of our chosen products and in the manufacture of new equipment to meet the pressing demand for lower costs and greater efficiency in the production of power." (In the excitement of the war's end, it was understandable that little notice was made of Dr. Fithian's 1945 retirement from the Cooper-Bessemer board. The Fithian name was absent only temporarily from the company's roster, however, because the Bessemer founder's son, also named Edwin, returned from Naval aviation duty in 1946, received an engineering degree from Purdue University, and joined the company in 1949.)

Planned expansion in the petroleum and natural gas industries, long served by Cooper-Bessemer, offered promise for retrieving old markets. Demand was expected to continue for locomotive engines. Municipal power plants should be ready to expand, now that materials would become available. But the company had undergone a transition that demanded emphasis on product innovation and new marketing, rather than simply a return to prewar concepts. It had experience in serving such new markets as light metals, aviation gasoline, synthetic rubber, and high explosives. It had established an international office. In 1944, it had been listed for the first time on the New York Stock Exchange.

Cooper-Bessemer had grown in employees, in facilities, and in reputation. The United Steelworkers Union had petitioned to have its organizing committee be recognized as representing the Grove City employees. And the U.S. government gave strong evidence of its intention to maintain, even increase, regulatory participation in the affairs of business and industry. Peacetime conversion could not become retrogression.

6

Emphasis on Engineering

Field service engineers become accustomed to varied problems. Perhaps the most annoying is recurrence of trouble, previously thought to be solved.

At the conclusion of World War II, many Cooper-Bessemer diesel engines were powering tow boats on the nation's inland waterways. But one boat, operating out of Paducah, Kentucky, became the nemesis of the company's Field Service Department. While others rarely needed attention, it broke down regularly. For several months, Field Service Department Manager Dennis Gallogly got calls for help every ten days. Each time, a service engineer went to Paducah then returned to report that the engine had required complicated adjustments, although nothing seemed to be broken.

Finally there were no more calls. Relieved but puzzled, Gallogly checked with the tow boat owner to make certain the engine was all right. "Yes," the owner said, "I straightened out the problem myself."

"How?" Gallogly asked.

"I'm paying my engine operator fifty cents extra a day to quit fooling with the adjustments," was the reply.

The range of field services had expanded appreciably since the days of attic accommodations and sow belly diets. Yet, similarities remained. Service engineers still went into the wilderness to "pile up iron," a term coined by "Uncle Ben" Paulson to describe erecting engines in the field. (With mandatory retirement not yet established in American industry, "Uncle Ben" had become known as the dean of service engineers. He remained active until the age of eighty-four.)

Frontiers of the '40s, where power was needed for development of natural resources, extended the periphery of service engineering. An increasing number of men were assigned to distant offices. "Before a remote area can blossom from mining, or oil, or lumber, it has to have power, so we always are among the first into undeveloped places," ex-

Towboat *Carcrosse*, powered by two Cooper-Bessemer engines, pushes its cargo down the Mississippi.

plained Bob Jones, who went into western Canada after the war to step up sales that had been carried out for several years through agents.

An important addition to the company's product line in 1945 was the Type FW supercharged locomotive diesel engine. Half of the one hundred on order were for locomotives being manufactured by the General Electric Company for shipment to South America.

Within two months after the Japanese surrender, Vice President Mike Pollock, head of the recently formed international sales office, announced the company's first sales-service branch outside the United States. Sent to Caracas, Venezuela, to head the office was Thomas E. Kraner, who had gone directly from Purdue University to the Cooper-Bessemer engineering department in 1937, and had been assigned to the Washington, D.C., office during the war. Times were set to change, and Kraner observed, "It was obvious that to really make a mark in international selling, it was going to be increasingly important to be on the scene; countries that had left everything to international oil companies were beginning to think about making their own decisions, including selection of suppliers." Still, for a time it seemed almost as if Kraner had never left home. A liberalized law in Venezuela made it possible to divide existing oil concessions, putting all segments up for bids, and the new C-B office was opened just as representatives from nearly all major oil producers were rushing to the South American country. Most of them were from the United States. "As far as doing business was concerned, it was about the same as being in Tulsa or Houston," Kraner said.

Another foreign market was opened when the company's first large postwar sale was made to the Soviet Union. Twenty-four compressor units were ordered for Russia's first big-inch natural gas pipeline to extend five hundred miles from the Ural Mountains to Moscow. One of the earliest orders placed directly in this country by Russia's purchasing agency in New York, Amtorg, it began an association that was to become even more beneficial in future years. It also tied in with one of the company's landmark advancements in engineering — development of the high compression gas engine.

For nearly twenty years, Cooper-Bessemer engineers had thought about increasing the efficiency of gas engines through high compression, similar to that developed in diesels. In the late 1920s they had experimented with increasing compression, but preignition brought such explosive results that the testing engine had been nicknamed "Old Dynamite." In each attempt, precautions had been taken to maintain the proper chemical ratio of air and gas to effect completion of combustion, but each time they would ignite in the cylinder ahead of the firing stroke. One day in 1945, C-B engineers were visited by a Russian representative of Amtorg, who hinted that someone was close to discovering how to make an engine run on either oil or gas at a moment's notice. Members of Cooper's Washington staff already had warned company engineers, in fact, that two rivals — Worthington and Rathborn-Jones — claimed to have prototype gas-diesel engines in operation. Faced with such a possibility, Chief Engineer Ralph Boyer (who was named vice president two years later) went to work on the project, even though he didn't believe such a thing could be done. Thinking back to the lessons of "Old Dynamite" and wondering what would happen if the mixture were not perfect, he reasoned that to exceed allowable compression, a mixture that was not chemically balanced would probably be required.

"I will never forget the comment by a colleague, John Hines, when I suggested the next day that we give it a try," Boyer said. "Hines asked, 'Who's going to turn the gas on the first time?'"

Someone did, and the experiment was a success. Efficiency resulting from the high compression quickly overcame any loss in efficiency due to improper chemical mixture. "Old Dynamite had tried to give us the answer back in 1927," Boyer said, "but it took us all those years to understand what he was saying."

Just one day after telling the Russian visitor it couldn't be done, C-B engineers demonstrated the gas-diesel engine. Applied first to four-cycle

Nineteen twin tandem gas compressors handled natural gas propane, ethane, and methane at a Carbon & Carbide Chemicals plant in Texas City. The photo was taken in 1947.

A Texas State Highway ferry, operating between Galveston and Point Bolivar, got its power from two Cooper-Bessemer supercharged diesel engines.

engines, high compression gradually was put to a two-cycle use. The principle was kept secret, with Cooper-Bessemer referring to it as "turboflow," a name with no telltale meaning. Competitors did not discover the simple secret of "turboflow" for two years.

Such creative advancements promised long-range benefits. But for the short term, directors were forced to boost the working capital base with loans. Cancellations of war contracts by 1945 totalled $11.5 million. That was more than the company's entire sales for the year preceding America's entry into the war. And it was nearly one-third of total sales in 1944. (It is interesting to note, however, that investors willing to take long-range gambles on the company's future eventually were well rewarded for their faith. Just prior to the company's sesquicentennial year, Dorothy Porter, assistant secretary of the corporation, reported on one person who purchased a dozen shares of stock at the conclusion of World War II. Without any further purchase, those 12 shares had grown to 440 in 1982.)

In the struggle to pick up slack from the cancellation of military contracts, extra effort went into the competition for large new domestic markets, as well as those overseas. Stanley E. Johnson, Sr., named vice president and sales manager in 1945, headed a company delegation traveling to New York to bid on a share of a multimillion dollar order for gas engines. Knowing that the purchasing gas company would be concerned about supplier abilities to handle sizeable segments of the huge order, Johnson decided to exude confidence and optimism. Just as he expected, the first question asked by the prospective buyer was, "Just how much of this order do you think your company can possibly bid on?" Without hesitation, Johnson answered, "Why, we came to bid on the entire lot." Visibly startled, the purchaser said he didn't think anyone was geared to that kind of production. But he was obviously impressed. Cooper-Bessemer received two-thirds of the order. Later, Johnson confessed that he wasn't certain the company could have handled the entire production. But it could, and did, meet the two-thirds commitment.

Diesel horsepower was being used widely in a vast ship salvage program carried out by the U.S. and British navies in reclaiming millions of tons of Allied shipping. One of the first salvage vessels was the *Lincoln-Salvor,* powered by six C-B diesel engines.

The transition to peacetime business was underway. Periodic spurts in sales raised spirits at times, but the overall pattern was sobering. Even B.B. Williams, rarely given to feelings of despair, admitted the lingering reconversion was being accomplished "with considerable strain," and that in many ways, the first postwar year of 1946 was "more difficult than any in recent times." He was particularly disturbed by what he called "concern over the present government-labor-management situation, which is seriously interrupting service to our customers," and by the nationwide steel strike that had resulted in a 1945 walkout by Grove City employees affiliated with the C.I.O. United Steelworkers of America.

He and President Lefebvre attributed much of the company's plunging sales and earnings to sharp increases in costs of labor and materials, with no relief from the Office of Price Administration ceilings until late in 1946, and to a decrease in volume of shipments brought about by work stoppages, not only in Cooper-Bessemer plants, but also in those of several suppliers.

The president also reported to the board that "obsolescence prevails in our factories," despite continuing efforts to squeeze out some expenditures for improvements. Consequently, the board launched a five-year replacement program, examining carefully each area of potential sales.

Much discussion centered on diversification, but only within the confines of established expertise. President Lefebvre defined the term as "finding new markets for old products, and new products for old markets, rather than moving into fields with which we are not familiar." That policy already had led to development of a new fluid pump and a line of motor-drive compressors known as the Types JM, he said. "And now we are studying problems in connection with manufacturing our own turbo-chargers as well as the feasibility of taking on the American Locomotive Company's spare parts business on all their obsolete models operating in marine and pipeline service and in the general industrial field."

Although diesels would continue to be important products for many years, the company looked upon gas-engine compressors as its principal foundation for future growth. Expansion was underway in American gas transmission, and market potential existed wherever a new pipeline was scheduled. While introducing high compression to gas engines, the company continued to gain strength in the transmission market with other innovative engineering as well. Convinced that engines on pipeline units could far exceed the normal 1,000 horsepower, Hewitt Gehres, who had been promoted to executive vice president and director of engineering, initiated a company effort to double that rating. Even potential customers at first opposed the idea, arguing that such an engine would be too large to be shipped preassembled. But Gehres, a man not easily dissuaded from an opinion, called on his chief engineer and others to assist him in proving it could be done.

Such was his reputation that the company was able to go out and sell large orders of the yet unbuilt engines, just from drawings (within the engineering department they were referred to as "paper engines"). In 1947, the GMW engine appeared, capable of developing 2,500 horsepower and shipped in one assembled unit. The unit was so large it was necessary to plan shipping routes that avoided railroad tunnels and other narrow passages.

The GMW engine, introduced in 1947, soon became the most sought after powerplant in gas transmission.

After some revisions in the field, the engines became the most sought-after powerplants in gas transmission. The combination of high horse-power and compact size saved pipeline companies hundreds of thousands of dollars in installation, housing, and operating costs. GMW engines were used exclusively to move gas through what in 1949 became the world's longest pipeline, stretching from Texas to New York.

The GMW was the last of many revolutionary designs Gehres contributed to the industry before he retired in 1956. Continued research based on his basic design principles gradually quadrupled GMW horsepower in the years that followed.

As an engine builder, Cooper-Bessemer gained momentum from the nation's upswinging economy in 1948. Industry and business had won the battle for removal of rationing and price controls, which were restraining production and creating stifling shortages of raw materials. Almost immediately, production across America leaped 18 percent. President Harry S. Truman, in an economic report to the nation, characterized construction as still being "below expectations and certainly below needs." A comprehensive survey by the Department of Economics and the Research Department of the McGraw-Hill Publishing Company led to the conclusion that, "With capital expenditures continuing at breakneck pace, all business is practically certain to keep on booming through most of 1948. In other words, the long heralded postwar recession doesn't show up on this year's calendar."

The working force enjoyed nearly full employment, and the only economic enemy of the United States was inflation. "Advancing prices are expressing themselves not in expanding production, but in expanding costs," warned *Business Week* magazine. But the editor of England's best-known business magazine, *Economist,* visiting the United States to make an indepth study of the economy, concluded that prices, production, and employment would not go any higher, but would turn down sooner or later. "My reason, based on study of available facts, says not just yet," he stated. "My instinct says in 1948."

The beginning of the Cold War led to restrictions on some civilian production, such as automobiles and television sets, but that did not detract from achieving peak nationwide production figures, because emphasis was shifted to armament requirements. Income originating from manufacturing amounted to $62.8 billion out of the total national income of $216.8 billion.

Nowhere was there more reason for optimism than in the natural gas industry. The American Gas Association and the American Petroleum Institute reported a rapid climb in gas reserves, brought about by new discoveries and extension of existing fields. Interstate pipelines were being laid as rapidly as steel pipe could be produced, serving hungry new markets and increasing capacities in areas where lines already existed. One natural gas transmission company even took over the government-built ("Big Inch") line, originally intended to deliver oil from the Gulf Coast to eastern Pennsylvania. All in all, the U.S. gas pipeline network had reached 230,000 miles, far exceeding the total mileage of railroad tracks, and 21,000 additional miles were on the drawing boards.

More than three-fourths of the natural gas was going to expanding industries, particularly chemical producers, iron and steel makers, petroleum refiners, paper producers, the food industry, nonferrous metals producers, cement plants, and makers of stone, clay, and glass products. But there seemed to be enough for everyone. "Luckily, this is a field where there's no sign of a raw materials shortage," reported *Business Week.*

Consumers were delighted with the low cost of gas, which actually appeared to be going down because of its relative slow climb compared to that of other fuels. Attempted protests from producers who foresaw a danger in keeping prices at what they considered artificially low levels, in the face of general inflation, were muffled by louder voices from majority sectors of the population. A temporary scare from isolated shortages during a severe 1948 winter was not enough to quiet those voices. With a seemingly infinite abundance of this cheap fuel, the solution was merely a matter of keeping the bulldozers, trenchers and stringers rolling to spread the network.

History would prove them to be as wrong as the London publisher who visualized an early end to rising prices. But history always makes heroes of second-guessers. Without the luxury of retrospect, the people who create progress were busy making things happen.

Cooper-Bessemer's five-year plan of recovery from the depths of 1946 was progressing ahead of forecasts. Sales were up. All machine tools and facilities were in use, and cost reductions were on schedule. Dividend payments to stockholders had been resumed on a regular basis in late 1947, after a virtual absence of sixteen years (with the exception of a few intermittent payments during the war years of 1941–45), and the board of directors was able to authorize further expansion of buildings and production facilities.

With the new machinery in operation, the company retired forty-six obsolete tools without reducing capacity. War surpluses were hurting marine engine sales, but with railroads beginning a final conversion from steam to diesel power, the worldwide locomotive market created a backlog of orders. A much greater backlog for gas engine-driven compressors was tied to the tremendous demand for natural gas, and its resultant increase in pipeline construction. Backlog alone exceeded the $16 million total sales figure of 1946.

Cities, finally able to get scarce materials, were building long-postponed energy, sewage, and water pumping plants. Refineries and general industrial plants were expanding. All represented prospective markets for Cooper-Bessemer engine installations. And Vice President Pollock, who continued to serve as export manager, forecasted warming trends in overseas sales.

America's business climate cooled slightly in 1949, fanned by what the government described as a shift in inventory accumulation, bringing about a minor decline in the gross national product. But Cooper-Bessemer's momentum carried it through the temporary recession only slightly scarred.

Markets outside the United States were continuing to grow. The earlier sales move into western Canada proved particularly fortunate when an immense oil field was discovered in Alberta. "We had sold all the equipment for small oil and gas operations in the southern part of the province," Robert Jones noted, "and when the big boom occurred three hundred miles to the north, operators were brought in from the south to develop the new oil patch. The equipment they knew best was ours."

To better serve the Canadian markets from coast to coast, the company expanded warehouse facilities at Edmonton, Alberta, and established a subsidiary sales unit, Cooper-Bessemer of Canada, Ltd., with offices in Edmonton and Calgary (also in Alberta), and in Halifax, Nova Scotia. Canadian tariff made it clear to management that the company would ultimately have to manufacture in that country to market there competitively.

Groundwork was laid also for the first overseas production of Cooper-Bessemer products when Vice Presidents Gehres and Pollock went to Ireland, exploring the feasibility of a licensing agreement with Harland and Wolff, Ltd., of Belfast. One of the world's largest shipbuilding firms, Harland and Wolff also had extensive manufacturing capabilities. The plan proved to be fruitful; Harland and Wolff was licensed to produce and sell Cooper-Bessemer engines and motor-driven compressors in all countries except the U.S., Colombia, Peru, Canada, Venezuela, Mexico and Saudi Arabia.

Domestically, Cooper-Bessemer continued to upgrade equipment, striving to improve production output. Departments equipped to produce three of the popular GMW engines monthly had to be expanded rapidly, because orders were coming in at double that rate. Units for the Texas to New York pipeline were completed in 1949 and the locomotive market flourished. Stockholders shared in what the president called a "period of progress" when a special stock dividend of 50 percent was declared in June.

At mid-century, the company was able to report that the major share of profits came from the sale of products developed since the end of World War II. Sales remained relatively steady, showing a slight gain over the previous year. An additional $1.5 million worth of capital equipment was on order, and nearly twice that amount was allocated for future modernization. Land was purchased for plant expansion at Mt. Vernon.

Some feelings were expressed that the company's fate was wagered on a single wheel of fortune — natural gas transmission — but there was no doubt about its current posture. The wheel was spinning, and Cooper-Bessemer held some winning numbers.

Compressors were being sold in India, Central and South America, and other points on the globe. With the 1950 Communist invasion of South Korea, however, the United States became entangled in another war, and Cooper-Bessemer priorities were to its own defense-supporting industries. Thomas Kraner returned from Venezuela to set up a sales and service center in New Orleans, and improvements were made at similar facilities in Houston, Odessa, and Pampa, Texas, and at Gloucester, Massachusetts.

Predictions of a downturn in the economy proved to be premature, as the index of industrial production continued to rise primarily because of the war, but partially on the strength of technological innovations heralding the coming age of high-speed computers.

In 1951, Cooper-Bessemer sales of $52,310,978 for the first time surpassed the $41,417,399 wartime peak of 1943. Net profits were more than double the 1943 figure, and book value, representing common stockholders' capital, had more than tripled.

One $15 million contract for thirty-three supercharged gas engines and generators, to be installed at a new Reynolds Metals plant in Port Lavaca, Texas, represented the largest single commercial order in the company's history and for many years to come. The sale involved lengthy negotiations and detailed presentations, including specific installation plans drawn by Cooper-Bessemer sales engineers, and participation by Charles Cooper, whose office in Washington gave him quick access to Reynolds Metals' main headquarters in Richmond, Virginia. Cooper liked to make the comparison that in spite of such a long, complicated effort by many persons representing both companies, he finally received verbal agreement for the order in a hurried call he made from an airport telephone.

Additional land was purchased in Grove City, with expansion of buildings, installations and new tooling continuing there, as well as at Mt. Vernon. Export sales remained strong. Opportunities to expand the Canadian market appeared even better than previously anticipated. An aggressive program of research showed gratifying promise of improved products at lower cost and better manufacturing methods.

Corporate life was not without its anxieties, of course. There were some flaws amidst the glitter. Troubles plagued the company's GMV supercharged turboflow engines in the field, reaching such proportions that the gigantic power plants, pushing gas from Southwest wells to homes and factories across the United States, had to be redesigned. Eventually the problem was solved by Cooper-Bessemer engineers, but in 1951 it was the cause of many furrowed brows and sleepless nights.

A less immediate danger, but greater potential threat, was recognized in the recent introduction of a competing product. After ten years and millions of dollars spent in experimentation, General Electric had developed a combustion gas turbine engine, purchased centrifugal compressors from another company, and produced a package that could revolutionize natural gas pipeline transmission. Cooper-Bessemer, despite its favorable growth, was not sufficiently capitalized to afford research and development for such a major change. For the present, at least, the company was limited to the continued improvement of the reciprocating engine-compressor that had made it the world's leader in the field of gas transmission.

The incident prompted more thought about Cooper-Bessemer's high degree of dependence on a relatively narrow line of products and how it would affect the company's future health. Lawrence Williams, by then promoted to corporate secretary and assistant to the president, was one of the men who expressed apprehension. He also felt that a wartime freeze on recruiting had created a large age gap between top and middle management, and the company should mount an effort to plan the succession of responsibility. He and his wife, Ruby, held special parties for

The Mt. Vernon plant in 1952 reflected post-war expansion.

young members of middle management, because he considered it important to have them become better acquainted and to know they were recognized as the company's future leaders. Williams was also instrumental in an effort to improve the base for future leadership, through an executive training program, initiated in the fall of 1951. Yet, the fact remained that the list of corporate officers showed no significant change in ten years, and, with the exception of President Lefebvre, it was the same as in depression days of the 1930s. Those men had served the company well, and continued to do so, but several among them agreed with Secretary Williams that closer attention to a youth movement was perhaps overdue.

Still, the bottom line in 1951 reflected the best year in the company's history. Even the high volume of production indicated only part of its success; at the end of the year unfilled orders were 40 percent higher than at the beginning. With the Korean War at its height, shipments were almost entirely to defense-supporting markets such as petroleum, aluminum, chemical, and railroad industries.

As business continued at the same high level in 1952, Cooper-Bessemer strengthened its capital structure by exchanging or buying all its preferred shares to become an all-common-stock company. Sales increased slightly from the previous year and continued development of higher compression and turbocharging produced engines with lower fuel consumption, while doubling power output.

Seeking a definite separation of domestic and foreign trade divisions, the board of directors first established designations of "Western Hemisphere" and "Rest of the World." Later they subdivided the latter into two wholly owned subsidiaries, Cooper-Bessemer International Corporation and Cooper-Bessemer Overseas Corporation. The board also authorized improvements at leased sales-service facilities, by then numbering twenty-three in this country and abroad. Another was added in Chicago the following year.

A highlight of 1953 was the success of reengineering the GMV engine to overcome the field problems that had persisted for two years. Thus, that important product was able to maintain its leadership in the gas transmission segment of the power industry.

Growing demand for synthetics requiring large supplies of petroleum and natural gas for their production, pointed toward increased emphasis on the petro-chemicals market and expansion of the company's product line. But sales were beginning to slip, and as the company moved into its 121st year, the slip became a landslide.

Attempting to pinpoint the cause of what one executive described as Cooper-Bessemer's "business disaster of 1954" was like throwing darts at a target with no bull's-eye. A veritable maze of contributing factors made scoring easy; any place a dart landed was worth points.

On the periphery was a nationwide recession, but the concensus of analysts, writers, economists and even politicians seeking public office portrayed it as mild. A strike at the Grove City plant shut down operations for seven weeks in the only production area that had been doing well, and operating difficulties with two of the company's newer products were costly to correct.

Probably nearer the center of the target, however, was a U.S. Supreme Court decision that brought a sudden, unanticipated suspension of several major pipeline projects. In what was known as "The Phillips Petroleum Case," the Court ruled that producers selling gas to interstate pipelines had to submit to jurisdiction of the Federal Power Commission. The case had been bouncing through FPC hearings and courts since 1946, and had prompted price-fixing legislation that had been vetoed by President Truman.

Prior to the Supreme Court decision, the federal government regulated interstate pipelines and state governments regulated local utility companies, but independent producers were subject only to competitive price determination. When the court's gavel fell on Phillips Petroleum, the reverberation was felt also by some eight thousand other producers, ranging from unincorporated owners of single wells to giant companies. Price controls now extended from well head to consumer delivery. With them came new regulations that required gas producers selling in interstate commerce to file rate schedules and apply for certificates of public convenience and necessity. Field prices were frozen at existing levels and the FPC was given authority to suspend future increases.

The aftermath brought a flood of applications and certificates that overwhelmed the commission with red tape. Legislatures in producing states moved to set their own minimum prices in attempts to block the FPC from reducing the figure too much. Many independent producers began to seek exempt markets within their own states, avoiding contracts with interstate pipelines. Amidst the confusion and uncertainties, pipelines added a freeze of their own, halting construction efforts until they could determine whether producers would renew contracts or continue drawing battle lines against the interstate regulations.

At the same time, Cooper-Bessemer's diesel engine sales, already providing a low profit margin, faced a serious new problem. General Electric wanted a new high-output engine for use on foreign lines. Cooper-Bessemer could remain the supplier, but heavy credit expenditures would have to be extended because payment for each engine would not be made until G.E. was paid by its customers for the total locomotive.

Adding to domestic woes was a difficulty in satisfying demands of foreign customers, particularly those in Latin America, because of their lack of U.S. dollars. Seeking a solution, the company explored myriad sources of funds, including government agencies organized for that purpose, and the Export-Import Bank. For Cooper-Bessemer, the accumulation of unfortunate circumstances, both interior and exterior, added up to a 38 percent decrease in net sales, and the first net loss since the depression year of 1938.

Logic provided hope for certain long-range improvement, because demand assured some kind of solution to the gas transmission stand-off. Natural gas was still considered the "wonder fuel" and the "most versatile of raw materials," into which investors had put billions of dollars. *Business Week* called it "the building block that is the key to thousands of chemicals, from ammonia to plastics." In Chicago, 135,000 names were on a waiting list for gas heating, and an Ohio gas utility reported a waiting list of seventy thousand for gas heaters. But cyclical dangers of the business were never more apparent. When a young engineer, Eugene L. Miller, was promoted to assistant general manager in the middle of 1954, one of the first reports he made to the board of directors was the critical need for diversification to level out fluctuations in natural gas markets. If doubts remained on the immediacy for such action, they were erased the following year by the emergence of a sudden, totally unexpected peril, posing one of the most alarming threats in Cooper-Bessemer history, but leading, ironically, to a more unified resolve to broaden the company's outlook.

Under the weight of multiple problems, Cooper-Bessemer stock had dropped to a level far below its book value. Recognizing the company's vulnerability, a wealthy New York investor, Robert New, was quietly putting together a substantial block of its stock. Early in 1955, he made his move to corral a majority interest and take control of the company. In the midst of the crisis, unforeseen circumstances brought about the resignation of Gordon Lefebvre. Lawrence Williams, who had taken early retirement in 1953, was summoned by the board of directors to return as president.

Investor New was a formidable opponent. "I was astonished at what that man had found out," President Williams said later. "He was an astute student of the market, and he knew our organization inside out before he ever showed up as a raider. If our entire board had not reacted fast, and in unison, he would have controlled our destiny. Since he was an investor, not an operator, we might very well have been liquidated. We had no idea what his plans were."

Led by Chairman B.B. Williams, still an inspirer of great confidence at the age of eighty, the board was eventually able to rally sufficient stockholder support to avoid the attempted takeover. New withdrew with a substantial profit from the stock he had purchased, but without the control he had sought.

"It was a pretty close call, but it actually was a very beneficial experience because it prompted us to turn the company around. We needed a youth movement in management and a great stability to guard against those tremendous up-and-down cycles of the heavy compressor business," the president said later.

Lawrence Williams had considered himself part of the Cooper "family" since childhood. After graduating from Oberlin College in 1926, he joined the company officially, starting as a mechanic's helper on the erection floor, then receiving general training in the repair, service, and sales departments before being named production manager of the Mt. Vernon plant in 1931. He was named works manager at Grove City in 1935, and was promoted to director of market research in 1938. The following year he was elected assistant secretary and a director of the corporation. In 1947 he was advanced to secretary and assistant to the president. Never really intending nor wanting to be president, however, he had taken early retirement to pursue other interests. He considered his return a temporary measure in a time of crisis.

Having avoided the attempted takeover, however, the company now faced a seemingly overwhelming challenge from the four-year-old General Electric combustion gas turbine engine, wedging progressively deeper into the pipeline transmission market. Its centrifugal concept appeared certain to overtake the reciprocating gas engine-compressor for use in pipelines, and Cooper-Bessemer's own recently developed centrifugal compressor could not check the swelling tide of competition.

The problem had persisted for several years, greatly troubling Lawrence Williams, who recognized an exact parallel with dinner table stories his father reiterated many years ago. Then, it was the company's steam engine confronted by steam turbines of competitors with stronger financial capabilities. Now, it was another turbine threatening Cooper-Bessemer's most important product. It was no exaggeration to again consider the situation critical to survival. The chief engineer of one important customer, El Paso Natural Gas Company, had, in fact, stated flatly, "We are going to be centrifugal — period!"

Vice President and Chief Engineer Boyer was well aware of both the problem and the concern of President Williams. "Once a day, Lawrence would open my office door and ask what we were doing about gas turbines," Boyer said. "What we were doing was searching almost frantically for a radical new concept we could afford."

If a possible solution could be found, President Williams would work to get board approval for quick action. That might not be easy, since even some sales management veterans preferred to stay with reciprocating compressors. (To that idea, one engineer responded, "If we don't somehow get into centrifugal compression, we might have to start manufacturing safety pins.")

Engineers reasoned that the difficulty could be reduced to one stumbling block, and that was the "hot end" — the gas generator where fuel is burned. Cooper-Bessemer certainly knew how to build a compressor, and the power turbine that received fuel from the gas generator was no problem. So what could serve as the generator portion of a gas turbine?

The possible answer? A jet! The idea was revolutionary, but it made theoretic sense. Desperation somehow made it even more plausible. Purchasing a relatively small, 600-hp jet engine from Continental Aviation, engineers set about converting it into what probably was the first jet turbine ever to run on natural gas. Its successful performance gave them confidence to experiment on a larger scale.

Aircraft engine manufacturers at first offered nothing but discouragement, pointing out that overhauls were needed every twelve hundred hours, obviously far too frequently to be practical on pipelines. But further investigation showed that nearly all wear occurred during take-offs. Under cruise conditions, the wear was almost negligible. After landing, the engine cooled down to outside temperature, before blasting off again with a sudden burst of heat. "That," observed a Cooper-Bessemer engineer, "is about the worst thing you can do to a piece of machinery; but obviously, we do not intend to take off in a pipeline."

After several months of negotiations, Pratt & Whitney Aircraft agreed to furnish a jet engine, converted to natural gas, for tandem with a Cooper-Bessemer power turbine and compressor. Experimentation was made affordable by using the engine manufacturer's sophisticated test cell at Hartford, Connecticut. Engineers agreed it was "the most thorough testing of any gas turbine the world had known."

An early jet power turbine takes shape in the 1960s.

Development consumed more months, but on October 3, 1960, with great ceremony, the first Cooper-Bessemer centrifugal compressor driven by a modified jet aircraft engine and power turbine went into operation on a Columbia Gulf Transmission Company pipeline. "I'll never forget that first great 'whoosh' when it started up," recalled Boyer, who was invited to push the red button at a control room in Clementsville, Kentucky.

The dramatic accomplishment of the world's first industrial jet-powered gas turbine represented a team effort. Its development spanned a period of many other changes, including the company's leadership. Several engineers contributed to the project, and Lawrence Williams indeed backed it with his best effort, working closely with other members of management in negotiating with Pratt & Whitney and guiding proposals through board of directors' authorization even after stepping down from active management.

Meanwhile, he had met another objective. "In spite of immediate problems that needed solving when I became president, I always viewed my principal assignment as turning the reins over to capable young leaders," he said. "My father was in his eighties. He loved the company, and he kept on there. And there were many others who had provided wonderful leadership for many years. But we simply had to renew the youth of the corporation."

Under the leadership of President Williams, a drive to elevate young executives to more responsible positions was initiated. "We had a second echelon ready, thanks to Gordon Lefebvre and the board for putting in the training program," he said. "All we had to do was reach down and bring them up another rung on the management ladder."

Gene Miller, who had been assistant general manager less than two years, became general manager in 1956, placing him in the position of chief operating officer. Stanley E. Johnson, Jr., who had left private law practice to join the company in 1951, had been named assistant treasurer the next year and served as negotiator during the long 1954 strike, working closely with the new general manager.

From lessons learned in a two-year period of frustration, the company set in motion plans for growth and the best possible use of available talents. Programs for immediate action were blended with a broad policy for the future. Whereas product and market diversification always had depended upon retained earnings and borrowing, the company expected to bolster growth potential with additional equity capital.

To answer the pending question of financing larger diesel locomotive engines, Williams and Miller negotiated a new agreement with General Electric, whereby the two companies would share the cost of development. Cooper-Bessemer would manufacture the engines for General Electric locomotives at cost, plus a fee of approximately 10 percent. General Electric was granted the option to manufacture these engines after payment of $2,125,000 in fees. In this way, Cooper-Bessemer avoided the responsibility of extending long-range credit, while satisfying G.E. requirements for eight- and twelve-cylinder units. The arrangement kept alive the longstanding relationships between the two companies and, although it would never be regarded as a major element of overall production, it generated some 10 pecent of the company's sales volume for several more years.

For a short time at the beginning of 1956, it appeared that gas producers would at least have the freedom from government regulation to boost production and, consequently, pipeline transportation. Following adoption by the House of Representatives, the Senate, on February 6, passed the Harris-Fulbright Bill overriding the 1954 Supreme Court decision on the Phillips case. A topic of nationwide pressure from many political and industrial sources, the bill was passed after a bitter fight by Senate opponents. It was considered a landmark case that would end a struggle dating back nearly two decades, when Congress established regulatory power with the Natural Gas Act of 1938.

"President Eisenhower's approval of the bill, expected this week, is all that is needed to relieve natural-gas producers from federal price control," reported Bertram F. Linz of *The Oil and Gas Journal.* Provisions of the new legislation were expected to assure that development of gas reserves would keep pace with demand, and that prices would be sufficiently regulated by free competition. Federal Power Commission control of pipelines would continue, serving as an additional price restraint, if such a thing were needed. Most important, supporters said, it would revitalize gas well drilling, which had continued to decline by 10 percent the previous year. This, of course, would help stimulate pipeline construction and the corresponding demand for Cooper-Bessemer compressors.

Backers of the Harris-Fulbright Bill never got a chance to test their theory. Instead, they found themselves in a state of shock when President Eisenhower unexpectedly vetoed the bill. Even Federal Power Commission members admitted to being startled by the President's action, because he had openly supported the basic objectives of the bill. Some persons attributed the veto to election year reluctancy to take a firm stand in such a bitter controversy. The President told Congress, however, the manner in which support was attained needed investigation that would take longer than the ten-day Constitution limit on signing a bill. At the same time, he restated support of the idea, saying "the type of regulation of producers of natural gas which is required under present law will discourage individual initiative and incentive to explore for and develop new sources of supply. In the long run, this will limit supplies of gas, which is contrary not only to the national interest, but especially to the interest of consumers."

There was no attempt to override the veto, and producing states reaffirmed intentions to offset federal control by keeping gas out of interstate commerce. Congressional supporters of deregulation talked of mounting a new effort, but having been denied an apparent victory after an exhausting battle, they found it difficult to rekindle necessary enthusiasm. It would, in fact, be another twelve years before any significant action would be taken to renew the effort.

There was some restraint in interstate transportation of natural gas, but much of the reluctancy to expand had been a phantom creature of uncertainty. The presidential veto, while disappointing to the industry, at least erased the suspense. There was a clear market demand, and American enterprise would not be subdued by obstacles. Besides, intrastate transmission, as well as interstate transmission, required pipelines. Thus, the legislative loss did not deter vigorous expansion through the late 1950s. One of the most extensive efforts was reaching the Pacific Northwest, the biggest area of the country not yet supplied with natural gas.

At the same time, Gulf Interstate Gas Company planned the biggest installation of engine-driven centrifugal compressors in the industry, stations all along the line to be equipped with Cooper-Bessemer's new

LSV-16 compressor units. The centrifugal stations were to be entirely automatic and remote controlled. This use of engine drive for centrifugal compressors was considered a pioneering effort, establishing a trend soon followed by others. Chemical and refinery processes, air conditioning and other markets picked up also.

In concert with such revitalized market demands, Cooper-Bessemer channeled $3 million into capital expenditures for new buildings and equipment. Sales bounced back from the depths of 1954–55 to an historic high of $61,214,437 in 1956. The cycle was swinging up again, but the company could not let the pleasant ride sway it from determination to avoid the return trip down. The new management team put its diversification plan into motion.

In retrospect, some early efforts seem minor indeed. But they were beginnings, and their importance should be judged by direction as well as distance. One such move was supplying engines for gas producers. Salesmen soon discovered a clear distinction between production and transmission markets:

In a transmission system packed with natural gas at between 800 and 1,000 psi, and with fifty miles or so between compressor stations, loss of an engine simply required temporary overloads on others until the problem was solved; the gas continued to flow through the line. On the other hand, engine loss in well production brought immediate shutdown. The well was temporarily out of business.

Cooper-Bessemer salesmen knew that transmission customers had the luxury of bringing in teams of engineers who wanted to discuss everything from power ratios to metallurgy. In contrast, they encountered an entirely different attitude from producers. "That production man didn't give a damn if the crankshaft was made out of green cheese," explained one salesman. "All he knew was that he evaluated his job performance on how much he produced out of those wells. If something happened to the engine, it was your fault if you supplied it."

It was a different marketplace, but one worth reaching. The company went after it with existing general products, then designed specialized engines for that specific use. It was the first of many new ideas that would be pursued by the new management group.

Perhaps symbolic of the changing of the guard was the fact that General Manager Miller was elected to the board of directors on October 23, 1956, the same day Chairman B.B. Williams tendered his resignation from the chairmanship. The feelings of more than fifty dedicated years were expressed in the humble ending of a hand-written letter of resignation: "I have enjoyed immensely my relationship with you as chairman, and your unfailing cooperation through the years will ever be for me a precious memory."

Lawrence Williams was elected chairman, as well as president. B.B. Williams remained a member of the board until 1959, and his dinner discussions continued to center on the welfare of the Cooper-Bessemer Corporation until his death on December 20, 1969, at the age of ninety-three.

————————

Oldtimers noted a nostalgic parallel between the 1956 retirements of B.B. Williams and Hewitt A. Gehres, vice president of engineering. Each combined genius with individual traits, reflecting a bygone industrial age that never could return. Accomplishments of Gehres, the engineer, had become legendary. Personal resolve of Gehres, the man, was no less renowned. Men in the shop remembered a particular incident that somehow illustrated the Gehres personality. Described as "a great engine man," he would create a new idea for increased efficiency, rough out a design, then have a prototype handmade to his specifications. Typically, he stayed as close to the project as possible, checking frequently on progress, and he felt personally responsible for its success or failure. The memorable event followed extensive machining in the shop, followed by assembly in the test laboratory. John Hines, who headed the test facility, was assisted on this occasion by a tool designer named Carl "Sky" Mahaffey, himself an inventor, and one of the best liked men in the plant. Mahaffey had strict orders that Gehres wanted to be on hand for the start-up, but he decided to hunch just a little to give it an early try. "I don't want 'Hew' to come out here and not even be able to start it," he explained to Hines. So he started the engine, and in the words of one observer, "it proceeded to tear itself to pieces, scattering metal and oil in all directions." In the aftermath, Gehres stormed into the test house to find Mahaffey standing silently beside the wreckage, hands on hips, just staring ahead. That posture also happened to be what the men called a "trademark" of Hewitt Gehres, so the scene became one of two men standing side by side, hands on hips, pondering the situation — almost a mirror image, the men recalled. Finally, the silence was broken by Gehres' voice: "Don't you say another damn word, Mahaffey." More silence, then Mahaffey quietly replied that he had not said anything. "No," Gehres snapped, "but you were thinkin'."

Lawrence Williams remembered a different situation when he was riding in a car driven by Gehres. Hurrying to return to Mt. Vernon from a trip to Grove City, Gehres failed to negotiate a curve at a high rate of speed. Veering sideways across an adjoining field, but maneuvered expertly by Gehres, the car came to a stop right at the edge of a lake. Looking the situation over carefully, Gehres concluded, "What a hell of a place to put a lake."

It was tough saying goodbye to a man like that. (Gehres remained active in retirement, and friends helped him celebrate his 100th birthday in the company's sesquicentennial year. His predecessor as chief engineer, James Debes, had lived to be 103).

7

A Youth Movement

On April 25, 1957, Eugene L. Miller became the youngest Cooper president since the original company's founder. At thirty-eight, he already was a management veteran who had essentially directed operations for the past three years, dating back to the latter months of his tenure as assistant general manager. But accepting responsibility at an early age was something he learned even before joining Cooper-Bessemer in 1946.

A native Oklahoman, Gene Miller graduated from a Tulsa Central High School class that also included Paul Aurandt, later known as newscaster Paul Harvey. (Miller also remembered two other students, Tony Rosenberg and Katy Fowler, who graduated in later Central High classes. They became known as actor Tony Randall and singer Patti Page.) The high school was so large, being the only one in Tulsa at the time, that student Miller never even met another classmate, Doris Cooley, until they both attended Oklahoma A & M University (now Oklahoma State University). She would also someday change *her* name — to Mrs. Gene Miller.

Having worked in a Tulsa refinery during his teens, and being familiar with other oil operations in the area, young Gene Miller decided to study engineering at Oklahoma A & M with emphasis on internal combustion engines. He received a bachelor's degree and was working on a master's degree in the winter of 1941 when the Japanese bombed Pearl Harbor. Already commissioned in the Army Corps of Engineers earlier that year, he was quickly called to active duty. Three weeks before going overseas, he and Doris Cooley were married. The fact that his college roommate, John Schwabe, subsequently married Doris's sister, Jean, would later have a coincidental effect on his professional career. At the time, however, there was a wartime duty to perform, and his assignment was in England, heading one of sixteen engineer aviation battalions constructing airdromes. Despite his youth, he was in charge of eight hundred men, building complete installations of concrete runways, brick buildings, sewage plants, water towers, emergency generator plants, barracks, kitchens, and even theaters. The emergency schedule was such that the battalions poured cement twenty-four hours a day. Bricks and steel and tools and men were in motion around the clock and the calendar, completing each totally self-sufficient airdrome in one year. Before his three-and-one-half year tour of duty was completed in England and then Germany, he became the youngest lieutenant colonel in the Corps of Engineers. He was just twenty-six.

It was the Christmas season of 1945 when Gene Miller came home to Oklahoma. To celebrate the return, he and Doris set out on what she called a "grand tour of the country," hoping to go into Canada, then down the East Coast to Florida, with only one specifically scheduled stop — Columbus, Ohio, to see Doris's sister and her husband, who had returned from Marine duty and was studying law at Ohio State University.

While they were in Columbus, Gene decided to look up two other good friends from college, Bud Darling and Arthur Able, who had taken jobs in nearby Mt. Vernon, with a company he had heard about, but of which he knew very little except that they built gas engines and compressors. Ironically, when he arrived at the Mt. Vernon Cooper-Bessemer plant, he discovered both his friends had been transferred to company sales offices in, of all places, Oklahoma. Although he explained he only came to visit friends, he was escorted to the plant by Personnel Director Carl Ferrel, then shown around by Abner "Buck" Buxton, when it was discovered he, too, was from Tulsa. There was little activity, however, because the plant was caught in the nationwide steel strike. As he left, still insisting he was not job hunting, Miller was asked to leave his name and address, along with the telephone number of his brother-in-law at Columbus, as Buxton explained, "just in case."

The trip to Canada and New York progressed as planned. But before they could continue to Florida, Gene and Doris received a call from her sister. A man named Buxton had been trying to get in touch with Gene, concerning a return visit to Mt. Vernon. Reluctant to alter their tour plans, Gene was persuaded by his wife that he "owed them the courtesy of going back." Yet, she was the one most surprised when the return visit ended in accepting the first position offered to him. He explained that the job, at $1.12½ per hour, meant getting involved with the kind of gas engines that most interested him. They returned directly to Oklahoma, gathered belongings, and moved to Mt. Vernon.

After his election to the presidency eleven years later, Miller was asked to comment on the unusual circumstances of his initial employment. "It was accidental, but it worked out well," he said.

Lawrence Williams, who became chairman, limited himself almost exclusively to board activities, but kept his word to offer strong support for new ideas, even when he sometimes was not personally convinced of their merit. An example was the hesitation he felt toward moving rapidly into computerization. Remembering disheartening experiences the company had with early calculators and first generation computers, he advised against moving again in that direction. Still, he respected the judgment of the new leadership to the extent of backing computerization when the decision reached board level.

R.F. Lay, who had been general sales manager for the past two years, became vice president and assistant general manager. Michael Pollock retired as vice president and export manager, yet remained a member of the board. He was succeeded in his operational position by Charles Cooper. Other officers in 1957 were Ralph Boyer, vice president and director of engineering; Stanley E. Johnson, Sr., vice president and director of sales; B.L. Potter, A.A. Burrell, F.M. Devin, Charles M. Reagle, and J.W. Reed, vice presidents and district sales managers; J.E. Brown, secretary and treasurer; F. William Kahrl, controller; E.S. Budd, assistant secretary; Stanley E. Johnson, Jr., assistant secretary; and R.M. Bone, assistant treasurer.

Boyer, Cooper, Johnson, Sr., and Reagle, also joined Miller, Williams and Pollock on the board. Outside board members included P.J. Bickel, an attorney with Squire, Sanders & Dempsey law firm of Cleveland, Ohio; P.A. Frank, president of National Rubber Machinery Corporation; E.P. Riley, vice president of Thompson Products, Incorporated; W.E. Stevenson, president of Oberlin College; Z.E. Taylor, president of the First Federal Savings & Loan Association of Mt. Vernon; F.C. Van Cleef, Oberlin investment advisor; and L.L. Warriner, Dayton, Ohio management and engineering consultant.

One of Charles Cooper's first moves as export manager was to establish a sales office in Toronto, to help solve problems of exchange and credit arrangements. He identified the primary need in Canada, however, as increased servicing of equipment. "The new highly rated engines and the increase in engine population require a rapid build-up of our trained service force to assure good performance and operating records," he told the board. "The company with the best record for field service, repair parts service and operating performance will be most successful in getting business in Canada."

In Mt. Vernon, a new centrifugal and engine turbocharger shop was completed, providing an additional thirty thousand square feet of floor space to meet the growing demand for rotary equipment. A line of expansion engines to produce liquid oxygen for missile propulsion was introduced, and a new model of packaged compressors was ready to help boost falling field gas pressures. Although marine sales remained relatively minor, they too were strengthened by improvements in the company's largest four-cycle power engines for towboats, dredges, and fishing vessels. Sales peaked at 14 percent above the previous year before once again encountering the cyclical drop that was beginning to appear inevitable in the manufacture of heavy machinery.

Almost as if programmed by destiny, sales suffered another periodic drop of 24 percent in 1958, even as the nation witnessed a record billion dollar natural gas transmission line construction. Nevertheless, management was confident it was building strength for growth, and more importantly broadening its marketing scope. New engine-driven compressor units were being designed for growing gas gathering requirements in producing fields and for the still rapidly advancing petrochemical processing business. New centrifugal compressors for refineries and petrochemical plants, along with new En-Tronic controls for automated operations were displayed for the first time at an International Petroleum Exposition in Tulsa. The word "En-Tronic" was coined from "engine" and "electronic" for the expansive control units covering entire walls of compressor stations.

Other newly developed products marketed as the year progressed were large centrifugal blowers for sewage aeration, compressor machinery for soot blowing and pressure charging to help central power stations increase steam boiler efficiencies, compressors and expander engines for oxygen production in the steel and missile programs, and both centrifugal and reciprocating compressor machinery designed specifically for the aircraft industry's wind tunnel research. Since many of these went to markets not previously served by the company, it was felt the potential offered a much brighter picture than was shown by the unfavorable general business figures. President Miller confidently reported that "All indications, including orders at hand, point to an early return to the sales and profit trend lines established as part of our ten-year, long-range objectives."

He noted also that the youth movement was progressing on schedule. "Were you to visit our various departments, you would see the teaming of less experienced but highly promising young men with those rich in experience," he told stockholders. In keeping with that movement, the company strengthened its pension plan and established a definite retirement age. "It seemed unfair to tell one person he must retire at an age when others were permitted to continue," the president explained. "To avoid that kind of discrimination, we had to have a definite plan, so we put one in."

Like other American companies, Cooper-Bessemer moved into a new industrial era sometimes described as the "Management Revolution," brought about by computerization, changing tax structures, increased government controls, fluctuations in monetary exchanges throughout the world, labor policies, continued technological advancement, and a logical progression of management capabilities. Innovation was as real as ever, but it was taking on a new depth to encompass the varied complexities of any business concern.

President Miller initiated a ten-year plan for Cooper-Bessemer, calling for internal growth, increased effort to supply such rapidly developing markets as petrochemical industries, and a program of diversification through acquisition and merger. Behind the scenes, he was investigating a possible merger that could accelerate the plan in one swift surge, possibly changing the course of the company almost overnight.

Gardner-Denver Company of Quincy, Illinois, a recent addition to the five hundred largest manufacturing corporations in the U.S., had been sought as an acquisition by the much larger Dresser Industries for more than a year. Negotiations between the two companies had been covered by the press, sometimes speculatively, and an agreement appeared to be imminent until December 5, 1957, when Dresser announced that the proposed merger had been cancelled. The sudden change was prompted by a letter from Gardner-Denver Chairman Gifford V. Leece, explaining to Dresser management that he believed the growth psychology of the two companies was "not at all compatible." His principal objection was the lesser degree of importance he felt Dresser placed on a proposed Gardner-Dresser group, as compared to other acquisitions.

The next day, Cooper-Bessemer President Miller telephoned his good friend, "Giff" Leece to propose an "equal merger between two fairly equal companies." Receiving a warm reception to the idea, Miller flew to Quincy for a talk that prompted several more discussions during the early weeks of 1958. Gardner-Denver products were being used in the exploration and development of oil fields and mines, as well as construction of highways, dams, tunnels, bridges, and pipelines. This included a broad range of air compressors, industrial power tools, and mud pumps. A combination of the two companies seemed compatible and desirable — just right for the times.

President Miller made several more trips to Quincy, meeting with officers and directors, observing operations, and continuing talks with Chairman Leece, who made similar journeys to Mt. Vernon. "Things seemed to be progressing beautifully, when Gardner-Denver just decided not to go through with the merger," Miller said later. "We never even received a hint of why they backed off." Miller did not discover until twenty-one years later, when Gardner-Denver was acquired by Cooper Industries, that Gifford Leece, who was twenty years older than the Cooper-Bessemer president, felt his leadership would become precarious, even though the plan called for him to become chairman and chief executive officer, with Miller serving as president.

The company's 125th anniversary in 1958 brought the creation of a Texas subsidiary, organized to fit a highly competitive marketing concept enjoying acceptance in the gas production field. Several companies were finding success in "packaging" compressors, engines, piping, air-starting, and other equipment into complete, self-sufficient units for ready-to-go delivery on portable steel skids. Cooper-Bessemer was involved, through an arrangement whereby it provided compressors to Southwest Industries, Inc., which in turn did the packaging and selling.

The time seemed ripe, however, to do its own packaging, preferably at a location central to the major markets. That meant Texas, not Ohio.

While management leaders pondered such a move, Thomas Kraner, branch manager of the New Orleans sales office, left the company to join J.L. Cannon, former president of Southwest Industries, in establishing their own packaging business, Creole Engineering Corporation. Rather than organize a competing group, Cooper-Bessemer executives persuaded Kraner and Cannon to convert Creole Engineering into a subsidiary, in which they would hold key positions. The agreement was made and a packaging plant was built in Houston. By October, the subsidiary, CB/Southern, Inc., was in operation, with Kraner serving as president and Cannon as secretary-treasurer. It was the first Cooper-Bessemer subsidiary formed for sales in the United States since 1910. While it did not fit the company's strict definition of intended diversification (it assembled existing products) CB/Southern indicated a willingness to extend the corporate vision.

The following year, Cooper-Bessemer's intentions gained more substance with negotiations to acquire Rotor Tool Company of Cleveland, Ohio. This time the diversification was clear cut. The thirty-year-old Rotor Tool manufactured pneumatic and high-cycle electric portable tools for automotive and appliance markets, foundries, fabrication, and general manufacturing plants.

In reporting management plans to the board, President Miller predicted the acquisition would "achieve greater stability of earnings and wider market diversification," as well as "open up more possibilities for compressor business for the company's present product lines." At the same time, he explained, Cooper-Bessemer contacts would create opportunities for Rotor Tool to expand its business into areas west of the Mississippi River and into world markets. The Cleveland company fit another preferred criterion also, because the older men who had built its business were willing to stay on and help train younger management people.

As an outside director, L.L. Warriner backed management by asserting that the proposed acquisition was the best of several that had been suggested, and he considered it the diversification breakthrough that would lead to new horizons. He voiced a word of caution, however, that the company should not "superimpose large corporation practices upon a small closely knit operation." Chairman Lawrence Williams, who had not taken part in final negotiations because of an illness that necessitated taking a leave of absence, characteristically sent a message from the hospital, stating that he was "wholeheartedly in favor of this merger and wish to extend my most enthusiastic congratulations to you who have worked out the agreement. I am convinced that the merger represents a real step forward for both companies."

As part of the merger agreement, Rotor Tool President Herbert P. Bailey, was to become a member of the Cooper-Bessemer board. An impressive man with great inspirational qualities, he had guided Rotor Tool since it was spawned on the eve of the Great Depression.

With unprecedented securities speculation feeding the optimism of new business ventures, 1929 seemed an appropriate year for a man of ambition to satisfy dreams of launching an independent industrial enterprise. Herbert P. Bailey, advertising manager for Warner & Swasey, Cleveland, Ohio, manufacturer of turret lathes and other machine tools, was such a man.

Gathering a group that included two colleagues and two competitors, he set about establishing an organization based on combined experiences of the participants. The others were Donald S. Linton and John J. "Scotty" Goodwin, both Warner & Swasey employees, and Fred B. Engeln and Frank Hejduk of Cleveland Pneumatic Tool Company.

Leasing space in a small building adjacent to the Warner & Swasey plant, the quartet founded its firm, Rotor Air Tool Company, at East 55th Street and Carnegie Avenue. Beginning with a purchased patent for an external blade horizontal grinder, the company soon designed a line of pneumatic grinders. Bailey, the major stockholder, became the first Rotor Air Tool president.

Rotor Air Tool managed to stand its ground in the Great Depression, even extending its product line to include drills, sanders, and wire brushing tools. In defiance of the monster depression, its early recovery was attributed greatly to financial constraint. The experience left company founders even more skeptical of taking risks. Len W. Dwors, who joined the company in 1935 (and later was to serve as president from 1971 to 1972), remembered several instances when he heard Bailey and Linton assert, "We are not in the gambling business." Dwors was one of only a few employees at that time, since the depression had stunted Rotor's initial growth, but business was beginning to improve, certainly ahead of many others. For the first time the company began to manufacture electric products, taking over a line of high-cycle grinders and drills manufactured originally by the Burke Electric Company in Erie, Pennsylvania. Appropriately, it soon dropped the word "Air" from its name, and became the Rotor Tool Company.

Rotor Tool never entered the retail hardware market, preferring to manufacture tools only for industrial uses. Consequently, all its products were precision items, with parts ground to extremely close tolerances for high-speed performance. Since portable tools are perishable and therefore subject to handling abuse, nearly half of its business was in the manufacture of spare parts. The company for the first time built its own modern manufacturing plant in 1952, leaving quarters it had leased since 1932. Located on six and one half acres at 26300 Lakeland Boulevard in the Cleveland suburb of Euclid, the new plant was air conditioned for comfort, efficient operation, and the constant temperature control needed to maintain exacting manufacturing tolerances. The plant was expanded in 1957 and again in 1962 (after the acquisition by Cooper-Bessemer) reaching 78,000 square feet, exactly twice its original size.

———————————

On October 13, 1959, Rotor Tool Company became the first Cooper-Bessemer acquisition in the thirty years since C. & G. Cooper and Bessemer Gas Engine Company became a single organization. During the next twenty-four years, there would be seventeen more.

Before the acquisition, all Rotor Tool Company stock had been closely held. It never was sold on the market. After Cooper-Bessemer's straight stock purchase, Rotor Tool became a wholly owned subsidiary, and later a division of the corporation.

Herbert Bailey, Donald Linton and Fred Englen, who had continued with the company since its founding, retired from active management, although Bailey became chairman of the subsidiary board as well as the parent company board.

Shortly after the merger, Cooper-Bessemer Chairman Lawrence Williams resigned his position, although he continued as a director and member of the Executive Committee. Upon his recommendation, L.L. Warriner became the first outside director ever to serve as chairman of the board.

A director for fifteen years, Warriner had top executive experience with the Fairbanks-Morse Company, A.O. Smith Corporation, Summitville Consolidated Mines, and the Master Electric Company. He resigned from the Master Electric presidency in 1956 to become a management and engineering consultant. His Cooper-Bessemer chairmanship involved presiding at meetings, but not operational or management concerns.

As predicted, sales rebounded to a healthy $66,875,601 — the second highest level in company history — contributing largely to a 52 percent increase in net earnings per share. Sufficient strides were made in development of En-Tronic automatic controls for engines and compressors to warrant organization of engineering, manufacturing and sales facilities for those products into a new Control Division, located in Mt. Vernon. Development of the gas turbine power unit was nearing fruition, and the step-by-step advance of export selling was picking up speed.

Although marketing in other nations had made considerable gains since World War II, Cooper-Bessemer's coordinated program of serving worldwide customers was merely on the threshold of development. The International Division, headed by Charles Cooper, was destined for many changes dictated by fluctuations in world markets.

Cooper reasoned that "The primary objective of the Division is protecting the world's market position of Cooper-Bessemer, resulting from the superiority of the company's products for the gas transmission and petrochemical industries." He told the board that, in his opinion, the company would eventually be required to produce some components in engine and compressor units in foreign countries. "If a foreign project is economically sound," he said, "we should proceed with its worldwide marketing even though we are fully aware that there is always some political risk involved." His ideas soon were to be translated into action.

The International Division was already represented by sales agents in ten countries, by licensees in Ireland, Italy and France, by the recently established Cooper-Bessemer, S.A., headquartered in Chur, Switzerland, and by franchises in The Hague, Netherlands, and Mexico City, Mexico. It faced a problem in Canada, however, where a strong feeling of nationalism reverberated all the way to Mt. Vernon.

The First Trans-Canada Pipeline was being built after years of planning and political wrestling, and Cooper-Bessemer had the preferred equipment designs to furnish compressors all along the line. The Canadians, however, insisted that anyone who received such a large contract should manufacture the compressors in that country. The presumption seemed reasonable enough, but the problem stemmed from locating a facility that could accommodate such a project. The pipeline schedule disallowed time to build a new plant, and the only buildings with sufficient room and one hundred-ton crane capacity were the big railroad shops overhauling locomotives.

Needing an "instant plant," Cooper-Bessemer was able to make an arrangement with the Canadian National Railway, whereby it could lease part of a building at Stratford, Ontario, left vacant by the phasing out of steam locomotives. The other part was still being used, although workers were being laid off regularly. Cooper-Bessemer's share of the building was stripped to bare walls and floors, except for the necessary overhead cranes.

With C. Robert Jones as vice president and general manager, and C. William Gilchrist as works manager, Cooper-Bessemer wasted no time in making the conversion. Sharing the building with the remaining Railway work force, the group installed machinery to manufacture the GMW engine, a 2,500-hp behemoth that would require all the lifting power available. Gilchrist recruited workers from railway personnel as they were laid off and was delighted to discover that the new employees had skills compatible with building, fitting, and testing the big GMW's. (As the Stratford operation grew and prospered in the years ahead, most of the original recruits remained with the company, and many became supervisors.)

Only one major mishap was reported during the rush toward initial production. Late one night, an engine backfire sent a charge of natural gas into an exhaust system, ripping open a pipe before the gas could reach a silencer mounted outside the building. The ensuing explosion was felt all the way along an adjacent residential street. In addition to cleaning up piles of rubble in the plant, the company had to replace dozens of residential windows, myriad sash, and one canary. When a cub reporter questioned Gilchrist about the explosion, the works manager explained that it was not an explosion, merely a backfire. The next day's newspaper reported, "Gilchrist claims the loud sound was a backfire, and that such a big engine, when it backfires, makes a lot of noise."

Engines and compressors began "rolling out the back door" just in time to serve the pipeline. But that was just a beginning. Canada was in the early stage of vast industrial expansion, with its attendant markets for compressors, engines, and controls. Products from the Stratford plant would soon be going to many areas of the country, then to South America, Europe, Russia, and the Far East. Gradually the company converted most of its facility to build turbine centrifugal compressors, but it continued to produce occasional large gas engines, because the plant still had the test stands, crane service, and machine tools to put them together.

The International Division built its program to be flexible, as specific needs indicated whether the most feasible pattern called for a license agreement, a joint venture, or a wholly owned subsidiary. "It was not good business to set firm, long-range policies," explained Jones, who later succeeded Cooper as head of the division. "We were too susceptible to changing political whims in countries where we operated."

8

Age of Conglomerates

Something about the beginning of a new decade stirs one to ponder the next ten years with a fresh outlook and revitalized enthusiasm. Perhaps it is tradition. America takes a new census, calculates shifts in population and economics, and attempts to weave threads of the past ten years into a completed vestment. It's time to begin a new pattern. Looking back, we label each decade — the Roaring '20s, depression '30s, wartime '40s, placid '50s — as if there had been no overlap. It's a means of pigeonholing music, dress, legislation, habits and teenagers. And with old slates wiped clean, we compose the prelude to what we thoroughly expect to be a unique new composition, always entitled "Today's Modern Times."

Thus, America faced the modern '60s with an intense presidential campaign that would put John F. Kennedy in the White House, rapidly spreading automation aided by high-speed computers, thriving industrial and agricultural productivity, and a Peace Corps designed to help implement human resource and economic development around the world. In a message to Congress, President Kennedy urged commitment to "landing a man on the moon" before the end of the decade. Nothing in the crystal ball revealed a Vietnam War that would change the nation's optimism into a mood creating the next label, "A decade of protest."

In the world of business, however, the 1960s would more appropriately become known as the age of conglomerates. Many mergers would join companies in unrelated industries, and federal antitrust action would flood the courts as the trend escalated to a point where few companies felt safe from being absorbed by an organization interested more in their ready assets than their continued health. Survival often depended on a company's early ability to scrutinize its management philosophy and respond with aggressive methods of growth. Cooper-Bessemer, remembering well the lesson of 1955, was one of those companies.

Although certainly not considered large in such terms as the Fortune 500, Cooper-Bessemer had built a strong image in the marketplace by virtue of its technical skills, dependable service to customers, and development of equipment as it was needed in the industry. It had been around a long time and survived many adversities by adjusting and taking advantage of situations. The most recent example was the 1959 introduction of its long-sought jet gas turbine, utilizing a natural-gas version of the engine that powered Boeing 707 and Douglas DC-8 aircraft. *Oil and Gas Journal* praised that innovation as "bringing well known jets down to earth to be harnessed as stationary gas engines."

Understandably, the company looked inward, relying on development and production expertise to solve problems. Strong family influence had progressed through the generations from its founding until the election of Gene Miller to the presidency. While that was no criticism — indeed, it typified industrial modus operandi of those years — it nevertheless was one criterion corporate raiders considered favorable to their cause.

There were great advantages to being located in small midwestern communities, away from pressure centers of the world. It was comfortable. That was one of the reasons many companies in the industry did not consider extensive growth to be a virtue. But looking ahead to the '60s produced a clear vision of what must be done. "We had to convince everyone in the company that it was time to lift up our heads and scan the horizon," President Miller said. Rotor Tool had been a start, but it was only a blip on the scope.

Even sales methods were being overhauled. In the days when individual entrepreneurs put together financing and created pipeline companies, Cooper-Bessemer salesmen like Art Burrell, C.H. Sanders, Charlie White, Fletcher Devin, Bill Arthur, Jim Reed, and B.L. Potter sold compressors directly to the owners. (Burrell, Devin, Reed, and Potter had been promoted to district sales managers and corporate vice presidents in the '50s.)

As time moved on, salesmen were required to make technical presentations to customers' engineering staffs, then to purchasing agents. "Ambassadorial selling" to owners was being replaced by "blueprint selling" to evaluation committees. Younger salesmen like Bob Humphries and George Edick depended not on contacts but on demonstrating by analysis that the company's product was superior to others. The change was not sudden; it was a gradual evolution that was still going on in the early '60s.

Energy companies and their supply industries were changing dramatically, competing for efficiency, productivity and strong market positions. One of the men who worked closely with President Miller in laying the groundwork for a broader, less institutionalized company was James E. Brown, vice president, finance, and treasurer, who had joined the company in 1927 and served in various financial positions including chief accountant and controller. Another was Stanley Johnson, Jr., corporate secretary who worked on both labor negotiations and investigation of possible acquisitions. In 1960, Alan E. Riedel, a young lawyer who had successfully handled a major arbitration case for the company, was lured away from the Cleveland firm of Squire, Sanders and Dempsey to join the Cooper-Bessemer management group as general attorney. A graduate of Ohio University, Riedel received his law degree at Case Western Reserve University before joining Squire, Sanders and Dempsey.

In the Cooper-Bessemer factories, men on the machines were well aware of changes that were taking place, and the great majority supported them. Stanley Johnson, Jr., who had grown up in Mt. Vernon and gone to school with many of those men, was often questioned about administrative changes and such activities as the acquisition of Rotor Tool. "There still was a family feeling about being a part of Cooper-Bessemer," he said. "It was a whole lot different than running a string of cars or such products through an assembly line. There were personal relationships and skilled craftsmanship involved, and they had a great pride in what their jobs meant to the company. That was very important. I would talk to someone who operated a $400,000 machine, and there was no doubt that he felt the responsibility of making sure it ran well, and it was accurate and didn't make scrap. That hasn't changed. A guy who pours a twenty-ton ladle of iron on three big engine beds — you can't believe how big until you watch — that man has to be right in five minutes. He might be pouring out of two ladles at the same time. And if he makes a bubble or a bad pour, it is ruined. It is a dramatic thing. You see that man pour that iron, and he is sweating when he comes out of there. Then he smiles and says, 'Well, we got that one down.' Well, you know right then, you are representing him, as well as the stockholders, when you make a management decision. And I think that those men knew any group headed by Gene Miller would be doing just that. So the decisions being made at the corporate level weren't paper decisions, they were human decisions."

President Miller set a goal of nearly quadrupling sales to a quarter billion dollars by 1970, establishing a solid corporation with strong stock market appeal, and producing important products for a wide range of markets. He placed great emphasis on combining individual talents into a well defined team effort. Board action, he asserted, should be at a policy level, excluding debates over operational procedures. To help bring those things about, he reasoned, the company should seek another strong management leader with current ideas and expertise in financial management. Vice President Brown was assigned the responsibility for finding such a person to work with him in the financial section of the company.

The company's newest outside board member, A.E. Palmer, Jr., a partner in the New York investment banking firm of White, Weld & Company, assisted in the search by asking some of his business colleagues for suggestions. One of them recently had left Standard Oil of New Jersey (later changed to Exxon) to join White Weld. He highly recommended a friend from Standard, but doubted that Cooper-Bessemer could hire him away from the nation's largest corporation. The man's name, he said, was Robert Cizik.

When Jim Brown and Stan Johnson, Jr., made their first recruiting visit to Bob Cizik, they knew he was the man they wanted. But his friend had made a valid judgment; Cizik was well established in Exxon's management, working in the treasurer's department and about to embark on an exciting new assignment with the company. He had heard of Cooper-Bessemer, but not Mt. Vernon. However, he was willing to listen to what Brown and Johnson had to say.

Their story of a company determined to become an important force in the industrial world intrigued Cizik. Subsequent discussions with President Miller convinced him that an unusual opportunity existed at the ground level of Cooper-Bessemer's projected new look. In 1961, he joined the company as executive assistant for corporate development, concentrating first on establishing uniform accounting procedures to create a financial framework that would support the intended reconstruction.

To understand the change that began with the 1960s, it is necessary to make some comparisons with the past. Earlier management policies, not only at Cooper-Bessemer, but throughout the heavy machinery industry, were functionally oriented. Executive headquarters was part of a plant. Members of top management had specific operational responsibilities that understandably narrowed their primary concerns into separate channels, yet they were responsible as a group for getting finished products off the end of the production line. Their indoctrination was in a single industry, and it developed great pride in being "an engine man" or "a steel man" or "an oil man."

Cooper-Bessemer's president had only to walk across the street to witness the danger in unwavering pride. Mt. Vernon Bridge Company had once been a construction leader. Its main office was lined with plaques attesting to its award-winning history. Declining markets had taken their toll, however, and the company was in financial trouble. Yet, Gene Miller's repeated suggestions that Mt. Vernon Bridge could produce steel fabrications for sale to Cooper-Bessemer brought stubborn refusal. "We are bridge builders," he was told, and that ended the discussion. Nothing could change the established policy. The company stuck stoically to bridge building until it went out of business. (Afterwards, Cooper-Bessemer purchased the former Mt. Vernon Bridge plant, where it developed manufacturing, drafting and data processing operations.) "I could see a parallel," President Miller said. "There certainly was nothing wrong with the pride we had in our work; it's something I hope we will never lose. But we didn't dare limit ourselves to being engine builders, with perhaps a few sidelines to get us over the rough spots. We had to continue working toward a radical change in our outlook. No one doubted that it would take lots of time. Leaping too quickly can be as dangerous as dragging one's feet. But if you waited too long in the 1960s, you might find yourself belonging to another company."

Cyclical was a word that probably seemed to be overworked, but there was no question it continued to describe the natural gas industry. The company's corresponding ups and downs on sales charts were monotonously in tune with that industry, and each dip brought with it a vulnerability. The cycles had to be leveled out to avoid being subject to the vicissitudes of the natural gas marketplace. A basic requirement was acceptance of the management concept that freed policy making from the restraints of day-to-day operations.

"Across the country, managements were becoming more professional," Miller explained. "More and more persons were being trained as business managers, through business schools; they knew how to analyze data, how to analyze a company. I'm not saying they were better than their predecessors. It's just that the changing business scene brought a fresh cast of characters. Some of the groups specialized solely on acquisitions."

Cooper-Bessemer chose not to be predatory, looking only at acquisitions that would be mutually beneficial. Sometimes the company was threatened by that stand. An example was when one investment banker, without the knowledge of his firm, warned Miller that "If you don't make a tender offer for (a company he named), someone's going to tender you."

There were also general threats of a continued recession. The economy was not receiving the spurt ordinarily associated with a new administration, as consumer income and retail sales fell to levels well below the previous year. "Some companies are merger-minded because the recession reveals internal weaknesses," reported *Business Week*, which described the rash of takeovers as "a fast game of corporate musical chairs."

Chairman Warriner sounded Cooper-Bessemer's positive outlook by telling stockholders, "I would feel remiss if I didn't counter the fear of industry's future, brought about largely by our constant reading and our constantly being told we must expect to bend or be swayed by changes. Cooper-Bessemer has no ring on its finger. It has not been given in marriage to others. It has no ring in its nose to be led around by others. As we grow in stature we shall give ground grudgingly in the loss of flexibility through regimentation to serve. We shall, to the best of our ability, retain the big single advantage to think for ourselves. Cooper-Bessemer, confident in its decisions, and having the courage to accept conditions beyond its control, will move ahead."

Meanwhile, the company's first modest acquisition was off to a good start. Rotor tool shipments showed a marked increase in volume, while rival tool companies were experiencing decreases. Cooper-Bessemer also acquired a small Galena, Ohio, company, Kline Manufacturing, adding high pressure hydraulic pumps for machine tool, earth moving, missile, and ground support applications to its product line.

At the beginning of 1962, the prototype 10,500-hp jet turbine on Columbia Gulf's gas transmission line completed eight thousand hours of operation, confirming the Engineering Department's confidence and prompting the president to describe its performance as "a highly satisfying experience for all of the many people who have dedicated so much effort and talent to the success of this revolutionary power concept." Orders for five more of the compact, fully automated units were being filled, and customer inquiries were arriving regularly. Having proven itself in gas transmission, the turbine was offered to electric utilities for economical generation of power during peak loads. Although Cooper-Bessemer did not intend to neglect other products, development of gas turbines with a wide range of horsepower ratings held top priority.

Expenditures for capital equipment for automated and higher speed machinery to improve production and reduce overall costs were nearly $2 million in 1962. They were scheduled to more than double the following year. For a company custom-building large equipment, investments in numerically controlled machine tools offered real advantages, first by reducing machining time, and second, by eliminating handling and storage of the large jigs formerly needed to manufacture its products.

Although it remained in the shadow of other production, locomotive diesel engine sales continued to act as one stabilizing factor to counteract relatively low first and fourth quarters brought on by the more seasonal nature of the natural gas transmission business. Under terms of the contract signed in 1956, General Electric exercised its right to assemble sixteen-cylinder diesel engines from components supplied by Cooper-Bessemer. For the time being, Cooper-Bessemer continued to manufacture, assemble and test eight- and twelve-cylinder units. But General Electric, whose locomotive sales had been entirely in other countries, was attempting to penetrate the domestic market dominated by General Motors Corporation. And since the larger engines would be required for U.S. locomotives, Cooper-Bessemer's future in that area would probably be limited to building components. Yet, the long association had been beneficial and it was the consensus of directors that management should continue the attitude of cooperating fully with G.E.

Uncertainties abroad at that time necessitated regular monitoring and even a touch of professional guesswork to organize export sales programs. Fluctuations in the economies and politics of Europe required regular adjustments to keep in tune with policies orchestrated by the Common Market and its rival European Free Trade Association bloc. Business arrangements were delayed by regulations and formalities varying among the very countries trying to create a unified trade group.

Member countries could not agree on whether decisions in a single economic union should be made in the interests of the group as a whole, or represent the highest common factor of the constituent national interests. Each year seemed to bring a new transitional period. The latest change, made in 1961, abolished limits on goods passing among member countries, but permitted quotas to be levied against other nations "in accordance with special arrangements," which were not defined. Political influence exerted so much pressure on economic decisions that Walter Hallstein, president of the European Economic Community, made a well publicized assessment that "we are not in business, we are in politics." The statement proved to be prophetic. Some years later, the word "economic" was eliminated, and the organization became simply the European Community.

Other economic maneuvers within the Free World also threatened the global sales position Cooper-Bessemer had gained by its reputation for quality products and continuing after-service. "It is with some natural concern that we view action already taken or currently under consideration by the governments of a few countries to finance the exports of local manufacturers under terms with which no private enterprise can compete," President Miller told stockholders. "Frequently, especially in the developing countries, such terms are so liberal as to overcome all other considerations in the eyes of the purchaser. To date the export assistance programs sponsored by our government are not competitive with these greatly expanded foreign plans."

From his vantage in New York City, International Director Charles Cooper reaffirmed his contention that indicators pointed more than ever toward "investments in manufacturing facilities in Europe, to properly serve world markets." He added that foreign imports of many types already were on the increase, although there was as yet little competition from European producers in the domestic U.S. market on compressor products of the type manufactured by Cooper-Bessemer.

In response to the situation, the company intensified existing studies of the international markets and operations to determine a long-term course of action. Miller explained to the board that "international sales are a significant part of the company's overall business; we must be continually alert to the danger of losing our position in the world market, as well as being aware of the potential for growth that these markets offer." He promised definitive results from the study in a short period of time.

Other specific objectives were outlined for the board as the first real attempt at annual planning, stemming from the financial planning headed by Robert Cizik, who was promoted to corporate treasurer when James Brown contracted a terminal illness.

Among objectives listed in the plan, which went into effect in 1963, were: (1) sales of $98.9 million with earnings of $4.4 million, the equivalent of $2.84 a share for the coming year; (2) to establish Cooper-

Bessemer division as a separate operating unit with division management obtaining control over facilities there; and (3) to define a Cooper-Bessemer corporate organizational structure and establish clear lines of communication between parent and divisions, and between divisions.

For the first time, Cooper-Bessemer Corporation was to have a sharp distinction between administrative and operational management. President Miller commented that "considerable progress has been made in 1963 toward establishing a corporate group capable of administering many relatively independent divisions, with each division manager responsible directly to the president for profitability of his division." It was a concept that would remain the core of successful management systems as the company grew into a major industrial leader.

To emphasize the importance of separating overall policy making from operations, corporate offices were moved from the Mt. Vernon plant location on Sandusky Street to the First Knox National Bank building on the city square.

The company was already arranging further expansion into northwestern Pennsylvania, near the spot where the nation's first oil well was drilled just a little more than a century earlier.

Cooper-Bessemer first became interested in the Ajax Iron Works in 1958, when the Corry, Pennsylvania, manufacturer of small two-cycle gas engines developed a line of integral gas engine compressors and a new water flood vertical pump for oil and gas production. Since that time, a management group had studied Ajax and its potential in the $3 billion-a-year oil and gas production market it served. Sales projections for 1963 were some $6.5 million, almost identical to those for Cooper-Bessemer's larger products in that particular market. Primary recovery of oil and gas (direct pumping and free flowing wells) was growing at a rate of 1.2 percent per year. Secondary recovery of oil and gas from fields where rock pressures had gone down (water flooding and other pressuring methods) was growing 3.5 percent annually. Ajax was among the companies serving this secondary recovery market. Chase Manhattan Bank's petroleum department reported equipment purchases for natural gas production growing at an annual rate of 8 to 10 percent. Ajax products were being well received in the marketplace, and it was felt the addition of Cooper-Bessemer talent could make it even more competitive.

On September 30, 1963, Ajax Iron Works was acquired for $3,648,000, broadening Cooper-Bessemer's marketing base and providing an established distribution system of oilfield supply houses. Like the parent company, Ajax could trace its lineage well into the nineteenth century and the early days of energy development in the United States.

9

Ajax

In the industrial scramble that followed the 1859 drilling of the world's first oil well at Titusville, Pennsylvania, men of great vision matched wits to gain a competitive edge. Oil deposits lay beneath the entire region of northwestern Pennsylvania. A revolutionary new trend in energy development was imminent, and prosperity awaited the front runners.

One early leader was Bostonian Samuel Downer, who decided to build a refinery in the heart of the oil fields, thereby gaining an advantage over rivals who were shipping crude over hundreds of miles of railroads. His choice of location was a railroad junction just twenty-three miles north of Titusville. It was to this point that men were hauling oil-filled barrels by wagon, for shipment via the Philadelphia & Erie and the Atlantic & Great Western railroads. A small settlement was already emerging among the immense pine and hemlock trees. Downer's refinery, built on land purchased from a man named Hiram Corry, gave it such impetus that one early writer was prompted to note "People from every section flocked in by the thousands, many of them men of uncommon dash and fertility of resource." Although real estate was in great demand, the generous Mr. Corry had sold property to the A & GW Railroad at such a reasonable price that the railroad's general manager named the station after him. As was common in the nineteenth century, the station name was passed on to the town. Within a decade, Corry leaped to a population of nearly seven thousand, with oil the most common subject of conversation and the principal basis for growing business activity.

Among those who moved to Corry was the Lewis L. Bliss family, from Nunda, New York. Mr. Bliss's reason for leaving Nunda is not documented, but it is known that his vigorous fight as a prohibitionist had gained such wrath from Nunda saloon keepers and patrons that his life and property had been threatened. In 1877, Lewis L. Bliss joined his brother-in-law, Clifford H. Bagley, and two other Corry businessmen, Clarence G. Harmon and George H. Gibbs, in organizing a company to manufacture steam drilling engines to replace manpower with motor power. His 25-year-old son, Frank L. Bliss, also joined the company and

102

Ajax began manufacturing gas engines in 1895.

soon became shop manager. Named Harmon, Gibbs & Company, the group purchased a segment of the Downer Refinery property, constructed a three-story building, and began production of 12-hp steam engines.

Despite the oil hysteria of the day, there is evidence that Harmon, Gibbs & Company was not totally preoccupied with thoughts of black gold. The third floor of their building was planned as an "opera house." Written records and even handed-down memories fail to explain why Messrs. Harmon, Bliss, Bagley, and Gibbs designed a theatre on the third floor of their factory building. Some persons attribute it to civic mindedness. Others suggest that the founders may have been hedging their industrial gamble with an extra use of their building. Competition was fierce, with many other drilling engines already on the market. Whatever the reasons, archives fail to unveil any mention of a theatrical performance in the opera house. The only production ascribed to the building is industrial.

As oil wells grew deeper, the young company increased the size of its engines, reaching 150 horsepower in just a few years. Business was supplemented with a general line of machine and foundry work and the manufacture of such specialty products as the Sheldon Pinch Bar, used to move railroad cars by compounding muscle power.

George Gibbs died a few years after the company was formed, and his estate shared in the group ownership. Then, in 1892, the company was incorporated as the Ajax Iron Works. The name Ajax, with reference to the Greek hero from Homer's *Iliad*, had been adapted for several years to one of the company's drilling engines. Corporation rights were grant-

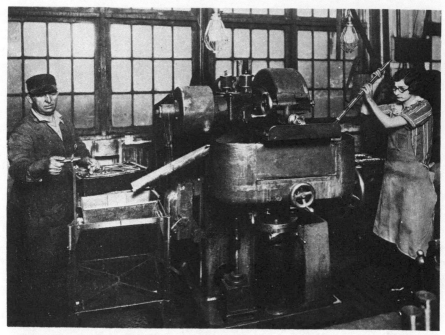

Grinding on a centerless grinder at the Ajax plant in 1935.

Partial view of the Ajax erecting floor for twin engines, 1935.

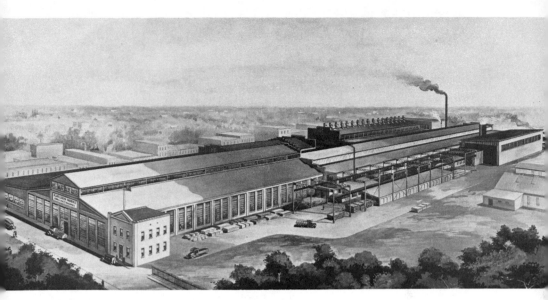

Illustration of Ajax Iron Works in the 1920s.

ed to Ajax as "machinists, founders, and engine builders." Corporate officers were Frank L. Bliss, president and plant superintendent; J.M. Arters, vice president; and Clifford H. Bagley, secretary-treasurer.

Known for his infectious smile and genial greeting, Frank Bliss was a vigorous, cigar-chomping industrialist with creative ideas and the organizational ability to put them in motion. He served several years on the Corry City Council and was mayor from 1903 to 1906. Friends called the Ajax president "Pap" and spoke of his skills as a leader and an engineer. While the company was struggling to grow, "Pap" Bliss invented and patented a steam engine reversing mechanism that was promptly appropriated by nearly every competitor in the business. For years, Ajax waged a bitterly contested battle in the courts, attempting to stop the encroachment on its valuable patent. Finally, the Supreme Court of Pennsylvania upheld its patent rights. On the day of the decision, Ajax closed its plant, chartered a train, and took all employees and their families to Niagara Falls for a celebration. When Frank Bliss died suddenly in 1909, stores and factories in Corry closed for two hours during the funeral. The procession of carriages and more than three hundred persons walking to the cemetery was reported by the newspaper as resembling a large parade on Center Street.

Ajax business grew rapidly after the turn of the twentieth century. An Ajax gas engine was already added to its line, the first having been produced in 1895. By 1911, more than twelve thousand Ajax engines had been sold, and the following year a night shift was added to help meet increasing orders pouring in from western oil fields. The manufacturing plant was expanded farther into the property where the Downer Oil Company refinery had been discontinued many years earlier. Lewis L. Bliss, oldest son of Frank L. Bliss, succeeded his father as president, inheriting, among other things, the reputation as a connoisseur of cigars.

Natural gas engines shared popularity with the steam engines, and in developing new models the company held doggedly to a previous decision that it would not sacrifice quality in favor of price. Its prices were high because it chose to remain in the top-of-the-line market. "It's the best market in the business," one executive explained. "Our products are sold primarily out in the oil patch, the middle of nowhere. When you have to deliver a new bolt out there, it becomes a pretty expensive bolt."

Oil field operators were progressing from cable to rotary drilling. To meet the changing need, Ajax pioneered development of a smoother operating twin-cylinder steam engine. Meanwhile, National Supply Company became exclusive oilfield distributor of Ajax engines. In 1920, National Supply bought the Union Tool Company, a leading manufacturer of rotary drilling equipment under the trade name "Ideal." One of Union Tool's lesser developed products was a steam drilling engine, putting National Supply in competition with the more advanced Ajax product it already distributed. That conflict of interest was resolved by pooling design features and introducing a new product, the "Ideal-Ajax" rotary drive steam engine. At the same time, Ajax discontinued its gas engine, returning to an exclusive steam engine line. Some opposed the move, believing that the Ajax gas engine design compared most favorably with that of competitors. But it was felt that the plant did not have sufficient capacity to continue manufacturing both gas and steam engines. Said one advocate of steam power, "A steam engine will run forever. It just gets a little noisier and a little looser, but as long as you put the steam to her, she'll run." Indeed, the first Ajax engine built in 1877 was going strong, and continued to do so until 1968 when it was retired to a Corry museum, still fully operable.

Lewis R. Bliss died in 1922 and was succeeded by his younger brother, Clifford F. Bliss. Because of a wide age difference, Lewis had been more like a father than a brother to "Cliff" while the latter learned the business from the time he became an apprentice machinist at the age of eighteen. After completing his apprenticeship, he had joined the Sales & Service Department in a position involving field work on both gas and steam engines. Later, he became shop superintendent, secretary, and vice president of the company. One of the new president's initial moves was to contact his late brother's son-in-law, Dr. John H. Castor, and convince him to leave the veterinarian profession and join Ajax. "Doc" Castor made the move, beginning a series of machine operation training jobs that would prepare him for a most significant role in the company's future.

During the 1920s, Ajax designed its engines to increase the speed of drilling at oil fields being brought in at widely divergent depths. The company increased the size of its twin engines as wells went deeper and deeper. In 1926, it became the first manufacturer to produce a totally enclosed drilling engine and the first to use roller bearings on recipro- cating engine crankshafts. In subsequent years, more than three thou- sand of the new engines were built and shipped, primarily to the busy oil fields of Oklahoma, Texas, California, and South America, with steam pressures being increased from the usual 100 pounds to 350 pounds. Harvey Loveland, who became head of purchasing the year the new en- gine was introduced, recalled that the company was willing to try any- thing a customer needed: "For an oil company that wanted to drill deeper and faster, it built ten big devils that developed 2,250 horsepower at a steam intake pressure of fifty pounds." Later, the company devel- oped a piston-valve cylinder feature for effortless reversing against the new high pressures. That brought praise from drillers who had been re- versing the heavy drills manually.

Surviving the depression doldrums, when oil business had dwindled to a trickle, Ajax set about developing new engines that could expand its marketing periphery. Charles I. Rainesalo, a Finnish-trained internal combustion specialist, joined the company soon after arriving in the United States and began research on new steam engine applications. As a result, in 1937, Ajax introduced a two-cylinder vertical steam engine to oil drilling. An independent rotary drive connected to an Ideal-Ajax steam engine beneath the derrick floor bypassed the draw works of a drilling rig. Consequently, work could be accomplished on the draw works and hoisting engine during drilling, adding both efficiency and safety. The engine also represented one of the company's most success- ful departures from oil field sales. Its variable, stepless speed proved adaptable for process and chemical industries (forty-five engines went to Du Pont alone), and for making plywood, where uniform acceleration was essential to the operation of veneer lathes.

Sidney Steward, vice president and general manager for many years, died in 1937. Doc Castor, by then trained in all areas of the plant, was promoted to that position. A native of Philadelphia and a graduate of the University of Pennsylvania, he had practiced veterinary medicine in the Corry area for several years. In 1921, he had married Florence Bliss and spent one year with a milk company in Bedford before returning to Corry as an Ajax employee. Although he had made the conversion from veterinarian to industrial executive with no regrets, Doc Castor retained not only his professional nickname, but also some characteristics from association with medicine and milk production. Numerous stories have been told of his unrelenting dedication to cleanliness. Under his management, the Ajax plant became a paragon of industrial housekeeping. His wife insisted that she could have walked through the plant wearing a long white gown without getting it dirty. Employees claimed the most sanitary manufacturing complex in existence. One said Doc would follow any trail of oil to find the dripping bucket. An assistant remembered protesting, "Doc, there is no way you can run an industrial plant like a milk plant. The day you don't see a chip on the floor is the day we are out of business."

But the general manager continued to insist on the highest possible standards of sanitation and he converted many skeptics over the years. His motivation went far beyond sanitation. He stressed good housekeeping primarily as a means of maintaining well-marked aisles for efficient handling of materials, space conservation, reduction of hazards, and improvement of morale. The precedent he set remains evident throughout the plant. Doc owned a milk company in Erie that he visited frequently, adding to the long hours he spent as the operational head of Ajax. Working seven days a week, he paid little attention to clocks and calendars. "He used to call me at 9:00 a.m. on Sunday and ask me what I was doing," said a man who worked closely with the general manager. "I would tell him, 'I'm just sitting here waiting for your call!'"

When World War II engulfed the nation, low priorities for oilfield drilling equipment nearly created a shutdown at Ajax. (The low priority was a consequence of oil producers assuring the government they had sufficient drilling to sustain the war effort.) To keep the plant in operation, Doc Castor went searching for a product that would be vital to the war. His first step was to obtain the services of Herman Mueller, a nationally recognized steam and marine engine designer. Joining Ajax, Mueller quickly conceived the idea of a large marine compound uniflow steam engine. Ajax developed a unique engine and through extensive personal salesmanship, Doc Castor obtained a contract with the Maritime Commission. Mueller, the innovator, and Charles Rainesalo, knowledgeable in machining, combined engineering talents to create the only steam engine produced especially for the war. Sixty-eight of the engines, ranging from 400 to 3,000 horsepower, each requiring two railroad flatcars for disassembled shipment, were used primarily on coastal vessels that had to get into shallow water. For such high achievement, the men and women of Ajax received the U.S. Maritime "M" pennant and Victory Fleet flag on Sept. 23, 1944. The award was presented to President Bliss at a formal program attended by employees and guests. Also honored at the ceremony were seventy-nine employees serving with the Armed Forces and one who had been killed in action. During a wartime visit to Corry, members of the Chinese Naval Mission tried to convince President Bliss and Vice President Castor to build an Ajax engine plant in their country. The offer was declined, a decision never regretted by the company.

Like most manufacturers, Ajax faced a need to stabilize its business after war contracts expired. The situation was compounded because it was evident that steam engines were soon to be outdated in all but a few marketing areas. Returning to production of natural gas engines was a logical solution, but the company had been out of that business for a quarter of a century. To meet competition, it would need to purchase a gas engine that had been developed over the years. Superior Engine Division of the National Supply Company, located in Springfield, Ohio, had just such a design for sale. In 1945, Ajax bought the Superior line of slow-speed horizontal gas engines and launched a half-million dollar changeover of its plant facilities. Meanwhile, it began manufacturing steam traps and valves, purchasing the nearby Precision Products plant for additional space. That part of the business was later sold to the Strong, Carlisle & Hammond Company of Cleveland, as gas engine production increased on schedule. (An even closer association awaited Ajax and the Superior Engine Division in the future when they would become segments of Cooper.)

Lloyd Lanphere, liaison man between National Supply Company's Toledo sales offices and its Superior plant, joined Ajax as treasurer, soon assuming additional responsibilities as assistant general manager. During his 22-year tenure with National Supply, he had become well acquainted with Ajax as well as Superior products and often had visited the Corry plant.

The first Ajax gas engine utilizing the acquired Superior design rolled off the assembly bay production line in the fall of 1946. Thus, the balance scale was tipped unquestionably toward gas products, although steam engines were still produced and sold to both American and foreign markets. The company's Houston regional manager, Harry Minard, made a detailed analysis of deep wells throughout the world. He identified 70 percent of all wells below twelve thousand feet as being drilled with Ajax steam engines and estimated that a normal number of those which could not be identified positively by his study would bring the figure to 86 percent. One model, the Ideal-Ajax 14″ × 14″ Type "B" steam drilling engine, set many sales records among steam drilling and hoisting engines for the oil industry.

With the growth of its gas engines, the company entered the relatively new secondary oil-recovery market, bringing in oil from abandoned or unproductive wells by such methods as water flooding and gas injection. Still, the company suffered a severe business slump from 1949 to 1950, while proving its ability to manufacture gas engines. "In spite of our enviable reputation as builders of the world's best steam drilling engine, gas engine users at first were skeptical of our ability to redesign and build a gas engine of comparable quality," Assistant General Manager Lanphere explained. "Many prospects, in the beginning, bought engines on a strict 'let's try one and see' basis, then waited for cost and performance tabulations. Soon most of those customers were satisfied that we could build a good gas product, and they demonstrated their faith by buying in larger quantities."

As with most heavy industry, business progressed in cycles, linked to world oil prices that determined periods of heavy or light drilling activity and to steel industry strikes. One particularly long strike in 1952 dampened the company's plan for a Diamond Jubilee celebration. Responding to customer requests, Ajax developed a vertical plunger oil field pump, constructed for long life with minimum attention and maintenance. "Building to such specifications necessitated high pricing, so the product didn't catch on for a long time," recalled Phil Sample, an engineer who joined the company in 1948 and later became works manager. "It was not made to sell cheap. But we held fast to our tradition of top quality, despite cost." After a few years, the sturdy pump was known around the world.

A similar situation occurred in 1958, when Ajax introduced an integral engine-compressor, believed by many to be the company's most important product advancement in many years. The compressor end was purchased from Pennsylvania Pump and Compressor Company of Easton, Pennsylvania, another group with whom Ajax would later become associated in Cooper Industries. Used for gathering gas, boosting gas, repressuring, and gas lift service, the single and two-stage compressors were priced above most competitors but found great success in sales through long life and high performance.

In 1960, Doc Castor died after an illness that had forced him to accept a part time work schedule for several years. Lanphere, who had shouldered much of the management responsibility, was named vice president and general manager. Bliss moved from president to chairman of the board. Mrs. Florence Bliss Castor was elected president and treasurer. Ajax employed 325 persons at the time of the cash purchase by Cooper-Bessemer. This number grew steadily in the following years as plant facilities were expanded and renovated to support the company's move to additional markets. (Sales of Ajax products in 1982 approached $100 million, providing a profit contribution 10 times its 1963 purchase price.)

10

International Upsurge

Less than a month after the Ajax purchase, Cooper-Bessemer followed through on its announced plan to separate operational authority into divisions. Thomas E. Kraner returned from the presidency of CB/Southern to become vice president and general manager of Cooper-Bessemer Division, largest operating unit of the company. Dennis L. Gallogly was vice president of engineering, Harold C. Johnson was vice president of manufacturing, and G.C. Woodard was vice president of marketing. Lloyd Lanphere was named vice president and general manager of the Ajax Iron Works Division, and Richard Allchin continued as president of what became the Rotor Tool Division. The company sold Kline Manufacturing, acquired two years earlier, after a basic management decision not to enter the high pressure hydraulics market. The impact of that transaction on sales and earnings was relatively insignificant.

Another step in the company's plan was taken in 1964 when international offices were moved from New York City to Mt. Vernon and designated a division, headed by Vice President Charles Cooper. A branch of the division, however, was maintained in New York. President Miller said the move was made to strengthen the International Division and improve communications on product sales between Cooper-Bessemer Division marketing and engineering in Mt. Vernon and the overseas sales offices. The Hague office was closed, and greater emphasis was placed on the offices in Paris and London, where a key man, John Fighter, was moved from the United States to head United Kingdom sales.

Timing of the International Division reorganization could not have been better. The year brought a barrage of overseas activities. First came what Cooper called "a tremendous upsurge" in demand for Cooper-Bessemer products in the Middle East, when Arab countries began to follow the lead of Venezuela by banning the flaring of gas. In response, Cooper-Bessemer established an office in Beirut, and Vice President Cooper anticipated that it would soon be joined by warehouse facilities to supply parts and service. In June, a wholly owned British subsidiary, Cooper-Bessemer (U.K.), Ltd., began operations in London, and immediately entered into an agreement with Harland and Wolff, Ltd. for the manufacture of equipment and parts. The former license agreement with Harland and Wolff was terminated, as Cooper-Bessemer (U.K.) assumed all marketing and service responsibilities in the United Kingdom.

In northwestern Europe, discoveries of sizeable gas fields — promising to be among the largest in the world — were expected to lead to unprecedented growth of natural gas and related industries in that area. One of the most intriguing developments at that time was new emphasis placed on gas utilization by international oil companies. The program, strongly supported by the Organization of Petroleum Exporting Countries (OPEC), called for preservation of petroleum and gaseous products to provide maximum long-range return from each country's natural resources. It was a subject that would produce many meetings, heated debates, and vacillating policies in the years ahead. The company also experienced growth in marketing such products as centrifugal engine-compressors, resulting from a flurry of fertilizer plants being built in developing countries to increase food supplies.

Domestic acquisitions were working out well, as the year 1964 progressed. In its fifth year as an arm of Cooper-Bessemer, an expanded Rotor Tool showed 126 percent of planned profit. The newly acquired Ajax was off to a good start with 133 percent of planned profit. CB/ Southern was more than tripling expected profits. All contributed to Cooper-Bessemer meeting its third goal of the short-term plan with sales of $104,523,000 producing earnings of $4,793,000.

Management, stepping up active investigation of other possible acquisitions to further smooth the curve of business fluctuations, twice had made offers for Pennsylvania Pump and Compressor Company, without being able to agree on a price. The Easton, Pennsylvania, manufacturer remained at the top of some fifteen organizations being studied, however, and time for successful completion of the merger seemed to be at hand. Penn Pump had given oral acceptance of a third offer, pending approval by the Cooper-Bessemer board.

In reviewing the background of Penn Pump, Vice President Boyer told the board the company had not approached its growth potential in manufacturing heavy duty reciprocating compressors in the 10 to 250 horsepower range, industrial centrifugal pumps and valves, none of which was competitive with Cooper-Bessemer's current products. Acquiring the company presented an immediate alternative to the less desirable prospect of designing and marketing products in that range.

Penn Pump had begun as one of many small companies whose founders left larger organizations shortly after World War I to join the competition for flourishing postwar markets. Growth and good times were strong enticements for men who envisioned industrial ownership. Many responded to the lure, abandoning job security in the gamble, and losers outnumbered winners by a wide margin. Pennsylvania Pump and Compressor Company was among the survivors.

Four decades later, it had a good reputation in its field, but it admittedly needed management rejuvenation that meshed with Cooper-Bessemer's reorganizing efforts. Although Penn Pump fell somewhat below size guidelines preferred by the board, it added a market area not served by the larger Ajax and still larger Cooper-Bessemer products. Board approval was unanimous; Penn Pump was purchased for 45,655 shares of common stock, and it became a division of Cooper-Bessemer Corporation on November 30, 1964.

11

Penn Pump

History sometimes becomes distorted by a mania to define origins in terms of specific persons, dates, and events. We insist on knowing exactly who started what and when. In the case of Pennsylvania Pump and Compressor Company, the compulsion to establish a precise industrial genealogy invites frustration and almost certain error. Such attempts to trace the company's beginning have resulted in conflicting comments and credits.

The plan to form a manufacturing company was spawned somewhere within the discussions of several men employed by the Ingersoll-Rand Corporation of Phillipsburg, New Jersey. Identifying the originator of the idea remains a matter of conjecture, but as the plan developed the ranks of participants grew steadily, and some of the men pooled enough money to rent a basement room in Easton, Pennsylvania, across the Delaware River from Phillipsburg, where they spent several months designing a small air compressor. Meanwhile, they solicited prospective investors. By the spring of 1920, the group had sufficient capital to purchase a 55-acre farm three miles from Easton, on which they began construction of a manufacturing plant. One of two farmhouses on the property was converted into an office.

On April 19, 1920, with construction progressing, product designs ready, and a charter granted by the Commonwealth of Pennsylvania, an organizational meeting of Pennsylvania Pump and Compressor Company was held. Fifty stockholders were represented in person or by proxy, and leadership that had emerged informally over the months was reflected in the election of officers. Norman A. Messinger, who had been a purchasing agent and works manager for Ingersoll-Rand at its Phillipsburg plant and its Cameron Pump Division in Easton for twenty years, was named president. Ward Raymond, former Cameron Division chief engineer, became vice president. Frank M. Godley, a 22-year Ingersoll-Rand veteran auditor and cost accountant, was named secretary, and Ellis R. Snovel, youngest of the officers at thirty-five, who had been an Ingersoll-Rand purchasing agent, became treasurer. Other key positions

This was Penn Pump's office in 1925, five years after the company was founded in Easton.

soon filled by former Ingersoll-Rand men who helped found the new company went to William C. Merwarth, shop superintendent; William E. Anderson, chief engineer; Ellis Nathan, steam pump engineer; and William H. Noble, centrifugal pump engineer.

Manufacturing low horsepower reciprocating compressors and centrifugal pumps, the company found ready markets for its early products, although it maintained a modest production volume. Industries requiring reliable supplies of compressed air and those pumping water for steam boilers and cooling were the company's principal customers. Chemical companies also bought Penn Pump products to compress various gases used in processing. Through the 1920s, the company grew slowly, suffering some loss financially, but gradually building its basic product lines. President Messinger died and was succeeded by Ward Raymond, who had been responsible for most of the engineering leadership. Ellis Snovel, a forceful man with strong convictions, not only headed financial aspects of the business but also became increasingly involved in general company management.

One great source of company pride was a reputation for good service on its equipment. This was accomplished in several ways, one of which related directly to the farm location. While one of the farmhouses continued to serve as the company office, the other provided residence for a succession of employees, each of whom was expert at servicing company products. With such a man living on company premises, Penn Pump enjoyed early recognition among customers for having someone on emergency call twenty-four hours a day. As the years went by, the company property, which bordered picturesque Bushkill Creek, became the scene of diverse activities for employees and their families, judging from the unusual projects recorded in the corporate annuals. Each spring, the company hired a farmer to plow some of the ground. This provided family gardens for all employees who wanted them. During lunch hours, gardening activity was brisk. A pond was stocked for employee fishing (spring-fed Bushkill Creek also provided some of the area's best fishing), and in the fall, lunch hour hunting was a popular sport on the company land. At family picnics and clambakes, the company furnished food and drink.

Strong ties existed between jobs and family lives. Several times the company financed home mortgages for employees without charging interest on the loans. In periods of slack business, the company avoided many layoffs by assigning employees to duties developing the property and planting trees. Conversely, when the company's continued existence was threatened by the Great Depression of the early 1930s, employees responded by working at low salaries, sometimes even without pay, to maintain operations. Penn Pump employment became traditional with some families. Carl Deck, who at one time occupied the house on plant grounds, was among those who had left Ingersoll-Rand to join the company when it was started, serving as the first assembly floor foreman and second plant superintendent. Four of his sons later joined Penn Pump. One of them, Paul Deck, who advanced to general foreman, recalled making the rounds with the night watchman "almost from the time I could walk," and working summers at the plant before he was old enough to assume a full-time position. Another long-time employee and resident of the company house was William Schlough, whose brothers, Jacob and Whitney, were both Penn Pump foremen. Jacob's son, Connie, maintained the progression, starting with the company at an early age.

From 1935, the company had an uninterrupted record of annual overall profit. It continued to operate on a smaller scale than major competitors, but its customers included leading U.S. companies. The 1940s, with their improving economy, brought new successes in the air compressor and chemical markets. But the centrifugal pump line, while still significant, did not indicate comparable promise for the future, particularly since it began to encounter a proliferation of competition. Management leaders, most of whom had been with the company since its founding, were hesitant to expand into a large manufacturing organization. They preferred the closely knit personal relationships that characterized Penn Pump, and they depended on original compressor designs that had proven to be reliable. The company held a unique position in the industry by specializing in products that large compressor manufacturers such as Ingersoll-Rand and Cooper-Bessemer avoided. It made specialty products for such exotic applications as compressing toxic gases, often on a custom-made basis. A good engineering group and skilled operators teamed well in putting together products that did not overlap with those of many other companies. Customers knew that Penn Pump, although small, was able to handle intricate, specialized assignments and guarantee rapid delivery. Company executives, unpretentious men who lived in modest homes, restricted themselves to extremely low salaries. An employee noted that company success never altered the leaders' patterns of living. Similarly, there was little change in policies and methods within the company, and employee turnover was an infrequent occurrence.

Even after he succeeded Ward Raymond as president, Ellis Snovel continued to hold the position of treasurer. A very short, energetic man, he had a booming voice that could be heard throughout the office building. It was reported that President Snovel never bothered with an intercom system, and rarely made interoffice telephone calls. He just yelled. William Noble, who became chief engineer when William Anderson was named vice president in charge of marketing and sales, kept a wealth of technical knowledge in a tiny black book with tattered, yellowing pages. A colleague said that "Bill didn't really need the book, anyway, because all that information was in his head, and he could design or size a compressor without looking at drawings." Ellis Nathan, a native of England, also was described as a walking encyclopedia of technical facts, and played an important role in company development even though he suffered ill health for many years.

After World War II, company leaders recognized a need to update management procedures. Leroy W. Fegley, who joined Penn Pump in 1952 as assistant secretary and later became secretary and chief accountant, remembered an early assignment to change the original inventory system, one that could be interpreted by only two or three men in the organization. "If you are successful in making that into a system that the average person can read, you will have done the most for Penn Pump that you probably will be able to do in your lifetime," President Snovel told him. That and other projects such as modernizing routing systems, replacing old accounting methods, and mechanizing the laborious hand finishing of products, were followed by instituting the company's first retirement-pension plan. A sizeable percentage of employees became eligible for retirement immediately.

For many years the company built its own heat exchangers, aftercoolers, and innercoolers. But as competition grew, it began to purchase those units from other companies. It also manufactured an air check valve, providing an entree to new and existing air, gas, and steam compressor users. To offer a more complete compressor package, it purchased other accessories such as control equipment and filters for resale. Indicative of Penn Pump product longevity, nearly half of company sales were parts. At various times, the company also designed and built compressor cylinders for oilfield engine-compressors marketed by Superior Engine Company, Clark Brothers, and Ajax Iron Works. The Ajax agreement was made after each of the two companies attempted to purchase the other. In the resulting stand off, it was agreed that instead of a merger, Penn Pump would build a compressor to match an Ajax gas engine. The resulting Ajax integral engine-compressor was introduced in 1958.

Earlier predictions of a dwindling business in centrifugal pumps proved accurate. A member of the management team noted that ."anyone with two, three, or four machines and a nice big garage can produce small pumps now, and competitors number in the hundreds, compared with about half a dozen in small compressor manufacturing." But millions of dollars in patterns and expansion would be required to upgrade pump manufacturing into a complete line, out of the reach of "garage" competitors. Such investment was not in keeping with company philosophy.

By 1963, pumps and pump parts represented only 7.5 percent of Penn Pump sales. More than 82 percent of sales came from compressors and their parts, with the remainder attributed to the resale of purchased accessories. Sales were directed by Vice President Anderson, who worked through manufacturers' representatives and also by able company trained employees like Douglas S. Bush. Bush started in the assembly department, went into field service, became one of the top salesmen in company history, and later advanced to works manager.

After consecutive decreases since 1959, the company experienced the highest sales in its history in 1963. A new office building was constructed the following spring, and wings were added to the factory. The original office building that had been a farmhouse before the company was founded was torn down. No one could suggest a feasible disposition of the huge, antiquated office safe, so it simply was buried.

After the acquisition, Ellis Snovel, ill during most of his final year as Penn Pump president, retired at age seventy-nine. The only other founder in active management, Vice President Anderson, retired at age seventy-six. C. William Gilchrist, former works manager at Stratford, moved from Canada to become general manager, then president of the Penn Pump Division.

Former Penn Pump President Ward Raymond, although he had been retired for many years, remained active in other affairs, including serving on a bank board at the age of ninety-nine. He paid frequent visits to the plant, always stopping first at the office of the president.

"He would leave his cane in a corner of the office and remind me to not let him forget it before he left," Gilchrist said. "Then he would go out in the shop and watch employees using some of the machinery he had designed. After walking around without any problem at all, he would stop by for his cane and leave."

Some of the nostalgia of earlier years was preserved at Easton when acreage along Bushkill Creek, formerly known as the grove area, was deeded by Cooper-Bessemer to Palmer Township and opened to the public as "Penn Pump Park."

As in the cases of Rotor Tool and Ajax, the Penn Pump brand name was continued after the acquisition. Sales and employment began increasing almost immediately and factory space was doubled within two years.

12

Moving to Texas

The basic tenet of reaching wider markets in the United States and abroad was the hub of the company's industrial wheel, supported by spokes that might need changing from time to time. Progress could not be expected to follow a perfectly straight line, but it was important to keep moving. New spokes unquestionably had strengthened the wheel. Sales in the five-year period from 1960 to 1965 increased from $68,397,038 to $117,397,000. Five operating divisions served four principal markets: gas transmission and storage, oil and gas production, petroleum and chemical processing, and general industry. Product lines had been lengthened significantly since the acquisition of Rotor Tool. Yet, management realized that reliability on future earnings growth still depended on traveling new paths. Acquisitions to that date could be classified more as expansions rather than real diversifications. Opportunity in production areas influenced by entirely different business cycles was still being sought. Corporate management, walking a tight rope between too much and too little centralized control of operations, girded itself with a flexible policy that could be adapted quickly to both opportunity and opposition. It was more important to have responsibilities well established within operating groups than to be overly concerned with titles and categorical designations. At the same time, the corporate management team was honed to a size that could act and react swiftly and in unison.

Treasurer Robert Cizik, who also had become controller when William Kahrl died in 1964, continued to head financial and planning strategy. Alan Riedel had advanced to secretary and general counsel, also serving as head of personnel and chief labor negotiator. Stanley Johnson, Jr., headed the General Products Group, encompassing Rotor Tool and Penn Pump, and was charged with generating new products, both internally and by acquisition. Thomas Kraner directed the Energy Services Group, consisting of the Cooper-Bessemer Company and CB/Southern. Charles Cooper moved to Washington, D.C., as corporate representative for coordinating relations with the federal government. The average age of corporate officers and division presidents was forty-five.

Charles Cooper, last of the family to be associated with the company.

As chief executive officer, President Miller also presided at board meetings after the sudden death of Chairman Warriner on January 19, 1965.

Even with the corporate move to downtown Mt. Vernon, it was difficult to shed old habits and effect the separation of policy making and operations — particularly when the corporate name remained the same as, its largest division. The problem was accentuated in a telephone call that interrupted Miller in the middle of a policy meeting. The caller, who managed one of the out-of-town plants, was having an engineering problem. After explaining it to Miller, he asked, "How do you guys at Cooper-Bessemer do it?"

Coincidentally, at a board meeting a few days later, one of the directors, General Leslie R. Groves (a retired general who had commanded the Manhattan Project for development of the atomic bomb in World War II) asked, "How long are we going to maintain headquarters of the corporation at Mt. Vernon?" Miller replied that he was not prepared to answer the question at that time, but it was a question being voiced from several quarters. General Groves offered the opinion that he was not promoting the New York area where he lived, and recognized that divisions needed attention to operate effectively, but added that "the key in this age is accessibility, not distance alone," even though Chicago director R. Edwin Moore described Mt. Vernon as "God's pocket."

More immediate concern was felt for the lingering question of a corporate name change that would end confusion and more accurately reflect the company's new direction. This time, President Miller and his management group were prepared with an immediate answer. With its first name change since the merger of Cooper and Bessemer thirty-six years earlier, the company officially became Cooper Industries, Inc., on December 10, 1965.

In the annual report, Miller described the new name as representing one more positive step in a conscious program, begun some four years earlier, to "organize and otherwise prepare ourselves for a more rapid rate of earnings growth, and diversification. Currently, we have a relatively simple, yet highly flexible organizational structure consisting of a small corporate office, two groups, and five operating divisions. This organization is primed for growth — both through profitable acquisitions and the expansion of our existing business into new market areas. The name Cooper Industries more accurately describes our company as it exists today and as it will grow in the future."

Two months after the change of name, Cooper Industries was invited for the first time to have its president address the New York Society of Security Analysts. Telling the group that the new name was consistent with the determination to develop a corporate organization and group of executives capable of administering the operation of a multidivision enterprise, Miller emphasized that the role of Cooper would never be that of a holding company. "We have developed, in the past four years, comprehensive profit planning and reporting techniques, capital investment procedures, and accounting policies and procedures which are followed by each division," he said. "Profit planning, which comes from within each division, has been particularly meaningful for us during the past two years. We operate under a philosophy whereby everything of importance is measurable, and will be measured."

Cooper plants in Mt. Vernon and Cleveland, Ohio; Grove City, Corry and Easton, Pennsylvania; Stratford, Ontario; and Houston, Texas, employed six thousand men and women, a record employment for the company, and more than $4 million was budgeted for improving facilities in 1966.

Looking for opportunities outside the boundaries of existing markets, a management group headed by Stanley Johnson, Jr., studied the feasibility of purchasing Ken-Tool Manufacturing Company of Akron. Although relatively small, Ken-Tool enjoyed a reputation for producing high quality products for automotive and aircraft service markets. It was known particularly for efficient design of durable tools for tire changing, rim servicing, and battery servicing of passenger cars, trucks, tractors, and aircraft. The tools were sold through jobbers and warehouse distributors, which would represent a new marketing dimension for Cooper.

After board approval, Ken-Tool and its related operation, Kennedy Service Tool Company, also located in Akron, were purchased by Cooper in May of 1966, becoming part of the General Products Group headed by Johnson. In June of 1966, Gene Miller suffered a severe heart attack and the company was managed by a committee of Tom Kraner, Stan Johnson, Jr., Bob Cizik, and Alan Riedel until Miller returned to limited duty in the fall.

Cooper-Bessemer Division, directing a large share of its attention to the international market in 1966, entered into a joint venture, Cooper-mex, in Mexico. The move followed several months of searching for a suitable partner, after the Mexican government applied stringent restrictions on imports, informing Cooper and other suppliers that continued marketing would be tied to production within the country. It insisted that American manufacturers work with Mexican partners and hire labor forces from that country. Complying with those requirements, Cooper and its partner, a group of prominent Mexican industrialists, opened operations in Mexico City, providing manufacturing and service support for sales of Cooper-Bessemer equipment to a rapidly expanding oil and gas production industry in that country.

Cooper-Bessemer's complete line of jet gas turbines, becoming increasingly important in total sales at that time, was described in a full-color sixteen-page bulletin sent around the world. Models covering a range of 2,750 to 16,500 horsepower were available for gas transmission and storage; compressor, pump or generator drive for refinery, chemical and petrochemical plants; peaking or base load generator drive; and marine propulsion. The jets combined low installation cost with high performance and minimum maintenance.

Although it never enjoyed the allure of stardom, the repair parts and service business continued to be one of the steadiest performers in overall finances, accounting for 30 percent of the company's total sales. Marketing was reorganized from product to market orientation, providing a greater awareness of effective order selectivity, with concentration on selling more profitable products and eliminating those that were marginal. While the magnitude of that single change might have been overshadowed by total development of the new financial department, it would be basic to production-sales philosophy as the company grew at an accelerating rate.

One of the promising segments of the company's business at the time was CB/Southern, which expanded its scope of activities to meet demands from some sixty nations scurrying to explore offshore oil and gas production fields. Large reserves were discovered beneath the Gulf of Mexico, off the Nigerian coast, in the North Sea, at Cook Inlet near Alaska, and other areas of the world. As the search moved farther from shore, into greater water depths, economics of operations required large platforms that could be installed in one piece above the water, or unique equipment that could be set on the ocean floor.

CB/Southern, which had begun with skid-mounted compressor packages, lost little time in building a deepwater facility on the Houston Ship Channel, with access to world waterways. Soon it was producing "Unipod" preassembled, automated single and multidecked offshore production platforms for shipment to worldwide locations. The new manufacturing facility included a slip dredged eighty feet wide and two hundred feet long, with a fixed craneway capable of lifting five hundred tons for direct loading onto barges. Connected to high-pressure gas wells, the units separated water and oil from gas and metered production to shore through submerged pipelines. Production at a typical unit near Houston was twenty million cubic feet of gas per day.

For operation in marshes and shallow water, CB/Southern also furnished a "Unisub" compressor unit on flotation platforms that could be towed to a production site and ballasted to the bottom. One particular project brought widespread press and trade journal coverage. *Gas Age Monthly* carried this report:

> Five barge-mounted compressor stations, believed to be the largest and most powerful ever built, were put on stream by Petroleos Mexicanos (Pemex) at the Cinco Presidentes field in Vera Cruz, Mexico. The ocean-going compressor stations, valued at nearly $10 million, were built by CB/Southern, a division of Cooper Industries, Inc., at Houston, Texas. The stations are designed to be connected between the gas source and a delivery line. Three of the plants are equipped with six compressors with 6,600 hp each, while the fourth has eight units with 5,500 hp. Engines driving the compressors are fueled from the natural gas source. A heat exchanger at each engine cools the lube oil, jacket water and the gas from the compressors. The barge substructure, while supporting the compressors and their auxiliary equipment, also contains compartments for seawater ballast, fresh water, lube oil and used lube oil. . . . each barge may be refloated by using ballasting equipment built into the hull. Relocation involved preparing a bed by dredging, positioning, and flooding the barge. Operation is semi-automatic. Signals, both audio and visual, are generated by fluid amplifiers. This new nonelectric system is actually powered by the gas handled through the compressors. Each station will have a two-man crew. CB/Southern feels the barge-mounted compressor stations provide savings in manpower, transportation, and construction, as well as avoiding delays caused by bad weather.

Operations were also extended into the process market, through the purchase of Cooper Metals, based in Houston but physically separated from other segments of the division. This unit, where metal vessels were designed and fabricated for chemical producers and oil refiners, had equipment capable of handling special purpose metals and rolling plate steel up to six inches thick.

CB/Southern was not destined to play a major role in the company's history, but it provided a colorful chapter and it helped extend the reputation for decisive response to market needs. It also represented a step away from provincialism, which by coincidence was in a location that would soon take on great significance for Cooper Industries.

In the fall of 1966, a special meeting of shareholders was held to approve important changes in the Articles of Incorporation. Common stock was split on a two-for-one basis and the number of authorized shares was increased from three million to ten million. At the same meeting, a new class of preferred stock was authorized, consisting of four hundred thousand shares without par value, to be issued as needed under terms and conditions approved by the Board of Directors. This new class of preferred stock was created to prepare for further acquisitions.

Other reflections of continued earnings growth were directors' decisions to increase quarterly dividends twice during the year, for a total jump from 22.5 to 30 cents, nearly tripling dividend income considering the stock split.

President Miller noted that Cooper Industries had ranked among the top five hundred U.S. industrial companies in sales for several years. "More significantly," he said, "our average annual growth in earnings per share for the past ten years has been at a rate exceeding 13 percent. This puts us among the top one hundred companies in terms of earnings growth. While this standing is highly attractive, I hope our growth can be accelerated, especially since we now have a proven management system, a diversified base, and a cadre of thoroughly trained and experienced management personnel." Miller believed the company, at the end of 1966, had reached another pivotal point in its history. Events of the following year would document his perception.

Across America, the tempo of conglomerate mergers was picking up, heading toward a peak that would bring about the disappearance of 2,407 manufacturing and mining firms in a single year. Cooper Industries received several "feelers" from larger corporations asking if it might be available for purchase, but it held firm in its decision to grow through product generation and acquisition. Management, backed by the board of directors, thoroughly opposed the conglomerate theory that companies could diversify wildly, with the somewhat arrogant idea that professional managers could oversee any kind of business, regardless of products, markets, or manufacturing processes. Such a movement was doomed, Cooper leaders believed, and the need for effective management control should set limits on the degree of diversification and the timing of its own acquisitions. The character of management, the skills, experience, and interests a company encompassed as it grew, should influence decisions about areas into which it would diversify.

Having successfully assimilated Rotor Tool and Ken-Tool into its revamped system of management control, Cooper was prepared to take a giant step into an area it had been investigating with increasing interest — the growing hardware market. Concurrently, the company felt an intensifying pressure to move its corporate headquarters into the geographic mainstream of business. A decision seemed inevitable, but President Miller was adamant about making a carefully planned, smooth transition from the city that had been so closely tied to the company for 124 years. Obvious locations of New York City, Chicago and Cleveland were rejected, in favor of the bubbling business climate of the Southwest, ready to erupt dramatically in Texas. Dallas could be a good choice, but there appeared to be a concentration there on developing banking, insurance, and warehousing. As the study narrowed, the focus fell on Houston, a city poised for rapid growth as a communications and transportation center, close to many of the company's major customers, and in an area familiar to Cooper through its CB/Southern division, currently undergoing its third deepwater plant expansion.

President Miller fended off jibes that childhood roots in Oklahoma drew his vision toward the Southwest. Houston was chosen as the new headquarters location of Cooper Industries. To avoid premature speculation, Robert Cizik investigated site possibilities, ostensibly selecting space in the First City National Bank building for CB/Southern office expansion, until Miller revealed on January 18, 1967, that it would become the new corporate home of the parent organization.

The *Mount Vernon News* reported the president's announcement at a press conference in that city:

> E.L. Miller, president and chief executive officer of Cooper Industries, Inc., announced today that headquarters of the corporation will be moved to Houston, Texas, later this year. Miller emphasized that only 10 employees and their families are involved and that the move will have no direct effect on operations of the Cooper-Bessemer Company Division here.
>
> Miller said, "As recently as 1959 our company consisted primarily of what is now the Cooper-Bessemer Company Division of Cooper Industries. Today, growth and diversification have created a modern Cooper Industries with six operating divisions serving markets throughout the world. Our progress has been achieved in an atmosphere of keen competition. To continue to meet that competition effectively and to continue our progress, we have concluded, after long and careful consideration, that we will be better able to strengthen Cooper Industries and its divisions by relocating the corporate offices in a large industrial and commercial center. Now that the decision has been made, we want our friends in Mt. Vernon to be the first to know that during 1967 approximately 10 men and their families will be moved to establish the corporate offices at Houston. . . . Those few of us who will be leaving our friends and Mt. Vernon, after many pleasant years, do so with regret but also with confidence that this will strengthen the position of Cooper-Bessemer, bringing added security to our employees and added prosperity to the city."

The announcement was made to news media at the office of President Miller. At his side were Alan Riedel, secretary and general counsel for the corporation, Robert Cizik, treasurer and controller, and Floyd Lawrence, who had come to Mt. Vernon only Monday to join Cooper Industries as a public relations man. Lawrence formerly was with Ford Motor Co. at Dearborn, Mich.

From conversations at the press conference, it was obvious Miller, Riedel, and Cizik will be among those leaving. "Now you see why I couldn't run for City Council," smiled Riedel. The secretary and general counsel has served two terms on City Council, and it was disclosed recently he will not be running again, but without explanation at the time. Miller commented he will regret leaving Mt. Vernon. "After all, I have been here 21 years," he noted.

A few days after the news announcement, *Mt. Vernon News* Editor Fred Lorey published an editorial reflecting a city's feelings about the forthcoming relocation:

The decision of Cooper Industries, Inc., to move its headquarters from Mt. Vernon to Houston this year was not entirely unexpected. The handwriting has been plain on the wall for the past couple of years. It will still be painful for us.

The number of men leaving the community will be small. Present plans are that only about 10 will be going. The 10 have not yet been publicly announced, but it is certain they will be men who have been important in the community and in its several organizations. They are the kind of men who are valuable in the leadership of a community. But as we said, the move was not entirely unexpected. Several years ago, Cooper Industries, Inc., then Cooper-Bessemer Corp., appraised its future and established a course for itself. It had the choice of continuing as a small, rather specialized engine maker, subject to the mercies of a highly cyclical business, and competing against other companies who were giants or striving to become giants, or of making some radical changes.

Cooper-Bessemer officers decided, and properly so as time has shown, to get into the arena and try to compete with the big and the ambitious by becoming bigger and more ambitious. Largely a home-owned builder of engines, it began to diversify. It broadened its board of directors to take in men from several fields of manufacturing and finance. New officers took over several posts. It grew and it prospered. With the prosperity of Cooper-Bessemer Corp., Mt. Vernon also prospered. Workers, local stockholders, the merchants, and the public in general all benefited.

But the diversification, the changes in the board of directors, the broadening interests and activities of the company soon created talk of a possible removal of the company offices. The questions were not "if," but "how soon?" and "how much?" Two years ago there was a major change in the corporate structure, a step which has probably done more than anything else to soften the blow which some in Mt. Vernon sensed was eventually going to come.

With the creation of Cooper Industries, Inc., as the top management structure, separated from its several divisions, the way was cleared to retain Cooper-Bessemer in Mt. Vernon, largely as we have known it through the years. Cooper-Bessemer Co. as a division of Cooper Industries has grown to be a bigger operation in Mt. Vernon than the old Cooper-Bessemer Corp. ever was. We have every reason to believe it will continue to grow. The major developments of the past year are assurance of that — the new people brought in; the development of the data processing center; construction and remodeling of buildings; installation of new equipment.

We can be assured that Cooper-Bessemer will continue to be a major part of our community, and we can look for it to continue to grow as Cooper Industries, its parent, also grows. We can be grateful to the men who planned it this way — that Mt. Vernon's biggest industry will continue to be a growing, vital force in the community. What is happening is not a disaster. It is a normal development in a process of change taking place in a growing company. We must ride with the change and adapt ourselves to a new situation in our largest local industry.

At the other end of the line, *The Houston Post* welcomed Cooper Industries to its new corporate home and quoted President Miller as predicting "a lot of acquisitions after we move to Houston." *Post* Business Editor Sam Weiner reported that Cooper seriously examined perhaps a hundred companies a year and did indepth research on perhaps twenty-five. He also divulged that Cooper was about to acquire the Lufkin Rule Company of Saginaw, Michigan.

Hand tools represented the kind of business leveler Cooper sought. There was nothing spectacular about them — no revolutionary style changes and few precipitous market fluctuations. Products were used up and discarded, or simply lost, creating what manufacturers referred to as "good consumption qualities." They were both recognized and used by everyone — from the peasant setting up a hut in some poverty-stricken corner of the world to the engineering genius fashioning an exotic piece of equipment for delivery to the moon. Stanley Johnson, Jr., had done a study on the hand tool industry, analyzing such market leaders as Crescent Niagara Company, and President Miller had observed with great interest the success a major Cooper competitor, Ingersoll-Rand, had found in an auxiliary hand tool arm.

There was no deep philosophical reason for Cooper to select that particular field. It was just one of several logical areas of interest, with two concerns that would have to be resolved before a commitment would be made. First, top quality name brands dominated every segment of hand tool production; second, Cooper knew nothing about operating such a business, and certainly had no intention of abandoning its policy of moving only when assured of success.

Then, as if summoned by what one executive described as "a stroke of Aladdin's lamp," Lufkin appeared with a promising solution to both problems. The established quality leader in measuring instruments, it brought with it a matching quality of leadership. Interestingly, Cooper's intense search paid off not in a direct discovery, but in being recognized by brokerage and investment banking organizations as a serious effort to find new avenues of development.

"Duke Glenn, a man I had gotten to know at Pressprich Company, an investment banking firm in New York, came to Mt. Vernon one day and simply said, 'I've got a company we'd like to present to you'," President Miller said later. "The company was Lufkin, which we knew, of course, and after we followed up on the recommendation, we discovered we had the chance to get more than a company; we were offered the dream of a visionary man named Bill Rector."

The dream, shared by Lufkin President William G. Rector and Vice President Harold A. Stevens, who headed the company's sales program, was to build the world's best hand tool manufacturing group, putting together what they called a "tool basket." It would be composed of selected, quality brand leaders, joined under an umbrella of modern management and imaginative distribution.

The concept Rector and Stevens presented to an interested Cooper management was based on the nature of the hand tools industry, composed of many narrow-line companies that had grown through several generations of family management. In attempting to provide everything for everybody, most of the companies had extended single product lines beyond peripheries of feasibility. In some instances, profit making items were actually outnumbered by losers. Families often continued to dominate decisions through large stock blocks long after their interest in operations had waned. Very little money was put back into decadent multistory factories, which were deteriorating rapidly and becoming increasingly expensive to operate. This created the irony of losing competitive positions while maintaining quality and worldwide brand-name recognition. Unless the trend were reversed, such companies would surely be swallowed up or overtaken by competitors, including those emerging in Japan, Germany, and other nations.

If Cooper would launch a program of buying these companies, over a reasonable period of time it could be possible to create a carefully managed group of name-brand hand tool products, distributed through a central system that would offer customers top quality at sizeable savings in ordering, shipping, and invoicing. Profits could go back into modernization, creating a chain of efficiency and competitive pricing, as well as helping smooth the cycles of gas-related business.

Fulfillment of such a dream would necessitate tremendous long-term investment in acquiring and completely revamping outdated operations. Lufkin offered a substantial base, with production already starting at a new plant in North Carolina. Its metal, fabric, and chain measuring tapes, and folding rules were being sold throughout the world, and it had manufacturing facilities in Puerto Rico, Mexico, and Canada. As part of Cooper Industries, the "tool basket" would have the modern management and financial backing success required. Bill Rector and Hal Stevens would become key figures in seeing it through, with Rector becoming a member of the Cooper Board of Directors.

Negotiations reached the final stage just when Cooper management was about to move to Houston. The Cooper board met in Cleveland to consider the acquisition on the day the Israeli Seven Day War began and the stock market plunged. In his recommendation for effecting the acquisition, Miller told the board the plan represented not just a single purchase, but "the start of a building program to buy quality hand tool companies in the way Bill Rector envisioned it." Approval once again was unanimous, and in October of 1967, Cooper Industries entered the highly competitive hand tools business.

The merger was consummated through issuance of 201,631 shares of a Cooper Industries Series "A" cumulative preferred stock with a five dollar dividend. It was the first use of the four hundred thousand shares of preferred stock authorized for such action by shareholders at the special meeting in 1966.

13

Lufkin

When E.T. Lufkin began a board and log rule manufacturing company at Cleveland, Ohio, in 1869, lumbering had reached that general area in its slow sweep from New England to Middle America. Slightly north and west, across the thumb of Michigan, the city of Saginaw was a temporary center of the migrating lumber industry.

With virgin forests covering millions of acres of land, reforestation was not yet an American concern. As supplies were depleted, lumbermen simply moved farther west, selecting from seemingly inexhaustible resources those locations offering the best "lumber streams" where logs could be floated with minimum obstruction to sawmills. Such logs had to be measured for sale, as did the boards coming from the milling saws. Consequently, manufacturers of measuring rules popped up like bubbles in the wake of lumbering's westward movement. Most of them burst almost as quickly, lacking necessary knowledge and skill to produce quality products, so despite their proliferation, suppliers were hard pressed to find reliable sources of measuring rules.

The E.T. Lufkin Board and Log Rule Manufacturing Company proved to be an exception. Using only the finest second-growth hickory butts available, it produced rules that were shaved down by hand, always following the natural grain, attached heads of carefully tempered steel, and burned figures into the wood, thereby avoiding the weakening caused by the less expensive stamping process used by most manufacturers. Handles were formed by skilled craftsmen and a protective finish came from varnish that the company prepared itself, following an exacting formula of selected gums and pure grain alcohol. Lufkin proclaimed that while its goods were not the lowest in price, they were "the most durable and therefore the cheapest." Business success amidst a cluster of faltering competition seemed to support its claim. The Lufkin log rule, made of flexible hickory, contained scales that provided quick board-foot calculations from measuring the length and varying diameters of a log. Because of natural log tapering and bark cover, the rule simply provided the means of making a feasible estimate. It was produced with a variety

Lufkin employees standing in front of the company's first factory in Cleveland in 1869.

Measuring timber with a Lufkin rule.

of scales dictated by a strange situation that had developed with logging. Separate scales had evolved as standards in different geographic areas. Containing such names as Scribner, Doyle, Favorite, Baxter, Dusenberry, and Cumberland River, some favored the buyer, others the seller. As a manufacturer, Lufkin supplied whichever variety a customer requested, avoiding controversy with a published statement of policy: "We are often asked which scale is the nearest correct. We leave that question for the lumberman to decide. We can furnish rules figured with any one of them." The less flexible board rule, also containing calculation tables along with the measuring scales, enabled lumbermen to figure exact board feet after sawing. Within a few years, the company increased the size of its plant and added new manufacturing lines. It became the largest producer of forged boot calks — spikes that attached to the heels of logger's boots — in what was described then as "the West," and offered specialties ranging from large log calipers to tiny thickness gauges that could be worn on a finger.

As Lufkin grew, it gained the attention of a measuring rule supplier, Morley Brothers Company, located in Saginaw, where logging and lumbering continued to flourish. Morley Brothers had many good customers. In 1877 alone, a billion board feet of lumber were cut and floated along the 26-mile Saginaw River, where there was about one saw mill per mile. Small wonder that Morley Brothers was disturbed by the difficulty in acquiring adequate supplies of quality measuring rules. Four men from the company decided to solve the problem by acquiring interest in a good log and board rule manufacturing concern. Acting independently of Morley Brothers, they contacted E.T. Lufkin, and in 1883 the group was able to purchase half of the Cleveland company. Within two years, they bought the remaining interest from Lufkin, who moved to Chicago, where he organized another business venture. Fred Buck, a 25-year-old Morley Brothers salesman, was hired by the new owners to manage the reorganized and renamed Lufkin Rule Company.

Tall and rugged, the young general manager looked more like a lumberman than a salesman. He had moved to Saginaw from Adrian, Michigan, where his father was a hardware retailer. Seriously impaired vision had not deterred him from a successful career; declared totally blind at the age of twelve, he had somehow regained some of his sight, overcoming the handicap to such a degree that colleagues could never determine its true extent. Forceful leadership qualities and mechanical expertise made him a good choice to lead the Cleveland manufacturing operation. Albert M. Marshall, a Morley Brothers executive who had provided most of the capital to purchase Lufkin, was named president although he did not take an active part in operational management. Soon after the purchase, a young man named Theodore Huss from northeastern Ohio was hired to head sales. A small man, he was a physical contrast to the 250 lb. general manager. But the men were well teamed as a production-sales combination that was to provide the company leadership for half a century.

By 1890, the company had introduced the first steel measuring tape to be produced in the United States and extended other lines to include straight and folding steel rules, lumber marking implements, glass cutting boards, and a patented "magic pattern rule and chart" that reduced the time for elbow pattern cutting from half an hour to one minute. The still-popular wooden rules were improved by company designed metal heads and end hooks. A company spokesman reported that "There is scarcely a lumber market in the United States or Canada where Lufkin products are not in daily use."

Meanwhile, logging continued its steady westward march, from eastern to western Michigan, then into Wisconsin and Minnesota. In the language of the industry, the Saginaw area was "all lumbered out." With its principal source of income vanishing rapidly, the city offered new-business enticements in the form of free land and long-term tax exemptions. Lufkin Rule Company was receptive to such a lure. It needed a more modern manufacturing plant and it had management roots in the Michigan city. Constructing a new factory on twenty-three acres of land provided by the city, Lufkin moved in early 1892 to Saginaw, where it continued to expand into new markets requiring quality measuring instruments. Much of its specially designed equipment came from the fertile mind of Fred Buck, who visualized concepts, then described them to draftsmen who prepared the drawings. New buildings were added with the introduction of new products over the years, and the single factory grew gradually into a manufacturing complex. Well before the turn of the century, the company established sales offices in New York and London. Then, in 1907, it opened a small plant in Windsor, Ontario, becoming Canada's first complete tape and rule manufacturer. (Later, the London office was closed in World War I.)

Although Lufkin had been incorporated in 1901, it was not until 1910 that Fred Buck succeeded Albert Marshall as president. Theodore Huss, continuing to head the sales organization, became vice president. (An interesting sidelight to the Lufkin history is Marshall's later move to Duluth, Minnesota, to form the Marshall-Wells Hardware Company, which became the largest wholesale hardware organization in the world before it was liquidated after World War II. Marshall and representatives of his family were members of the Lufkin board until the company was acquired by Cooper Industries, Inc., in 1967.) Among the company's new products were surveyor's chain tapes, made of steel, and an extensive line of measuring tapes combining woven linen with metallic warp, often contained in leather cases with brass winding handles.

Just before World War I, President Buck became interested in the folding wooden rule being manufactured in Europe. Convinced that the product would find wide acceptance in America, he made investigative trips abroad, and in 1915 Lufkin purchased a plant in an area that was to become part of Czechoslovakia when that country was formed from sections of Austria and Hungary three years later. Lufkin produced the zig-zag folding wooden rules there for two years. Then the press of war prompted Buck to sell it and bring the process to the United States. In the years that followed, the folding "spring joint rule" became one of the best selling products in the company's long history.

As industrial advancement created increasing need for closer tolerances, Lufkin added a new division for the manufacture of precision hand tools. Starting slowly in 1919, it developed and produced such measuring instruments as micrometers, combination squares, precision scales, radius gauges, and related products. An engineer named Walter Schleicher was hired from an Eastern Seaboard company to develop the precision tools. Eugene Witchger, who had been with the company for several years, was head of engineering for other products, later taking over both segments when Schleicher left the company.

Entrenched competition made penetration of precision tool markets difficult during the 1920s, but the new Lufkin division survived early problems and became an important arm of the company, although it never challenged the leadership of tapes and rules. Product innovations spread Lufkin's reputation in that decade. Among the best known was the "push-pull" metal tape rule, with a concave configuration that held it rigid when extended. President Buck also invented a machine that greatly improved the printing of woven cloth tapes. Several years later, the inventive Lufkin executive wavered temporarily from his established course of producing only quality products, by creating what he admitted to be a cheap product. Motivation for this uncharacteristic decision came from the nation's Great Depression.

Layoffs from America's economic collapse of the 1930s spread through industry in a swath that left few companies untouched. There was no way Lufkin could escape, but Fred Buck was determined to preserve as many jobs as possible by developing a small, inexpensive measuring tape that wound like a telephone dial. Sold almost at cost, it was created solely to maintain employment, and during the few years it was marketed it kept one hundred workers on jobs that otherwise would have been vacated. Many employees did suffer layoffs, however, as the company inched its way through the lean depression years. But the experience was not entirely new to Buck and Huss. They could remember similar economic panics of 1890 and 1907, and they remained optimistic. Lewis Barnard, Jr., the president's grandson, who joined the company in 1932 just in time to experience the depression, remembered a story Fred Buck often told about the severe economic reversal of 1907. He recalled how his grandfather described walking along a Saginaw street with his close friend and business colleague, Huss. "Theodore," the president asked, "what have you got in your pocket?" Searching briefly, Huss replied, "Just fifteen cents." Buck thought a moment, then said, "I've got a dime; let's go have a beer."

Neither man lived to see the company recover completely from the Great Depression. Huss died in 1934 and was succeeded as sales manager by George Macbeth, a veteran company salesman, who later became a vice president. President Buck did lead Lufkin out of the worst part of the depression before he died in 1938 at the age of eighty. His successor as president and chief executive officer was Robert C. Thompson, who had headed the New York sales office and warehouse division as a corporate vice president for many years.

World War II brought a company commitment to defense industries. Precision tools were in great demand, as American industry tooled up for military production. Rules and tapes were needed also, and Lufkin went on a two-shift work schedule to meet its orders. As one of the company's fifteen hundred employees stated succinctly, "Everything that is built has to be measured." Obtaining material was a problem, particularly since a special steel, most of which came from the Roebling Company of New Jersey, was needed for Lufkin products. Chrome, used as a rust-proof coating for tapes and rules, was in scarce supply also. Even the high quality hard maple used in manufacturing spring-joint wooden folding rules was difficult to purchase; hard maple was used in the manufacture of army truck bodies.

When the war ended, Lufkin converted easily to peacetime marketing and began to search again for product improvements and new outlets. Lewis Barnard left the company briefly for further business study at Northwestern University, returning in 1947 as vice president. Canadian manufacturing operations, having grown during the war, were moved from Windsor to Barrie, Ontario, in 1948, occupying a new facility that in time was expanded fourfold.

In 1950, Lewis Barnard was promoted to president and chief executive officer of Lufkin, Robert Thompson moving to chairman of the board until his retirement six years later. The company set goals of increasing its precision tool business and maintaining leadership in widening lines of metal, wood, and woven cloth tapes and rules, to keep pace with accelerating American consumer and industrial needs. The company increased its sales force, continuing an historical policy of using company salesmen, rather than manufacturers' agents, domestically, and directing foreign sales through New York export houses. The company's own New York sales and warehouse division was closed. Explained President Barnard, "Although we had operated it effectively for a great many years, times changed, and it became more economical to ship directly from Saginaw."

Sales doubled during the 1950s, and the company expanded into several new areas of operation. The first was the purchase of Master Rule Company, a producer of tape rules in Middletown, New York. "That company might have been small, but we learned something from it," said Barnard. "We had thought for years that it was necessary to apply tension on a tape using large, expensive machinery to assure accurate printing. Master Rule had a method of printing just as accurately and a whole lot easier without tension."

Later, the company acquired a plant in Maine, where an independent operator prepared lath, the strips of wood used in manufacturing folding rules. Previously, Lufkin cut its own lath out of hard maple boards shipped in from lumber companies in the Saginaw factory. Since one-tenth of the board was usable, the rest became expensive sawdust, when viewed in the context of shipping weight. Purchase of the Anson Stick Company enabled it to prepare lath in Madison, Maine, near the source of hard maple, and send it waste-free to Saginaw. A manufacturing and sales outlet for Lufkin products was then established as a joint venture, Lufmex S. A., in Mexico City. Later it was transferred to Guadalajara. Moving into Puerto Rico, the company established a dial indicator business, Lufkin Caribe. "We also took a few fliers on some things that didn't work out as well as we hoped, so we got rid of them quickly," the president said of the 1950s.

Having dipped lightly into the manufacture of advertising specialties — products bearing a customer's name for promotional distribution — Lufkin in the early 1960s acquired half interest in Tigrett Industries of Jackson, Tennessee. John Tigrett, who had founded the company, had obtained a patent on a popular metal measuring rule that would roll up into itself. He also had patented a special spring in which Lufkin was interested. A few years later, the company bought the remaining half of the business, moved its own specialties production to Jackson, and Lufkin Specialties, Inc., became a wholly owned subsidiary. Lufkin Rule Company of Canada began exporting to foreign markets in 1963. Separate arrangements also were made to have product parts shipped from Barrie to a plant in Australia, where they were assembled and marketed.

In 1964, Lewis Barnard moved to chairman of the board, and William C. Rector, president of True Temper Company in Cleveland, who had served as an outside director on Lufkin's board, joined Lufkin as president and general manager. Another True Temper executive, Harold A. Stevens, became vice president, in charge of Lufkin sales. Following a feasibility study the company's precision tool line, which had reached more than three thousand items and accounted for approximately 20 percent of sales, was discontinued, with equipment, tools, parts, and patents sold to Pratt & Whitney, Inc. At the same time, a modern new manufacturing plant was constructed in Apex, North Carolina. Limited production was started at the Apex plant in May of 1967. Five months later the company was acquired by Cooper Industries, Inc.

After the acquisition by Cooper, Lewis Barnard served as a consultant for a short time, then retired. William Rector remained president of

Lufkin, with offices at the main plant location in Saginaw. Within a year, however, the antiquated Saginaw manufacturing facility was closed, and production was consolidated at the new Apex, North Carolina, plant, considered the most modern of its kind in the world. With Lufkin's transition to modernization, the first component of Cooper's "tool basket" was in place.

14

Poised for Expansion

During the move to Houston and merger negotiations with Lufkin, Cooper established a realignment of executive responsibilities to better position management at both corporate and operational levels for the long-awaited expansion campaign that seemed now to be on track.

Gene Miller, president since 1957, became chairman of the board and continued to serve as chief executive officer. Tom Kraner was elevated to president and chief operating officer. Creation of a Corporate Planning Department to oversee long-range strategy for all entities of the corporation was announced as the nucleus for establishing Cooper's direction in its advancement as a multi-market enterprise. Robert Cizik moved from treasurer-controller to become vice president in charge of the department.

John F. Woodhouse, who had been with Ford Motor Company and The Canadian Imperial Bank of Commerce before joining Cooper in 1964, was promoted from assistant controller for Cooper-Bessemer Company to corporate treasurer. James W. Neithercut, assistant corporate controller for the past year, became controller. He had come to the company in 1965 from the accounting firm of Touche, Ross, Bailey, & Smart, where he was senior consultant-audit supervisor at the Detroit office.

Stanley Johnson, Jr., remained vice president of General Products Group, and Alan Riedel continued to serve as secretary and general counsel, with Roger A. Scott promoted to assistant secretary and assistant general counsel.

The following year Riedel was named vice president of industrial relations and general counsel, and Scott became secretary and assistant general counsel. Robert G. Lambert, who had joined Cooper-Bessemer as controller in 1964 after working in financial and production control positions with Jones & Laughlin Steel Corporation, was promoted to vice president and controller when James Neithercut resigned to join a company in Toledo, Ohio.

When Charles Cooper announced in late 1967 that he would soon retire from the vice presidency and the board, sentiments of the entire company were expressed in the Cooper-Bessemer division's employee publication, *The Manifold*:

> A part of the 134-year old tradition will leave the company early next year when the last of the Cooper family . . . founders of the multi-million dollar corporation that still bears the name . . . retires. Charles G. Cooper, grandson of one of the founders, namesake of the other, marks the end of an era when he retires January 31 (1968), closing out a career that spans 42 years. Some persons might call 42 years a long time, but Charles Cooper had to do some squeezing to crowd all his interests and activities into such a "short" span of years. . . . Dozens of organizations outside the world of business have found Cooper a man of boundless energy, ready to serve almost any cause. A graduate of Yale University, he never forgets his old school ties, serving in a variety of posts as president of the Yale Club in Washington, vice chairman of the Yale Alumni Board and a member of the Yale Honorary Degrees Committee. He also is a past councilor of the American Society of Naval Engineers, the Society of Naval Architects and Marine Engineers, and the Washington Society of Engineers. . . . He is a past director of the Columbia Hospital for Women and a member of a variety of clubs in New York, Washington, D.C., and Mt. Vernon.

Cooper moved to San Diego several years after his retirement, but never lost his enthusiastic support of the company and continued regular correspondence with corporate friends until his death in 1979 at the age of seventy-six.

A framework on which the company planned to build its future was provided in a policy statement described by Miller as "a guideline, not a straightjacket." None of the company's objectives or guidelines was immutable, he said, and many would have to be modified as conditions changed and the company developed a clearer picture of opportunities in various segments of its business. Overall policy would, in fact, be reviewed and updated annually. Nevertheless, basic strategies offered a clear definition of the management's intended course of action:

> Over the long term, our basic corporate objective is growth. Specifically, it is a rate of growth that will increase earnings per share (before tax) at a compound annual rate of 11 percent. Growth by itself, however, will not be sufficient. We must also improve the quality of our earnings by reducing the fluctuations in income that have characterized our company in the past. Stability of earnings must, therefore, represent a collateral objective. This objective implies a careful examination of opportunities in less cyclical and countercyclical areas as well as a continuing effort to expand our current businesses. We will have achieved stability along with growth when our earnings in any one year never fall below those of the previous year.

There are two reasons why the achievement of these objectives is essential. First, the resulting earnings performance will ensure an above-average return on shareholders' investment, in terms of dividend income and increased market value of Cooper shares. Second, the growth inherent in this performance is necessary to provide the opportunities for individual growth and development that will enable us to attract and hold high talent personnel.

Precise step-by-step actions to be followed in achieving the above objectives should not be spelled out until the opportunities open to our existing divisions are more clearly in focus. Nevertheless, there are two general strategy guidelines that should be observed by division and corporate executives as they plan for the future. First, we should preserve, and where practical improve on the strong position we enjoy in our current businesses so as to ensure a solid financial base on which to build. Second, we should vigorously pursue acquisitions. These will include both those that represent logical extensions of existing operations and those that provide diversification into more stable areas of business. Diversification means we will be considering and acting upon a wide range of opportunities. We will ask for specific recommendations on (1) segments of our current business that offer attractive growth potential and the approach that should be followed to exploit them; (2) segments of our current business that will not contribute to future growth and profitability and the action to be taken with each (e.g., divestiture, retrenchment); (3) new product and market areas that appear to offer attractive growth opportunities and steps to be taken to capitalize on them.

Cooper Industries will continue to operate through a decentralized, yet balanced corporate organization with a minimum of necessary central control. The basic operational unit of the company will be the "semi-autonomous" division. Operationally, each division will be managed by a division president who will operate within the framework of the corporation's planning procedure. On this basis, he will have full responsibility for the implementation of approved plans. Divisions will operate on a worldwide basis. We do not anticipate a return to the formation of a centralized international group at the corporate level. Related divisions will continue to be grouped together for administrative purposes under a group vice president who will be a corporate officer. Currently, we have two such groups — Energy Services and General Products. We intend to form other groups whenever the group management job becomes too burdensome or complex, or when we acquire businesses that do not logically relate to either of these groups. Overall administration of the corporation will be provided by the corporate office. This office will consist of the chairman and chief executive officer, the president, and a corporate staff. The staff will assist in development of policy guidelines and provide specialized services to operating divisions. We will need to emphasize development and training of management personnel if we are to provide resources necessary to make this organization effective and support future growth.

For the present, we are splitting responsibility for our acquisition program. We want division management to seek potential acquisitions that represent logical extensions of their current operations. The corporate staff will be responsible for acquisitions that represent diversification moves.

Considering the present makeup of our company, we will strive to maintain an average long-term debt to total capital ratio of 25 percent, with a permissible maximum ratio at any year-end financial reporting date of no more than 30 percent. As this makeup changes, we will, of course, alter the policy to ensure the best return on stockholder equity. When a division's performance over a two-year period falls below the average return on assets of the corporation, corporate and division management will jointly undertake a thorough review of that division's outlook to determine how performance can be improved and whether it is in the company's long-term interest to stay in the business concerned.

Such ambitious goals would not be easy to achieve, and Miller said he fully expected the company to experience many frustrations in attaining them. "Yet," he said, "I am confident we have the courage and resourcefulness that will enable us to succeed."

One frustration emerged in the immediate wake of the policy statement. For months the company had been putting together a merger with Waukesha Motor Company, manufacturer of diesel, gasoline and natural gas engines in Waukesha, Wisconsin. Cooper had purchased 10 percent of Waukesha's common stock and arrangements were approved by shareholders of both companies when the U.S. Department of Justice suddenly served notice that it would oppose the acquisition and filed a suit to enjoin the merger.

After analyzing time consuming delays and potential costs associated with legal action that would be required to overcome the Justice Department's position, management of both companies concluded that such action was not in the best interests of shareholders. Accordingly, the merger agreement was allowed to lapse at the end of the year, and Cooper sold its Waukesha stock. The loss was a disappointment, to be sure, but time would do more than heal the wound; nine years later the scar would become a dominant asset in bringing about a more important acquisition.

A 52-day strike at Mt. Vernon seriously curtailed Cooper-Bessemer division business in 1967, causing delayed shipments of promised equipment and excessive costs when the company scrambled to catch up with customer delivery requirements. The strike kept earnings from reaching what *Wall Street Transcript* called Cooper's "spectacular" level of the previous year. But the *Transcript*, in its evaluation of the company, predicted a quick recovery and "reduced earnings volatility" stemming from the company's "improved internal efficiency, coupled with an active diversification program." Its advice to prospective stock buyers was that "a commitment in Cooper will not only benefit from a higher rate of average annual gains in earnings per share, but, moreover, this improved rate of gain will be progressively capitalized at higher ratios. Accordingly, we recommend purchase of Cooper stock, particularly to those accounts seeking capital appreciation." In light of this advice, it is interesting to note that each $1,000 of Cooper stock purchased at the time of the newspaper's prediction would have been worth $4,378 plus $631 paid in dividends, or a total return of 13 percent per annum fifteen years later.

As a step in overcoming the perennial problem of European import restrictions, the company joined a German ship and diesel engine builder, Bremer Vulkan, in establishing Cooper-Vulcan, producing gas compression equipment in Dusseldorf to serve the rapidly growing West European gas transmission industry. The joint venture, owned 50 percent by Cooper, soon led to a similar project in the Netherlands, where huge natural gas reserves were just beginning to be tapped in 1968.

Gascomij N. V. was formed as a joint venture between Cooper-Vulcan and Dutch interests. Through its facility at Hengelo, Netherlands, near the German border, the company soon became the principal supplier of gas turbine compressor packages for NV Nederlandse Gasunie, the major Dutch gas transmission company. Four huge units, totaling 60,000 horsepower were installed in the first natural gas pipeline station ever to be erected in the Netherlands. Located near Emmen, they were scheduled for start-up in 1969. Three other units, totaling 45,000 horsepower were installed soon afterward at Gasunie's Ravenstein station. Additional compressor power was scheduled to continue on a regular basis, with Gasunie anticipating that by 1970 the Emmen facility would become the most powerful compressor station for gas transmission in the world.

Units built by Gascomij for Gasunie were basically the same as those furnished by Cooper-Bessemer for cross-country gas transmission systems in the United States and Canada. Primary components of each unit were a Rolls-Royce light industrial gas generator, a Cooper-Bessemer power turbine to convert energy of the gas generator to rotative power, and a Cooper-Bessemer centrifugal compressor to compress the natural gas as required to speed it along the pipeline.

The Type RFB-36 centrifugal compressors designed by Cooper-Bessemer at that time were the highest capacity ever built for gas transmission. In concert with their gas turbine drivers, they enabled Gasunie, even in the initial phase of its project, to transport more than twice the volume of gas being handled by its earlier pipeline system. The mammoth station at Emmen, transmitting gas from the vast Groningen fields, was remotely controlled from a dispatch center at the production site.

Cooper formed a wholly owned company, Hengelo, Overijsel, in the same city where Gascomij was located, to manufacture Cooper-Bessemer En-Tronic control systems. The operation became so successful that it supplied En-Tronic controls not only for Cooper-Bessemer units, but also for those of Ingersoll-Rand, Dresser, and other competitors active in Europe. One Dutch employee, Henk A. Dekker, who learned the business at the Overijsel plant, several years later moved to Mt. Vernon as head of all Cooper-Bessemer En-Tronic manufacturing.

Holland also became a focal point of activity for a second Cooper division when Lufkin announced its intention to construct a tape manufacturing plant in Emmen. The plant, opened in 1969, was Lufkin's first entry into Europe. It was designed to serve world markets for metric measuring products. (Lufkin had plants in Mexico and Canada when it joined Cooper.)

Nations everywhere were taking measures to solidify positions in energy markets and other critical arenas of world trade. Political unrest was rampant, and no country seemed immune to its economic side effects. Yet, it was important to try; throughout history the ability of commerce to ride the waves of choppy political seas has kept societies from chaos. The year 1968 was an extraordinary test. There had been nothing like it since 1848, when smoldering revolutions broke out all over Western Europe.

Student uprisings brought clashes with police in London, Madrid, Tokyo, Warsaw, Prague, Belgrade, Berlin, Rome, Rio de Janeiro, Mexico City, dozens of cities in the United States, and even in the previously tightly disciplined city of Peking, China. Workers walked off jobs to join student demonstrators in Paris, almost toppling the De Gaulle government, and practically shutting down the economy.

Open rebellion on U.S. campuses and city streets, ignited by the widening war in Vietnam, the draft, and charges of university administration inadequacies, was intensified when smoldering civil rights embers burst forth again following the assassinations of Martin Luther King and Robert F. Kennedy.

In other countries, grievances seemed based on dissatisfaction both with governments and with societies in general. Students carried banners depicting Mao Tse-tung and Che Guevara as heroes, issuing a barrage of vague questions for which there were no answers.

Less than a year earlier, the United States and Russia had worked in harmony to prevent commitments during the Israeli-Arab Seven Days War from escalating into a military clash between the two big powers. Because of their cooperation, the United Nations was able to effect a cease-fire. Now they were locked in political combat over a full-scale Tet Offensive, raising questions about the capacity of U.S. military forces to end the war in Vietnam. And while that clash raged, troops from the USSR, Poland, Hungary, and Bulgaria invaded Czechoslovakia.

In the glare of blazing headlines, the continued dependence on a flow of goods was difficult to recognize. Talk of restricting it in a time of international temper tantrums might have made good political rhetoric, but it would have been devastating even to populations engrossed in the storming of streets. Production, being a long-range process, could not be switched on and off with shifting nation-to-nation relationships. In the case of heavy machinery, which can involve months of manufacturing a single item, the need for stability was particularly noticeable.

It was in this vein that a group of Russian industrialists approached Cooper through the company's Canadian office. With vast resources in northeastern Siberia, Russia was searching for new technology that could make it economically feasible to transport enormous quantities of gas fifteen hundred miles to Moscow, and hopefully on to France and Italy. The Russian delegation was familiar with Cooper-Bessemer compressors acquired through the lend-lease program of World War II, and still operating efficiently on their old pipelines.

Harold Johnson, who headed Cooper-Bessemer division international affairs at the time, explained that "The Russians were great on looking for people they could trust — people they had dealt with and felt comfortable with. So when they looked around the world for a builder who could supply the tremendous compression the proposed pipeline would need, they settled on Cooper-Bessemer."

There was a great deal of skepticism, and some outright opposition to even discussing business with Russians at that time. But it seemed obvious that the world's two most powerful countries could not let the political iron curtain completely block their economic growth. Times most certainly would be changing, and it was prudent to at least investigate the possibilities of obtaining what could become the largest contract in the company's history. A decision was made to follow up on the Russian inquiry, beginning a series of meetings that would be held in Moscow, Stratford, and Mt. Vernon for nearly four years. Beginning with polite, generally vague sparring, they eventually built to the intricate art that set negotiation with Russians apart from all other forms of business procedures.

Cooper's effort to maintain its pace of international commerce amidst the stampede of worldwide political protest obviously was not an isolated case. Trade among nations advanced strongly in 1968. United States exports increased about 10 percent, but were outstripped by imports that increased more than 20 percent, both to industrial and consumer markets.

Events of the year served to reinforce America's need for a more vigorous self-defense program, and to spur activities ahead. Cooper-Bessemer was awarded a contract by the U.S. Corps of Engineers to supply power generation equipment for thirteen Sentinel antiballistic missile sites near Huntsville, Alabama. Total value of the contract was in excess of $26 million, and could eventually exceed $60 million with tentatively planned options. The award covered sixty-nine engine-generator sets with related accessory equipment, each set capable of providing 3,000 kilowatts of precise electrical power for radar facilities in the Sentinel system. The sixteen-cylinder engines were more mature versions of those selected earlier by the Corps of Engineers for Nike-Zeus, the nation's first missile defense system to undergo functional testing.

In the event of an enemy ballistic missile launching, the Sentinel's detection system would immediately feed speed and trajectory data into massive high-speed computers that would program interception points for the outer perimeter defensive missiles. The Spartan, a three-stage missile armed with what then was considered the most highly advanced nuclear warhead, was designed to intercept and destroy enemy ICBM's four hundred miles from targets and one hundred miles into the ionosphere. At a second plant facility, on the missile site, Cooper-Bessemer engine-generators would provide power upon command from the computer complex. Transfer from perimeter to missile site radar functions would be accomplished automatically.

Cooper-Bessemer division also introduced a 10,000 hp Z-330 reciprocating engine-compressor, put into operation on a gas transmission line in Missouri. Design advancements enabled the engine to achieve a great amplification of horsepower (its forerunner in 1965 was 5,500 horsepower) without a comparable size increase.

At the same time, the company was preparing to add a second well-known brand name to its hand tool "basket." Even before it acquired Lufkin, Cooper had been interested in Crescent, a name synonymous with adjustable wrenches. Bill Rector also had been interested in the Jamestown, New York, manufacturer of high quality tools before his Lufkin organization merged with Cooper. Crescent Niagara Company, in fact, held a top priority position on his plan to penetrate deeper into the tools and hardware market. Crescent Niagara was not a profitable company, but Cooper management became convinced it was only scratching the surface of its potential. During the summer of 1968, Rector, Cizik, and Riedel met often with principal stockholders of Crescent Niagara, negotiating a friendly offer that settled finally on sixteen dollars a share. Cooper Industries purchased 96 percent of the outstanding Crescent stock by late October, through offers made to all shareholders, and the acquisition was approved officially by the board.

With Lufkin already established as part of Cooper Industries, the addition of Crescent Niagara was not considered a diversification, in the sense of venturing into unknown production and marketing territories. It did, however, expand the hand tools line considerably, adding a wide variety of high quality wrenches, pliers, and screwdrivers, utilized by professional craftsmen and "do-it-yourself" enthusiasts in many parts of the world.

15

Crescent

The shape of a Crescent wrench would lead to a logical conclusion as to how the product received its name, were it not for an interesting historical paradox.

When the Crescent Tool Company was founded in 1907, the Crescent adjustable wrench had not yet been invented. Neither of the new company's principal products, a combination ratchet-screwdriver-nail-puller and a "lightning" wrench, approached a crescent configuration. In starting his company at Jamestown, New York, Karl Peterson offered a modest prize to the employee suggesting the best name. The winner was machinist George Carlson, who prevailed over the other nineteen men at Peterson's small metal manufacturing plant, with the name "Crescent." Specific inspiration for the name was never recorded. George Carlson might have been glancing at a new moon. It is highly unlikely he was thinking about the symbol of the Turkish Empire, since he, like most residents of Jamestown at that time, was a Swede. But determining motivation is far less important than reflecting on results. The company name soon afterward became synonymous with its world-renowned adjustable wrench containing a movable jaw with a cylindrical-screw adjuster.

Even before he organized a tool manufacturing company, Karl Peterson seemed destined for success. Immigrating to Jamestown from Sweden in 1886 as a young man of twenty, he entered an area that had become a center for furniture making. It was not long before he designed, patented, and sold a machine to carve wooden spindle bedposts. Jamestown, located at the tip of Chautauqua Lake in the southwestern corner of New York State, had developed as a largely Swedish community. America's first Swedish immigrants settled in western New York in 1825, although the much larger influx in subsequent years was to Wisconsin. Jamestown, incorporated as a village in 1827, was chartered as a city the year Karl Peterson arrived.

After inventing the wood carving machine, Peterson joined the experimental department of the Art Metal Construction Company where he helped develop the forerunner of the modern voting machine. Later he started a small snuff factory. But an inventive nature led him to become superintendent of a bicycle parts manufacturing company, then to join a close friend, J.P. Danielson, an American of Swedish parentage, in starting a machine shop. The small shop, named J.P. Danielson Company, built machine tools to order and manufactured both an adjustable pipe wrench and a combination tool, but bicycle extension bars provided its most stable sales.

A philosophical difference ended the partnership of the two men, with Danielson insisting on high volume sales through private brand manufacturing, and Peterson holding out for company branded products, which he considered better long-range security. The schism was irreconcilable. So in 1907 Karl Peterson gathered a group of friends to incorporate a new tool company. Emil Johnson, also an inventive machinist, became superintendent of plant operations. Emil Nelson was named vice president and Charles F. Falldine, secretary-treasurer.

Although he selected highly skilled craftsmen for the machine work, President Peterson noted that there was not an engineer or technically trained man in the entire company. "We did a lot of impossible things in those days," he said many years later, "but since none of us had ever been to college, we didn't know they couldn't be done." Neither did they know that the year after Crescent Tool Company was formed, a Detroit manufacturer would turn out the first of more than fifteen million vehicles bearing the name "Model T." The plain black "Tin Lizzie" would have a notable effect on Crescent Tool's future.

But the most momentous influence came to the company unexpectedly, through a visitor from Sweden. In talking with Karl Peterson, the visitor described an ingenious adjustable wrench he had seen in Sweden. The conversation triggered Peterson's own ingenuity to the extent that he promptly sat down and carved a wooden model of such a tool. Using it as a guide, the company developed America's first open-end adjustable wrench, which it appropriately called the Crescent wrench. The wooden pattern still exists and is displayed at Cooper Industries' corporate headquarters in Houston.

Transferring the adjustable wrench concept from wood to steel proved to be far more complicated than simply making duplicate dies to forge the metal. Great difficulty was encountered in cutting a slot in which the adjustable jaw would slide. Unless the slot were perfect in size and shape, the wrench would bind. The seemingly insurmountable problem was solved, however, by Plant Superintendent Johnson, who invented a complicated slotting machine that produced the required precision cut.

When Crescent's revolutionary new steel wrench hit the market, the reception was dazzling. Customers were so enthusiastic that competitors moved quickly to meet the challenge by planning their own versions of adjustable wrenches. But none could match the exactitude of Emil Johnson's patented slotting machine. Attempted infringements abounded, but threatened court action and occasional lawsuits kept competitors at bay, without progressing to the trial stage. One company, thwarted from copying the Johnson patent, built a duplicate slotting machine in Canada, immune from U.S. law. For several years the competitor forged wrenches in the United States, shipped them to Canada for slotting, then brought them back to be assembled. But Crescent's early momentum had given the company a wide marketing lead it never relinquished. Through the years the original slotting machine design remained virtually unchanged, improved by a more modern bearing system for longer life and expanded for multiple slotting, but with identical casting and fixturing. Also continuing to match the test of technology was the original ring milling machine that produced teeth, called the rack, in the adjustable wrench jaw. Other companies emulated them when the seventeen-year patents expired.

To improve the strength and quality of his new wrench, and to add a line of slip-joint pliers, Karl Peterson went to Hartford, Connecticut, where he bought two Billings and Spencer drop-forge hammers. Housing them necessitated early expansion of the two-story Jamestown plant, the beginning of a continuing growth into a manufacturing complex. Early growth paralleled that of the emerging automobile industry, not coincidentally. Owning a tool kit was part of owning an automobile. Periodic adjustments of the brake and clutch bands on the family Model T Ford, along with unscheduled emergency repairs, could be handled best with an adjustable wrench, slip-joint pliers, a screwdriver, and some baling wire. Crescent produced two of these four necessities, even naming one the "motor kit pliers." And automobile manufacturers provided a set of motor tools with each new vehicle.

As a machinist, President Peterson remained convinced that quality, rather than price, would best gain and hold the loyalty of customers. He was not a man to waver from his beliefs. Small, but endowed with the boundless energy typical of those who launch private enterprises, he provided a fountain of ideas, following many of them to fruition. He had served an apprenticeship, together with his good friend Leonard Bloomquist, Sr., at the Anderson Machine Shop in Jamestown. After he started Crescent Tool Company, he convinced Bloomquist to join him as a supervisor. Some said being of Swedish descent was necessary for being hired by the Crescent founder, and being a Lutheran helped. But no one questioned Peterson's devotion to the Jamestown community. As chairman of the Board of Public Utilities, he led a drive to make electric power available to every citizen, spending much of his time for several years developing a city-owned system that reached the goal.

During Crescent's first twenty-five years, more than half of the plant machinery was designed by Peterson and Johnson, the latter a man of scant formal education but able to construct a hand-tool manufacturing machine from rough sketches on the back of an envelope. Another employee, Ernest L. Anderson, meanwhile developed a new method of hardening the surface of forging dies for longer life. Many out-of-town visitors appeared at the plant to ask about his processing secret.

The Crescent adherence to top-quality product lines brought opposition from a trade organization proposing a shared-market plan of stabilizing prices in the hand tools industry. Peterson refused to join the group, explaining, "In such a protected position we would have little incentive to improve." In retaliation, the organization's leader informed Peterson that other members would join forces to put Crescent Tool Company out of business. The Crescent president is said to have replied, "It is your privilege to try." Continuing to work toward product improvement, Crescent increased production and sales while competitors waged an intense price war. The result was an early armistice, with no compromise from Karl Peterson.

Crescent tools were sold almost entirely through correspondence with hardware wholesalers for six years before Wilbur Opdyke was hired as the first company salesman in 1913. A short time later the company hired a second salesman, Clarence R. Swisshelm, who later became sales manager and vice president.

Although the eastern United States understandably represented Crescent's major market, an event in 1914 brought a sudden shift in sales emphasis. After decades of planning and seven years of construction, one of history's great engineering feats was accomplished, and a forty-mile long canal joined the Atlantic and Pacific Oceans across the Isthmus of Panama. Western hardware dealers soon received their most favorable purchase prices from wholesalers large enough to buy in shipload quantities for delivery via the Panama Canal. Products built for long life were in greatest demand at distant markets, and nearly everyone was in need of hand tools. Within a short time, Crescent's top market was in the West.

The company's willingness to replace any tool returned by a customer, regardless of the reason, reinforced its growing reputation throughout the country. By the time America faced entry into World War I, Crescent's mortgage and all other indebtedness had been paid, its product lines were growing steadily, and sales were reaching into foreign lands, most notably Australia, New Zealand, Mexico, Central and South America, and South Africa. Crescent tools soon became well known also on the Allied European front, where large repair centers were set up behind fighting lines. Thousands of Crescent tools were shipped abroad for use by French mechanics manning the centers. When the war ended, the Crescent brand name was well established. Sizeable shipments were ordered by French industrial companies.

Postwar production continued to grow at a pace the founder admitted to be far ahead of his most optimistic forecasts. His only son, Marvin L.

Peterson, a graduate of Rensselaer Polytechnic Institute, joined the company in 1921 and the two initiated a plan that would lessen Crescent's dependence on outside sources for vital parts, supplies, and services. Steps were taken toward establishing in-house facilities for die sinking, forging, production of shipping boxes, and other means of improving company self-reliance. They also set sights on adding hand tools through the company's own engineering and development groups and through acquisition, if feasible. In 1926, purchase of the Smith & Hemenway Company of Irvington, New Jersey, enabled Crescent to expand product lines to include fixed joint pliers, hack saw frames, screwdrivers, punches, chisels, star drills, nail pullers, and line tools. These were supplemented further a few years later when the engineering department developed tinner's snips, wire grips, and sleeve wrenches.

The Crescent name continued to dominate the industry and news reports were often equivalent to high-priced advertising. Newspapers around the world carried the report that a young aviator named Charles Lindbergh, on May 20, 1927, piloted his *Spirit of St. Louis* across the Atlantic with a scant cargo of "gasoline, sandwiches, a bottle of water, and a Crescent wrench and pliers." Listed among the provisions of Antarctic explorer Richard E. Byrd when he established Little America two years later was a set of Crescent tools. British explorer Sir Hubert Wilkins took Crescent tools on a submarine expedition to the opposite polar region of the Arctic Ocean, and balloonist Captain A.W. Stevens carried them 72,395 feet aloft as he set a world altitude record in 1935. (Many years later the magic was proven to be still alive when media reported Crescent tools aboard the first Gemini flight.) Many attempts were made to usurp the name "Crescent," but both U.S. and foreign courts held that the name, when applied to wrenches, could be used only by the Crescent Tool Company. Even attempts to describe other wrenches by such references as "crescent type" or "crescent pattern" were declared illegal because they tended to confuse consumers.

In 1930, another trademark took its place in the Crescent hall of fame. "Crestoloy," a name given to an alloy steel developed by Crescent after several years of research, was introduced to the public. Crescent's participation in creating the strong, light alloy came at the request of the Army Air Corps. To further insure the quality of tools made by the new metal, Crescent engineers designed and built intricate new testing equipment. In time, "Crestoloy" steel replaced carbon steel as the preferred material for the manufacture of hand tools.

When the Great Depression struck America after the stock market collapse of 1929, Crescent remained financially sound even though it suffered sales slumps and accompanying personal adjustments by employees. At the depth of the depression, on June 30, 1933, Karl Peterson died and his son became president of the company. Strong-willed like his father, well trained for the position, and respected throughout the plant where he had spent much of his time, Marvin Peterson was able to maintain the company's stability while it survived the nation's slow, painful, economic recuperation.

By 1938, Crescent was manufacturing thousands of "Crestoloy" tools for the Air Corps. When the United States entered World War II, this production was multiplied several-fold and the plant went on an around-the-clock schedule, with 100 percent output for the war effort. Contracts were signed with the Navy, Signal Corps, and Army Ordnance Service, as well as the Air Corps. Tools were produced as regular equipment for trucks, tanks, half tracks, and airplanes, and for a wide variety of war industries. The company prided itself on meeting every delivery commitment, many far ahead of schedule. The effort was recognized in September of 1943 when Crescent received the Army-Navy "E" award for "accomplishing more than what once seemed reasonable or possible."

In the summer of 1945, between the May 8 surrender of Germany and the August 15 surrender of Japan, Crescent suffered a sudden assault that made it appear to have been a bombing target. Jamestown was hit by the most devastating tornado in its history, and the Crescent plant was among many buildings damaged extensively. In addition to repairing and rebuilding battered facilities, the company planned peacetime expansion for increasing markets. Unlike many industries, Crescent did not face a change-over lull in its manufacturing. Demand for restocking inventories of jobbers and dealers was immediate. Wartime restrictions had depleted their supplies. Moreover, the wide use of Crescent tools by Armed Forces throughout the world had introduced the products into areas that now became new markets. Foreign mechanics particularly liked the adjustable wrenches, and demand from overseas suppliers soared.

On the domestic scene, the beginning of a trend that was to mushroom in the years ahead offered further reason for optimism. The do-it-yourself urge was on the threshold of becoming a national passion. Homeowners began tooling up for personal attention to garden equipment, power motors, outboard motors, and many other objects of affection. Professional mechanics, too, were looking toward new tooling. Such complications as automatic transmissions created demands which Crescent met by introducing new lines of open end, box, and socket wrenches. By the 1950s, Crescent's plans for expansion reached the construction stage, and after the Korean War two major additions were made to the manufacturing complex.

As it approached the end of its first half-century, Crescent looked toward new needs and trends in producing hand tools the company president described as "the connecting links between man and machine." Still, many traditions remained, and the company's Swedish lineage was very much in evidence. Leonard Bloomquist, Jr., who had joined his father at Crescent and later was to head the company, recalled a day in 1951 when he introduced a visitor through the plant. "The first four men we met were Axel Carlson, Henry Carlson, William Carlson, and George Carlson," he said. "None was related to any of the others."

Men like T.F. "Fred" Angquist, chief engineer at that time, had developed designs that formed the basis for Crescent's steady maturation. They represented a wealth of knowledge and experience that led a young engineer to remark, "You got an education from those men that you could not get at any school." Little of that knowledge, however, was recorded in files, and time made it important to transfer such knowledge to paper. In reflecting on the accomplishment of that task, Henry Sievers, who succeeded Fred Angquist as chief engineer, vividly characterized an engineering era:

"One of my first assignments at Crescent was to approach the supervisor of the Trim Department, who had been with the company since it started, and acquire designs of several series of punches used to manufacture adjustable wrenches. Crescent had been making them for years, but specifications on those punches — dimensions and hardness — were carried in the heads of master mechanics. Many of those men were also design experts, but the designs were strictly mental images. They were fantastic men. Most of them were of Swedish descent. The supervisor hesitated to give such information to a green kid just out of college. Finally, though, he did. Later, other supervisors followed suit. We were able to draw up specifications on materials, geometry, heat treatment, and methods of fixturing wrench and plier parts in machinery. Those men had gotten along just fine without specs. They loved designing and manufacturing tools. And they kept all that complicated data in their heads. It hardly existed anyplace else. The only drawings I found of anything were on rough kraft paper. So we didn't really have a full set of formalized drawings until 1951."

By the end of the 1950s, a sixty-page catalog was required to picture the complete Crescent line. New tools were in the design and market research stages, and a fleet of specially equipped station wagons carried samples to assist in sales.

Crescent remained a family owned company until 1960, when Marvin Peterson sold it to Crescent Niagara Corporation of Buffalo, New York. A holding company, Crescent Niagara had been formed by members of the investment firm of Schoellkopf, Hutton & Pomeroy, Inc. Crescent Tool Company became a division of Crescent Niagara. Administrative and sales offices were moved to Buffalo. Crescent Niagara operations were headed by President Charles H. Stephens. Tools were marketed in sixty countries, with export trade accounting for 20 percent of gross sales. All domestic sales were made through distributors, who resold to jobbers and wholesalers serving industrial, hardware, department store, auto supply, and other markets.

In 1962, Crescent Niagara acquired Billings & Spencer, the company from whom Karl Peterson had purchased his first drop-forge hammers half a century earlier. Barcalo Tool Company of Buffalo was purchased the following year, and Bridgeport Hardware Manufacturing Corporation, Bridgeport, Connecticut, was added as a subsidiary in 1964. All three companies were later dissolved and their major products added to the Crescent hand tool lines. The company continued to develop completely new products also, some for professional craftsmen, others for the booming do-it-yourself markets.

There were signs of changing times. Supervisors accustomed to working "with the boys" were finding an increasing number of shop positions assigned to women. They received some expected initial complaints from both male and female employees but sometimes were at a loss to determine which sex needed protection from the other. Industrial Relations Director William A. Hauck received a grievance from men in one department soon after women were employed there for the first time. The men complained that they lacked privacy to change clothes at the start and conclusion of their shifts. "The women, however, neither were concerned with, nor interested in, the men or their problems," Hauck said. "To them the state of male dress or undress was no particular problem."

Alaric R. Bailey succeeded Charles Stephens as president of Crescent Niagara and held that position until the company was purchased by Cooper Industries in October of 1968.

16

Doing the Mundane Better

Following the acquisition of Crescent, Bill Rector became a corporate vice president and president of the Hardware Group, which also included Lufkin, Rotor Tool and Ken-Tool. Bill Gilchrist was named vice president and general manager of Crescent. His first responsibility was cutting the Crescent product line, closing some satellite plants along with the Buffalo headquarters, and consolidating the entire operation in Jamestown.

The stabilizing influence of diversification already was being felt by 1969, when President Miller reported to shareholders that sales of tools constituted approximately 30 percent of the company's total $176,313,000 revenues. Still, overall company earnings continued to be influenced heavily by fluctuations of heavy machinery sales, and the objective of steady year-to-year growth was not yet attained.

Although 1969 proved to be a disappointing year in sales, management believed events of the past few years had positioned the company where it wanted to be on the long-range planning chart. The company's mood was reflected in its annual report, which looked back over the "two deliberately charted growth routes" it had followed during the decade about to come to a close: extending management and technological expertise into fields closely related to traditional markets, and acquiring companies in industries reflecting stable growth rates to lessen dependence on inherently cyclical sales of machinery and equipment.

Development of increased engine power illustrated the technological advancement. The largest reciprocating engine-compressor in operation at the beginning of the decade was 3,500 horsepower. In 1969, the capacity was increased to 12,500 horsepower without a proportionate increase in the physical size of the engine.

A second example was the introduction of a new jet engine-equipped gas turbine, the Coberra, destined to be developed further and to represent a significant portion of sales for many years to come.

155

The 1969 version, preassembled and tested at Cooper-Bessemer facilities for shipment to field installations, had a 12,500 horsepower rating. It was capable of operating more than three years between overhauls, three times longer than early jet models. The gain was developed by redesigning and upgrading major components and intermatching them with auxiliaries. Primary among them were a power turbine, control system and centrifugal compressor, designed and manufactured by Cooper-Bessemer, and a light industrial gas generator engineered by Rolls-Royce for continuous base-load duty.

The Coberra was introduced on the tenth anniversary of the company's pioneering installation of the world's first gas turbine using an aircraft-type jet engine for gas transmission. Less than a year later, a 25,000-hp unit was added to the Coberra line.

Cooper remained the leading supplier of compression equipment to gas transmission companies. During the sixties, this market was subject to many influences, including fluctuating capital costs and government regulations.

"Charting the installations of pipeline compression equipment over any extended period of time results in a line as jagged as shark's teeth," said Bob Cizik. In describing the unpredictability of earnings produced by that market, Cizik paraphrased a well-known nursery rhyme: "When they were good, they were very, very good, but when they were bad, they were horrid."

Cizik, who was elected executive vice president and chief operating officer in 1969, explained that programs to build the company were designed to improve the "low quality" of earnings that come from such a cyclical market. Looking back on questions the company faced at that time, Cizik later said finding answers "required that we settle on some basics about our corporation identity or image and the direction of our growth — on a theme, if you will. Our fundamental decision in that regard established our identity as a *manufacturing* company. That was where our managerial, technological, and marketing expertise lay, and we wanted to build on our strengths."

The management team eliminated any thought of delving into non-manufacturing businesses such as insurance, retailing, and banking. By that decision, Cizik said, the company relegated itself to "a segment of the business spectrum that many regard as lacking romance and glory, but one we viewed as offering great opportunity." He said the team determined that success could be found "by doing the mundane better, by paying attention to manufacturing processes, producing a good quality product at a fair price, and still making a decent profit." It was a key to solving U.S. productivity problems, Cizik believed, and something that was slipping from the sights of too many industries.

Cizik said the company set about achieving the "identity" of which he spoke by providing a disciplined approach to evaluating risk exposure and market opportunities. A "complementary" acquisition or merger, was defined as a logical extension of existing products or markets, carrying less risk than a "diversification" acquisition or merger, which is a new experience. With the latter, no matter how thorough the preparation, "there always is the chance that something was not anticipated, always the possibility of losing control for a time, of encountering a surprise," Cizik said. (Cooper in 1969 was considering expansions that would fall into each of the categories described by Cizik — a complementary acquisition of Weller Electric Corporation of Easton, Pennsylvania, and a diversification acquisition of Dallas Airmotive, Inc.)

Cizik also emphasized that progress could involve subtraction as well as addition. "People often think success is measured only by adding, adding, and more adding," he said. "That's extremely important, but you have to keep examining what you have, and you can't be afraid to get rid of the things that have served their useful time, or are costing you money or not taking you where you want to go. You eliminate by product line, or even entire segments of the business."

The importance of that concept would become evident during the 1970s and '80s, involving some areas still showing promise in 1969. On the other hand, Cooper would gain advantages at times by bucking trends toward elimination of products considered by others to be over the marketing hill. Strategic maneuvering was by no means an exclusive military property.

The company's approach to certain general industry markets already had changed substantially during the 1960s. Cooper-Bessemer phased out production of locomotive diesel engines, a major product for many years, to permit more profitable redeployment of assets and technology into dual-fuel, engine-generator sets for municipal power plants, and integral gas engine compressors. Two new engines were well accepted in 1969. The twenty-cylinder LSV-20 was capable of generating up to 5,600 kilowatts in municipal power plant application, utilizing low-cost natural gas as fuel. The KSV engine series of diesel-powered electric generator sets focused principally on the substantial electric power generation standby and peaking market that blossomed when well-publicized city blackouts created fears of similar emergencies for years to come. Capable of accommodating severe overloads for limited periods, the KSV seemed just right for its time.

One business segment that could be counted on to withstand the fickle passions of public concern was the sale of parts and services. Like the "second banana" ever on the alert to relieve a falling star, replacement parts and their attending services brought in revenues of $44.3 million, representing 25 percent of total sales for the year. To help assure its continued performance, Cooper entered the field of contract overhaul, updating equipment no longer on warranty. Another significant service program was geared to maintaining compressor equipment on a contract basis outside the United States. The first such venture was into the Middle East, and Cooper planned to capitalize on spreading popularity of contract service in gas and oil industries elsewhere.

Competitive pressure for sale of new engine and compressor systems to oil and gas producers was intensifying with another surge in exploration. The company's most vulnerable pressure point was CB/Southern, where Thomas E. Naugle became division president in 1969. Several companies had copied versions of CB/Southern's deep-water facility, and had begun to offer compression systems for offshore production when an oil spill at Santa Barbara, California, led to sharp restrictions on activities there and cancellation or deferral of scheduled lease sales in other locations.

The Santa Barbara oil pollution incident brought such a public outcry that various federal studies signaled possible changes in government policy which would adversely affect the domestic petroleum industry through increased tax burdens or changes in import controls. Additionally, the accelerating capital requirements of gas and oil producing companies placed greater reliance upon borrowed funds at a time when interest rates reached what seemed at the time to be astronomical.

In looking ahead, Cooper envisioned one of its most promising opportunities in petroleum production products on Alaska's North Slope. Eight energy companies sharing ownership in Alyeska Pipeline Service Company were preparing to build a pipeline, forty-eight inches in diameter, from Prudhoe Bay oil fields to the ice-free port of Valdez, eight hundred miles away. Gas separated from crude oil at gathering stations would power turbine engines at pump stations along the way. Cooper engineers were working closely with Alyeska, hoping to be in a favorable position to supply compression and power equipment required for what then was the most expansive project of its kind in history. No stranger to Alaska, Cooper had provided machinery and equipment for various uses there for thirty years, becoming the leading supplier of production compressors in Cook Inlet.

By the end of 1969, Cooper was ready to expand its hardware and tools division again. With the first full year of Crescent operations completed, hardware and tools showed a 51 percent increase over 1968. Normal growth rate of the markets it served was higher than that of the Gross National Product. Even with conventional home sales lagging, Lufkin and Crescent products benefited by increased activity in other segments of the industry. Output of mobile homes, for example, grew from 240,000 in 1967 to 400,000 in 1969, and the trend was expected to continue. (As it happened, 1969-72 sales of 1.9 million mobile homes equaled those of the previous two decades.)

It was estimated that the rate of home and apartment construction would leap in the next few years, cutting into the backlog of unmet needs. Since everything built must be measured, and most would need screwdrivers, wrenches and pliers, sales of Lufkin and Crescent products could be expected to grow. They should be boosted also by manufacturing and marketing efficiencies taking place at both plants.

At the November 5, 1969, meeting of the board, Chairman Miller presented the management's plan to acquire another market leader, Weller Electric Corporation, whose brand name was known throughout the world. Built on the strength of Carl E. Weller's invention of the electric soldering gun, the Easton, Pennsylvania, company had grown from a basement workshop business in 1945 to the world's leading manufacturer of soldering tools, with plants in Canada, England, West Germany, and Mexico.

Contact had been made with the company through Bill Rector and Hal Stevens, who knew Carl Weller. Cooper's case also was helped by Carl Weller's acquaintance with Bill Gilchrist, Cooper's first general manager of Penn Pump, and Weller's observations of the improvements made in Penn Pump after its acquisition by Cooper. A quiet but extremely energetic man, Weller wasn't the kind of person who might reveal his reactions readily. After listening to Rector and Stevens describe how his company's reputation for high quality production matched Cooper's goals, Weller said, "I'm going fishing in Florida and I'll have my mind made up when I return." Two weeks later, Rector received a telephone call that was right to the point. "I'm back and I'm ready," said Carl Weller. "Let's talk."

During subsequent negotiations that included Cizik and Riedel as well as Rector and Stevens, Weller revealed that he believed diversification was "the way to go in the tool business," and he had been looking for an alliance that would give his company greater marketing power. After what he called "a lifetime of working for myself," he didn't think he could blend into a large corporate structure, however, and would retire if the acquisition came about. He and his family owned the company, and none of the others had a desire to run it. Cooper's board enthusiastically accepted the merger proposal, and an announcement was made before the end of the year, although the transaction became official on February 26, 1970.

17

Weller

Patience generally is accepted as a virtue. But if Carl E. Weller had subscribed to such a philosophy, he might have spent his career repairing radios instead of founding a company that reached international proportions in the space of two decades.

As a young man growing up in western Pennsylvania in the 1920s, Weller became interested in electricity and a relatively new phenomenon known as radio. Leaving high school, he traveled across the state to Easton, where his two older brothers, Everett and Dale, offered him employment in the basement repair shop of their downtown appliance store. Although he was just sixteen when he began repairing appliances, he bolstered his natural flair for electrical craftsmanship by completing courses with international correspondence schools.

Radio was growing so rapidly that it changed family patterns of living. News became instantaneous. Music reached millions. Hundreds of new broadcasting stations appeared every year after Pittsburgh's KDKA became the first to go on the air in 1920. The first syndicated show, "Amos 'n Andy," introduced radio serial entertainment in 1928, the year after Carl Weller arrived in Easton, and sales of superheterodyne receivers rocketed. Among those benefiting from the boom were the Weller brothers. Radios became important sales items in their appliance store, and house calls were added to the duties of their repairman. Within a few years, Carl Weller gained such repute in Easton that other technicians came to him for assistance in solving problems. But he had one particularly bothersome problem of his own — he became exceedingly impatient waiting in homes while an important tool of his trade, the soldering iron, heated to its required temperature. After he had repaired the radio, he was forced to wait again while the iron cooled enough to be put away.

There were other frustrations. Parts distribution in the 1920s consisted principally of traveling salesmen carrying merchandise in the trunks of their automobiles. Delivery was so uncertain that Carl Weller started making transformer replacements for his own use, preparing himself for the new responsibility by taking night courses at Lafayette College. The idea evolved into a sideline when he and his brothers purchased used machinery from a defunct company to wind coils and produce transformers for a national distributor.

The young repairman had solved one dilemma. Now if he could just find a soldering tool that would heat fast, maintain a steady temperature, then cool in seconds rather than minutes, he could avoid the irritating delays in radio repair. Since no such instrument existed, he decided to make one of his own. Utilizing knowledge he had gained from electricity and transformers, and experimenting with designs and metals, he put together a tool built around a transformer that reduced line voltage, transferring sufficient heat in seven seconds through heavy twin conductors to a copper tip, which had a high negative temperature coefficient of resistance. Starting from a cold state, the tip of the tool had a low resistance, so a surge of power went into it. When it got hot, resistance increased, automatically reducing the flow of electric current and power. Thus, it produced fast heat, then held a steady temperature. A few seconds after the trigger was released, the tip again became cool. Carl Weller had invented the soldering gun.

With a sample that performed exactly as he had planned, the inventor put it to use immediately, even before he applied for a patent. However, he had taken the precaution of making drawings and filing his idea with an association of inventors, thereby establishing conceptual priority. Soon afterward he did make a patent application, then produced another sample to register with the U.S. Bureau of Standards. A physics professor with whom Weller had studied at Lafayette College delivered the sample to Washington D.C. After seeing it, technical representatives of the Bureau ordered two more for their own use. Notifying Weller of the purchase request, the professor asked what he should quote as the selling price. "I really don't have any idea what to charge," Weller replied. "Well," suggested his friend, "why don't you just say fifteen dollars each?" That sounded reasonable enough, and the first two Weller soldering guns were sold to the Bureau of Standards for thirty dollars. Several years later Carl Weller was to consider himself fortunate that the professor made a feasible guess.

To test the product's market potential, Weller made more samples, giving twelve to one of the automobile-trunk salesmen who called on him. One of the inventor's brothers later revealed that the salesman told him he took the soldering guns only because he didn't have the heart to tell Carl they would not sell. But in a few days, the salesman telephoned to ask how quickly he could get two dozen more.

Despite such encouragement, hopes for commercial development of the gun had to be shelved when America entered World War II. Materials for such things were suddenly unavailable. The same was true of household appliances. So the Weller brothers closed their retail store and began manufacturing electrical meter coils for army aircraft altimeters. With a patent pending, Carl also tried to interest soldering iron manufacturers in his invention. But no one considered it a marketable product. Consequently, when the war ended he decided to organize his own company and manufacture the soldering guns in the basement workshop. Since he had the necessary tools, the major investment was in purchasing a mold for the Bakelite handles.

In the summer of 1945, Weller Manufacturing Company was started as a family partnership with Carl as president. Ten employees produced soldering guns using a minimum of automation, and sales promotion consisted of advertisements in technical magazines reaching radio repairmen, supplemented by word-of-mouth throughout the Philadelphia area. With production underway, the president reflected with a sigh of relief on the good judgment of his faculty friend from Lafayette College. The war had ended, but the Office of Price Administration lingered on. Price controls were established on "roll back" to previous listings, and it was ruled that a Weller precedent had been set by the quote to the Bureau of Standards. Fortunately, the company would be able to make a profit on a retail price of fifteen dollars.

Although the president had confidence in his product, he was surprised at how quickly business grew. Less than two years after start-up, it was necessary to construct a factory. By 1950 that building was outgrown and an administrative reorganization was in order. Two corporations were formed to support the partnership, which continued to serve as the U.S. manufacturing arm of the business. One corporation began manufacturing soldering guns in Puerto Rico. The other, Weller Electric Corporation, handled sales and distribution for both manufacturing groups. (Later, the Easton manufacturing partnership was merged into Weller Electric Corporation.) A large new factory was constructed for manufacturing in Easton, leaving sales and distribution departments in the existing building.

"I remember that we used to sit and discuss magazine reports on how many radio repairmen there were in the country, and calculated that we must already have sold each of them four guns," said Edwin Y. Thompson, one of the original Weller employees who was named general manager of manufacturing operations in the 1950 reorganization. "It seemed that we should be thinking about other products, but the demand just continued to grow for soldering guns." Other products were tried in Puerto Rico, where the company had two plants, one of them headed by Everett Weller. Separate companies were established there, one to manufacture electric sanders, the other electric saber saws. Both prospered temporarily, until excessive competition made continued production impractical and they were dropped from the Weller line.

Another kind of competition developed during the early 1950s in the United States when a company began producing electric soldering guns in what Weller considered an infringement of his patent. Lengthy court proceedings, including appeals, brought a 1956 ruling in Weller's favor, and the competitor was ordered to make restitution of a reasonable percentage for all sales that had been made. However, agreement was reached for it to continue manufacturing the guns by paying royalties to Weller until the patent expired seven years later. The infringement did little apparent damage to Weller success. New construction at Easton was necessary in 1952 and again in 1958. "I thought we were set forever with those buildings and five acres of land," President Weller said later, "but that was more like a beginning compared to what happened later."

With the soldering gun continuing its popularity in domestic markets and penetrating those of other countries, President Weller decided to explore the possibility of expanding overseas. Although he did not ordinarily become involved in marketing to a large extent, preferring to concentrate on experimental work in the laboratory, he broke precedent and did much of the preliminary foreign sales development personally. He also hired one man to work exclusively in Europe. The first foreign marketing was carried out through sales representatives. But evidence pointed increasingly toward establishment of a manufacturing plant in Europe.

An additional factor in determining future growth was progress of a new product design. After considerable experimentation, President Weller had filed for patents on an industrial soldering iron containing a temperature control mechanism. Even though it appeared to be a promising product, space limitations deferred production until the additional construction in 1958. In that year, several business considerations meshed into the framework of broadened company operations. With its increased factory space, Weller began production of industrial soldering irons. Except for the brief period of producing sanders and saws in Puerto Rico, this was the company's first major new product to supplement the soldering gun. Simultaneously, the company organized Weller Elektro-Werkzeuge G.m.b.H., in Besigheim, West Germany, to manufacture temperature-controlled irons and soldering guns for markets throughout Europe and the Near East. "The industrial soldering tools were what really made the West Germany plant get started successfully," President Weller said later. Similar moves into other countries followed in subsequent years. A sales branch in Kingston, Ontario, grew into Weller Electric Canada Limited, producing both guns and irons. Another in Horsham, Sussex, England, became Weller Electric Limited, with guns and irons assembled from components supplied by the Easton plant. Weller Electrica, organized in Mexico City, also assembled products from Easton-supplied components. Meanwhile, the plants in Puerto Rico were closed, helping provide capital for the company's foreign expansion and for another construction project at Easton.

In 1966 the company doubled the size of its parent facilities with purchase of 170 acres and construction of a new manufacturing unit. Although the corporation had just passed its twentieth birthday, the era when it produced exclusively for electronics repairmen seemed far in the past. Weller had long ago established itself in the blossoming hobbyist market, and was already a principal manufacturer of industrial soldering irons.

The question of diversification was continuous and over the years the company had considered a wide variety of products. Thompson, who became executive vice president at the beginning of overseas expansion, remembered several items, not always related to hand tools. "We made the prototype of an ice crusher at one time," he said. "Then we even came up with an electrified ice cream scoop that worked on the principle of the soldering gun. With its instant heat, it could slide right into hard ice cream. The scoop and the ice crusher both worked just fine, but you don't sell them to the same people who buy soldering tools, so we decided to stick with the things we were organized to sell."

Growth and steady improvements of the company's soldering gun and iron product lines were accompanied by increased market penetration both in the United States and abroad. As electrical equipment became more complex and compact, Weller soldering tools were designed to reach into small areas with precise, controlled heat. By the time Weller was acquired by Cooper, its soldering tools were utilized worldwide in the professional radio-television servicing trade, by hobbyists, and in the manufacture of delicate electrical and electronic circuitry such as printed circuit boards, transistor radios, computer circuits, and hearing aids.

The modest, casual manner of Carl Weller makes it difficult to associate his invention with a spirit of impatience. But there are other signs. Retiring after the Cooper acquisition, Weller moved temporarily to Venice, Florida, where he encountered a problem finding adequate docking for his power boat. His solution was to form a partnership to build a marina complete with motel and restaurant, which became one of the finest marine facilities on Florida's west coast.

18

Weaving a Tool Basket

Carl Weller often told friends that he was glad to know the company he had spent his career developing was sold to an organization "with the best sales force in the tools business." He referred to a sales strategy that evolved with Cooper's "tool basket," which now included Weller products.

At the heart of the plan was consolidation of the three companies into one cohesive merchandising operation, while retaining the brand name of each product line. The idea was not particularly startling, but as sales Vice President Stevens pointed out, "It never has been done before. There has never been an effort on the part of an individual or a company to put together a group of high quality lines."

The essential ingredient, acknowledged when Cooper first became involved in the plan with the acquisition of Lufkin, was that each brand name be either first or second in its field. Now there were three in the group, and all rested at the top: Lufkin in measuring tapes and rules, Crescent in wrenches and other hand tools, and Weller in electric soldering equipment.

Headquartered in Apex, North Carolina, in a modern, efficient complex adjacent to the Lufkin manufacturing plant, a tightly knit distribution organization marketed all the products through centralized facilities. "This gives us a lot of leverage with a distributor," Stevens explained. "We can go to him with top brand names in several commodities, showing him that it will be economical to buy from us. He has to go through the same motions to buy one line that he does to buy three from us — ordering, processing, handling invoices, receiving shipments. There are sizeable savings just from receiving a group of products through a single order, because of minimum shipping costs."

Nearly all merchandising was carried out through two basic channels: (1) hardware distributors who purchased products for resale to retail dealers who in turn sold to consumers, and (2) industrial supply distributors who sold directly to clients in service industries. "We sell equal amounts to both," Stevens said, "because we have man-on-the-street consumer products and also expendables used in factories."

165

The basic philosophy of the "tool basket" concept was to effect economies in production, sales, and distribution that would give customers top quality products and profits competitors could not match. If a distributor or retailer could sell a wrench or tape rule with a name he didn't have to worry about, and make one dollar profit as compared to fifty cents for a competing wrench or tape rule, it would not be difficult for him to determine which product he would prefer to handle. Making him more profitable could in turn make the producer more profitable, and if the theory worked, a chain effect would build more volume, more economies, and more price advantages. Implementation involved certain measures that could be put into motion immediately, and others that would take a few years to accomplish.

The first step was to establish a small, efficient sales force representing a blend of the top salesmen from each of the acquired companies. By 1970, the streamlined group was smaller than that of Lufkin alone when it was acquired three years earlier. Five domestic regional managers were appointed, but there were no separate regional offices. Four were headquartered at the Apex control center and the fifth worked out of his home on the West Coast. Salesmen reporting to these managers were trained extensively to handle products bearing all three brand names.

A merchandising manager for each of the brands was charged with the responsibility to update packaging and marketing techniques, and to be alert for ideas that could improve products. Most of those ideas came from the salesmen, who were encouraged to give frank appraisals of changing moods at the market place. Strong competitive pressures made constant surveillance necessary because products always were on open display. "There is no secret in this business," Stevens said.

On the manufacturing side of the ledger, the most immediate step in bringing about economies essential to the plan was elimination of unprofitable products. Through the years, hand tool manufacturers had clung to the tradition of supplying everything their customers requested, without particular regard for profit. Examples of companies manufacturing tools selling at the rate of a dozen per year were not uncommon. If someone asked for a left-handed widget, it was put in the catalog. Consequently, product lines became so overwhelming it was difficult to even compute their relative values. Inventory analysis was seldom, if ever, carried out and warehousing became a costly extravagance. Yet, it was a known rule of thumb in hand tool manufacturing, as in nearly any business, that 20 percent of the products represented 80 percent of the sales volume. Cooper management considered it poor business practice not to respond to such obvious guidelines. Hand tool product lines were trimmed to profitable levels in all the plants; Lufkin items alone were cut from 3,500 to 500. The company also realized that manufacturing facilities for both Crescent and Weller needed to be updated. Plans for new plants and machinery capable of mass production would have to be on the drawing boards as soon as possible.

As redesign of products and equipment progressed at its plants, the management organization at Apex carried out a continuous program of modernizing warehousing and distribution. With a new name, The Cooper Group, it brought out such new lines as the Weller Mini-Shop portable hand grinder, the Crescent multi-plier, and the Lufkin yellow blade rule, but continued to lop off unprofitable products.

Bill Gilchrist moved from Jamestown to Apex as Group vice president of manufacturing, and was succeeded as general manager of Crescent by Leonard Bloomquist. A thirty-year veteran of the company, Gilchrist had helped supervise the opening of Cooper-Bessemer manufacturing operations in Stratford, Ontario, and served as the first manager of Penn Pump at the time of its acquisition, before going to Crescent.

C. Baker Cunningham, who had been a member of the Corporate Planning Department in Houston for a year after receiving his M.B.A. from the Harvard Graduate School of Business Administration, was appointed vice president of administration and finance for The Cooper Group. Among his responsibilities was supervision of a new computerized data processing system, bolstering the efficiency of inventory control, sales, ordering, billing, and other financial matters. Cunningham considered the planning function supported by intelligent use of computer technology to be a key to outstripping competition. "I think as business organizations become larger, more complex, they have to interact and react to many more influences, trying to anticipate the consumer groups and government, not just customers in the immediate neighborhood of a factory," he said. "Things are becoming much more global in scope, so there are many more variables that have to be taken into consideration. So everyone is looking for a common denominator everyone can understand. That means the financial function, which reduces everything to terms of dollars and cents, tends to be the eventual collector of this information. I think as people become more educated, they are aware of various things. We say it becomes one of the key variables of success, if you will, to be able to anticipate what might happen and plan accordingly, so you are able to react faster and more sensibly than the competition — at least not get caught flat-footed. So the more complex things get, the more important the planning function becomes."

International activities of The Cooper Group were centered in London, England, under the leadership of Donald R. MacPherson, who was vice president and general manager of Lufkin's Canadian operations at the time of the merger. As international vice president of The Cooper Group, he was on a management level with Stevens, Gilchrist and Cunningham. Geographic dispersity and the legal requirements of individual countries made it more feasible to maintain an international center in

Toronto rather than join it with Apex offices. So MacPherson's responsibilities covered sales, finance, and manufacturing for the Group's international business.

Not being as bound by traditions as the U.S. market on individual brand names, international merchandisers were able to use the Cooper Group umbrella to even a greater extent than their counterparts working out of the Apex Center. In a country where one brand was particularly popular, international salesmen could explain that it now was part of The Cooper Group product lines that contained other top quality tools with names not as familiar in that area of the world. Because all three of the Group's major acquisitions had established some overseas markets, brand recognition varied from area to area. This became a basis for selecting important points of sale.

"We identify markets where we have acceptance on one or more brands," MacPherson explained, "then we work toward establishing either a field sales force or distribution center there." A case in point was Washington New Town, England, where Weller had a small manufacturing plant serving United Kingdom markets. "There were other places in the United Kingdom where customers insisted on Crescent end-nippers, or Lufkin rules," MacPherson said, "so we took the reputations of Lufkin, Crescent and Weller and fused them together at Washington New Town. We developed our own sales force and distribution and The Cooper Group name became as well known as the brand name. Essentially we considered the U.K. a domestic market, not a foreign or export market."

In the years ahead, the same technique was used to extend International hand tool operations of varying kinds into France, Italy, Germany, Mexico, Brazil, Colombia, Australia, The Netherlands, and more areas of Canada. MacPherson was well equipped by experience to carry out such an assignment. In the preacquisition days of Lufkin he had traveled to more than eighty countries, introducing Lufkin to markets and testing acceptance.

The staggering volume of small tools sold every minute of every day was mind boggling. Even those closest to the scene found it difficult to explain. "We know the market is far from saturated; in fact, it continues to grow," said Leonard Bloomquist. "You sometimes wonder where all these tools are consumed, particularly since they last so long under normal circumstances. Many are lost, of course, but the only logical explanation is that a world population in the billions is nearly impossible for the human mind to comprehend."

Ken-Tool, although successful as a small manufacturing unit, did not fit The Cooper Group pattern of top brand-name recognition and was sold in 1974 to the Warren Tool Corporation. Rotor Tool was continued as part of The Cooper Group administratively, although its pneumatic and high-cycle electric tools were sold through sales representatives to automotive plants, appliance markets, foundries, and many types of general manufacturing and fabrication plants. It pioneered special design tool sets for assembly use, such as multiple nutsetters used for attaching automobile doors, and could point to several design and marketing "firsts" that brought steady progress in lowering noise levels and increasing the safety of tools.

Cooper looked long and hard at the power tool business, but decided against wavering from its policy of including only market leaders, and could not at that time envision realistic prospects of acquiring such a dominant company as Black & Decker. The company preferred building upon proven successes in nonpowered hand tools, using money generated by the gas compression business for financing.

The strategy proved to be a life saver. In the dawn of the new decade, earnings from The Cooper Group sustained the company during a dismal period of Cooper-Bessemer division operations. Many felt The Cooper Group strength saved the company from falling prey to the conglomerate movement that was experiencing a last hurrah before fading under pressures of overextended management. The situation would someday reverse, giving further credence to the value of diversification, but as 1970 drew to a close optimism was focused on modernizing the company's hand tool business and continuing the search for other qualified candidates for its basket.

With the hand tool business in a position to expand and gas compression in a slump, Cooper was in the market for another acquisition that could serve three important purposes: increase the value of trading stock through better name recognition, provide another leveler to cyclical sales charts, and add size that would help lessen vulnerability to organizations who had not yet lost their predatory instincts. Several areas were examined, but in the realistic world of business, decisions boil down to what is available at a given point in time. Dallas Airmotive, Inc., was an interested candidate with operations compatible to Cooper's industrial philosophy. The well-managed, highly respected company, based in Dallas, repaired, overhauled, and leased jet engines and distributed parts and supplies for all types of aircraft. There appeared to be a close manufacturing relationship with Cooper's own expertise in light industrial jet engines.

As to market growth potential, one needed only to look at what was happening in aviation for obvious answers. Domestic airline passenger travel had grown from 92 to 153 million annual passengers in the past five years. Domestic ton-miles of express and freight had gone from 943 million to 2.2 billion in the same period of time. "Jumbo jets" carrying up to five hundred passengers were in service on domestic and international routes, dramatically increasing the need for feeder lines served by Dallas Airmotive. Dallas Airmotive's management and skilled work force were well prepared to handle the larger, more complex engines already slated for the immediate years ahead. Furthermore, it was one of only two companies holding an unlimited FAA license for this purpose. In addition to serving scheduled airlines, it rebuilt component systems for piston, prop-jet and pure jet aircraft engines used by air cargo carriers, corporations, the Air Force, and other governmental agencies. It also operated a spare-engine inventory program, unique in the industry, by which customers could achieve 48-hour change-out on their aircraft for certain engines. Nine hundred employees worked at plants in Dallas and Frederick, Oklahoma.

Cooper management had studied Dallas Airmotive for a long time, receiving board approval of an acquisition as early as the spring of 1969. But negotiations were terminated temporarily when Cooper stock declined and while Dallas Airmotive pursued a separate possibility of merging with a competitor, Southwest Airmotive. The latter plan was abandoned, and on July 1, 1970, Dallas Airmotive was purchased by Cooper Industries in a straight stock trade.

Most people complain about problems. Others develop successful careers out of solving them for the complainers. The story of Dallas Airmotive began with two such men, both young, who discovered an imaginative way to weave government red tape into the framework of a new private enterprise.

During World War II, the U.S. government assumed total control of the aviation industry. To meet the exhaustive demands of war, it regulated all manufacturing of aircraft and aircraft components. Even the purchase of spare parts for nonmilitary use required special authorization from the War Production Board, and most requests were understandably denied. As a consequence, small airlines became starved for supplies.

When the war ended, tens of millions of dollars worth of new aircraft engine parts sat in war production plants or at depots around the world, no longer needed by the government. Most had not even been uncrated. Domestic airlines, struggling to revive after dormant war years, desperately needed the parts. But they were not easy to obtain. Their disposal had come under supervision of a War Assets Administration. Explained one airline representative, "You got parts only by going to the proper office in Washington, filling out a mountain of forms, paying in advance, and agreeing to accept the merchandise 'as is' and 'where it is.' To that, you could add the question of 'if it is.' You had no guarantee of getting anything at all."

The man who made that statement, Henry I. McGee, Jr., decided to do something about the problem not only for his employer, TACA International Division of Trans World Airlines, but for all commercial aviation. His determination was shared by a friend named Jack Ingram, who was attempting to get surplus parts for Braniff Airlines. The two men devised a plan to form a company that could serve as an agent in distributing the government's aircraft engine and parts inventory to legitimate users, providing a profit for themselves and for the government, while making certain each customer received full value for money spent. Their approach was three-fold. First, they convinced the government that their proposal would benefit all concerned parties. Then they received endorsements from the domestic airlines and the Civil Aeronautics Administration, predecessor to the Federal Aviation Agency. Although they were unable to get exclusive representation for all equipment, they did obtain it for Pratt & Whitney engine parts. That represented sufficient potential to put them in business.

When partners McGee and Ingram made the move to self-employment, their major asset was confidence. An early colleague said later, "We didn't start on a shoestring. We started on half a shoestring." Backed by a three-year contract with the government, the men formed Aviation Activities Company on February 19, 1946. They soon sold a one-third interest to General Robert J. Smith, an Air Force veteran who had become president and general manager of Pioneer Airlines.

Aviation Activities, with McGee serving as president and chief executive officer, opened in a warehouse that had been constructed by the federal government at Grand Prairie, Texas, a suburb of Dallas. The Dallas area was selected because it was considered a hub of air, railroad, and highway transportation, and materials would be coming in from myriad locations for subsequent shipment to customers throughout the United States.

Aviation Activities, Inc., later bought Dallas Airmotive by issuing McGee and Ingram its stock. Five members of the organization acquired the bankrupt Texas Metal & Manufacturing Company as individuals, primarily to obtain its prime property on Forest Park Road, just two miles from Love Field. Another corporation, Industrial Plants, was then formed to build a modern engine overhaul shop on the Forest Park site. Completed by the end of 1950, it became the last independent large-engine shop to be built in the United States. Subsequently, the entire organization was consolidated into Dallas Airmotive, Inc., with stock issued to the general public.

The distribution of parts, on which the company had been founded, continued through a network of fixed-base operators, although it was relegated to a supporting role in the company's overall business. Field service representatives in Detroit, Houston, Miami, New York, and Washington, D.C., provided extensions of service from the Dallas headquarters at the time of Cooper's acquisition.

Henry McGee continued to head Dallas Airmotive operations after the merger and was elected to the Cooper board of directors. At the same time, Tom Kraner retired from the Cooper presidency. Chairman Miller assumed the additional office of president, and Robert Cizik became executive vice president and chief operating officer. A few months later, Thomas E. Naugle was promoted from president of CB/Southern to corporate vice president for planning.

The synergy of aircraft and fixed-based jet operations within the company never crystallized. "Our airmotive business continued as a totally separate operating unit," said Cizik, "so we decided to build it that way, using the same methods that were working well for The Cooper Group. Through modernization, cost cutting, financial planning, and vigorous marketing, we would transfer it from an individual proprietorship type of business into a major corporate entity."

The early 1970s found ecologists and economists at each other's throats, the former demanding a no-growth policy, the latter seeking trade-offs between environmental concerns and social progress. "The ecologist sees growth and technology as part of the problem," wrote Walter W. Heller, chairman of the Council of Economic Advisors to the President. "The economist, viewing the huge costs and difficulties of reducing resources to rescue the environment, regards the bounties of growth as a vital part of the solution." Caught in the stand-off, energy transmission once again suffered the squeeze of indecision. Projects such as the proposed Alaskan pipeline were forced into limbo and shrouded in red tape, depressing the demand for heavy machinery to levels as much as 30 percent below those of 1970.

It was a time of deep concern for Cooper. Problems from several sources, both internal and external, converged to strike a series of blows, most of them landing on the already vulnerable machinery division: a shift in demand from reciprocating to rotating products, new competition, continual cost increases, the rising trend of foreign nationalism, and disappointment in results of the company's own attempted countermeasures. History could not be accepted as a guarantee that riding out the cycle's downswing would carry a company to the next upswing.

Taking a critical look at the long development of Cooper-Bessemer, corporate management decided to apply some proven hand tool strategies to its heavy machinery business. Specifically, it would capitalize on strengths and eliminate weaknesses. That meant concentrating resources where it was the industry leader, namely the manufacture of compression equipment for oil and gas markets. It would cease building centrifugal compressors for process applications where it did not have marketing leadership.

The decision was made with some regret, because Cooper-Bessemer had done an excellent job of developing centrifugal compression technology. Its quality matched the best in the business. But it had been a 'Johnny-come-lately" in that particular field, and its products were designed to cover a wide range of markets. Competitors, on the other hand, had concentrated expertise on specialized targets. One company became the leading supplier for the ethylene market, others for ammonia, nitrogen, oxygen, and on down the line. Every application commanded costly individual engineering. Supporting engineering for them became a burden compounded when all the markets went sour, as in 1971. Cooper reasoned that individual leaders in those markets would not be unseated by anything short of a revolutionary breakthrough in technology, and none was in sight. Bob Cizik later explained to *Forbes* magazine, "We could probably have gone ahead and invested $100 million over four to five years for the latest technology. But the competitors weren't going to be standing still. I thought we could come out of that and still be third or fourth in many of those lines." *Forbes* gave the decision an "A" rating.

So the company retrenched. It phased out products for the process industry in favor of holding its leadership position in manufacturing machinery to handle oil and natural gas. In doing so, it moved against prevailing winds carrying competitors in the direction of centrifugal compression, which had become the glamour segment of the industry. Dresser, Worthington, and Ingersoll-Rand all were hurrying into rotating equipment, leaving behind what was considered a dying business in reciprocating compressors.

Cooper gambled that the reciprocating business not only would survive, it would prosper if the price of natural gas should rise to levels where efficiency would become a major factor (reciprocating compressors were more fuel efficient than centrifugal compressors). In 1971, gas was selling for 30 cents per mcf. When Cizik predicted it would rise to one dollar in the next four years, friends insisted he was wrong. They were correct; his prediction was too low.

19

Valleys and Peaks

Even when business is bad, it generates some cash. Although most 1971 cash was going into hand tool expansion, some was applied to research and development of a Quad integral gas engine compressor, an extremely gas efficient unit. Cooper advertised that it was going to specialize in natural gas compression equipment. While it received very little market enthusiasm at first, it was laying groundwork for the anticipated comeback few others seemed to expect. As it happened, however, there were some other believers.

Respected throughout the industry as a man of high integrity, Gene Miller presented his frank appraisal of Cooper's business to a group of analysts in Philadelphia. One young analyst, Paul Mecray, never forgot his introduction to the company at that meeting. Ten years later he recalled what he described as a most unusual presentation:

> I've followed Cooper for a great many years. My first memory dates back to 1971 when Gene Miller appeared in Philadelphia to give a talk to analysts. I was with Wellington Management Company, and had a background of geology and finance with Atlantic Richfield, so I knew about Cooper-Bessemer products and something of the company, but not much. And I didn't know Gene Miller at all. Well, he told the analysts that, quite frankly, business was lousy. I had never heard a president of a company be so candid. I was so impressed that I began to talk quite a bit to Cooper people, particularly Bob Lambert, then their controller, but to others as well. I was struck by the honesty of the entire management — the impression I had received from Gene Miller obviously was a true one. Well, I thought if they were that honest about business being poor, they might be just as believable when it was improving. And that's what happened. We had a thesis at Wellington that this country was seriously underpricing natural gas. So we were looking for investments that would grow when that situation turned around. One, of course, was the natural gas producers. But we thought also we should look at companies who would be associated in less direct ways. More pipelines would be forthcoming, if our thesis was correct, and I became well enough acquainted with Cooper people to think they would be direct beneficiaries. The management was capable and, as I mentioned,

174

honest. Gene Miller always was accessible to a young analyst and patient in helping a person learn about such unfamiliar things as the difference between centrifugal and reciprocating compressors. He also made me feel genuinely comfortable, and he asked my opinions on industry conditions. It was more an exchange of ideas than a one-sided conversation. That has been true of others in Cooper management also. Wellington invested heavily in Cooper and has maintained its holdings for ten years. It has been a totally pleasant and profitable association.

To further aggravate an already difficult year, confusion resulting from a White House announcement of a wage freeze in August, 1971, precipitated a nineteen-day strike by workers at the Grove City plant, cutting into second-half earnings. The presidential action followed an earlier price freeze, followed by a longer range program of price controls. CB/Southern also was forced to revise its annual plan, while searching for business opportunities not directly associated with its regular products.

In addition to dropping "special application" centrifugal process compressor production, Cooper-Bessemer evaluated every product and prototype in the reciprocating and rotating lines to determine how best to reduce costs and improve production efficiency. Some costs were cut by shifting production facilities, and by simplifying organization and communications within the division. Mt. Vernon retained production of some rotating line products, with turbines emphasized at Stratford. Reciprocating line production and associated foundry operations were centered exclusively at Grove City. Products and services that could be handled more efficiently in small, specialized operations were moved to Penn Pump.

The evaluation indicated also that sales trends had traditionally influenced development and prototype efforts, resulting in proliferation of new models at the expense of older profit makers such as parts and services. A division planning function was established to seek better understanding of markets on which to base product development, particularly with regard to turbines and pipeline centrifugal compresssors and parts.

Operating earnings had dropped to $1.12 a share, compared with $2.75 the previous year. Restructuring equipment during the latter part of the year resulted in extraordinary expenses equivalent to seventy cents a share, so actual net income in 1971 was forty-two cents a share.

Meanwhile, Mexico's nationalistic investment policy, which was causing more production and assembly of machinery there, prompted sale of Cooper's 40 percent equity interest in Conjuto Manufacturero to its Mexican partner. Increased Mexican input had resulted in abnormal costs and management problems in manufacturing reciprocating equipment there. After the sale, Conjunto Manufacturero continued to do business with Cooper-Bessemer as a licensee.

There was a ray of hope for Cooper-Bessemer division during 1971, however, and it emanated from Moscow, where negotiations initiated in 1968 were progressing nicely. Discussions with the official Soviet Union licensing agency, Licensintorg, centered on supplying that country with equipment and technology to help develop its proposed natural gas transmission network. Cooper also worked closely with the U.S. Department of State, making certain it conformed to international policies that fluctuated with administrative changes and the natural course of world politics.

Harold Johnson, who still headed the Cooper-Bessemer negotiating team, was able to resolve some emotional problems within the division by explaining that State Department guidelines were being followed, so the company was doing nothing that could be construed as unpatriotic. Cooper was, in fact, encouraged by the State Department to move ahead with the project, because it helped establish a basic relationship that could build confidence in SALT talks being carried out between the two countries. Other industries likewise were supported by the Nixon administration in establishing friendly business rapport with the Soviets.

During 1971, the group met so often with Russian representatives that Johnson said both sides were "playing hop scotch between Mt. Vernon and Moscow." But there was a lot at stake. In a year when the division was suffering severe setbacks, here was a possibility of securing long-range, multimillion dollar contracts. Licensintorg had made an exhaustive study of companies, and had decided Cooper-Bessemer technology was what it wanted. All that remained was the negotiating, but the complexity of that far exceeded anything the company ever had encountered. It involved dealing with separate trade agencies for machinery, imports, licensing and technology, the Soviet Gas Ministry, and even the U.S. and Canadian embassies in Moscow.

Johnson always studied the cultures of nations with whom he would deal, because "you play each ball game with a different set of rules." For instance, he said, "A Frenchman does business like a man in a rowboat; he progresses in the opposite direction that he faces. A German beats his path straight ahead." With the Russians, the "ball game" was slow, deliberate, and comparable to friendly, but high-stakes poker. "All we talked about was dollars," Johnson said, "but we had to hedge our bets a little to be in a position where we could accept gas or oil products in lieu of cash, so we also were talking to German and French banking interests, who might be interested in taking the products and paying us the dollars. We realized all this was very time consuming, so we wanted to make it worthwhile by negotiating not just for a single contract but for a relationship that would lead to far-reaching business over a long period of time."

After a delegation of seven Russian technical representatives visited Mt. Vernon, it appeared both sides were close to agreement. Four Cooper-Bessemer executives traveled to Moscow for a meeting that continued almost without interruption for four days. Stanley Johnson, Jr., who headed the Cooper-Bessemer division at that time and was one of those joining Harold Johnson at the deliberations, recalled an incident that dramatized the art of Russian-American bargaining:

> It was a great experience, because the chairman of their negotiating team, a chap named Kuzmin, was an extremely competent man in his early fifties who headed a trade agency. We used a woman interpreter who was an expert in linguistics, but we had the feeling Kuzmin understood English even though he tried hard not to let on he knew what we were saying among ourselves. Finally, Kuzmin made a proposal that struck us as wanting a great deal from Cooper without giving up much in return. So, speaking slowly and deliberately, as you do with an interpreter, I said, 'Mr. Kuzmin, it seems to me you want us to give you a bear and you give us a rabbit.' As I said that, his eyes twinkled. Then, when the interpreter told him what I said, he leaned forward and seemed to correct her. That made us pretty sure he understood English. Later we found out the interpreter had mistakenly translated my comment as saying a cat for a dog, instead of a rabbit for a bear. That, of course, was completely away from the point I was trying to make. Kuzmin could tell he had blown his cover, and confessed he understood us. We all laughed and chatted briefly in English, then went back to formal negotiating, using the interpreter.

After several more sessions, Cooper, in 1972, signed a ten-year agreement with Licensintorg. The pact, expected to generate $18 million in revenue, called for Cooper-Bessemer's Grove City plant to build a large engine compressor to be used as a prototype by Russia in producing similar machinery in that country. During the ten years, Cooper-Bessemer would continue to furnish component parts, including power cylinders, and the technical assistance required by the Russians to design, develop, and produce the equipment. Although the prototype was a 7,500-hp model, Cooper-Bessemer was to provide know-how enabling Russia to produce models up to 12,500 horsepower. The license arrangement was the first of its kind between Russia and an American industry, and it did indeed open the door for opportunities that would soon enter.

Other overseas activities also helped offset weak domestic markets in 1972. Sales hit record highs in Germany, The Netherlands, and the United Kingdom, as those countries stepped up the installation of production and transmission systems to utilize reserves of North Sea oil and gas fields. Petroleum development elsewhere in the world led Cooper to open a warehouse in Singapore and a sales office in Algeria, and to seek joint ventures in several other nations.

Donald E. Steele was hired from Allis-Chalmers Corporation to become president of Cooper-Bessemer. A graduate of Whitworth College and the University of Washington, and a former Naval officer, Steele held various marketing and general management positions at Allis-

Chalmers, the most recent being general manager of the large pump and compressor division prior to joining Cooper.

By the middle of 1972, pipeline construction in the United States was beginning to reverse its downward spiral. Approximately $1 billion worth of construction was underway or planned by July 1, although some awaited Federal Power Commission approval. Cooper-Bessemer anticipated a boost in sales, because long-time customers were involved in those projects.

But the biggest news from Cooper's Houston headquarters was a recently completed acquisition the financial world considered a benchmark in modern day mergers. *Business Week* magazine succinctly described it as a story of "how Cooper Industries squeezed its way into control" of Nicholson File Company, "while three other companies battled openly to take it over."

The Providence, Rhode Island, manufacturer of files, rasps, and saws had been high on the original "preferred list of possible acquisitions" inherited with the Lufkin merger five years earlier. In 1969, Cooper had attempted to interest Chairman Paul Nicholson in a merger, but he was opposed to ending family control dating back to 1864. In keeping with its policy against "unfriendly" acquisition, Cooper reluctantly abandoned the proposal. The desirability of purchasing Nicholson was later described in a compilation of outstanding case problems in finance, edited by three members of the Harvard Business School faculty and published by Richard D. Irwin, Inc.:

> A relatively poor sales and profit performance in recent years, conservative accounting and financial policies, and a low percentage of outstanding stock held by the Nicholson family and management all contributed to its vulnerability. Annual sales growth of 2% was far behind the industry growth rate of 6% per year, and profit margins had slipped to only one-third those of other hand tool manufacturers. In 1971, the Nicholson common stock was trading near its lowest point in many years and well below its book value of $51.25. Lack of investor interest in the stock was reflected in its low price-earnings ratio of 10-14, which compared with 14-17 times earnings for other leading hand tool companies. The stock was clearly selling on the basis of its dividend yield, with only limited hopes for capital appreciation.

> What made Nicholson so attractive was its basic competitive strength — strength that the family-dominated management had not translated into earnings. The company was one of the largest domestic manufacturers of hand tools and was a leader in its two main product areas. Nicholson held a 50 percent share of the $50 million market for files and rasps, where it offered a broad high quality line with a very strong brand name. Its second product line, hand saws and saw blades, also had an excellent reputation for quality and held a 9 percent share of this $200 million market. Only Sears, Roebuck and Company and Disston, Inc. had larger market shares.

Nicholson's greatest asset, however, was its distribution system. Forty-eight direct salesmen and 28 file and saw engineers marketed its file, rasp, and saw products to 2,100 hardware wholesalers in the United States and Canada. These wholesalers in turn sold to 53,000 retail outlets. Overseas the company's products were sold in 137 countries through 140 local sales representatives. The company seemed to have all the necessary strengths to share fully in the 6-7 percent annual sales growth forecast for the industry.

Such vulnerability was not likely to go unnoticed. Nicholson became a clear target for other companies, among them Pittsburgh-based H.K. Porter Company, manufacturer of industrial equipment with wide ranging interests in tools and other products. On March 3, 1972, Porter's ebullient chairman, Thomas Mellon Evans, announced an attractive offer of forty-two dollars for Nicholson stock, then trading at thirty dollars, well under its book value. The Pittsburgh conglomerate, having previously purchased 44,000 Nicholson shares, sought 437,000 more to gain majority interest that would give it management control of the company. Evans set a deadline of April 4 for the tender offer.

Nicholson President George Williams, who had managed a Porter tool division at one time, greatly feared a take-over by his former boss. "Mr. Evans sees things from a financial, not an operating or even humanitarian point of view," he told *Business Week*. "He's gone into companies before, closed operations, and put people on the street. We wanted to give our employees a better shake."

When they received the news, Bill Rector, Bob Cizik, and Alan Riedel met with Nicholson management, assuring the company that Cooper would make a more favorable tax-free proposal than Porter if action could be taken without delay. After waiting several days for a decision that did not come, however, Cooper withdrew its offer as it was too risky for a time when the previous bad business year had depressed its own stock. Porter might even retaliate with a tender offer for Cooper.

A few days later, Nicholson and Walco National Corporation made a sudden stock exchange merger agreement that would not be taxable — an apparent advantage over the taxable Porter plan. But within a week, Nicholson paid Walco to scrap that agreement so it could tentatively accept a $50-per-share stock offer from a diversified Cleveland manufacturer, VLN Corporation. At the same time, it got a temporary court order to delay Porter's tender. Nicholson management, pointing out the benefits of a tax-free VLN merger with preferred-stock price advantages, received approval from its directors. Porter countered with a different interpretation of financial figures, showing that VLN had not paid common stock dividends for two years. Adding to the confusion, speculators began buying stock in hopes that the battle would become a price war.

Cooper decided to take advantage of the dilemma facing Nicholson stockholders by quietly reentering the scene. Chairman/President Miller credited Executive Vice President Cizik with "molding the imaginative plan" that became a classic in the industry.

As stockholders scratched their heads, Cooper was busy purchasing twenty-nine thousand Nicholson stock shares, driving the market price above the H.K. Porter tender offer, and hoping to use them as a bargaining tool, or at least defeat the offer. Evans, meanwhile, was weighing problems that could develop if the Nicholson-VLN merger should be approved by stockholders. He would end up with VLN preferred stock, with its relatively low dividend rate and poor trading posture.

Cizik reasoned that Evans was not going to reach the tender goal and would be better off converting his Nicholson stock to Cooper stock if an acceptable exchange rate could be arranged. In addition, Cooper earnings were recovering from 1971 and the company's liquidity was superior to that of VLN. Armed with that ammunition, Cizik presented his proposal to Evans at the latter's New York City office. Asked by a *Business Week* reporter if it were true their voices echoed through the halls of the office building, Cizik replied, "Evans talks with a loud voice, and he uses colorful language with abandon."

When negotiations concluded, Cooper was able to acquire Porter's 30 percent holdings in Nicholson in a one-for-one exchange for a new Cooper convertible preferred stock. Having by that time acquired an additional 30 percent on the open market, the company gained control of Nicholson. Evans could hardly be described as a loser, having exchanged Nicholson shares purchased at forty-two dollars in March for Cooper preferred worth sixty-five dollars a few months later, creating a paper profit of nearly $4 million. Nevertheless, an analyst who followed events closely told *Business Week*, "As everyone battled to control Nicholson, Cooper cleverly snuck into the middle of a stalemate and snatched up all the cookies."

20

Nicholson

We desire to call the attention of our friends and the public to a dangerous and most injurious means of deception, which we have found practiced at different times during the past few years. We refer to old or worn out files of our make which have been treated by immersing them in an acid bath, and afterwards selling them in packages bearing a label of similar appearance to ours, having the words *Nicholson* or *Nicholson Files, Increment Cut*, etc. printed thereon; thus palming the same off as our original goods. As this fraud is of a most dangerous character, we advise caution against it — as files, so doctored, are comparatively valueless for use. We warn all parties that if detected in this, or any doctoring of our files, with the intention of trading upon our hard earned reputation, they will be presented to the courts for treatment.

Within these plain words of warning from the original edition of William T. Nicholson's *A Treatise on Files*, published in 1878, are reflections of a man, a company, and an industry.

As the inventor of a file-manufacturing machine and the principal founder of a company bearing his name, William Nicholson was convinced of the superiority of his product and aware of the competitive nature of an industry where secrecy was considered essential to survival. Representatives from another company had already appeared at his Providence, Rhode Island, plant to blatantly offer employees wage increases to switch allegiance.

The scenario appears to be much ado about a simple hand tool. But part of the intrigue lies in the extraordinary complexity of creating such simplicity. The humble file is fashioned from a special steel with carefully controlled carbon content in an elaborate process consisting of shaping, annealing, grinding, draw-filing, machine-chiseling, hardening, finishing, and individual testing for soft spots. A seemingly infinite variety of sizes and shapes is demanded by nearly every shop, factory, farm, and household in the world. And no arrangement of standard machining equipment will produce a file. Specialized machinery exists only in a few

Typical of harsh nineteenth-century apprentice agreements, this indenture nevertheless provided young Henry Barnett with experience that led to his founding a company producing the famous "Black Diamond" file. Early in the twentieth century, the Barnett company was merged into Nicholson.

file manufacturing plants, their designs known by just a small cadre of engineers. Attempts to alter basic manufacturing processes that have remained essentially unchanged for more than a century have failed to meet quality requirements.

Yet even a century is little more than a moment in the history of files, which, according to the Old Testament of the Bible, were used more than a thousand years before the birth of Christ, during the reign of King Saul. As late as the mid-nineteenth century, they continued to be produced by laboriously raising each cutting edge from smooth metal blanks with hand-held chisel and hammer. Mechanizing the procedure had defied even the likes of Leonardo da Vinci. Finally, some file-cutting machines were produced, the first in America about 1853, but none proved competitive with the handmade products of skilled craftsmen, the best of whom were located in Sheffield, England.

Developing such a machine became a great challenge to many inventors, among them young William T. Nicholson, whose early patents already included "Nicholson's Improved Egg Beater" and other somewhat less than essential utensils. Born in 1834 at Pawtucket, Rhode Island, Nicholson, like many boys growing up in mill towns during the Industrial Revolution, had become an apprentice machinist at the age of fourteen. He gained experience in two factories and a small machine shop in Providence. During his tenure at the machine shop, where he became proficient at mechanical drawing and was promoted to mechanical manager, he made rough sketches of a proposed file-cutting machine. The idea was tabled for several years, however, when he joined a partner in opening Nicholson & Brownell, announcing the intention to "build to order every description of light machinery, machine tools, etc. used by jewelers, silversmiths, and others, of the newest and most improved construction." The partnership soon dissolved, but continuing as sole proprietor, the now confident young businessman moved to larger quarters, doubled the size of his plant by purchasing assets of another company, and expanded production. Within a year, cannon fire at Fort Sumter, South Carolina, prompted a change in William Nicholson's plans. Asked to aid in production of Springfield rifles for the Union Army, he formed another partnership, Nicholson & Company, manufacturing ten thousand rear gun sights per month. Nevertheless, he found time to complete drawings of a file-cutting machine. Patents were acquired, an experimental machine was built, and in 1864 the thirty-year-old inventor sold his partnership interest to launch a new career.

Unlike much manufacturing of the time, production of machine-cut files could not be started on a modest scale. It demanded heavy capitalization, a sizeable labor force, enough volume to compete with established companies, and a quality that could overcome a universal preference for handmade files. Several machine-cutting manufacturers made matters worse by turning out inferior products that provided more ammunition for already well-entrenched hand craftsmen. Financing was well beyond the means of William Nicholson. But files produced by his experimental machine attracted the interest of a wealthy Providence investor named Byron Sprague, who had abandoned a lucrative family cotton milling business to form a varied series of new enterprises. Sprague garnered necessary funds from other investors, most of them successful businessmen who could afford to join a highly speculative venture, and in the summer of 1864, the Rhode Island legislature chartered a new Providence corporation, the Nicholson File Company.

Although he had initiated the idea, invented the machinery, and had the company named for him, William Nicholson did not have sufficient capital behind the project to be elected an officer, or even a director. Instead, he was named agent, a position comparable with today's general manager, and given a generous block of stock for company title to his patent. It was not until 1871 that Nicholson was elected fourth president of the corporation, following Byron Sprague, lumber merchant William Mowry, and retired cotton merchant Alexander Farnum, all prominent in providing the original capital of $300,000. Even that large sum by nineteenth-century standards proved insufficient. With a factory constructed and equipped, initial employment of approximately one hundred, and investment in high quality steel that had to be imported from England, additional stock subscriptions had to be made soon after the first files were sold midway through 1866.

But tenacity prevailed. When William T. Nicholson at last assumed the role of chief executive officer in 1871, the file company was double the size of any other in the United States and equal to any in the world. The next year, Nicholson File declared its first dividend, beginning an unbroken record of annual stockholder returns.

Some prospective customers still resisted change from hand-cut files, convinced that irregular teeth were superior to machined uniformity. Rather than argue the point publicly, William Nicholson introduced an "increment cut" file, machine-made but with irregular rows of teeth. It was advertised as being patterned after the hand-cut file, an ingenious concession that helped overcome the holding power of the status quo. Gradually, Nicholson increment cut files became standard for the industry.

The company president had prepared well for such leadership in the industry. A compulsion for thoroughness drove him to learn minute details of anything related to his product. He traveled to Europe where he studied the heat treatment of steel. He experimented with machines and processes, tested persistently to see if any new shape or degree of coarseness could improve cutting edges, and practiced myriad techniques of using the product. His *Treatise on Files* was a compilation of terms, techniques, descriptions, and illustrations summing up one man's encyclopedic perception of the subject. While generally impartial in detailing features belonging to all files and rasps, it was sprinkled with what he admitted to be "the special points of merit claimed for the goods made by the Nicholson File Company," as well as the caution on "doctored" products. The first hardback edition was published in 1878. Later renamed *File Filosophy*, it reappeared in a long series of twenty editions, unchallenged as the most complete and scientific compendium ever written on filing. One illustration in the *Treatise* pictures an intriguing design made of 554 files attached to an exhibition rack for the nation's 1876 centennial exposition at Philadelphia. One hundred years later, when the United States observed its bicentennial, the historical display was in The Smithsonian Institute. To a casual observer, the files could have been purchased in 1976.

By 1879, Nicholson lines had been expanded to include hundreds of sizes, styles, and cuts of files, supplemented by such specialties as brushes, stub files, and bent rifflers. A new office building was erected. More than three hundred employees produced six hundred dozen products in each ten-hour working day. Among new faces at the plant was that of a young man who would be tutored carefully by the assiduous president for company leadership. Samuel Mowry Nicholson, the president's son recently graduated from high school, began training in the mechanical phase of company operations.

Enlargement of facilities and development of products continued through the next decade, with a "South Works plant within a plant" constructed for production of extrafine (X.F.) files to compete with precision tools being imported from Switzerland for use by jewelers and watch makers. Operations were so secretive they were conducted behind barred windows. But the company's most dramatic growth began in the 1890s, when it plunged into an acquisition program that would bring a tenfold magnification within a few years.

Although some 150 American companies were producing files, only 10 used machinery, and they supplied 90 percent of the market. Court dockets teemed with legal battles over patent infringements and sales wars abounded in the marketplace. Aggressiveness seemed essential for victory. One bitter rivalry was dissolved in 1890, when Nicholson purchased the New American File Company of Pawtucket, Rhode Island, in a move described as bringing relief to all persons concerned. The purchase increased production 25 percent and provided another step toward William Nicholson's goal of international prominence for his company. Working closely with his father in that effort, young Samuel Nicholson traveled throughout the United States and into several Canadian provinces to establish new channels of distribution and improve customer relations. A contrasting personality to his father, he was more interested in dealing with people than experimenting with machinery.

He had a flair for selling imaginative ideas in a conservative business, and numerous stories were told of his ability to solve marketing problems with personal charm.

The company presidency came much earlier than anticipated to Samuel Nicholson when his father died suddenly in 1893. Death at age sixty followed a strenuous seven weeks in Chicago, where the elder Nicholson characteristically gave his close personal attention to even the smallest details of exhibiting company products at the Columbian World's Exposition. Arriving home, he worked late to catch up on more details that had accumulated in his absence. Finally, he closed his big roll top desk, locked the door of his office, and drove home in the gathering dusk. The next morning as he prepared to leave home for the office, he was stricken with an attack of apoplexy. The following day he died.

At age thirty-two, Samuel Nicholson was in charge of long-range growth plans already set in motion. He quickly condensed them into a short-range pattern. Whereas the company once was concerned with defending against superior forces of European imports, the new president intended to reverse the situation. Traveling to Europe, he personally established contacts that he believed could be cultivated into fertile fields of overseas marketing. Upon returning to Providence, he was convinced that the best offense could be mounted by a full-scale export program supported by continued acquisition of American production capabilities. Such an ambitious combination called for new capital investment. According to a story handed down through three generations, the Nicholson president sought assistance from a talented fund raiser, Arthur Watson, who in turn recruited his son, Byron Watson, and an influential millionaire named Marsden Perry for a meeting in the Watson summer home near Rhode Island Sound. There President Nicholson set forth his plans, prompting a discussion that lasted through the night. By dawn he had assurance that sufficient backing would be forthcoming.

Within a few years the company established a London office marketing full lines of Nicholson files, then a separate foreign sales department with a full time representative, Harold C. Field, canvassing Australia, South Africa, and the Orient. It purchased the Great Western File Company of Beaver Falls, Pennsylvania; the McClelland File Company of Saginaw, Michigan; M. Buckley & Company of Pawtucket, Rhode Island; Eagle File Company of Middletown, New York; Kearney & Foot Company of Paterson, New Jersey; Arcade File Works of Anderson, Indiana; The J. Barton Smith Company of Philadelphia; Globe File Manufacturing Company of Port Hope, Ontario; Mechanic's Star File Manufacturing Company of Levis, Quebec; Toronto File Works of Toronto, Ontario; and the most important acquisition of all, the G. & H. Barnett Company of Philadelphia, manufacturers of the well-known "Black-Diamond" file. The variety of products reached into the thousands, and the company motto, "A File for Every Purpose," was almost a

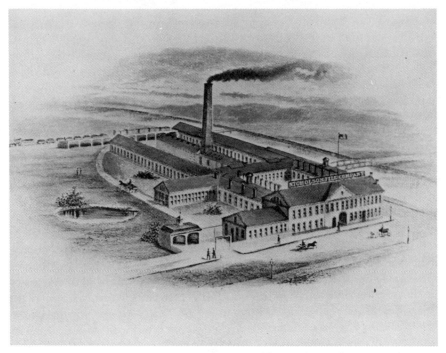

An artist's rendering shows Nicholson's Providence, R.I., plant near the turn of the twentieth century.

literal truth. Addition of rasps further extended the lines of supplementary products as well.

The great acquisition surge was accomplished in a single decade. With the twentieth century less than five years old, Nicholson was marketing in forty nations. Only the Collins Axe Company of Collinsville, Connecticut, had preceded it in the tool export business.

Nicholson consolidated its array of purchased companies into five plants: Providence, Philadelphia, Anderson, Port Hope, and Paterson. An equal marketing balance between agriculture and industry was expected to tilt toward the latter, under the additional weight of America's manufacturing explosion. But economic shifts posed no particular cause for either elation or alarm. Everybody needed files.

Samuel Nicholson not only withstood the pace and pressures of expansion, he was energized by them. A man of diversified interests, he seemed to make friends and accomplish tasks effortlessly and with great pleasure. Friends described him as handsome and proud, a super salesman who always wore a boutonniere and pursued business and yachting with equal zeal. Governor Elisha Dyer of Rhode Island appointed him to a state military position, carrying the rank of colonel. The commission essentially was honorary, encompassing ceremonial duties with the governor and other political figures, but he applied his customary enthusiasm to the role and thereafter was referred to as "Colonel" Nicholson.

Despite his flamboyance, Colonel Nicholson was far from reckless in business ventures. His seemingly impulsive injections of creativity into sales and distribution were in fact calculated meticulously, to the extent that he considered himself a conservative businessman. With the spectacular drive toward world prominence accomplished, Nicholson File Company settled into a pattern of steady, albeit less dramatic, progress. The president's son, Paul C. Nicholson, joined the company in 1911 after graduating from Yale University. Although he had studied liberal arts, he was intrigued by mechanics and he felt more comfortable involved in operations than in sales.

The company's worldwide reputation continued to grow. World War I requirements on America's industrial front triggered another boost, ushering in a period of expansions at existing Nicholson plants lasting into the 1920s. Production secrets continued to be guarded assiduously. Early patents had long expired and file companies rarely applied for new ones. Experience indicated that it was better to develop machines under wraps than let competition see patent papers providing descriptions for anyone who wanted to investigate them. Clever modification of patented designs made litigation difficult, if not impossible. Consequently, Nicholson's experimental department was considered impregnable. Joseph Redinger, company development engineer for many years, assumed personal responsibility for the department's security, and employees reported that Fort Knox would be safe in his hands.

In Canada, the Port Hope plant concentrated on domestic markets. A British "preferential tariff" changed that, however. Under terms of the act, nations of the British Empire could import from Canada without paying duties. Those markets previously had been supplied by the Providence plant, but a shift was in order and Port Hope expanded to meet its new opportunity in the early 1920s. So while industry generally hibernated to withstand the chill of a Great Depression, Nicholson's Port Hope plant erected a series of new facilities. United States operations enjoyed no such immunity. From a prosperous year in 1929, they slumped with the rest of the nation after the stock market crash. Layoffs were extensive. Ray Sokol, who joined the company in 1939 and many years later became general manager of file manufacturing, remembered his father working as a file cutter at the Anderson plant in the depression: "He was raising a family of nine, and he considered a three-day work week exceptional. That was as much as a person could get, and it was considered big income compared with most other people."

The most serious casualty of the depression was the Paterson, New Jersey, plant which had to be closed, its machinery sent to Philadelphia and Port Hope. The total corporation did not reach a point of financial desperation, however, and it revived more rapidly than most industries. Colonel Nicholson suffered a stroke, and although he returned to the office (with difficulty), his son directed the company activities during much of the economic recovery. In 1939 the Colonel died and Paul C. Nicholson became president. A retiring, shy man, the new president provided a quiet leadership with widely delegated responsibilities. Having worked closely with his father, he continued established policies with very little change but with a resurgence of production sparked by the beginning of another war.

Port Hope was the first Nicholson unit to feel the tide of World War II, when Britain declared war on Germany September 9, 1939. Put on a crash schedule, the plant upped production to capacity. The need for increased facilities forced realization of the fact that there was no more room for expansion, setting the scene for a later decision to build an entire, new factory complex at another location. War was not a time to make such a move, however, and plans had to be postponed until early in the next decade.

Just before America entered the war, the president's son, Paul C. Nicholson, Jr., represented a fourth generation of the family to become associated with the company, although his initial tenure was brief. A graduate of Yale, as was his father, he joined the U.S. Navy after graduation, received a reserve commission, then went to work with the company in January of 1941 while awaiting call to active service. Seven months later he was assigned to a subchaser, beginning a five-year tour of naval duty.

No changeover in tooling was required for Nicholson plants to join the war effort. The need for files was universal. They were, in fact, designated essential items in the War Production Board's allocation of steel. When the war ended, Nicholson expanded further. While many industries suffered postwar slumps, demand for files was heightened by distributor competition to fill depleted inventories. The tradition of supplying files for every purpose continued, with Nicholson and Black Diamond brand names heading the long list. Requests, however small, were met whenever possible. Records showed sparse and therefore unprofitable sales of such specialty items as bowling ball files, carcass files, and toenail files.

One top salesman was intent on having a special dog nail file added to the line. Because of his good record a full set of samples was prepared. With great enthusiasm he set off on a round of dog shows, convinced that the special files would capture the imagination of dog owners throughout the world (and that represented no small market). Unfortunately, he couldn't even get rid of the samples. Despite its wide variety of demands, the world was not yet ready for dog nail files.

Employees gather in the Nicholson grinding room after exceeding a production goal in the 1940s.

In fact, world opinion was fluctuating regarding the purchase of American products. United States dollars were in short supply in many countries, so they were rationed for top priority imports. Whenever possible, nations purchased from their own manufacturers or from those in countries where currencies were less restrictive.

In 1952, Paul C. Nicholson, Jr., who had rejoined the company after the war, was named president, succeeding his father who became chairman of the board. His immediate objectives were twofold: to modernize existing plant facilities and to study the feasibility of establishing production in Europe. Property was acquired and construction begun on a long-awaited new manufacturing plant at Port Hope the following year. In June of 1955, it was ready for occupancy. Long-range rehabilitation projects were started at the three U.S. plants in Providence, Philadelphia, and Anderson, all of which had deteriorated with age. Meanwhile, the company, prompted by the so-called "soft and hard currency question" and formation of the European Common Market, decided to extend manufacturing overseas. With the exception of purchasing a 40 percent interest in Wiltshire File Company of Melbourne, Australia, in 1941, Nicholson had confined foreign production to Canada. Now it launched a search for a feasible location in Europe. Studying factors of economic and political stability, labor supplies, and competitive file companies, company management narrowed the field to Italy, Scotland, and Holland, finally choosing the latter. In 1954, it purchased that country's only file-making company, a very small organization, then made plans to construct a modern plant at the town of 's-Hertogenbosch, where a promotion-minded mayor had worked diligently to attract the new industry.

President Nicholson traveled to Holland for the ground breaking ceremony, which proved to be unusual by American standards. Instead of turning a shovel of dirt, he operated a pile-driving machine, setting the first foundation piling into the sandy soil. But that formality was a pale prelude to the program announcing the plant opening in 1957. Such an occasion is observed in Holland with great fanfare. On the well-publicized day of opening, His Royal Highness Prince Bernhard of The Netherlands came to 's-Hertogenbosch to speak and officially open the new plant. Instead of cutting a ribbon, he was to use a special goldplated Nicholson file to sever a thin strip of silver that would then spring apart, close electrical circuits, and turn on plant machinery. All went well until the prince began to file — and file and file and file. Using a sawing motion that would have made the author of *File Filosophy* shudder in horror, Prince Bernhard made little progress. His dilemma was heightened by the facts that gold plating had dulled the file and the silver strip offered an extremely slippery surface. Finally, he turned to the company president at his side and asked politely, "Mr. Nicholson, does this file cut?"

"Oh, yes, Your Highness," came the reply. "Just keep filing." After more seconds that seemed like hours, the silver band broke, lights went on, and machines whirred. Several hundred observers cheered, and all was well. But President Nicholson remembered it as "a very long moment." Nicholson File Nederland, N.V., had entered European manufacturing with a flourish.

While it had been studying foreign manufacturing sites and possible new markets, the company also had been contemplating diversification. The resulting decision was to purchase companies that would add products complementing its lines of files. In 1956, Nicholson acquired the Danielson Manufacturing Company, later the Danco Division at Putnam, Connecticut, and W.O. Barnes Company of Detroit, Michigan. Danco produced custom-molded and extruded plastic products, among them handles for files. It also made soft-faced hammers which could be sold through the same channels as files. Barnes was a small independent manufacturer of hack saw and band saw blades.

At the same time, Nicholson faced the prospect of overcapacity in its domestic file plants, brought about by a combination of national economic decline, Port Hope expansion, and opening of the Holland subsidiary. Consequently, an accounting firm was hired to study Nicholson operations and determine which should be eliminated. Most company leaders expected it to be Philadelphia. But the recommendation was to close the Providence plant and expand operations at Anderson. "That jolted us," Paul Nicholson recalled, "because here was the home base, the place where the company started, the traditional part of the company. But the study was so clear that the board of directors voted to close the Providence plant." Over the period of a year, manufacturing facilities were integrated into those of Anderson, and main offices were moved to a building in east Providence.

Nicholson clearly dominated the world's file market, selling in more than one hundred countries. Its products were used on exotic machinery of a fast moving technological age, in do-it-yourself workshops, and in the cane fields of underdeveloped nations. An astounding number of files were used to sharpen machetes in Central and South America and Caribbean countries, at least one million a year going to Jamaica alone. In his remarks at the company's centennial party in 1964, the president pointed out that if all files in Nicholson history were laid end to end, the line would reach to the moon and back. Yet, with high investment and a predictable stability of file sales, further diversification seemed vital to new growth and financial safety. Stockholder interests could be served better by broadening the manufacturing base. Furthermore, it was important to have a more extensive product package available for industrial and hardware distributors.

To that end, Nicholson made its largest acquisition in 1966, purchasing Atkins Saw Division of the Borg-Warner Corporation, a modern plant located in Greenville, Mississippi. The founding of Atkins actually had preceded that of Nicholson. It was started in Indianapolis in 1856 by Elias C. Atkins, a young man of twenty-three who had learned saw manufacturing at his uncle's plant in Connecticut. Choosing Indianapolis because of its location in the center of a hardwood lumber industry, he began to make round, drag, and cross-cut saws in a one-room building, designing and constructing his own machinery as he expanded into other lines. Among his many patents was the formula for producing "Silver Steel," which became an Atkins trademark in 1873 and enabled him to become the first producer of band saws in America. The company soon offered a full line of hand saws to supplement its heavier products.

E.C. Atkins and Company became a corporation in 1885. Soon after the turn of the century it was distributing a variety of saws throughout the world. By then it employed six hundred persons and was headed by H.C. Atkins, who had assumed leadership when his father died in 1900. During World War I, the company supplied cross-cut saws for the forest regiments of the A.E.F., but much of its production was switched temporarily to armor plate. Growing in the 1920s and surviving the 1930s, it again went into military production in World War II, producing armor

A formidable task awaits these two men, ready to put their Atkins Saw to work.

plates for tanks. Wartime development of a segmental cold saw to reduce costs of shells and torpedoes proved valuable to the company after its return to normal production.

When H.C. Atkins died in 1944, the company was run by his two sons until 1952, when it passed from family ownership with acquisition by the Borg-Warner Corporation amidst a long, damaging strike. Eight years later, Borg-Warner moved its Atkins Saw Division to Greenville, Mississippi, where the city had constructed a building and offered a long-term lease with a property tax moratorium as inducement. When Nicholson bought the division in 1966, it was producing fourteen major lines with

Playing a "musical saw" frequently featured introduction of new Atkins products at hardware stores.

so many variations in sizes and styles that records showed manufacturing instructions for thirty thousand separate items.

In 1968, Nicholson File Company took part in a joint venture with some citizens of Mexico in establishing a manufacturing plant. The company owned 49 percent of Nicholson Mexicana S.A. de C.V. in Tlalnepantla. A decision on other plans was forced quite unexpectedly by the state of Pennsylvania when it condemned Nicholson's Philadelphia plant for construction of a freeway. Faced with a choice of whether or not to remain in that city, the company studied alternatives, then elected to rebuild there. Typical of the times, costs far exceeded projections but the new Philadelphia plant was completed on schedule, opening in 1969. That same year, Paul C. Nicholson, Jr., resigned the presidency to become chairman and was succeeded by George Williams, who had been with the company since 1965 as vice president of operations. For the first time in nearly a century the chief operating officer was elected from outside the Nicholson family.

As Nicholson entered the 1970s, it no longer was a single purpose manufacturer, although 85 percent of its business continued to be files and related tools. Little change was made in the policy of producing small volume specialties, and the company catalog listed sixty-two hundred separate items, most available in many sizes. Duplication of manufacturing led to thoughts of closing the Anderson Plant.

21

"Cooper's Comeback"

After the acquisition by Cooper, consummated officially on October 31, 1972, Globe, Arcade, and K & F brand names were phased out in favor of consolidation under the name Nicholson. Because of high recognition, the Black Diamond file name was continued, but in "dual-branded" form; the Nicholson name was placed on one side, Black Diamond on the other. An immediate result in some sections of the continent illustrated the value hand tool customers placed on brand names. "We had an adjustment problem for a while," said Ray Sokol. "Before the merger, you couldn't sell anything but a Black Diamond file below the Mason-Dixon Line. Talk about an image, they would reject any other kind, just out of tradition, I guess. After we dual-branded them, we had a hard time convincing people they were getting the exact same file we always sold them. Some of them swore they could tell a difference." Eric Carr noted similar situations in Canada, but not for long. "There were a few raised eyebrows," he said, "but the transition took place without much upheaval; and it certainly was a pleasure for us, because we didn't have to process all those different brands, try to keep them separate, and hold cut blanks in soft condition until branding time."

The number of basic files and related products was slashed from thirty thousand to three thousand, cutting off sales to the three or four persons a year who ordered bread rasps, used to eliminate burnt crust. Saws were limited to four lines — circular saws, hack saws, hand saws and band saws. But the standard file, still the best seller among Nicholson products, remained identical in appearance to those pictured in William Nicholson's famous file treatise of 1878.

Plants in Canada, Holland, and Mexico became part of the Cooper Group International. "Acquiring Nicholson was a big breakthrough internationally," said Don MacPherson. "The company had pioneered world sales more than a century ago; we have letters delineating policy problems they had in 1870 with their trade in India. Believe me, they found niches in agricultural markets everywhere, including remote bush country. We discovered that peasants sharpening knives or machetes or

195

whatever cutting tools they used in their particular areas couldn't read brand names, but could recognize Nicholson's crossed-file trademark as assurance of something that would last ten or twelve times longer than any other file. If a competitor's box contained twelve files, you might find a dozen different quality levels. Not with Nicholson. The same top quality was there in every file. We didn't have to tell people that; they told us. That file had become an institution in agrarian economies. Nicholson had a tremendous international reputation that opened some new avenues for the whole Cooper Group."

International headquarters in London directed an extensive sales and distribution network throughout England and Western Europe, The Balkans, the Middle East and continental Africa. This, in turn, made possible more efficient utilization of manufacturing capacity whereby the Lufkin plant in Holland produced some Weller products, while Weller plants in Germany and England produced some Lufkin products. During the year, a plant was established in Australia to manufacture Lufkin and Weller products for that country and New Zealand, and a sales and distribution system was organized to serve the broader Australian area.

Although only two months of Nicholson's sales figures were included in the 1972 annual report, The Cooper Group accounted for about 38 percent of total corporate sales. Earnings rose from the shattering 1971 plunge to a respectable $2.52 per common share, beginning an upward trend that would continue unbroken through the remainder of the 1970s and into the next decade.

In a year end article entitled "Cooper's Comeback," *Financial World* magazine observed, "It isn't often a stock will hit a new high only a matter of months after it has trimmed its dividend. But that's what's happened at Cooper Industries, Inc., which cut the payout from 35¢ to 20¢ quarterly dividends in March. Since then, things have picked up nicely and the Houston-based firm's stock recently posted a new peak for '72 on the Big Board."

Cooper entered 1973 a more balanced company than at any other time in its 140-year history. Despite problems in the machinery segment, Miller believed the company was well prepared to cope with uncertainties that still existed, and The Cooper Group had shown it could provide a holding action until the basic business could revive. Growth of the aircraft service business seemed assured by projected statistics. Frustrations surrounded the anticipated Alyeska Trans-Alaska Pipeline business, but Cooper had sold ten turbine engines to drive oil pumps there and was favored to get more orders in that new market if barriers to its progress could be removed. The past year had produced little more than further environmental reviews in federal courts, while the nation's biggest oil and gas discovery remained a frozen asset. One thing that might hasten its thaw was a brewing energy crisis that observers in the oil and gas industry correctly predicted as about to come to a boil.

────────────

Outside members of the board — men not directly associated with the company's day-to-day operations and in positions to make objective comparisons with other leading industrial organizations — identified the willingness to transfer leadership smoothly as one important factor in Cooper's success. Certainly, Gene Miller assigned high priority to such transitions, having witnessed management uncertainties early in his career. Severe adjustments sometimes were required when plans did not work out exactly as expected, but Cooper's management evolution progressed without the jarring repercussions that make business page headlines. Within the changing corporate structure brought about by growth and merger, operational officers from acquired companies were assimilated into existing management; performance, not personal allegiance, was the criterion for success at all levels.

In early 1973, Robert Cizik was elected president and chief operating officer of Cooper Industries. Gene Miller continued as chairman and chief executive officer. Other corporate offices were held by Alan Riedel, senior vice president, administration; Bill Rector, senior vice president, operations; Dewain Cross, vice president, finance; Tom Naugle, vice president, planning; and Roger Scott, secretary and general counsel. The newest member to the group was Mr. Cross, who came to Cooper from Arthur Young & Company in 1966 and held positions of director of accounting and taxation, assistant controller, and treasurer, before being promoted to vice president in 1972.

Energy shortages, well known throughout history but not yet accepted seriously by the public nor by several governmental agencies, were receiving less attention than expected, causing Cooper's energy services business to continue waiting in the wings. Natural gas prices were rising, however, as Cooper's new president had predicted two years earlier and the company's product development continued to emphasize fuel efficiency. Cooper-Bessemer division adapted the Rolls Royce RB-211 jet engine, used on the L-1011 Airbus for gas transmission on a Canadian pipeline, and expected it to become popular also in Alaska and Europe.

Hand tools and aircraft services now represented well over half of total sales. Both those areas were growing, and each would soon be bolstered by another acquisition. Southwest Airmotive, which had considered merging with Dallas Airmotive before the latter joined Cooper, was interested in renewing discussions. Following the deaths of two principal executives, the company considered itself in a position to be acquired and it asked Cooper to make an offer. The company, with executive offices and primary manufacturing facilities in Dallas, served the aircraft industry through overhaul and repair of engines, installation of electronic equipment, and a modern Love Field terminal for private and corporate airplanes. It also was a major distributor of engines and parts. In 1968, it had branched into another area of jet service by acquiring Executive Aircraft Services, Inc. The latter, based at Redbird Airport and also in Dallas, designed, installed, modified, and maintained business jet airplane interiors and avionics systems. Unquestionably, Southwest Airmotive could supplement Cooper's relatively new, but steadily growing aircraft services business.

Cooper offered a financial package, pending further study to confirm certain assumptions, but it was rejected by Southwest on the basis of having better offers from other companies. When those did not materialize, a mutually satisfactory arrangement was worked out, and Cooper acquired the company for $26,057,000 in cash.

Southwest Airmotive was founded in 1932 by Edward F. "Doc" Booth, West Point graduate, Air Corps veteran, and flying enthusiast. With financial backing from his rancher-oilman father-in-law, Charles Pettit, he opened Edward F. Booth, Inc., to provide "airline maintenance for the private owner." Despite the depression and its obvious threats to new business, oilmen were becoming interested in private airplanes. From such early jobs as repairing a cracked-up Stinson and repainting a bi-wing Stearman, the business grew enough that operations were moved into a new building in 1934. Booth took on a new partner, and the company became Booth-Henning, Inc. An instrument shop with one calibration bench evolved into a facility for complete airframe, instrument and propeller maintenance, and engine overhaul for what Booth described as "about everything that flew." Among regular clients were pilot-actor Wallace Beery and pianist Jose Iturbi, who would fly into Love Field "just to have the spark plugs changed," according to Booth.

The company became an authorized Lockheed service station in the late 1930s, and in 1940 its name was changed again, to Southwest Airmotive Company. Winston Castleberry, George W. Jalonick, and J. Harlan Ray became principal owners. Castleberry and Jalonick actually ran the company as vice presidents, with Ray serving as chairman while pursuing other interests. It was not until Ray died in 1970 that Jalonick was named chairman and Castleberry president and chief executive officer. By then the company had a jet-service complex on thirty-five acres of land, a modern business terminal, and a distribution division with sales offices in major cities of the Southwest and West. The following year Castleberry suffered a fatal heart attack while playing golf, and was succeeded by Lou V. Emery, who remained president until the sale to Cooper.

Emery had been a founder and head of Executive Aircraft, started in 1945 as Harry M. Chase, Inc., to convert military Lodestars into corporate airplanes. As trends in corporate aviation leaned toward larger aircraft, the company moved from surplus to airplane conversion. In 1968, eight months before it merged with Southwest Airmotive, it formed the avionics division to engineer and install navigation, communication, radar, and guidance systems, often more extensive than those in airlines.

———————————

After the acquisition by Cooper, Southwest Airmotive was combined with Dallas Airmotive to form Cooper Airmotive, Inc., a wholly owned subsidiary of the parent company. Robert Lambert, the former vice president of operations of Cooper-Bessemer, was named president of Cooper Airmotive. While that was taking place, The Cooper Group was just as busy adding a new line of screwdrivers, nutdrivers, and other small tools through acquisition of Xcelite, Inc., a 52-year-old manufacturing company located in the Buffalo suburb of Orchard Park, New York. Like most other companies that had joined the group, Xcelite had facilities badly in need of modernization, but a brand name known and highly respected in specialized fields of electronics. Veteran management leaders were looking toward retirement, and Cooper was able to formulate a purchase plan that would meet their needs. The acquisition took place on July 31, 1973.

22

Xcelite

It has been said that the decade of the Roaring Twenties was named for the sound of automobiles bringing changes in lives and livelihoods. Both the thrill and the practicality of rapidly increasing mobility were spurred by the end of war and the beginning of prosperity. Not surprisingly, the automobile industry leaped ahead, like a Model "T", toward first place in American production. Entrepreneurs reacted by relating their own ideas to the obvious trend. Among them were founders of the Park Metalware Company of Orchard Park, New York, a suburb of Buffalo.

No specific event identified the company's origination. The plan emerged within a group of friends and relatives, all residents of Orchard Park, who pooled their money, incorporated on September 2, 1921, and started business in a small barn that had served as a machine shop for one of their number, John Zilliox. An expert machinist and prolific inventor, Zilliox was a logical choice for president. Sales expertise was provided by F.B. "Birney" Farrington, a thirty-year-old former Dodge Motor Car salesman. John Petre, a carpenter and son-in-law of the president, was plant superintendent. The president's son, Arthur Zilliox, worked as a machinist. Two other investors, Farrington's brother Lewis, and their brother-in-law, George Colby, were not active in manufacturing operations. However, Colby, a bank cashier, was financial advisor and it was he who first suggested converting the Zilliox machine shop into a manufacturing plant.

Business was automotive oriented. Among the first products were expansion metal carriers for running boards, battery connectors, a flat-headed adjustable wrench for which John Zilliox had a patent, and a tire iron for which Birney Farrington somehow acquired manufacturing rights. But the youthful company did not put all its trust in supplying the motor car industry. It also manufactured toy tin boats, bottle cappers, and custom-made tools and dies. With a small machine-shop operation, the company never manufactured many products at one time. Instead, production shifted back and forth, matching sales fluctuations and displaying what a member of the group described as "a willingness to try anything."

In its second year the company sold stock to about ten other persons, among them Howard Langworthy, who would later serve a brief term as president. Then in 1923, it bought land and constructed a wooden structure on Thorn Avenue, where it expanded gradually through the years. The most consistent company product on the market was its Gillette solderless electrical connector, used by utility companies to connect service taps with main power lines. Strong and inexpensive, the connectors also prevented the possible shock effect of using solder to secure electrical couplings. Meanwhile, the company was selling screwdrivers made by another manufacturer. Although they had wooden handles, those tools did not protect fully against electrical shock.

With experience in making shock-resistant electrical connectors, company leaders decided to apply similar logic to screwdrivers. The result was a first step toward international recognition, although it would take many years to reach that status. In 1925, Park Metalware manufactured the world's first plastic-handled screwdriver. Company management was not driven by visions of widespread recognition. President Zilliox preferred inventing to manufacturing. A quiet, relaxed, former wrestler, he enjoyed the comfort of his drawing board where he sketched original plans leading to patents on gear arrangements, a boiler cleaner, and a wide variety of tools. Those most important to the company evolved from his special interest in the interchangeable use of parts.

The formal patent description of one new idea in 1930 is familiar now to even the unhandiest of handymen: "This invention relates to a wrench and more particularly to an open end machine wrench in which a plurality of open end machine wrench heads having different sized jaws are employed in connection with the same handle, thereby decreasing the cost of a set of such wrenches, as well as permitting the convenient, compact nesting of the same in a kit."

That same year, John Zilliox sold all his company stock and started his own small machine shop, explaining to friends, "Whenever I have more than four employees, I am ready to cut back." Many years later, when he was in his nineties, Zilliox still sketched imaginative new designs. For exercise he would make one trip a month to downtown Buffalo, riding the twelve miles by bus, get off to walk two or three miles up Main Street, have lunch, then walk back to the same bus stop for the return trip home. Stockholder Howard Langworthy succeeded Zilliox as president, although the company was essentially managed by the other men. Two years later, Birney Farrington was elected president. John Petre, who patented several inventions of his own, continued as plant superintendent and treasurer. Langworthy was named secretary and Arthur Zilliox vice president.

The small company barely survived America's Great Depression. Even its own auditor admitted to officers that he fully expected it to go bankrupt. Good products were of no value without customers. Sales were so infrequent that management leaders cut their own salaries to minimum levels. At one point the president's salary was thirty dollars per week, with others adjusted accordingly. Credit became extended to the limit and payments from customers were slow to arrive. The determining factor in meeting a weekly payroll often was the content of Friday's mail. In a small town, friends sometimes helped each other. For one critical order, the company needed payroll money to make the product. A bank loan for that payroll could be extended only if proof could be shown that the order was "in transit." But how could you ship something that was not yet manufactured? To solve the problem, a friendly Railway Express agent signed the receipt shipment. The receipt was then used to get a loan which enabled the company to hire men who produced the tools that quickly made up the shipment. Such was the Great Depression.

Even while the business struggled to survive, two related events brought reason for optimism. The company introduced the nutdriver, and met a man named John Olsen. The word *nutdriver* was coined by Park Metalware for its version of a hand speed wrench, an effort-saving tool whose invention was claimed by several companies. John Olsen was a manufacturer's representative from Cleveland, Ohio, and a former partner in one of the first radio stores in Pittsburgh. In 1936, he attended an electronics parts show in Chicago, where Park Metalware Company had an exhibit. One member of management described it as "a last desperate effort before collapsing." Olsen expressed a strong desire to represent the company in Ohio. Park Metalware had always marketed strictly through manufacturers' representatives, so the new appointment was made on the spot. Immediately, Olsen collared friends attending the show, brought them to the Park Metalware display, and talked several of them into filing orders.

The company had not seriously considered electronics as a specialized sales field even though it was aware of the growth of radio. But prodded by Olsen and already armed with suitable product lines, it set out to capture the exciting new market. Nationally, the manufacture of radios and related apparatus grew from a $15 million to a $338 million business in the 1930s. Industrial electrical appliances went from $46 million to $976 million. Park Metalware Company never regretted its decision.

Manufacturers' representatives reported the needs of customers, and Park Metalware supplied them. John Olsen became a stockholder and a director. He attended each directors' meeting carrying a list of new product suggestions from which he and his colleagues could make selections. Some never made it past the first debate, but others, such as color-coded handles for nutdrivers, became instant hits in the marketplace. By 1940, Olsen was chairman of the board although he remained Ohio sales representative and did not become a part of plant operations.

A Special Tools Division was launched in 1941, providing variations of standard tools that would provide special angles and edges for changing models of electronic equipment. An adjustable socket wrench had been given the trade name "Xcel." The latest plastic handle was named "Xcelite," simply as a means of identification. Both names became well known in the radio and electronic industries, if not with the public. The company concentrated on making high-quality items for professional use, not entering the low-price, mass marketing field. When World War II forced a temporary detour in the nation's industrial direction, Park Metalware still had only eighteen employees. Although it maintained its regular line of screwdrivers, nutdrivers, and specialty tools during the war, selling most of them to the Air Corps, the company adjusted its main sights toward munitions. Park Metalware was selected to produce steel grips, ammunition feeders, and air cooling tubes for machine guns, subcontracting through the Buffalo Arms Company. Plant superintendent John Petre secured the contracts after two other machine companies had attempted unsuccessfully to meet complicated production standards. Employment rose to nearly one hundred, half of whom were on part time schedules. Park Metalware's success helped broaden its reputation, but directors realized the need to prepare for postwar competition.

Peacetime reconversion proved to be a slow process, not on machines, but in the market. Most manufacturers' representatives had become inactive. Many of those who remained were still automotive specialists, and the company clearly saw its future in the electronics field. Arch Warden, an eastern New Yorker who married the daughter of George Colby during the war and joined the company in 1945, remembered his first sales call on a large radio manufacturer in Chicago. "The president of that company was miffed because he previously had inquired about purchasing Xcelite and Xcel tools, and had been referred to an automotive distributor," Warden said. "Afterward, he never let me live that one down." Warden was named sales manager the following year, with responsibility for reaching electronics distributors throughout the country. At the same time, the company began molding its own handles and developing new products such as a handle with spring attachment accommodating an assortment of blades.

The company enjoyed a popularity within the electronics trade because it developed a continuous flow of new shapes and sizes of tools as they were required. Park Metalware contracted with other manufacturers to expand production of such items as Xcelite pliers and adjustable wrenches, which it sold along with its own screwdrivers and nutdrivers.

As business grew, the brand name eclipsed the company name. Much of the incoming mail was addressed to the "Xcelite Company." Moreover, the Park Metalware name was causing confusion. Orders were received for pots and pans. One person telephoned to purchase a well cover. So in 1951, the thirtieth anniversary of its founding, Park Metalware became Xcelite Incorporated.

The 1950s brought a steady growth as television added new impetus to the electronics industry. Often faced with problems in meeting customer demands, Xcelite nevertheless moved forward conservatively. Explained one officer, "When most of management has been through a devastating depression, you don't take sudden big steps — you take hesitant small ones." New products were again introduced, however, and plant facilities were expanded. Miniature screwdrivers and nutdrivers with blades molded into the handles became important items in an expanding product line.

In 1960, the board of directors elected Arch Warden president. F.B. Farrington became chairman of the board, actually entering semiretirement (he died in 1962). Clarence F. Schwabel, who had become increasingly active since 1947, was elected vice president and treasurer. A son-in-law of John Petre, he had started his association with the company on a part time basis while operating a private accounting practice in Orchard Park. The Xcelite name spread worldwide. With a high priority on overseas marketing, the company advertised in export publications and set up sales channels through manufacturers' agents by mail. In many areas of the world, Xcelite became better known than companies fifty times its size. "Sometimes visiting customers were startled," Warden recalled. "They would come in from some place like New Zealand and look at the plant. Then, invariably, they would ask to see the main plant. They couldn't believe they were looking at it."

As before, Xcelite did not opt for mass-market retail selling. Sometimes, however, company officials recognized these designs on discount house shelves. One foreign manufacturer made a screwdriver set identical to a popular Xcelite item in every aspect except the quality of material. Even a tiny hole in the handle was matched precisely. Retail price of the copy was 99 cents. Xcelite's own materials and production cost of the original was $1.50.

As the 1970s approached, Xcelite was the largest employer in Orchard Park with approximately 125 persons working full time. It leased warehouses across the country and in Canada. Hand tools were sold in hundreds of sizes, most of them to radio, television, electronics, and industrial supply distributors. The company made screwdrivers and nutdrivers, still filling out its line by purchasing pliers, adjustable wrenches, electricians' knives, reamers, socket sets, seizers, and other tools from other manufacturers. All corporate stock was held privately when the company was sold to Cooper.

23

The Energy Crisis

Completion of the Xcelite acquisition was just one of a succession of news events describing The Cooper Group's exceptional year, in which sales increased 90 percent over 1972. Others announced new products in existing lines, groundbreaking for a new file plant in Sorocaba, Brazil, plans for expansion of Nicholson's plant in Philadelphia, and the beginning of two major construction projects, one a sixty-thousand-square foot distribution center at the group's headquarters site in Apex, North Carolina, the other a new Crescent plant in Sumter, South Carolina, less than one hundred miles south of the distribution center. The latter news was afforded a particularly warm reception in a Sumter *Daily Item* newspaper editorial.

> John T. Jones, chairman of the Sumter County Development Board, hailed the new industry (Crescent), which will hire 400 persons, as a "blue chipper" that will have a substantial impact on the economy of the Sumter area. The plant's decision to locate in Sumter was the result of a joint effort by the Chamber of Commerce and the Sumter County Development Board, in cooperation with the State Development Board.

But good news of any kind, even at a local level, faded quickly into obscurity as one event captured headlines across the nation. A new crisis was born. This time it was energy, and Americans found plenty of time to read all about it while they waited in line at neighborhood gasoline service stations.

Shortages of heating oil had forced midwinter shutdown of some schools and factories early in the year. Industrial voices had warned of an end to cheap energy. Trade associations had published studies showing the opposing trends in consumption and production. But it took an Arab-Israeli war twelve thousand miles away to make the energy squeeze hurt. When it came, the pain was sudden and easily diagnosed: the source was an October 17, 1973, announcement by eleven Arab states of an embargo on crude oil sales to countries deemed friendly to Israel. Primary offenders were the United States and The Netherlands, but before it ended, the energy crisis became a worldwide affliction. How could a leading industrial nation like the United States get caught in such a crisis? Was the government to blame? Was it a business plot? Was it even real? Volumes could be written, and have been written on the "sudden" problem, but William O. Doub, then commissioner of the U.S. Atomic Energy Commission, managed to sum it up in a single paragraph in a report to the General Assembly of the World Future Society:

> In ten short years we have shifted from a cavalier indifference toward energy to a preoccupation with the subject, and our energy status has changed from cornucopia to crisis. There was no conspiracy. The crisis was not contrived. It was spawned by a sacrifice of long-range interest to secure short-run objectives — or, if you will, a case of the irresistible force of accelerating energy demands colliding with the irrefutable principles of finite supply and "you get what you pay for." Artificially low prices were achieved either by omitting the full costs of energy production — especially the steadily increasing costs of minimizing environmental impact — or by regulating popular prices, as in the case of natural gas. The situation was further exacerbated when overdue, but to some degree unexpected, environmental controls forced the use of less available fuels. Then came the catalyst that precipitated the most recent chaotic energy situation — the Arab oil embargo.

Society was forced to reorient its way of thinking about, and coping with, what was finally recognized as an energy evolution, not a momentary fright. Controversies concerning fair prices, ecological impact, and the extent of government control would by no means end, but they might at least be based on a more realistic set of rules. (One point was made when an FPC-approved hike in intrastate and interstate natural gas pricing was followed by a 33 percent gain in gas-well exploration, compared with the same period of 1972.) If Cooper Industries wanted to extract a specific, earthy message from the torrent of philosophizing, it might find an endorsement of the earlier decision to improve upon, rather than abandon the fuel-efficient reciprocating compressor.

The annual report characterized 1973 as "a most successful and gratifying year," establishing records in sales ($320,392,000) and earnings ($4.04). It concluded that "while it is gratifying to report a return to previously high earnings levels, it is also satisfying to note that more than three-fourths of these earnings came from our hand tools and aircraft services businesses — activities that were not a part of Cooper when previous records were set. We are assured by the belief that we have built a strong base of highly efficient businesses which are relatively more resistant to the fluctuations of an uncertain economy, and that we have properly prepared for an upturn in the fortunes of our more cyclical business. In short, we believe we present a company that is not only more diversified in its business interests, but also one that is fully capable of adapting to the ever-changing environment in which it must exist."

In looking ahead to the challenge of setting new records, there was reason also to notice a retirement in Mt. Vernon that reminded one of the company's roots. Sam Trott, a machinist at the Cooper-Bessemer plant there, retired after forty-six years on the job. He was the last employee to have been with the C. & G. Cooper Company before its merger with Bessemer Gas Engine Company, having started as a shaper in the small machine shop in 1927. The retirement was duly recorded by the *Mt. Vernon News,* which quoted Trott as saying he had "worked all over the place" and was the first to operate several machines installed by the company over the years.

Attempts to deal with energy shortages in the early months of 1974 brought dramatic changes. Nations over reacted in making adjustments to new high prices of fuel, sometimes cutting back on factory production, then tried to reverse that trend to meet increased demand for goods. Balance of payments among countries bounded out of control as prices at Middle Eastern wellheads jumped 100 percent. The energy problem clearly added a lasting dimension to future business relations among nations. In the United States, the economy drifted into a paradox of suffering the highest inflation rate in several decades, coupled with a deepening business recession. That unlikely combination would also become a long-range concern in business computations.

Cooper found that most traditional concepts of costs, prices, and relative performance were painfully distorted by the new "shortage economy." Yet, the embargo scare had not been without its benefits to the company. Cooper Ajax was soon operating at full capacity, as domestic crude oil price increases prompted development of previously uneconomical oil and gas reserves. Compressors and pumps were sold on an allocation basis well into coming months.

Congress, with help from the White House, finally had settled the Alaskan pipeline dispute in 1973 by directing agencies to issue construction permits in keeping with the National Environmental Policy Act. Within a year, Cooper received an order from Alyeska totaling more than $15 million for fourteen Coberra gas turbines. The order, representing all pumping requirements for Phase II of the Trans-Alaska project, was in addition to ten similar units delivered previously.

Before the year ended, the company also received orders for seventeen centrifugal compressors to be used for gas transmission in Russia, and four Coberra turbines for a feeder pipeline between London and the Leman North Sea gas production field.

With previous administrative problems solved, Cooper-Bessemer, Ajax, Penn Pump, and CB/Southern divisions were organized into an Energy Services Group. The consolidation facilitated coordination of marketing and sales, manufacturing, resource procurement, facilities planning, and product development, thereby improving prospects for increased profitability from anticipated sales growth. Separately, the divisions had sold power and compression equipment ranging from fifty to forty thousand horsepower, and services to many of the same companies. The group plan established a worldwide marketing organization, using the combination of skilled sales personnel, distributors, and agents to offer a wide range of products and services wherever they were needed.

For the Energy Services Group, 1974 seemed to mark the beginning of a return to pre-1970 prominence, and, indeed, year-end figures would reveal a healthy 70 percent increase over 1973.

In listing the characteristics of a successful corporation, President Cizik often included the ability to adjust effectively when faced with unexpected situations. Cooper had a chance to measure its own aptitude in that respect during April of 1974.

The test arose in Roebling, New Jersey, where a branch of Colorado Fuel & Iron (CF&I) produced a high-carbon strip steel for Lufkin power tapes. The plant's primary business was manufacturing heavy wire rope — it had supplied cables for the Brooklyn Bridge, for instance — and the high carbon "flatwire," rolled thin, hardened, and tempered precisely to Lufkin's quality standards, was produced in a separate section of the building. Competitors had fallen by the wayside over the years, leaving the New Jersey manufacturer with a U.S. monopoly in the specialized line. No wonder a shock wave went through Cooper Group headquarters when Vice President Gilchrist received a telephone call from CF&I, informing him that "We are closing down production of our 1095 steel."

With no other supplier readily available, Cooper looked for alternatives and found only two. One was to buy from the only other source in the world, located in Germany and certain to be an expensive choice. The other, determined to be more desirable, was to purchase the strip-steel portion of CF&I operations. "We made a deal with the owner to buy the equipment and operate it right there in the plant," Gilchrist said. "Then legal problems forced the owner to change his mind, and we were given ninety days to move 1,250 tons of such equipment as 150-foot tempering lines and huge brick-lined annealing furnaces to another plant, which we didn't have."

After searching rapidly for a feasible site, the company located and purchased a former auto parts manufacturing plant near its Nicholson saw operation in Greenville, Mississippi, then somehow met its deadline in moving the massive equipment from Roebling to Greenville. Three months after the move, the plant conversion was completed, employees were trained, and Cooper Steel went on line. Without adding it to the list of guidelines for acquisition, Cooper nonetheless admitted to another criterion for growth — desperation.

Moving heavy equipment became a way of life for The Cooper Group that year. The new Crescent manufacturing facility in Sumter, South Carolina, was finished and screwdriver production was shifted from the Jamestown, New York, plant, beginning a gradual changeover lasting through 1976. Moving equipment one thousand miles while phasing out operations in one plant and starting them in another created what Manager Len Bloomquist understated as "a challenge," but deliveries to the Group's distribution center suffered only slightly. The Jamestown plant was not shut down completely. Drop hammer and die forging operations remained there.

The beautiful new $10 million Sumter plant, encompassing eight acres under one roof, contained well over $1 million in new, highly automated machinery, in addition to that brought from Jamestown. Most of the special purpose machines were developed internally. Henry Sievers, chief engineer of Crescent who had joined the company in 1943, helped develop some of the new designs. "Our greatest thrusts have come from being acquired by Cooper, and moving to this plant," he said. "Now we have a chance to really show what we can do."

The Cooper Group also completed expansion of its Nicholson Philadelphia plant, and moved corporate headquarters to Two Houston Center in 1974.

In a year-end summary of Cooper operations, *Barron's* concluded that the company was weathering the unstable economy and benefitting from the new energy awareness:

> So far the slump has failed to make a noticeable dent in Cooper's operations. A hint of a dip in sales of hand tools appeared recently as some distributors began cutting inventories, but part of this is believed to be seasonal. True, a prolonged and deep recession could cut into hand tool sales. One favorable factor for Cooper, though, is the strong acceptance of various Cooper brands, which are among the best known in the hand tools business. Cooper's energy services business, however, currently is the beneficiary of the worldwide energy crunch. . . . About a year ago demand began picking up, and indications are that volume will continue rising for some time. . . . Both hand tools and energy services are benefiting from higher prices as well as operating efficiencies. Extensive relocation of hand tools plants to new facilities has resulted in lower unit production costs. By the end of next year the company expects to have all of hand tools production in new plants. Facilities turning out pumps, compressors and turbines also have been modernized in recent years, accompanied by reductions in overhead costs, improved management controls, and elimination of some unprofitable lines. . . . Fortunately, too, most of its aircraft services revenues have been coming from sources either unaffected or favorably affected (such as oil companies) by the energy crisis.

In the spring of 1975, President Robert Cizik became the tenth man in Cooper's 142-year history to hold the position of chief executive officer.

Eugene Miller remained active in company operations, serving as chairman of the board and of the executive committee. In one sense, the change reflected the widespread management evolution throughout industry, in which top executive responsibilities were shifting from leaders with engineering backgrounds to those whose training and experience were focused on areas of finance and law. But presenting Cooper's transition strictly as an example of changing eras not only would be attempting to fit an event into a convenient historical pattern, it also would elicit protest from President Cizik, who liked to quote Mark Twain as saying, "Few things are harder to put up with than the annoyance of a good example." Miller and Cizik had worked together closely in the company's recent transformation, and they would continue to do so during and after the transfer of executive authority.

Cooper's new CEO had discovered early in life that he wanted to pursue a career involving some degree of finance. Born in Scranton, Pennsylvania, he was one of five children whose father had worked as a coal miner since the age of fourteen. In the early 1940s, when Bob was twelve years old, the family moved to Norwalk, Connecticut, where proximity to a heavy concentration of defense plants offered better employment opportunities. Academic achievement came easily to Cizik, and a special love of mathematics led him to the University of Connecticut, where he majored in accounting and economics. Following graduation, he fulfilled a dream of becoming an accountant by joining Price Waterhouse in New York City. Soon afterward, he married Jane Morin, whom he had met in high school, and the young couple moved to Newark, New Jersey, within easy commuting distance from his job.

Having been a member of ROTC during his college days, Cizik was on his first job less than a year when he was called to active Air Force duty in 1954. With the United States still involved in mutual defense affairs in South Korea, he was converted from civilian to lieutenant, then given an immediate overseas assignment in such rapid order that he was stopped by a military policeman on a California Air Force base for having his officer's bars attached sideways on his new uniform. In Tokyo, however, the intended Korean assignment was stopped short when a lieutenant colonel checked Cizik's academic record. The Air Force was just introducing double-entry accounting into its system, and he was a recent college graduate who must obviously have the necessary basic expertise. With few questions asked, a change of assignment was arranged; instead of continuing on to Seoul, Lieutenant Cizik headed for Air Defense Force headquarters in Nagoya, Japan, where he was thrown into a major's job with responsibility for accounting procedures in Japan, Okinawa, Korea, and all other Far Eastern areas of U.S. operations. It was his first taste of management, and he discovered he savored the flavor.

During frequent travels to other bases in the Far East, Cizik became increasingly intrigued with the idea of broadening his career beyond accounting. With the encouragement of experienced Air Force officers, he applied for admission to the Harvard Graduate School of Business Administration. The application was accepted at the end of his military tour of duty, and he went on to receive an M.B.A. degree with "high distinction," picking up the honor of being elected a Baker Scholar along the way. Having become extremely interested in financial management, he looked around for an opportunity that would expand his knowledge in that area. The search led to Standard Oil of New Jersey, a company in the forefront of financial analysis as a core of management strategy. Three years in that company's Treasurer's Department were rewarding and enjoyable, but his career plans were rechanneled once again when Gene Miller and others convinced him an even greater challenge would be found in organizing an effective acquisition plan for Cooper.

A strong leader who spiced incisive observations with humor, Cizik believed in delegating responsibility, but without a formalized chain of command. "Everyone likes to categorize," he said. "It's convenient to draw an organization chart with units that lead to groups that in turn lead to some sort of business sector, giving you a nice pyramid. But it's easy to become obsessed with style — form for the sake of form, perfection for the sake of perfection. I think one should strive for perfection, but not get hung up with achieving it overnight, or with sacrificing accomplishment for form. Of course, a company needs some kind of organizational structure in writing. But getting too formal with terms and lines of authority can stifle thinking. I will even go so far as to say that keeping things upset from time to time makes people happier."

Flexibility, the president believed, enabled a multimarket company like Cooper to move according to needs, "because not everything will be clicking at the same time." A company with all of its areas tied to the same general market cycles could not have the "movement back and forth between businesses as you need them," he said, explaining that "if you have no choice in what you must do, you have no strategy. All you do in that case is respond to each demand. The only way you can lay out a strategy is to have the opportunity to say, 'well we'll take certain losses, or we'll spend money here while we invest there.' Without alternatives, you can't have a strategy."

Cooper's successful build-up of its hand tools business during a prolonged depression of energy services had already provided one positive assessment of the strategy. It was now time to prove that the "back and forth" movement described by Cizik would be equally effective with the emphasis reversed. Heavy capital investment in The Cooper Group peaked out just as the compressor business was in a position the president referred to as "ready for another take-off." Consequently, the flow of capital expenditures was rerouted toward energy services.

Interestingly, a teeter-tottering economy seemed to synchronize the change as if it had been designed as a test case for the company's strategy, the rise of energy services prosperity balanced by a lowering of demand for hand tools. Cooper had experienced some softening of hand tools markets, through the "dip in sales" reported in *Barron's*. But the first few months of 1975, later recorded by *Americana* as one of the worst periods for the U.S. economy since the Great Depression, drove hand tools sales well below anticipated levels.

Cooper Group Sales Vice President Stevens referred to the problem as "the most precipitous drop in the history of business." Although hesitant to make specific judgments, he pointed to the ability of well-financed hardware and industrial supply distribution companies, most of them family owned, to build large warehouse inventories as a hedge against inflation. "They discovered at the end of 1974 that they had more inventory than they could sell to customers suddenly hurting for cash," he said. "As a result, our business has gone down with a boom. Ordinarily it drifts up and down slightly, never with a drop of more than 8 percent at the very most. Now it's plunged something like 20 percent."

Stevens was concerned, but confident that the setback would be brief, lasting only until inventories needed to be replenished, because, "recession or no recession, people are going to need hand tools — whether it's because they have money to spend, or because they have to spend the least amount possible to keep the old equipment running." His analysis was confirmed the next year when hand tools sales rebounded even sharper than they had dropped. Sufficient gains were in fact recorded throughout the American economy in the last half of 1975 to change the year's earlier pale image into one of strong recovery.

The simultaneous recovery of energy services, the decline of hand tools sales, and the stable volume of aircraft services, with an overall 32 percent increase in corporate net income, proved that Cooper was strengthening its defenses against external economic assault. Miller and Cizik urged stockholders to measure the company's success by "overall performance — how our three business areas interact over time — not performance of any one business area at a specific point in time."

Cooper's earlier decision to stick with the generally forsaken reciprocating compressor began paying reassuring dividends, as the cost of natural gas reached $1.20 per mcf in mid-1975, showing no sign of leveling out for some time to come. But management was less concerned with patting itself on the back than with stretching the lead it had obtained in that segment of business (it had installed more than 40 percent of the horsepower requirements for gas transmission in North America). The new Quad integral engine compressor was introduced, along with another generation of the Coberra centrifugal unit.

In keeping with its policy of focusing investments on areas of greatest profitability, the company discontinued CB/Southern operations, selling its plants, facilities, and real estate, and transferring the work force to another compressor packager to handle commitments on a remaining backlog of orders. CB/Southern had performed well in its heyday, and it had provided a colorful episode in the company's history. But the market had become marginally profitable, spread thin by such a proliferation of compressor packagers that for a manufacturer, packaging evolved into what Cizik described as "a green stamp business; if you buy my compressor, I'll package it for you." Selling the assets of CB/Southern enabled Cooper to reinvest in higher return projects.

Energy Services Group was restructured and renamed, with cessation of CB/Southern and the combination term of "Penjax". In a booklet distributed to customers, the revamped operating division announced, "We've got it all together," with the brand name of Ajax, Cooper-Bessemer and Penn Pump continuing, but under a new banner, "Cooper Energy Services." Division officers included Thomas E. Naugle, president; Donald E. Steele, executive vice president; Samuel D. Greiner, vice president, product management and development; and Burwyn B. Bender, vice president of manufacturing. Research and development called for upgrading Ajax products to cover an increasingly wider power range, ultimately filling all gaps in the total engine-compressor market. A mixed-flow compressor in the higher Cooper-Bessemer horsepower range was also at the development stage.

The company made another move to strengthen growth potential by increasing trading stock value, when it listed its common stock on the Pacific Stock Exchange. President Cizik told security analysts at a meeting in San Francisco, "We have taken this step for two reasons. Though we are listed on both the New York and Midwest Stock Exchanges, we feel listing with the Pacific Stock Exchange will give broader recognition to our stock and, with the longer trading hours, will benefit investors making trades late in the day."

To increase the general awareness of Cooper Industries nationwide, the company launched a two-year advertising campaign in financial publications, primarily *The Wall Street Journal.* Creative full page ads announced Cooper's "Escape from Anonymity," in a series touching most segments of operations. An introduction in the first advertisement expressed the essence of the campaign by confessing, "It's terribly irritating to be one of the fastest growing companies in the Fortune 500, yet seldom meet anyone who has heard of you. Starting today, we're going to do something about that." Being recognized more widely in the financial community would not in itself bring automatic investment increases, but it would help. "Investment organizations always want to know *why* they should purchase a company's stock," explained Vice President Cross, "and it certainly doesn't help if you have to first explain *who* the company is. That was the reason for the ad campaign. When brokers recommend a certain stock, they have a double selling job to perform if they have to explain both why *and* who."

Several possible acquisitions were being studied at that time. One of them, Standard Aircraft Equipment of Garden City, New Jersey, was soon to become a part of the company's aircraft services group.

Well established as a service leader in overhaul and repair of jet engines for regional and commuter airline carriers, and for the corporate and general aviation markets, Cooper Airmotive sought to strengthen its position as a distributor of parts and supplies. Standard Aircraft offered a network of sales outlets that would double the size of Cooper Airmotive's distribution division. Although fifth in size among American companies distributing aircraft parts, it ranked first in the categories of instruments and accessories, the latter including such products as brake parts, generators, starters, alternators, and actuators.

Founded in 1933 at Roosevelt Field on Long Island (take off point for Charles A. Lindbergh's historic flight to Paris), Standard Aircraft advanced in lock step with aviation. Its history closely paralleled that of Southwest Airmotive, acquired by Cooper in 1973. Louis J. Bollo, who started the company, built his business steadily through the depression and World War II, expanding greatly after the coming of the jet age, then selling a majority interest to Pittsburgh Coke and Chemical Company. By that time, its main headquarters had been moved to a Garden City office building. Roosevelt Field was but a memory, having long since given way to the construction of shopping centers, business buildings, and a race track.

Cooper purchased Standard Aircraft on July 22, 1975. Two years later, the Garden City offices were moved to MacArthur Airport on Long Island.

The changing balance of Cooper activities was reflected in 1975 year end figures, showing energy services accounting for 49 percent of operating income, compared with 29 percent in 1974; hand tools declining from 63 percent to 39 percent (although holding steady in total sales); and aircraft increasing slightly from 8 to 12 percent.

The temporary setback in hand tools performance was overshadowed, however, by several projects considered certain to enhance long-term profitability. Xcelite manufacturing was relocated to the Crescent plant in Sumter, closing down inefficient facilities at the Orchard Park plant. A 248,000-sq. ft. plant on a forty-acre site in Cullman, Alabama, was purchased from Monogram Industries, Inc., to be renovated for consolidation of Nicholson file manufacturing being carried out in Philadelphia and Anderson. And two months after America entered its bicentennial year, Cooper announced purchase of a plant in Cheraw, South Carolina, as the new home of Weller manufacturing operations. The move from Easton was completed before the end of 1976.

With those changes underway and the distribution center expansion nearing completion at Apex, The Cooper Group was completing its modernization program on schedule and looking toward another acquisition that would add yet another name-brand item to its tool basket.

J. Wiss & Sons Company of Newark, New Jersey, was recognized as the premier name in quality scissors, shears, and snips, and it had added the well-known "Tree Brand" knives to its product line through purchase of the H. Boker & Co. plant in Maplewood, New Jersey, in 1970. Founded in 1848 by a Swiss immigrant name Jacob Wiss, the company was headed by succeeding generations of family descendants until 1973, when Paul G. Richards was brought from a West Coast consulting firm to be president. Richards had cut back on unprofitable products, much as Cooper did in its hand tools plants, and he had effected other efficiencies in the operation, but the plant itself needed more extensive rehabilitation than the company could invest; heavy blocks of stock were still owned by family members not interested in long-range capital commitments. Under such circumstances, Cooper management felt certain its established hand tools manufacturing-distribution formula would bring excellent financial returns on a Wiss acquisition. The board of directors required little persuasion beyond The Cooper Group's previous track record, and a successful offer was made to Wiss.

24

Wiss

When Jacob Wiss immigrated to the United States from his native Switzerland in 1847, he supposedly was headed for a job awaiting him in Texas. At Newark, New Jersey, however, his modest funds gave out and he was forced to accept employment before continuing the journey. Having apprenticed as a cutler and gunsmith, the thirty-year-old craftsman took a job in the factory of Rochus Heinisch, an Austrian who had come to America twelve years earlier, perfected a method of facing malleable iron with steel in manufacturing shears, and established a cutlery business. Work became slack, however, and Jacob Wiss not only lost his job; he had to stay in Newark awaiting back pay. Rather than continue the struggle to reach Texas, he opened his own small business in a former stable, forging out surgical instruments and shears. His decision may have been influenced also by the Mexican War raging in the area of his intended destination, although no mention is made of it in historical accounts. Whatever the motivation, his assessment was destined to become an important factor in making Newark a world center of quality shears and scissors.

For several generations, the skills of cutlery makers were passed down through European families, their secrets carefully guarded and protected through guilds. One of ten children, Jacob Wiss had learned precision craftsmanship that typified Swiss expertise in delicate cutting tools and watches. Had he remained in Europe, he might well have followed the traditions of other master cutlers in rejecting the use of power machinery and new abrasives. But in a fresh environment a young man was free to adapt acquired skills to modern developments. Consequently, he eventually would surpass the quality of his Old World mentors.

Jacob Wiss did not break tradition abruptly. In his small shop he used natural stone for grinding and a wooden wheel for polishing, just as he had been taught. But he did introduce power to the one-man operation. The grinding and polishing wheels were turned by a Saint Bernard running on an attached treadmill. Within a year, business grew to the point where he employed a second dog. Taxes apparently posed only petty an-

216

noyance to business enterprise in nineteenth-century Newark. A tax receipt dated August 1, 1848, shows a total tax of four dollars for Jacob Wiss, cutler — all of it for the two dogs.

As business increased, apprentices came under the tutelage of the shop owner, and each came to realize that the foremost objective was quality. Jacob Wiss was determined to make the finest shears and scissors available, regardless of cost. Few precision tools were made in America at that time. Within a few years the company outgrew its quarters. Two moves were made to successively larger shops on Bank Street, and the dogs were replaced by steam power. Married in 1849, Jacob and his wife Maria always lived in rooms above their place of business, even after they had two sons and two daughters.

Early products were shears, scissors, table knives, surgical instruments, and razors. Word of Wiss quality spread beyond the boundaries of New Jersey, and by the time America entered the Civil War, Wiss was an established rival of R. Heinisch Sons Company for whom the founder had worked when he first reached Newark. During the war, the Wiss shop was called upon to make scissors (two round-handled rings of equal size) for Union Army medical units, and shears (one round-handled ring and one oblong ring into which more than one finger could be inserted for additional leverage) to cut uniforms. The introduction of power driven sewing machines in the manufacture of military uniforms, boots, and shoes brought those industries into the factory system, creating extensive new postwar markets for Wiss scissors and shears. The company benefited also from development of home sewing machines and from lowered textile costs created by a proliferation of New England mills. And improvement in crucible steel provided better raw materials for the manufacture of Wiss products.

As the owner's children grew, the firm's name was changed to J. Wiss & Sons Company. The sons, in fact, were brought into the business at early ages. Frederick C.J. Wiss, the older of the two, arose early each morning to fire the boiler before going to school so that workers would have steam by 7:00 a.m. By the time he was twelve, he was a competent fireman. At seventeen, he took over management of the company when his father became ill. In 1880, Jacob Wiss died and Frederick became president at the age of twenty-two. His brother Louis, twenty, joined the company at that time and the two young men soon initiated an ambitious program of promoting Wiss products as superior to European imports. The latter had been losing ground because of the hesitance to accept new manufacturing and processing methods. The sons shared their father's determination to stick with top-of-the-line quality, despite competition from numerous less expensive scissors and shears.

Major products in the 1800s included several lines of shears and scissors, trimmers, pruning shears, and tin snips. Manufacturing and wholesale-lot shipping were supplemented by the company's own retail outlet at the shop site. With its rapid growth of business, Wiss made plans for large-scale construction and company realignment. A block of property at Littleton Avenue and West Market Street was purchased, and work started on a new two-story brick factory building. When the plant opened in 1887, the company divided into three operations: manufacturing, retail, and real estate. All manufacturing was moved into the new building, but the retail segment, Wiss Store, remained on Bank Street. Later it was moved to another location where it began specializing in jewelry. Subsequently expanding to include branch operations in neighboring towns, it became the largest retail jewelry firm in New Jersey. The third division, established in 1887, was Wiss Realty Corporation, a real estate holding company. In 1903 it built the city's first skyscraper. Frederick Wiss described the move into a new manufacturing plant with a letter to customers:

> It is with pleasure we announced the completion of our New Works, the erection of which was found necessary to accommodate our constantly increasing trade, which has grown so rapidly that we have been unable, for some time past, to fill orders as promptly as desired. The many details incident to moving, transfer and placing of machinery, have caused some delay in filling orders, and we would express our appreciation of kind indulgence for any annoyance that may have been experienced. Our new factory has been supplied with everything needed in improved machinery, etc., and all departments enlarged to an extent that will enable us in a very short time to promptly meet all demands. We now have what is conceded to be as fine, if not the finest works of the kind in the world, and intend to fully sustain our well-known reputation of manufacturing only strictly first quality and fully warranted goods.

The guarantee was no idle claim. Wiss replaced any broken product, regardless of the reason for damage.

The Wiss chain of ownership was broken temporarily in 1898 when its manufacturing segment was purchased by the National Shears Company, better known as the Shear Trust. Organized in New Jersey but with main offices in Manhattan, Shear Trust quickly purchased five plants, among them J. Wiss & Sons. The leading man in the drama was J.H. Clauss, head of one of the purchased companies, who was voted president of the new trust. Three of the companies were closed, but by operating Wiss and Clauss Shear Company, the trust controlled from 65 to 70 percent of the shears and scissors output in America. Success seemed assured, but in less than two years the organization was declared bankrupt. Production continued for a short time under receivership, then in May, 1900, the Wiss family bought back its factory. A few days later the business was incorporated as J. Wiss & Sons Company, and business continued with Frederick Wiss again the president-treasurer and Louis Wiss elected secretary.

Additional plant construction followed, and in 1906 power drop hammers for hot forging steel shears frames were installed, making it possible to weld tough high-carbon steel blades to softer, more malleable steel. This new process, which made shears and scissors virtually indestructible, prompted the Wiss brothers to launch the industry's first spirited national advertising campaign through such popular magazines as *The Ladies Home Journal.* Most sales at that time were to cutlers and grinders who sold to tailors, dressmakers, and milliners, but Wiss wanted to clear additional channels to the customer market through hardware and cutlery retailers. Louis Wiss did not live to see complete results of the advertising effort. He died in 1908 at the age of forty-eight.

A vigorous sales campaign, bolstered by the national advertising, put Wiss products with inlaid cutting edges on counters and in show windows across the country. The push was accelerated in 1912 when the company perfected a process of forging steel handles. Until that time, the steel blades of tailors' shears were attached to handles made of malleable iron, which tended to crack. Contours of handles were considered by tool and die makers too complicated for drop forging, but Frederick Wiss overcame a series of experimental failures to add another improvement to his scissors and shears. His "steel forged" process was completed with the welding of inlaid blades of high carbon crucible steel to the forged steel frames of tailors' shears.

Still competing at prices above those of most other manufacturers, Frederick Wiss remained convinced that customers would pay more money to avoid pulling and tearing their fabrics. On the wall of his office was a sign bearing the words, "The recollection of quality remains long after price is forgotten." The company even began making its own screws, bolts, and nuts since it was impossible to buy supplies that met the standard of what the president referred to as "watchmaker accuracy," and it became the first manufacturer to apply the technique of blade-edging to the production of garden cutting tools.

By purchasing R. Heinisch Sons Company in 1914, Wiss became the world's largest producer of fine shears and scissors. World War I brought further gains when imports from European cutlery centers of Sheffield, England, and Solingen, Germany, were halted. Production soared to plant capacity during the war and continued at a high level until 1920. Then disaster struck. In its haste to rehabilitate a defeated enemy and encourage it to pay war debts, the government permitted Germany to dump large quantities of duty-free goods on American markets, including scissors priced at less than half the cost of domestic merchandise. Before the tarriffs of 1923 rescued American industry, several plants that had expanded to join the wartime production armada were capsized. Wiss was among the survivors, but many months were required to reestablish its position with a price conscious public amidst the leftover glut of cheap goods. One method it used was to direct a new sales effort toward department stores, which were growing rapidly in size and number in the '20s.

By the end of the decade, the company manufactured annually more than two million pairs of shears and scissors in 250 varieties. At age seventy, President Wiss was still one of the first men at the factory every morning, even when he commuted from his summer home at Avon. His daily routine included a mid-day visit to the downtown jewelry store, then a return to the plant until evening. A believer in recreation, the president backed employees in their request to stage boxing events during lunch breaks. Gathering on the second floor, spectators would form a human ring around the participants flailing away with big gloves. Intrigued, President Wiss came up with an idea that could be unique in the annals of personnel relations. Whenever he learned of friction among plant employees, he checked to see if the men involved were of comparable age and weight. If so, he arranged to have them settle differences in the ring. An employee who attended the bouts reported that the system worked well. Arguments ended with exhausted, laughing reconciliation. Frederick Wiss died in 1931 and was succeeded as president by his older son Robert. His other son, Norman, was elected vice president and treasurer.

The third generation Wiss president faced an immediate problem shared by most Americans, the Great Depression, which already had taken a heavy economic toll. Wiss did not close its doors, but employees worked what they dubbed appropriately "short weeks." Sometimes that meant two days a week, every other week, for a total of four days per month. The company set up a program where employees could spend nonworking days selling products door to door. But families who could barely find money for food could make an old pair of scissors last. Textile companies without customers did not need tools. When at last the nation began to recover, Wiss helped encourage sales by introducing such new products as pinking shears with zig zag edges and a new Metalmaster line of industrial cutting tools.

The depression appeared to etch lasting memories into the personality of Robert Wiss. Long after production returned to normal levels, he walked through the plant once each morning and again each afternoon. Joseph Rega, who joined the company in 1929, learned every job in the factory, and later became head of quality control, said, "Robert Wiss had production control in his head when he walked through the plant. The men worked on piece rates, and when someone told the president he did not have enough work to finish out the day, I would be told to send him more shears or scissors. If I said we already had that requirement filled for a month, he'd say to send them down anyway, because he didn't want the man out of work."

Wiss products were converted to military applications during World War II, sometimes in unusual ways. Cuticle and nail scissors proved ideal

Assembling scissors at Wiss. This photograph of the inspection and rework department of Wiss, in 1948, was part of a group of photographs taken in honor of Wiss' 100th anniversary.

Of 360 J. Wiss & Sons Company employees in 1936, there were 28 father and son combinations. Twenty-nine sons are standing behind fathers, with the odd number attributed to one man having two sons in the firm. J. Robert Wiss, company president, is seventh from the left in the first row, with his son, Richard, behind him.

for the manufacturer of precision radar and radio systems. Pruning shears were adapted to preparing poultry for overseas shipment, and pinking shears were utilized in the manufacture of airplanes. Several Wiss products were used to barter with natives in remote parts of the world where American money had no apparent value. In more conventional applications, metal snips were used building ships and tanks, and surgical scissors went to hospitals on every fighting front.

As sales reverted to civilian markets after the war, the company's position was strengthened by its military record, particularly in the manufacture of industrial shears. When the company observed its 100th birthday in 1948, five hundred men and women were employed at the Newark Plant and plans for expansion were in the blueprint stage. The manufacture of scissors and shears remained more manual than mechanical, however, and a large percentage of the craftsmen were veteran employees. A 25-year service club was established during the centennial, with 117 employees eligible for immediate membership. As part of its birthday celebration Wiss publicized the art of manufacturing its products, explaining the approximately 176 operations required to make dies and tools, forge, grind, heat, treat, polish, finish, and test a pair of scissors or shears.

In 1954, Vice President Norman F. Wiss died. The following year, President J. Robert Wiss died and was succeeded by his only son Richard. That same year the family sold the jewelry business it had formed at the turn of the century. Four years later, the Wiss Realty Corporation was dissolved.

Manufacturing continued to expand in 1957 with the purchase of the Kroyden Golf Club Company factory at Maplewood, New Jersey. As a division of Wiss, the plant produced snips and garden tools. In the decade that followed it bought the Crook-Miller Company of Hicksville, Ohio, manufacturer of wooden garden tool handles, and started a three-stage expansion program at the Newark plant. Construction of a warehouse, manufacturing facilities, and a new office was completed by 1970. But the most important event of that year was the purchase of Boker Manufacturing Company's factory adjacent to the Wiss division plant at Maplewood. With that acquisition, Wiss became producer of the renowned Boker "Tree Brand" pocket and hunting knives.

Boker predated Wiss in America. Founded in 1837 by Herman Boker, a descendent of an old family of Prussian merchants, it imported and manufactured cutlery sold primarily to hardware jobbers. Operating from quarters in New York City, the company earned its reputation principally by selling German and English hardware and cutlery for many years. Among its products was the celebrated "Tree Brand" knife, manufactured by Heinr Boker & Company of Solingen, Germany. H. Boker & Company, Inc., of New York was exclusive distributor in the

American market, but there was no other official connection between the two companies beyond the founders tracing their ancestry to the same family. Eventually, a royalty arrangement permitted the American firm to apply the Boker Tree Brand name to its own manufactured products. This was halted in World War I when all German patents and trademarks were dropped in this country.

In 1926, John R. Boker, Sr., president of H. Boker & Company, expressed concern that business had not grown for many years, having been "just allowed to be kept alive." To instill new momentum, he built a manufacturing plant at Hilton, New Jersey. Later the town name was changed to Maplewood. It was not until 1949 that the company again was able to acquire rights to produce knives under the Boker Tree Brand trademark. Two years later a vigorous advertising campaign opened worldwide markets, ironically putting Boker in competition with the Solingen, Germany, firm from whom it obtained trademark rights. In 1965, the plant was purchased by The New Britain Machine Company, which was acquired later by Litton Industries. When Wiss bought the building and certain assets, it acquired the Tree Brand trademark.

In the years after Paul Richards became president, increased mechanization cut the cycle time for producing a pair of shears or scissors from nine months to fifteen weeks. Induction hardening improved the process and a patented set-easy pivot provided individual adjustment of the cutting action. Yet some operations, such as the final angling of blades, continued to depend on personal craftsmanship.

25

Need to Free Free Enterprise

Wiss became a part of The Cooper Group in December 1976, and Richards continued to head its operations for a year before he left to join another company.

With seven major brands being marketed in 140 countries through consolidated international corporations, The Cooper Group launched an intensive television advertising campaign linking its group name to products bearing individual labels of Crescent, Lufkin, Nicholson, Weller, Wiss, Boker Tree and Xcelite.

Lufkin tapes already had received an unsolicited promotional boost when they were selected for official measurements at the Olympic Games in Montreal. The tapes were used for laying out the track and field events, as well as measuring the shot-put, high jump, hammer throw, and pole vault. To make certain the selection did not go unnoticed, Cooper produced a series of television commercials featuring gold-medalist pole vaulter Bob Seagren suggesting that viewers "judge Lufkin for yourself . . . the Olympics did."

Most notable of The Cooper Group's international events during the year was the opening of a Nicholson file manufacturing plant at Sao Paulo, Brazil. President Cizik visited the new plant, then went on to Cali, Colombia, where he met with partners in a proposed hand tools joint venture to serve the Andean Common Market countries of Colombia, Bolivia, Ecuador, Peru, and Venezuela. That manufacturing operation went on stream the following year.

Cooper Energy Services also shared the international spotlight in June, 1976, when it was awarded a contract in excess of $30 million to build eighty-eight pipeline compressors for AEG-KANIS TURBINEN-FABRIK Gmbh, of Essen, Germany. The compressors were to be installed on Russia's 1,440-mile pipeline stretching from Orenburg to the Austrian border. AEG-KANIS and an Italian company, Nuovo Pignone, shared a contract for the project, obtained through the official

Cooper Group Executive Vice President Hal Stevens and President Bill Rector discussing Lufkin's role as official supplier of measuring instruments for the 1976 Olympic Games.

importing agency of the USSR. "Several American firms have signed substantial support agreements with the prime contractors," reported *Gas Turbine International* magazine. "The most significant order went to Cooper Energy Services."

Just six months later, however, even that contract was dwarfed by another awarded to Coberrow, Ltd., a United Kingdom company owned jointly by Cooper-Bessemer of Canada, Rolls-Royce Ltd., and a British affiliate of Williams Overseas Ltd. The $165 million contract from the Soviet foreign trading organization, V.O. Machinoimport, was for equipment to be installed on a 56-inch, 800-mile natural gas pipeline in Western Siberia. Cooper's part was valued at $70 million, representing the largest order ever received by the company.

Fierce international competition among the world's major gas turbine manufacturers had followed Russia's announcement of the proposed project. Cooper Industries was in a favored position with the Soviets, because of earlier dealings and success of equipment already being used in that country. Unlike the United Kingdom and Canada, however, the

United States did not participate in financing projects for sales to Russia. To overcome that obstacle, Cooper (through its Canadian manufacturing division) joined the two British companies in forming Coberrow, a consortium headquartered at Surrey, England. The name of their joint venture was an acronym of Cooper-Bessemer, Rolls-Royce, and Williams.

The agreement, one of the largest in the history of trade between Russia and the Western World, took several months of discussion and negotiation to conclude, while financing was arranged in cooperation with the Vneshtorgbank of Moscow, the Export Credits Guarantee Department of the United Kingdom, the Export Development Corporation of Canada, and Morgan Grenfell, & Company Ltd. of London. It called for Cooper to supply light industrial gas turbine-centrifugal compressor systems, Rolls-Royce to furnish jet-derivative gas generators to power the turbines, and Williams to supply project engineering, management, and accessory equipment. Full systems were to be installed at six compressor stations between Western Siberia and the city of Chelyabinsk. Spare parts, repair facilities, and technical services were also included in the contract. Equipment provided by Cooper would be manufactured in its plants at Liverpool, England, and Stratford, Canada. It would consist of 18,200-hp Coberra turbine-compressor systems similar to those used extensively in Canada under similar climatic conditions and applications.

In addition to being Coberrow's initial business venture, the contract marked the first sale of light industrial turbines using jet engines for pipeline service to the USSR. The compact units, capable of delivering large amounts of horsepower, were considered ideal for use in remote Russian areas; should the power source fail, it could be removed and replaced in a matter of hours and sent to a special repair facility.

Performance of the compressors, following installation that began in 1977 proved to be another door opener for Cooper participation on other major pipelines constructed by Russia in the years ahead.

Competition for the Russian pipeline exemplified the rapidly expanding scope of industrial capabilities among the world's manufacturers. As it celebrated two hundred years of democracy, America found its system pitted more and more against those of other nations. Automobile and steel industries were among those feeling the greatest pressures, and more would follow. Many industrial problems could be attributed in large part to a company's own failure to recognize changing market demands. Even conceding that point, however, some industrial leaders warned of what Cooper's president identified as "The need to free free enterprise." Cizik elaborated in remarks to shareholders at the April 28, 1976, annual meeting in Dallas:

> The current attitude that bigness in business is an inherent evil that requires legislative correction can have dangerous consequences. The goal of

all business is to grow. Growth is our measure of success, our measure of how well we are doing our job of providing the goods and services which our consumers want and need. In the free competitive system, there are winners and losers. If growth is punishable, there is no incentive to take the very real risks necessary to produce that growth. Without the willingness to take risks, we cannot have a system of free enterprise.

Accordingly, the job of preventing possible abuses of concentrations of economic power should be viewed as one that requires a great deal of judgment and reason. Our primary concern should be to protect ourselves against possible flaws in our system without endangering the system itself. Free enterprise is now, and always has been, supported by the American people. A poll taken several years ago showed that 93 percent of Americans expressed their willingness to make personal sacrifices, if necessary, to preserve the free enterprise system. This system includes all business, large and small.

In our current reformist mood, however, we have neglected the judgment needed to legislate wisely. We have forgotten that laws already exist to protect our country from many economic abuses. Indeed, we seem to have forgotten that it is the abuses and not the system that the laws should attack. Some lawmakers act as though they have a mandate to legislate against business, and this imagined mandate is producing a tyranny of regulation that is enormously wasteful and destructive to initiative, innovation, efficiency, and productivity.

The multitude of government regulations imposed on business is absorbing more and more of our time, our capital, and our freedom to seek new ways to satisfy our consumers' demands. Laws are being proposed that would dismantle our nation's largest industries, not because they have abused their economic power, but because they are big. More and more of our free market mechanisms are being destroyed and replaced with central planning and control.

Thus far, big business generally has been able to endure the legislative onslaught. However, the large number of smaller enterprises that have found themselves incapable of meeting the plethora of regulatory requirements and have consequently been forced to close their doors is a poignant indication of how lofty legislative goals can go awry. While big business is condemned for its very size, the increasing degree of government intervention is permitting only the larger enterprise to survive, and one of the cornerstones, indeed the foundation, of our free enterprise system — the small business — is being legislated into oblivion.

Over the years, government has proven its effectiveness in endeavors that cannot be undertaken by private institutions — national security for example. But in many areas, government action cannot be as effective as other mechanisms. Government is not a panacea. It cannot solve all our problems today, nor will it do so in the future. What we must have is a return to a balance of roles among all our great institutions — sound and responsive government to be sure, but within an environment of free enterprise, coupled with the essential contributions of religion and a sound educational system. As to the role of business, the marketplace can, if allowed to do so, regulate through freedom of choice, many of the problem areas we are attempting to control through burgeoning bureaucracies. This will be particularly true if we reestablish profits as an essential and desirable part of our economic system.

The period in which we are living is a critical one for our nation's future. We are facing major problems — inflation, energy shortages, high unemployment, national security, and crime control. If we are able to apply our energies to the solution of these problems, the future benefits will be great. If, on the other hand, we pursue misguided goals that weaken our free enterprise system, we will find a future devoid of the strength that has supported all of our past advances. You and I pay the costs of our nation's mistakes. We should work to avoid those mistakes. The key to preserving free enterprise is involvement — involvement in our educational system and our political system. It is time to become involved. . . . The prospect of all that we stand to lose is too overwhelming not to inspire wholehearted dedication to the goal of freeing our free enterprise system.

One organization that had suffered from economic pressures of the mid-1970s was the Cleveland-based White Motor Corporation, which ran into severe financial difficulty when the truck market collapsed. Unable to meet loan agreements and short of operating capital, it launched a program of retrenchment. Among its intended cutbacks was sale of its White Superior engine division in Springfield, Ohio.

Cooper Industries was quick to respond. Superior's engines and reciprocating compressors fit precisely into a gap between the largest Ajax and smallest Cooper-Bessemer products. Cooper had attempted to fill that manufacturing segment in 1967, through a proposed acquisition of Waukesha Motor Company, but had been stopped by the Justice Department. Now, management was hopeful that changes in the company would provide a new opportunity to complete its compressor horsepower range, and Superior offered an even more desirable acquisition than Waukesha. Its heavy-duty engines and compressors were used widely in natural gas production and gathering, which should experience rapid growth. The range of gas, diesel, and dual-fuel engines was approximately 400 to 2,650 horsepower. Its direct potential for profit growth was supplemented by the good-will benefit of offering an unbroken product line to customers. And its manufacturing plant was located less than one hundred miles from Cooper Energy Services headquarters in Mt. Vernon. "There's been a home waiting for Superior in Cooper Energy Services for some time," said the division's president, Tom Naugle.

Agreement for a cash purchase was reached with White Motor Company, but it too was challenged by the Justice Department. In response, Cooper, under the leadership of Senior Vice President Riedel, prepared a thorough study of all possible areas of contention. Cooper's case was built around three principal precepts that Riedel invited Division representatives to investigate: (1) Cooper's withdrawal from the separable compressor business in 1974 and the liquidation of CB/Southern in 1975 removed any possible competitive overlap that may have existed previously between Cooper Energy Services and White's Superior Division; (2) sale of the Division was essential to White Motor Company continuing its basic truck and agricultural implements businesses; and (3) a 1974 acquisition of Superior's leading competitor, Waukesha, by Dresser Industries was reviewed by the Justice Department and not challenged, providing precedent for a similar opinion in favor of Cooper's proposed purchase.

The Great Lakes field office in Cleveland was unpersuaded and the case was then reviewed in Washington by Thomas Kauper, head of the Anti-Trust Division of the Department of Justice on July 14. Justice Department approval was announced on July 15, and on July 16, 1976, Superior became part of Cooper Energy Services, which was able to announce to its customers, "Now we can singularly accommodate your power and compression equipment needs from 40 horsepower to 36,400 horsepower across the board." For Riedel, who had guided and managed the antitrust aspects of Cooper's acquisition program since 1960, the decision on Superior was sweet atonement for the only loss suffered — the Waukesha case.

26

Superior

When Patrick J. Shouvlin opened a small machine shop at Springfield, Ohio, in 1889, he didn't intend to pioneer an industry. His immediate objective was to put engineering skills to work servicing existing industries in the area. Ohio at that time was producing 20 percent of the world's oil supply, largely as a result of the bountiful Lima-Indiana oil field discovered just a few years earlier. Machining expertise was in great demand, and the 26-year-old entrepreneur quickly established a thriving business with oil pumpers and drillers. Some of the repair work was on steam engines being used to bring in oil, while natural gas escaped as a waste product. The natural gas engine was in its infancy, having been invented little more than a decade earlier in Germany. But many persons were developing models of their own, and P.J. Shouvlin became one of them, hoping to utilize escaping wellhead gas to power oil-pumping engines.

By the early 1890s, the Shouvlin machine shop on Washington Street had a new name, The Superior Gas Engine Company, describing its new product. P.J., who was always known by his initials rather than his first name, sold his first gas engine for oilfield pumping to a Findlay, Ohio, organization, later to become the Ohio Oil Company, and then Marathon Oil. There was great excitement in the gas engine business. Several companies were appearing, particularly on the Eastern Seaboard and in Chicago, as internal combustion challenged steam as a source of power. Probably the best known among the new companies was the Otto Engine Works of Philadelphia, licensed in the United States to manufacture a "silent gas engine" invented by Dr. Nicholas A. Otto of Cologne, Germany, and acclaimed by the scientific world for its simplicity, economy, and ingenuity of design. Otto advertisements spread the gospel of gas engines with the slogan, "No boiler, no danger, no engineer."

Superior, with its engines adapted particularly for oil fields, proved to have a strategic market location. At first, Shouvlin sold directly to customers, but the volume soon required the services of a distributor. Consequently, arrangements were made for a newly organized group known as the National Supply Company to become exclusive agents for Superior sales throughout the oil production industry. National Supply was formed in 1894, when several men who had been supplying operators in Ohio, Pennsylvania, and West Virginia pooled their resources and experience into a corporation headquartered in Pittsburgh. Both the National Supply Company and the Otto Engine Works were to figure prominently in the future of the Superior Gas Engine Company.

A solidly built man of medium height, P.J. Shouvlin was well conditioned for the rigors of heavy industry. He was born in Ireland, but moved with his parents and brother to the United States when he was just three years old. His father, an engineer, had previously spent several years at Allentown, Pennsylvania, operating blast furnace engines. After the death of the elder Shouvlin, his widow moved with her two sons, Patrick and Daniel, to the anthracite coal region of Pennsylvania. With only a common school education, young Patrick became a miner, with the responsibility of looking after machinery. He supplemented that practical experience with enough formal study to become a mechanical engineer. At age twenty, Shouvlin moved to Springfield, where he worked in a locomotive shop. That led to positions as assistant master mechanic for the Chicago, Burlington & Quincy Railroad at LaCrosse, Illinois, and Tacoma, Washington. But in 1889 he returned to Springfield, this time with a wife, Catherine, to begin a company and a family. Both grew rapidly; P.J. and Catherine Shouvlin had two daughters and four sons.

Straining limitations of the original machine shop by 1900, Superior Gas Engine Company moved to a new location on East Street. Four years later, it moved across the railroad tracks to a new plant at 1401 Sheridan Ave. By its twenty-fifth anniversary in 1914, Superior was selling a line of standard engines from 20 to 100 horsepower, tank-cooled and open jacket engines from 2.5 to 15 horsepower, both stationary and mounted on all-steel trucks, throughout the country. The plant had expanded to a complex of foundry, pattern room, erecting floor and several machining areas.

Although it limited production to natural gas engines, Superior was well aware of the increasing impact of diesels. Shouvlin experimented with oil-burning prototypes, and in 1920 he added a semidiesel engine, identified as the Type PS, to the product line. A writer at that time described the new engine as "destined to become one of the wonders of its kind." Still, there were many things to be considered before determining the extent of commitment to diesel development. Superior was prospering as a gas engine manufacturer. In the early 1920s it employed an average of five hundred persons, whereupon the Clark County Historical Society claimed it "the largest singly owned company in the world." Diesel engines had few power applications, particularly in the oil and gas

When "Mount Vernon," the home of George Washington, was restored in the early 1920s, a 50 horsepower engine produced by Superior was installed to provide electricity throughout the estate.

fields where Superior had great strength. A progressive engine manufacturer, however, could not overlook such a promising newcomer. P.J. Shouvlin decided that the company must become involved in diesels, and he wanted to make the first step a substantial one. That meant utilizing established European diesel experience. Specifically, Superior needed designs, patents, and engineering advice from Germany.

Motoren Fabrik Deutz of Cologne, Germany, participated in the original development of the diesel many years earlier. Its affiliate in the United States, Otto Engine Works, the early leader in gas engines, now was well along in diesel production. In 1923, Superior entered diesel competition by purchasing Otto Engine Works, securing also the Deutz license. President Shouvlin sent one of his sons, Raphael, a World War I veteran, to Philadelphia, as head of the acquired company. A few years later, the Deutz license was dropped in favor of following a course of Superior's own diesel engine refinements. The Superior model of a vertical diesel was completed in 1926, expanding possible future uses to such familiar territory as oil fields, although the first units went to Cuban sugar plantations. Appropriately, the word "gas" was dropped from the company name, making it the Superior Engine Company.

At the age of sixty-three, P.J. Shouvlin had seemingly lost none of his vigor. He walked through the plant daily and headed a management team that included all his sons. In order of age they were Daniel, John, Raphael (in Philadelphia), and Joseph (more commonly known as Dan, Jack, Ray, and Joe). The president himself was called "Mr. P.J." Explained a former employee, "Out of respect, we thought we should address him with the title "Mr.", but with so many Mr. Shouvlins around, that name would have been confusing." Mr. P.J. was an even-tempered Irishman who enjoyed people in and out of the plant. Active in his church and community, he was elected a city commissioner while traveling abroad, serving many years in that position. He was also a delegate to the Democratic National Convention that nominated Woodrow Wilson for the presidency. One observer called him "a Democrat with independent proclivities."

The family-management structure of Superior was changed in 1928. The National Supply Company, whose growth had paralleled the oil industry it served, acquired Superior in a straight stock transaction. P.J. Shouvlin continued to head the newly named Superior Engine Division, and his family, in fact, became the largest stockholder in National Supply. Ray Shouvlin remained in charge of the Otto Engine plant in Philadelphia. An employee remarked that the only changes noticeable to the man at the machine were on the signs and the stationary, and he didn't see much of the latter.

The family tree of the National Supply Company had many roots, all nourished by oil. From the group that had organized it in 1894, the company had expanded to blanket oil production territories with sales outlets. National Supply stores followed oil exploration so closely that they became barometers of the industry. Opening of a new store was good indication that a wildcat strike would lead to an important new field.

National Supply opened a store in Bartlesville, Oklahoma, when total production for the territory was only 139,000 barrels. One year later, it soared to 1,367,000 barrels. When wildcatters hit black bonanzas in Texas, a National Supply store was close behind. But there was no company claim of infallible judgment. Sometimes the prediction was wrong and the store closed early, along with the field. Yet, National Supply stores had become as recognizable as drilling rigs in the barren plains and bayous that were oil country. Drillers received mail "% The National Supply Store." They left messages for each other on large blackboards provided by storekeepers, borrowed the use of a store's telephone, and stood in line at the back door, awaiting their turn in the area's only bathtub.

Along with its nationwide distribution, the company manufactured a variety of oilfield equipment. Acquisition of Superior gave it an impor-

Patrick Shouvlin, founder of The Superior Gas Engine Company.

tant engine line at a time when oilfield operators were demanding a single source for power equipment and other supplies.

In 1930, Superior diesels were applied for the first time to rotary drilling. Generators connected to the engines provided power for a wildcat drilling operation in a Mississippi delta marsh south of New Orleans. The project caused a flurry of excitement, as engineers visited the site to obtain data. But diesel development for rotary drilling was stunted temporarily, along with other industrial progress, as America's Great Depression depressed the flow of capital. The plant never had to shut down during the depression, but the work force went on half time schedules and pay checks reached levels of bare subsistence. It was not until 1939 that Superior felt the market warranted introducing a specialized line of Type PTD diesel engines, designed specifically for oilfield drilling. Most, if not all others, were adaptations of general purpose engines. Joseph Shouvlin had succeeded his father as head of the division in 1937 and also became a director of the parent company. P.J. Shouvlin continued to be involved in company affairs, however, maintaining an office and assisting in management until he retired in 1940 at the age of seventy-seven. He lived to the age of ninety-two.

National Supply continued to grow, acquiring in 1937, Spang, Chalfant and Company, one of the oldest names in American industry dating back to 1828, and a leading manufacturer of steel pipe. Three years later, it purchased Central Tube Company, which had started at the turn of the century as Pittsburgh Steel Construction Company.

By the beginning of World War II, the entire Shouvlin family had left Superior. Joe was the last to leave, in late 1940, to join Bauer Brothers, manufacturers of machinery used in the paper industry. David C. Peterson was appointed works manager of both the Springfield and Philadelphia plants at that time. Frederick W. Burns became works manager of Superior in May 1942, a year of notable achievement for the division. In a major consolidation and rehabilitation effort, the Philadelphia plant was closed and all equipment was transferred to Springfield. Martin H. Miller, who had joined the company in 1934 and would later become works manager, was in charge of the movement of equipment. "Someone estimated that it would take sixteen train cars to carry the equipment, and it turned out to be exactly sixty," he recalled.

The Superior Engine Division ended 1942 by receiving the Maritime Commission "M" award and Victory Fleet flag for its record of building diesel engines for U.S. Liberty Ships. The engines were designed by George F. Noltein, chief engineer who had been with the company since 1927. Born and educated in Russia, he taught in German universities before emigrating to the United States. With a wartime employment of eighteen hundred men and women, Superior also built engines for Naval LST landing-craft vessels and for lend-lease to other Allied nations. John D. Spalding transferred from a National Supply plant in Torrance, California, to become Superior works manager in 1943 on a temporary basis. He was succeeded the same year by W.F. Tiemann.

Postwar planning brought extensive streamlining of production and marketing. Basically, the objective was to eliminate enough models to concentrate on more efficient production of medium-weight and heavy-duty, slow-speed diesel engines. The division's high-speed diesel line was sold to Sterling Engine Company of Buffalo, New York. At the same time, in 1945, the Ajax Iron Works of Corry, Pennsylvania, purchased the Superior line of slow-speed horizontal gas engines. (Ajax and Superior themselves would become united thirty-one years later as units of Cooper.)

A cost conscious management built a plant addition, changed production procedures, updated equipment, and redesigned the use of floor space to gain efficiency. Great effort also was made to strengthen existing sales channels and pursue new markets opened by mushrooming technology. Oil firms were poised for offshore exploration in a formidable array, similar to the horde of settlers waiting for the gun that would send them rushing across the Oklahoma plains. Diesel power was needed for ocean liners, tugboats, locomotives, municipal light and power plants, refrigerating facilities, factories, quarries, irrigation, and many other uses. The organization that had started with the manufacture of

Post-war production in 1947 concentrated on these Superior engines, manufactured primarily to produce power for municipal plants.

gas engines and later pondered the advisability of including diesels had made a complete turn. It was virtually out of the gas engine business.

In 1950, the marine aspect of Superior's business was boosted with the purchase of certain assets, primarily service outlets, from the Atlas Imperial Diesel Engine Company of Oakland, California. With products listed under both the Superior and Atlas Imperial brands, the Springfield operation underwent another name change. It became known simply as the Engine Division of The National Supply Company. By the mid-1950s, the division's engines were being used in practically every petroleum-producing area of the world. Through development of dual fuel and turbocharging applications, they were being used extensively in pipeline pumping. They were performing on oil tankers, harbor tugs, river towboats, and tuna clippers. They were helping to turn the wheels of railway transportation and industry. And they were drawing increasing attention from other companies. One organization, the White Motor Company of Cleveland, Ohio, at that time was expanding into product lines closely allied to its position as one of the country's leading manufacturers of large, heavy-duty trucks and tractors. One of its priorities was adding the production of diesel engines.

After extensive negotiations, the National Supply Company in April, 1955, sold its Diesel Division to White. The cash sale included an agreement that National Supply would continue to distribute Superior and Atlas engines throughout the oil industry. The president of National Supply explained that it was in his company's best interest to dispose of the engine manufacturing operations and aggressively expand its engine sales in the oil country, where it had 120 stores. Several years later, National Supply was acquired by the Armco Steel Corporation of Middletown, Ohio, becoming a division of that organization.

With the acquisition by the White Motor Company, the Springfield facility officially became the White Diesel Engine Division. William F. Burrows, who had been in charge of White's diesel activities in Cleveland, was named president of the new division, succeeding F. Howard Kilberry, works manager since 1950.

When the U.S. Department of Defense began its expansion program of building a network of radar detection and missile launching stations, Superior engines proved to be well suited for exacting requirements to power generating equipment. In 1957, the first of several government contracts was received for diesel engine-generator sets destined for the Air Force Semi-Automatic Ground Environment (SAGE) system of air defense and the Distant Early Warning (DEW) line in the Aleutians. In the years that followed, Superior engine-generator sets helped produce reliable ground power for Bomarc, Atlas, Nike-Zeus, Nike-Hercules, Mace, and Titan II missiles. They played important roles in air traffic control and warning, down-range missile tracking, and antiaircraft mis-

The "V" engine assembly room of Superior is shown in 1970.

A Superior W-64 Compressor goes on line at a Cities Service Oil Company plant at Desert Springs, Wyoming, in 1981.

A drilling rig, powered by Superior units, operates in the Gulf of Mexico, near Shreveport, Louisiana, in the 1970s.

A clean burn unit, developed to lower emissions well below requirements of the Clean Air Act and vastly improve fuel consumption, was installed in 1982 at the Pioneer Gas Company in Texas. Senior Development Engineer Jay Serve (pictured here) was involved in clean burn development. He supervised the installation.

sile systems. In total, White Superior Division diesel engine-generator sets provided power for more than 175 missile sites and eighteen major defense programs. The Bell System installed Superior sets for precise electric power to control, compute, and track its Telstar communications satellite.

Gradually, the Diesel Division restored production of gas engines with basic characteristics much like those of the diesels. The greatest impetus came in 1960 when it introduced a new line of compressors, engineered to match Superior gas engines or to be turbine or motor-driven. The compact, matched design, engine-compressor package was instrumental in revitalizing sales to oil and gas producers. Much of the design work on the compressors was done by James Buchwald, who learned engineering design at the Cooper-Bessemer Corporation of Mt. Vernon, Ohio.

The decision to develop the gas engine-compressor proved to be a masterpiece of market timing. It was the right product at the right time for the right market. It complemented rather than competed with existing products, it could be sold to the same customers by the same salesmen and, most important, it could be produced in the same plant with minimal investment. One example of timeliness came unexpectedly and near home. In 1964, Ohio experienced another substantial oil boom, again not far from Springfield, and gas-fueled Superior engine-compressors were installed as units there.

With gas engines reestablished as important products, the name was changed once again in 1965, this time from White Diesel Engine Division to White Superior Division. Refinements of both engine and compressor lines continued, including a twelve- and sixteen-cylinder Vee gas engine, fully packagable to be transported via truck for use as an engine-compressor, engine-generator, engine-blower, or engine-pump. William Burrows retired in 1968 and Arthur F. "Pete" George became president of the division. He was succeeded in 1972 by Samuel F. Lamb. Both were former Cooper-Bessemer employees. By then, heavy-duty engines and compressors were clearly established as the primary division products. The range of gas, diesel and dual-fuel engines was approximately 400 to 2,650 horsepower. But while the division's path pointed once again toward dependence on gas engines and compressors, selective sales of the right diesel and dual-fuel products seemed appropriate to fill out schedules.

The majority of Superior markets were in the oil and gas industry, with some among municipalities and only occasional sales to government groups. The division had withdrawn completely from marine diesel production when it was purchased by Cooper.

27

Selective Diversification

The $32.8 million acquisition of Superior easily fulfilled Cooper's hopes; in succeeding years its operations were expanded at Springfield, then extended also into plants at Mt. Vernon and Stratford, Ontario. Both the Superior and Ajax product lines were in great demand when increased development of previously marginal wells created needs for more small equipment both in the United States and abroad. Small engines were installed also at nuclear power plants, as emergency stand-by equipment.

Cooper Industries passed the half-billion dollar milestone in 1976, with record sales of $554,453,000. The year produced a two-for-one stock split of common shares, and a fourth consecutive annual increase in dividends. Having made ten acquisitions in ten years, the company had tripled its total assets in that time, to $452,544,000.

Unlike many corporations, Cooper was able to secure external funds for expansion even during the recession and unstable capital market conditions of 1974. Through prudent use of debt, combined with increasing cash flow from operations, the company preserved its financial flexibility, enabling it to pursue new opportunities and continue existing programs irrespective of the general economic climate. The two acquisitions in 1976 required more than $64 million in cash, adding to other capital expenditures of $14.4 million for internal growth. Yet, the company's total debt-to-capitalization ratio of 35 percent was essentially unchanged from 1975.

Management was strengthened further, early in 1977, with election of new corporate officers in legal, corporate development, and financial areas of responsibility. The slate of corporate officers now read: Eugene L. Miller, chairman; Robert Cizik, president; William G. Rector, senior vice president; Alan E. Riedel, senior vice president, administration; Dewain K. Cross, vice president, finance; Robert B. Dyer, vice president, planning and analysis; Roger A. Scott, vice president, secretary and corporation counsel; and the new members, Edgar A. Bircher, vice president and general counsel; C. Baker Cunningham, vice president, corporate development; and Frederick B. Hegi, Jr., treasurer. (Hegi later left the company in 1982 to become president of Valley View Capital Corporation in Dallas.)

In April, Cooper Industries received the 1977 Peter Hilton Award from the Association for Corporate Growth, an organization whose membership included more than thirteen hundred representatives of leading corporations, consulting firms, banks, and investment institutions. The award is presented annually to one company in the United States or Canada that has achieved an outstanding record of growth over the previous five years, without sacrificing quality of earnings or financial stability, and a high degree of social responsibility. In the five-year period of 1972–77, Cooper Industries' compound growth rate was 25 percent in revenues, 38 percent in net income, and 32 percent in share earnings. Return on shareholders' equity improved consistently from 10.5 percent in 1972 to 21.5 percent in 1976.

Growth that brought the award to Cooper was accomplished at a time when terms such as "conglomerate" and "multinational" were losing the grandeur that had made them seem synonymous with "invincibility" for nearly two decades. The "growth for growth's sake" philosophy that had created some giants with what proved to be unsteady legs, made monsters of all expanding corporations in the public eye. Ironically, even businesses introducing developments in technology, medicine, communications, and energy had to defend themselves for being successful. Acknowledging the confusion that lumped all diversification into a category of undisciplined growth, Cooper explained its position by introducing the word *non-glomerate*. Although President Cizik considered the term "too Madison Avenuish" and later officiated at its burial, he did not hesitate to answer the repeated question, "What sets Cooper Industries apart from the conglomerates that have given the word such a bad connotation?" His address to the Association for Corporate Growth in essence became a "position paper" on Cooper's philosophy:

> In general, our diversification program has been very selective, carried out at a methodical and deliberate pace. That does not mean to say we have not moved quickly to exploit unexpected opportunities. My point is that on every occasion, top corporate management controlled each major move. No move was made unless it offered Cooper the opportunity to become a principal factor and potential leader in a major and growing market. New diversifications were never attempted until earlier ones were thoroughly understood and under control.
>
> . . . Products become outmoded, markets decline and disappear, plants and equipment deteriorate, and despite the advances of science, we still measure man's life span by the biblical "three score and ten." Nothing is permanent except change, and companies that fail to acknowledge this fact will find that success is indeed "last year's nest from which the birds have flown." If products become obsolete or markets vanish and a company has

not already identified and begun to supply new needs, its wealth will vanish and its organization deteriorate.

. . . Diversification is the means by which an organization is preserved and temporal resources are replaced. As management strives to strengthen and adapt its organization to changing economic conditions, markets, and environments, untapped talents and capacities will emerge, creating opportunities for expansion into new areas. By diversifying into new products and subsequently exploiting new markets, acquiring new facilities, and infusing new blood into its organization, a company can restore depleting resources. Diversification is the natural outcome of foresight and the instinct to survive in a changing world, and it is made possible through the wise use of financial assets, or more specifically, cash. In its early years, a business is likely to be a net consumer, rather than a net producer of cash. With maturity, the opportunities for profitable investment decrease, and assuming funds are not invested merely to stay in business, more cash will be generated than consumed.

Throughout its existence, an organization must deal with the challenge created by the cash flow cycle — that is, cash into the business and cash out of the business. It must continually search for sources of funds and opportunities for investment. In a very real sense, its health and survival depend on its success in these searches. If a company cannot finance its growth, financially stronger competitors will relegate it to the corporate backwaters. Similarly, a mature company that fails to translate today's cash into tomorrow's profits will decay. The latter problem can be solved in part through diversification. When businesses are combined, those with cash flow surpluses can feed those with a need for cash. Later, as investments made in one line of business come to fruition and opportunities emerge in another their roles can be reversed.

Management of a diversified company which understands the dynamic nature of business and is responsive to organization potential is more likely to achieve higher returns with lower risk. It can build strengths and capitalize on them. It can anticipate and prepare for change. Conversely, single-product, single-market companies face serious perils. They are condemned to suffer the problems of their product. If demand for that product is cyclical, they are cyclical companies; if the product is highly technical, new technology may put them out of business.

. . . Whether we examine organizational structure, the products, markets, facilities and people, or the cash flow of a business, we are led inexorably to the conclusion that diversification is a natural phenomenon in the life of the ongoing business enterprise. It offers the possibility of preserving the valuable aspects of an organization indefinitely, of replacing perishable resources, of regenerating those that are transitory, and of maximizing the use of all assets, expecially cash. In my opinion, it is not a question of whether diversification should occur, but rather how much and in what direction. Assuming this to be the case, "What," one may ask, "went wrong with the conglomerates?" After all, they were, in fact, the ultimate in diversified companies. What brought about the disasters of the seventies, which now cause investors to shy away from conglomerates, and also cause companies, including Cooper, to bend over backwards to avoid the conglomerate label?

I have emphasized diversification as the logical response to challenges common to all business organizations. In the sixties, however, it materialized as an instrument of corporate wizardry and a catalyst for rampant acquisition. It was found that through a combination of normal internal growth and unrelated business acquisitions, an impressive cumulative growth rate could be obtained, fueling other acquisitions in turn. Custodial responsibility succumbed to expediency.

In my opinion, the conglomerates that rode to disaster did so on a distorted philosophy of management control. They viewed management as a sure science with infinite potential. Companies diversified wildly with the idea that professional managers could oversee any kind of business — regardless of divergent products, markets or manufacturing processes. All control was based on a system of financial reports. The recipe for success and instant paper profits was relatively simple: to a goodly measure of free-form management, add several completely divergent companies; combine as loosely as possible while creating the illusion of maximum synergy; spice liberally with creative accounting techniques; garnish generously with greed; package in Chinese paper and label appropriately with future earnings projections; then market aggressively until the package self-destructs.

It did self-destruct, mainly because the system of financial controls on which the concept of the conglomerate was founded did not work. In the long run, those reports probably would have indicated whether an operating executive was doing a good job. In the short run, they probably would not. This is particularly true if the compensation, or even the job, of the executive depended on the report — because he would have a powerful incentive to distort its results. By the time top management discovered the problems, it was too late to prevent major losses.

Real management control must go deeper than a series of financial statistics. I believe that to exercise such control, management must thoroughly understand the company's activities — its production process, products, and markets; the laws that relate to its various activities; and the cultures and customs of the areas in which it operates. These complexities, as well as the personalities of the managers, dictate the organization of reporting needs of the company. Since these factors vary from company to company, there is no single formula of how to achieve solid control. Management formulas must change as the business evolves. Regardless of the system used, the involvement necessary for corporate management to control the company's operations properly is extremely time-consuming. The amount of time required is dictated by the number of areas in which the company operates and the affinity that exists among them. In the final analysis, these factors determine the degree to which the company can successfully diversify; the more the operations differ, the fewer they can number. The need for management control sets limits, not only on the total degree of diversification, but also on the timing of new acquisitions. Management must be certain each new business area is understood and controlled before the next move is made. The particular character of management — the skills, experience, and interests it encompasses — must also influence the decision about the areas into which a company diversifies.

When I say it is top management control that distinguishes Cooper, I am clearly referring to more than an intimate, high-level involvement in the degree, speed, and process of diversification. I am also referring to the conviction that it is the very nature of that management — the personalities, talents, and interaction of its members — that must determine the distinctive direction and limits of a company's diversification. As Cooper continues to grow and diversify into areas compatible with the skills and experience of the current generation of management, this philosophy will perpetuate our disciplined growth.

Cooper's flexible structure made labeling of segments less important than understanding responsibilities of operational units — whether they were "groups" or "divisions" or other designations that would change with realignments brought about by acquisitions or to conform with such exterior influences as Federal Trade Commission regulations.

In 1977, the company had three basic operational units: Energy Services, The Cooper Group (hand tools), and Aircraft Services. Each was given the individual responsibility for planning, research and development, manufacturing, marketing and sales, both in the United States and abroad. Each had control of its own financial and human resources, within policy constraints established by the corporate staff, and each was headed by an executive officer with direct responsibility to corporate management. There was virtually no comingling of operations, nor of functional responsibilities. (Thus, for example, no corporate sales and marketing function existed.) "We consider it unrealistic to think a person selling wrenches could or should be good at selling 20,000 horsepower compressors too," said Senior Vice President Riedel.

Working within a framework of management, each unit developed a strategy to justify its objectives, procedures and proposed capital investments, subject to periodic review at the corporate level. Production, sales and profit projections were set forth in annual budget plans, broken down by quarter and month. Management programs explaining the means of carrying out those projections were presented, adjusted when necessary, and monitored through monthly reports, with the performance of each unit evaluated according to its contribution to overall company earnings. Capital investment was evaluated through a system designed to determine specific potential gains that could be expected from a new plant or machine tool. Performance later would be weighed against expectations. The company made no claim of having a set of unique business concepts — "Just the basic blocking and tackling fundamentals of management," said Riedel — but many business failures could be traced to a lack of such tight controls. Cooper considered them essential to ambitious plans for not only continuing, but greatly accelerating its growth. Shifts in nomenclature were to take place, as predicted, in the next five years, but there would be no compromise of the fundamentals.

Cooper's philosophy, of course, was based on successful reaction to, not elimination of, risks inherent in expansion. Each time period presents its memorable contribution of new factors that successfully prohibit the design of a "sure thing." One of 1977's offerings was a proliferation of federal bureaucratic juggling that boggled the mind, clouding efforts to anticipate business trends, particularly in energy services. A Cabinet-level Department of Energy was formed to envelop, but not eliminate the Energy Research Development Administration (ERDA), the Federal Energy Administration (FEA), and the Federal Power Commission (FPC), among others. The Nuclear Regulatory Commision (NRC) was not affected by the change, except that its research function previously had been transferred to ERDA. The Federal Power Commission functions were largely included in the Department of Energy's Federal Energy Regulatory Commission (FERC). An understatement from Washington warned that some functions of the new Department of Energy might come into conflict with each other; as it happened, the primary disagreement that surfaced concerned control of natural gas prices. President Jimmy Carter proposed increased regulation of both the interstate and intrastate gas markets. Opponents argued that regulation had caused the shortages and that higher prices expected from deregulation would encourage both conservation and production. The subject became a topic of legislative debate, with the House favoring the Presidential plan, and the Senate backing deregulation. By the end of the year no compromise was in sight, despite the fact that the winter of 1977 had been the most severe in decades, resulting in the closing of factories and schools from lack of gas.

It was not surprising that Cooper Energy Services found its most advantageous markets in foreign countries eager to develop their own energy resources. To expand and improve its international marketing, Cooper doubled regional sales offices and established a direct sales presence in Moscow, Latin America, and the Middle East. The scope of products offered directly to all international markets was expanded to include Ajax and Superior lines of engines and compressors, as well as products manufactured by the company's joint venture partners. Further support for international marketing was initiated by a program aimed at doubling capabilities to provide after-market parts and services.

As to prospects at home, where major markets were for low-horsepower compression equipment used in gas production, Donald Steele, executive vice president of Cooper Energy Services, reported optimistically, "Despite government indecision, there is one overwhelming certainty — an energy shortage exists. As long as that shortage is not satisfied, individuals and companies will be trying to find new oil and gas resources. As in past years, Cooper Energy Services will be there to assist them."

The uncertainties of 1977 did not deter Cooper from reaching record revenues ($678 million) and earnings ($4.68) for the fifth consecutive year, and increasing dividends from $.84 to $1.08 a share. The next year dividends were increased again, to $1.44 a share in February, then to $1.84 in November. "Under the direction of a highly cost-conscious management, Cooper's return on equity has risen dramatically to nearly double the average for all U.S. companies," reported *Duns Review*. "Cooper now dominates the international market for natural gas compressors, with about half the worldwide business for big pipeline equipment."

Two additional orders, totalling $30 million, were received early in 1978 to supply natural gas compression turbomachinery offshore in the North Sea. The orders, by Shell UK Exploration and Amoca (UK) Exploration, were for eight Coberra gas turbine-compression systems manufactured at the Cooper Energy Services plant in Liverpool, England. They marked the first application of new 30,600-hp Coberra models utilizing the Rolls-Royce light industrial gas generator in the North Sea. With installation of the eight units (completed the following year), Cooper had more than 320,000 horsepower in natural gas compression equipment operating in North Sea offshore fields. Soon after those sales, Cooper Energy Services and Rolls-Royce Ltd. organized a joint venture, Cooper Rolls, Inc., whereby Coberra light industrial turbine-compressor systems, using Rolls-Royce gas generators, were marketed by a unified sales force.

Barron's predicted that "Cooper Industries, having racked up peak sales and earnings in 1977, seems likely to score fresh highs again this year." *Financial World* named President Cizik a "Silver Winner" in its annual "Chief Executive Officer of the Year" competition, explaining that "the forceful 46-year-old chief executive officer of Cooper Industries just closed the books on the most successful year in the company's history at a time when capital goods makers in general are keeping a low financial profile."

After years of heated debate, Congress in 1978 finally enacted a compromise National Energy Plan that did little to end the controversies, but at least provided what a major proponent, Senator Henry Jackson (D-Washington), labeled as "the best possible bill we could get; it's a good beginning." Most industries, including Cooper, would have preferred deregulation, but were not altogether disappointed in the legislation. Pipeline and distribution segments of the gas industry believed the plan brought some improvements, such as early decontrol of deep gas and possible eventual decontrol of new gas, both of which would stimulate drilling. Neither industry nor Congress had illusions about the plan solving energy problems, but at last the tide seemed to be turning toward economic incentives as a means of strengthening domestic oil and gas production.

U.S. gas well production did increase significantly during the year. That trend, coupled with corresponding increases in Canada, created sufficient new demands for engines and compressors in Cooper's Superior horsepower category to justify major plant expansion plans at Springfield and Mt. Vernon. At the same time, new electric furnaces and machine tools replaced less efficient equipment at the Grove City plant, and a modernization effort to double Ajax manufacturing and assembly capacity at Corry was well on its way to completion.

Indeed, all three operational units of the company were in the process of expanding to meet increasing market opportunities. The announcement that The Cooper Group would move its Wiss manufacturing operations from Newark, New Jersey, to a recently puchased plant in Statesboro, Georgia, capped the relocation plan that had been in effect since the company's entry into the hand tools business. With Nicholson file manufacturing in the completion stage of a move to Cullman, Alabama, the Wiss relocation marked the final step in vacating antiquated facilities that once plagued the hand tools companies acquired by Cooper. During the ten-year modernization program, more than $80 million in capital expenditures and $30 million in associated transfer expenses had been invested in shifting production to geographic locations offering cost advantages in manufacturing efficiency, land costs, taxes, availability of labor, and proximity to the central distribution complex at Apex, North Carolina. With additional new plants operating in Brazil, Colombia, Germany, and The Netherlands, Cooper was the world's largest manufacturer of nonpowered hand tools. (Bill Rector, who had dreamed of the "tool basket" concept and directed its successful development, died of a heart attack while hurrying through Chicago's O'Hare airport in January of 1979. He was succeeded as president of The Cooper Group by Bill Gilchrist, who held the position until he retired in 1982, and was succeeded by Don MacPherson.)

Cooper Airmotive in 1978 maintained a level pace, after a spectacular 80 percent jump in earnings the previous year. The leveling out was anticipated, however, as Airmotive withdrew from the military engine repair and piston engine markets, which did not offer adequate long-term profit opportunities. A series of capital expenditures was launched, increasing capacity to serve more favorable airline, general aviation, and industrial segments of the market.

Events of the eleven years since Cooper had moved its corporate offices to Houston and initiated its major diversification movement were impressive. Both revenues and total assets had nearly quadrupled. The number of employees had grown by 50 percent. The value of plant equipment had more than tripled. The enhancement of shareholder investment was such that shares held since 1967 had shown a compounded 9 percent per annum yield (principal gain plus dividends) into 1978. And if Chairman Miller had not yet been reprieved from colleagues' ribbing about alleged prejudicial selection of his home area of the country as Cooper's new headquarters (including one incident in which President Cizik presented a blank piece of paper as Miller's "exhaustive study on why we should move to Houston"), he must have been exonerated by an editorial appearing in the October 16, 1978, issue of *Oil and Gas Journal:*

> The world is beating a path to Houston's doorstep, and the *The Journal's* Gulf Coast office is getting caught up in the rush. Gulf Coast editors used to be doing their jobs if they kept up with the Texas Railroad Commission, covered Wilcox and Frio drilling plays, and reported Gulf of Mexico lease sales. But as Houston has risen in national and world energy importance, so have the editor's regional responsibilities. And the pace is picking up. For example, we cover the Baltimore Canyon from here. That's because most of the operators working off the U.S. East Coast are headquartered in Houston. Another example is the flood of federal energy people into Houston to keep industry posted and to sample industry reaction on the latest regulations. In our international coverage, Houston is playing an increasingly important role in worldwide energy development. Many of the major construction projects in the Middle East and elsewhere are engineered and supervised here. The World Bank a month ago stopped in Houston to present its annual report. Houston was included in the world tour because the bank expects much of the capital needed to support energy projects in developing countries to be mobilized here. Houston also is playing a key role in U.S. hopes for a share in Mexico's dramatically growing oil and gas development. Although the controversial planned sale of Mexican gas to the U.S. is stalled, four of the six pipeline companies involved are based in Houston. And the Gulf Coast continues to be a major source of drilling equipment and services for Petroleos Mexicanos. Probably the most obvious sign of Houston's strategic international role is the annual Offshore Technology Conference. Begun in 1969, the OTC has become the world's largest energy meeting and draws thousands of overseas visitors. The "Gulf Coast" has grown.

Like the city of Houston, Cooper Industries had progressed to a position of international strength. But the next few months were to bring a single monumental surge that would equal the scope of its total growth since 1833.

In 1978, Cooper saw a potential opportunity to realize a long-held dream of acquiring the internationally known Gardner-Denver Company.

Cooper had established its credentials through viable planning strategy, successful diversification, a proven structure of management controls, and most importantly, a seasoned management team. Supposition had matured into actuality, investment into profit. There was no doubt concerning further acquisitions; the only questions were who and when.

In contrast, Dallas based Gardner-Denver was suffering from problems of inefficiencies brought about by frequent management turnover and reorganization, ailments not uncommon among growing corporations. "Gardner-Denver is a company notorious for lack of planning or cost controls," reported *Forbes*. "In 1971, it developed a blasthole drill for mining that turned out to be 'gold plated' and therefore uncompetitive. In 1975, it opened a $33 million foundry in Oklahoma whose economics depended on sales to outside customers. The customers never materialized, and the foundry lost $16 million until Gardner sold it at a further $5 million loss in early 1978. It is a company known by its competitors for cutting prices at just the wrong time and for a sales force that is, in the words of one competitor, 'looking for nothing but payday and five o'clock.' But it also is a company, dating to 1859, that is respected by every competitor for excellent products that need only the management they deserve."

The *Forbes* description closely paralleled the general profile of companies Cooper had acquired and returned to prosperity in recent years — but with one dramatic exception: it was approximately the same size as Cooper. Estimated revenues of $642 million and net income of $50 million were slightly smaller than those of Cooper, while total assets of $503 million and equity of $293 million were slightly larger. The company's three major business segments — mining and construction; petroleum, water well, and exploration; and general industry — offered product lines not unfamiliar to Cooper, yet different enough to avoid duplication. Cooper management was confident it could greatly improve Gardner-Denver's posture through a merger.

The Dallas company's stock, which traditionally had been among the most substantial in the machinery industry, had slipped to a P-E ratio below competitors, prompting the financial press to speculate that it could be taken over. Analysts agreed it had become vulnerable, and a German company was rumored to be buying its stock with just such an objective in mind. With that background information, President Cizik presented a merger proposal to Gardner-Denver Chairman-President Lynn L. Leigh at a luncheon meeting in July of 1978. He was rebuffed, in a situation reminiscent of the 1958 discussion between Gene Miller and Gifford Leece, but not discouraged. Determined to find a favorable course toward his objective without reversing the company's long-standing policy against unfriendly mergers, Cizik shifted his tack later in the year, this time approaching an outside Gardner-Denver director, Stanley E.G. Hillman, a Chicago industrialist and a member of Gardner-Denver's executive and finance and planning committees. Hillman was sufficiently interested to take it before the Gardner-Denver board.

The heart of Cizik's proposal was to acquire (1) 45 percent of the company's outstanding common stock through a cash offer of thirty-three dollars for shares trading at about twenty dollars on the New York Exchange, and (2) the remainder by a tax-free exchange for Cooper common and newly created cumulative convertible preferred stock. It was structured to offer Gardner-Denver shareholders those alternatives (succeeding events confirmed the wisdom of those who opted for the exchange), while making certain Cooper shareholders would still own 65 percent of the combined assets. The formula brought such a positive reaction from Gardner-Denver directors that Cooper's management team was thrust into a highly confidential crash program to move ahead with immediate merger planning. On January 18, 1979, trading in Gardner-Denver common stock was suspended by the Stock Exchange, following a market price rise to $22 ⅝ a share. Four days later, the Cooper plan was announced.

Cooper paid a premium price of $634,792,000 for the acquisition ($347,082,000 representing the fair value of securities and $287,710,000 cash), twice the amount of its own book value, in what *Forbes* reported to be "one of the 10 largest mergers in U.S. history." In doing so, it raised its debt from 20 to 37 percent of its total capital, eliciting some raised eyebrows among conservative investors. But in a single move, it doubled the size of the company and entered the exclusive ranks of firms surpassing billion-dollar-a-year revenues. It moved from 301st to 225th place among *Fortune*'s "500" and gained the complementary strength of products carrying not only the respected name of Gardner-Denver, but also of Martin-Decker, Apex, Demco, Funk, Dotco, and others obtained by Gardner-Denver's own acquisitions in previous years.

28

Gardner-Denver

Although Gardner-Denver's roots penetrated history somewhat less deeply than those of Cooper, the merger revealed interesting parallels of two companies growing with America, reacting similarly to the forces of democracy and to the development of her natural resources. They were nearly equal in size, each having emerged from a combination of several companies that had come together earlier. Now united, they seemed to represent what the young French visitor, Alexis de Tocqueville, might have had in mind when he wrote in 1833, "those who live in the midst of democratic fluctuations have always before their eyes the phantom of chance; and they end up liking all undertakings in which chance plays a part . . . the Americans make immense progress in productive industry, because they all devote themselves to it at once."

Robert W. Gardner was born in London, England, on February 18, 1832, one year before Charles and Elias Cooper opened their Mt. Vernon foundry. Most of his youth, however, was spent in Scotland where he attended school, then studied at the University of Edinburgh. Influenced by a father who had achieved scientific prominence in both Great Britain and France, the young man became proficient in mathematics and its application at the Royal School of Design.

Many years later he recalled how his father provided a lesson in self-discipline. Seeing his son slouching at the dinner table, the elder Gardner immediately ordered the butler to saw off the back of his son's chair. "No child ever sat straighter after that," he later said, and the principle of adherence to standards was imprinted into his personality.

Failing to receive an expected appointment after completing his studies at Edinburgh, Robert Gardner came to the United States in 1849, taught mathematics at a country school in Illinois for two years, then returned to Scotland. Not happy with changes taking place there, however, he went back to Illinois, settling in Quincy. With teaching positions unavailable, he decided to master the practical side of science by accepting an apprenticeship in the small machine shop of Edward G. Turner. He left the city for a brief period to work with an Alton, Illinois, engine building company, but returned to join Henry Mitchell in purchasing the Turner shop. When Mitchell died, Gardner formed a partnership with a machinist named John Robertson.

Although it is difficult to pinpoint the beginning of what was to grow into a manufacturing organization, the most accepted year was 1859, when Gardner invented a "fly-ball" governor that for the first time provided control of the speeds on steam engines. Until that time, steam engines — the major source of power in America — ran only at peak power, regardless of work load. When the load was reduced, as in the case of a lumber-mill saw completing the cut of a log, the engine could run wild, tearing itself apart and sometimes even exploding. Gardner's governor used the centrifugal force of two lead balls that swung in an enlarging arc as speed increased, closing a valve before a danger point was reached. Gravitational pull of a weighted level opened the valve again when the speed was reduced to an established level. Patented in 1860 and improved later with the addition of spring action, that one invention brought world acclaim and prosperity to the Gardner Governor Company during the next three decades. An article in an 1888 issue of the *Quincy Daily Herald* recorded the progress:

> The magnitude of this establishment (Gardner Governor Company), devoted entirely to the manufacture of a single specialty, must be seen to be fully appreciated, In 1860, Mr. R.W. Gardner, the patentee, introduced to the world his invention, and for a long time was unable to get the recognition his device merited. After several years of hard work and many competitive tests in which he was able to demonstrate the superioriy of his device over all others then in use, the business began to grow, and a season of prosperity set in that has culminated in its being recognized as the leading device for governing engines now in use in this country. The business was incorporated in 1883, with R.W. Gardner, president, L.C. Neustadt, secretary and treasurer, and J.W. Gardner (the founder's son who joined the company in 1880), superintendent, and since its incorporation has manufactured and sold over 25,000 governors. There are now nearly 55,000 in use all over the world, and it is no unusual event for the company to send their governors to China, Japan, Australia, Europe, and South America. Agencies carrying stocks of governors have been established in London, Amsterdam, and all the leading cities of the United States. From 75 to 125 men are constantly employed in the manufacture of these governors, which vary in size from one-half inch to twelve-inch steam pipe, weighing from six pounds to two thousand pounds, and designed for every class of engine from one-horse to six hundred horse power.

It is possible the article's flattering prose could be attributed in part to the fact that Gardner's brother Henry had moved to America and become co-owner of the *Quincy Daily Herald* — but its accuracy was well documented.

Robert W. Gardner, founder of the Gardner Governor Company.

An early advertisement of the Gardner and Robertson partnership features the fly-ball governor that led to the formation of the company.

During the years of early growth, Gardner had bought out his partner, Robertson, and survived an 1880 fire that destroyed his facilities. This forced him to construct a new buiding where he incorporated and started preparing his young son for management responsibilities. Among the company's best customers were oil drillers, whose rigs and hoisting mechanisms were powered by steam. But the versatile governor also was used on engines at construction, mining, and factory sites, on packet boats plying the nearby Mississippi River, and even on merry-go-rounds. At the 1883 Southern Exposition in Louisville, Kentucky, the Gardner Governor Company was awarded a medal for the best steam engine governor made in the United States.

It was not until 1890 that Gardner decided to diversify into a second product, a steam pump, and that move was not made without admitted "feelings of trepidation" because of well-established competition. Early attempts to enter the market were geared to underpricing other manufacturers. Prospective customers, however, equated the low price with inferior quality, and Gardner quickly determined that his company henceforth would fight its marketing battles at a top quality price level. It was a policy that would guide his thinking from that point forward, and the

Gardner employees pose outside the Quincy plant in 1901.

Gardner duplex reciprocating pump eventually captured a profitable niche in the industrial marketplace.

Expansion toward the end of the century led to construction in 1900-01 of a new plant on South Front Street, which would become the heart of a continuously growing manufacturing complex for many years. Dedication of the new building was a gala affair, with one area of the factory floor waxed for dancing to the music of Louis Rischar and his fifteen-piece Empire Theatre orchestra.

Just prior to completion of the building, the company also introduced its third major product, a vertical high-speed air compressor. Like the C. & G. Cooper Company, Gardner was taking steps to meet the foreseeable decline of steam power, on which its business had depended for many years. The Gardner Rix vertical compressor was a positive step in that direction, as well as a pioneer in an area it would come to dominate.

Meanwhile, Gardner pumps were becoming increasingly popular in a new market — the oil fields of Texas, where a business boom had been created by the 1901 discovery of the great Spindletop Oil Field there. The pumps, originally designed to provide water for pressurized boilers generating steam power for general industry, were easily converted to what became the original "mud pumps" for circulating mud used as a lubricant in rotary drilling by the host of wildcatters basking in what became known as "Texas rain." Quincy's Mississippi River location provided a direct delivery route to the Gulf of Mexico, giving Gardner an advantage over its eastern competitors.

J. Willis Gardner who succeeded his father as president in 1905, improved the company's position further by introducing the "Gardner Booster," a duplex steam pump specifically designed for mud service. (The elder Gardner died in 1907, shortly after capping a record of diversified philanthropy by purchasing a beautiful 23-acre area which he bequeathed as a park to the city of Quincy.) Continuous development of its pumps created a link with the growing petroleum industry that would extend into a chain of products used in drilling operations through the years. A turret-type reciprocating pump in 1913 was overshadowed by a large slush pump of 1923, which was paraded on the back of a truck through the oil fields of California to impress operators, but in turn was dwarfed by later models. Open frame crank-shaft construction gave way to the first enclosed eccentric driven duplex power pump.

Sales of all company lines were marketed through agencies or manufacturers with complementary products. One of those was the Denver Rock Drill Company, a customer-agent selling Gardner compressors in conjunction with its own air-powered drills. The Denver Rock Drill company had been founded by a transplanted New Yorker, William H. Leonard, who had gone West at the age of eighteen when the discovery of gold at Cripple Creek started the historic rush of 1891. There are discrepancies in accounts of the company's beginning, but 1905 has been considered acceptable because it was the year a man named F.M. Iler, with whom Leonard was associated, designed a rock drill he hoped to market in the gold mine camps. The drill, which resembled a huge brace and bit, was too heavy and inefficient and only half a dozen were sold. Undaunted, however, Iler and Leonard leased the ground floor of a Denver building and continued to work on improvements that might give them a marketable product. Having made a great deal of money in smelting and cattle raising, Leonard could afford to finance the venture. "While we were struggling with the assembly of our drills, Mr. D.S. Waugh appeared on the scene," Leonard later wrote in an article for the *Mile-Hi News*. "He was an able machinist and mechanic and had a well-developed inventive mind. He had previous experience making pneumatic chipping hammers in a little shop in Chicago prior to coming to Denver. His claim for recognition was that the automatic valves he used in his pneumatic hammers could be made to operate a hammer drill. His first stopping drill had an air feed in line with the hammer cylinder, chuck, etc., and was a departure from the Iler type of drill."

On the strength of Waugh's invention, Leonard formed the Denver Rock Drill Company in 1906, as successor to the operation he shared

D.S. Waugh, machinist-inventor, designed products that enabled the Denver Rock Drill Company to thrive in its early years.

William H. Leonard, founder of the Denver Rock Drill Company.

A Gardner air compressor is used to power Denver rock drills for a Denver equipment demonstration in 1925, two years before the companies merged.

with Iler. The first design was followed by a series of improvements, as well as new product lines, all created by Waugh. By 1910, the company was established in new quarters on thirty-five lots in Denver, and two years later it built a shop containing what was considered "the last word" in forging equipment. Waugh products for mining, contracting, quarrying, and other industries became known in many parts of the world. They included a wide range of drills and such other products as concrete breakers, trench diggers, steel punchers, fans, automatic air line oilers, and even full-scale derrick rigs for large hammer drills, each containing the Waugh name. So prolific was the inventory that company salesmen for a time were referred to as "Waugh-iors."

The company operated without a president for a year during World War I when Leonard served as a captain, heading an engineering company of men that included several Denver Rock Drill employees. After he returned to the presidency in the summer of 1918, he continued to be called "Captain" Leonard by friends and colleagues. The company resumed its expansion, after a brief postwar recession, building a foundry containing the first large electric furnace in that section of the country, then adding the best available machine tools, grinders, milling machines, and automatic lathes. As its market areas grew, the company attempted to produce a portable compressor to round out its line but found that it could not compete with established manufacturers.

With both companies seeing benefits in combining interests, negotiations for a merger began in 1926. J. Willis Gardner was instrumental in working out a satisfactory arrangement, but when the Gardner-Denver Company was formed in 1927, Leonard became its first president and chief executive officer, with Gardner chairman of the board. The products complemented each other so well that not a single item in either line was eliminated by the merger. The new company was able to supply equipment for oil wells, pipeline trenching, mining, dam and tunnel projects, highway construction, and other projects representing the nation's greatest growth potential.

The Great Depression following the stock market crash of 1929 brought a temporary about-face in the company's forward march, but recovery came relatively soon, as large-scale construction programs such as the Hoover and Grand Coulee dams were organized by the government to revitalize the nation's economy. When H.G. Myers succeeded Leonard as president in 1935, the company already was introducing new models of former products and entering the air motor and hoist manufacturing business. Canadian and overseas markets grew, particularly in the heavy mining regions of South Africa.

When America entered World War II, Gardner-Denver production was sidetracked entirely to the armed forces and merchant marines or their suppliers and contractors. Nearly all wartime products, however, represented the company's standard lines so little conversion of facilities was needed. The largest war contracts were for pumps used on submarines and Liberty Ships (which had Cooper-Bessemer and Superior power shafts). Air compressors and drills were used in the construction and maintenance of distant bases, including excavation of underground caverns for fuel and ammunition storage. A variety of Gardner-Denver products went to airplane, tank, and gun plants, and to shipyards. Employees received the Army Air Corps "E" award for extraordinary effort, and 652 served in the armed forces, merchant marines, and American Red Cross. Thirteen died in the line of duty.

Edgar F. Schaefer became president when Myers retired from active management in 1947, heading the company during another period of war production supporting armed forces in Korea, then into peacetime expansion of manufacturing facilities at Quincy (where executive offices also were located); Denver; LaGrange, Missouri; Brantford, Ontario; and Johannesburg, South Africa. An Export Department, developed and headed by long-time executive Gifford V. Leece several years earlier, had seven branches in Canada and eleven in other nations on four continents. Leece subsequently had been named general manager, then vice president and a member of the board. When Schaefer died in 1954 Leece was elected president, beginning a period of growth, much of it through acquisitions, that would make him one of the well-known chief executives in the country, often sought out as a spokesman for the industry. Ralph G. Gardner, grandson of the founder, was named chairman of the board.

At Gardner's suggestion that the company consider adding a pneumatic tool line, the new president initiated an acquisition of the Keller Tool Company. Located in Grand Haven, Michigan, Keller designed and manufactured pneumatic tools used in high production assembly plants of automotive, electronic, aircraft, telephone, and other industries. Organized in 1912 at Fond du Lac, Wisconsin, by William H. Keller, the company actually represented the rebirth of a business founded at Philadelphia in 1893 by Keller's father, then sold to a Chicago firm in 1906. The newly formed company was incorporated in 1914 and moved to Grand Haven three years later, manufacturing portable air-powered tools sold under the brand name "Keller-Made Master-Built." Early products, many of them used in the war effort, were chipping and riveting hammers and some tools custom designed for the automotive industry. During the next two decades it added grinders, drills, screwdrivers, and nutsetters, showing steady profits but only minimal growth.

Sizeable expansion was sparked by World War II military production needs, shortly after E. Vincent Erickson became vice president and general manager in 1939. Many Keller tools accepted by manufacturers at that time gained inroads for postwar sales. In 1948, Keller purchased the Dunning Manufacturing Company of Charlotte, Michigan, one of its principal suppliers of parts. In continuing the design and manufacture

A Denver Rock Drill Company coal drill chips away at the wall of a Pennsylvania coal company mine in 1922.

William H. Keller, left, talks with another Grand Haven, Michigan, industrialist shortly after his company was moved to that city in 1917.

This photo was typical of those in World War II, demonstrating Gardner-Denver going "over the top" in a war bond campaign.

Workers use Gardner-Denver sinking drills to prepare blast holes on the famed Pennsylvania Turnpike project of the 1940s.

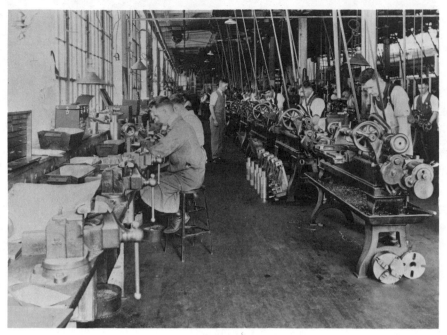

The inspection and turning room of the William H. Keller, Inc., plant in 1918 (inspection employees on the left, turning on the right).

of its expanding numbers of products, the company combined precision and light weight with ruggedness that could withstand the abuse of assembly lines. It dominated the market in customized specialty manufacturing, but experienced difficulty in combining that type of effort with high-volume production. Still, it ranked third or fourth in overall sales volume of pneumatic tools, and in 1953 it opened a screw machine plant in Reed City, Michigan, producing Keller "Wire-Wrap" tools and parts used in the assembly of its pneumatic tools.

The acquisition of Keller in 1955 expanded Gardner-Denver by approximately 25 percent. Erickson, who by then had become president of the Grand Haven company, was named executive vice president and board member of Gardner-Denver. "Vin Erickson did a remarkable job in assuring his people that the merger was mutually beneficial," said Gifford Leece. "I think one of the weaknesses of any merger can be the domination by the larger company. You can find quite a few road blocks and a lot of suspicions. Fortunately in the Keller merger we didn't experience a great deal of this." Erickson later became a key figure in handling other Gardner-Denver mergers.

With products and markets growing, Gardner-Denver in 1956 formed a subsidiary manufacturing company in Brazil and purchased new office

This unusual air tools plant in Westhausen, West Germany, originally was a German munitions factory in World War II.

and plant facilities in Woodstock, Ontario, closing operations at Brantford. Negotiations also were completed for production in Belgium, and construction started on a new forge plant near Derby, Colorado.

In a move to manufacture air tools in West Germany, Gardner-Denver made a lease arrangement involving one of the most unusual industrial plants in the world. Located in a valley near the small village of Westhausen, the factory was twelve meters wide and approximately one mile long, with cement walls nearly one foot thick. It had been built into adjacent hillsides by the German government to make munitions during World War II. With contours following the natural lay of the land, surrounded by trees and shrubbery and covered by camouflage nets, it had never been discovered by Allied bomb crews. Peter Niess, one of two German industrialists who worked out the lease arrangement for what became Deutsche Gardner-Denver, was a former tank commander serving with Germany's famed Field Marshall Rommel. He managed the plant from the time Gardner-Denver began operations there in 1958 until a short time after the 1979 merger with Cooper Industries.

Having abandoned merger proposals of both Dresser and Cooper in 1958, Gardner-Denver acquired the Mayhew Machine Company and Mayhew Supply Company of Dallas, moving for the first time into the heart of the oil industry it had been serving for many years. Founded in

1923, Mayhew had become the largest producer and distributor of seismograph and geophysical drilling equipment for oil exploration, and a manufacturer of small oil well drilling rigs. It also made rotary drilling equipment for the construction and mining industries. Mayhew had been a Gardner-Denver customer for many years, so the companies had what Leece called "a personal acquaintance," making negotiations "an altogether different approach than we had in the case of Keller, in which both of us came in cold turkey to talk." Charles Mayhew, son of the founder, was named to the Gardner-Denver board and served in various consulting roles until his retirement in 1972. The addition of Mayhew moved Gardner-Denver from what one executive characterized as the "fringes of the petroleum business" into the mainstream. Renamed the "Dallas Division," it was expanded after a struggle of several years into basic drilling components such as drawworks and rotary tables. Reported *Business Week,* "Leece is determined to broaden its (Gardner-Denver's) line to include just about everything needed to drill an oil well."

The company continued to spread in other directions with a quickening tempo of acquisitions. In its centennial year of 1959, it added Cyclo-Blower Company of York, Pennsylvania, to its compressed air manufacturing group. CycloBlower manufactured a complete line of helical screw and rotary lobe type blower/compressors, providing high volumes of air at lower pressures for pneumatic conveying, waste treatment, and other industrial applications. Established just two years before the acquisition, the company represented combined efforts of several men having long experience in pressure and vacuum air applications. Its president was C.J. Surdy, who had left the vice presidency of an Erie, Pennsylvania, company to design a new line of screw-type blowers and assemble a group of former colleagues and outside investors in the new venture. The company's products brought both early success and interest from Gardner-Denver. After the acquisition on October 28, CycloBlower became a wholly-owned subsidiary with the founders serving on its board of directors.

During a special tour billed as an occasion to view Gardner-Denver's entry into its second century of progress, President Leece took a group of fifteen New York analysts (via chartered airplane) to visit what a *Finance* magazine reporter described as "the company's vast manufacturing complex turning out a line of equipment used in general industry, construction, the oil fields, mining, and electronics." He explained that the company "checked out as the 482nd U.S. firm in volume of sales that reached nearly $75 million in the centennial year of 1959." The hard driving chief executive, who had been with the company since 1922, explained also that Gardner-Denver would continue to follow a pattern of acquisitions complementing its established areas of strength.

His projection was well founded. Less than a year after the CycloBlower acquisition, the company broadened its pneumatic tool line by acquiring the Apex Machine & Tool Company of Dayton, Ohio, a leading manufacturer of bits and sockets used with electrical and air tools, and a producer of universal joints for machinery and aircraft.

Founded in the late 1920s, Apex went into receivership after the 1929 stock market crash. In 1933, a group headed by Carl A. Lange purchased it from the receivership trustee and resumed the manufacture of tools, accessories, and small universal joints. With the automobile business one of the first to recover from the depression, the new company also developed a line of gauges and pricing scrolls for gasoline pumps. This association with Detroit led Lange to the decision that a need existed for top-quality universal joints, sockets, and screwdriving tools. Further investigation reinforced his idea, and within a few years, Apex became a leading producer of industrial screwdriver bits and universal wrenches, which quickly improved the ability for assembly operators to drive bolts, nuts, and screws in relatively inaccessible areas. When power tools came into vogue, the company responded by adapting its products for pneumatic equipment. Rented manufacturing quarters were abandoned in 1941 when the company acquired land on Patterson Boulevard and built a one-story plant.

During World War II, Apex manufactured all the universal joints used in military aircraft. It also produced sockets to drive nuts and bolts for a major aircraft engine builder. Both of those ventures led to continued product expansion in the postwar years. A Phillips insert bit and bit holder, invented by the company's sales manager, Harry Fisher, became standard in all industry. The addition of a heat treating plant and several expansions under the leadership of Julian Lange preceded the Apex merger with Gardner-Denver in 1960. Other expansions were to come later, including the addition of another manufacturing plant in 1973. (In 1982, two years after the merger of Gardner-Denver and Cooper Industries, Julian Lange retired, having served Apex for forty years, and Arthur E. Aspengren became vice president and general manager. The Apex Machine & Tool name was shortened to "Apex.")

Sales to the construction industry constituted the largest single segment of Gardner-Denver business in the early 1960s, as the nation accelerated efforts to build dams and tunnels for hydroelectric power, and a 41,000-mile interstate highway system. A 1963 issue of *Investor's Reader* dramatized an example of this growing market:

> Though not generally celebrated for its mineral deposits, New York City nevertheless is one of the major users of mining equipment. This fact causes Gardner-Denver Company of Quincy, Illinois considerable pleasure. The big city is regularly riddled from Battery to Bronx and river to river to allow subways, autos, water and power to make their way under-

ground. For instance, 80 feet below the Avenue of the Americas, Gardner-Denver "jumbos" — carriers for compressed air drills — are boring their way into the mica and quartz-laden Manhattan schist as a new 4th-to-34th Street express tunnel is added to the Sixth Avenue subway. . . . On the street level above, a bank of four brand-new Gardner-Denver Rota-Screw machines compress air for the platform of the jumbo and the four drills mounted on it.

An aggressive research and development program brought new products also for oil fields, general industry, and a rapidly expanding electronics market. President Leece noted that, "With our products, price is not the top consideration for our customers. Performance and quality of service come first." His words echoed the policy described by the company's founder three quarters of a century earlier.

Leece retired from active company leadership in 1963, becoming chairman of the board, but turning the chief executive reins over to a new president, Cedric H. Rieman. Before becoming the seventh president, Rieman had served as executive vice president since 1961. He had joined the company in 1936 as a salesman and advanced through various management positions.

In 1965, the company widened its stake in the petroleum industry with the acquisition of Martin-Decker Corporation, a producer of recording instruments for oil drilling rigs as well as weighing devices and test instruments for industrial applications. Martin-Decker instruments monitored the flow of mud in a drilling hole, the weight on the bit, the level of mud in tanks, and other information that told a driller what he should be doing. The new wholly-owned subsidiary had a highly successful worldwide sales and service organization supporting its manufacturing facilities in Santa Ana, California. It had been founded in 1927, the same year that Gardner and Denver companies combined operations.

Actually, the company was a successor to Martin-Loomis Corporation, formed in 1927 to manufacture and sell a weight indicator for the oil drilling industry. Two thirds of the corporate shares were owned by the Loomis Oil Well Control Company of Long Beach, California, and a few friends. The remainder was owned by a Loomis employee, Walter R. "Frosty" Martin, who had conceived the idea of an indicator that would weigh a drill stem continuously during all drilling operations. A former roustabout, driller, and salesman who had grown up in the oil fields of Pennsylvania, Martin had drifted west, joined Loomis and developed his idea for a weight indicator. After the separate corporation was formed to produce it, however, his new colleagues had second thoughts about its possibilities. Their feelings were intensified by litigation concerning the use of a diaphragm that formed the nucleus of the indicator, and the belief that any blacksmith could produce the simple instrument or something similar, under patent terms acquired by Martin. As a result, Chairman Loomis asked a young salesman, Elmer L. "Deck" Decker, to find a buyer for the two-thirds interest in Martin-Loomis. (A former oil driller and automobile salesman, Decker had joined the Loomis Oil Well Control Company after selling its chairman and several officers new Willys Knight touring cars.) Unable to find a buyer but convinced the product was sound, Decker worked out a financial arrangement of his own, which included some money from "Frosty" Martin in an agreement that made the inventor a two-thirds owner. On July 20, 1928, the two men became partners in Martin-Loomis. Martin was fifty-five years old, and Decker was thirty. Included in their agreement was a "sell, transfer or dispose of" clause that later would make the younger man sole owner of the company.

Launching a sales campaign through the mid-continent and Gulf Coast oil fields, Decker preached what he labeled as "a straight-hole sermon." His theme was "the shortest distance between two points is a straight line — a Martin-Loomis weight indicator will keep the hole straight." He recalled later that old timers were impossible to convince, and the company's successful beginning was attributed to the interest of young technical men who convinced their superiors that the ability to drill straight holes would solve "sucker rod problems" and reduce production costs. After that, Decker said, "The young company could hardly keep up with orders." Financial obligations to the Loomis Oil Well Control Company were settled by the end of the first year's business, and the company name was changed to Martin-Decker. A new plant containing all new machinery was constructed on three Long Beach lots.

Decker considered the successful dedication of the plant in February 1930 to be a good omen. An orchestra played for a dance inaugurating the new facility, and nonalcoholic punch was served, since Mrs. Martin was a prohibitionist. Nevertheless, Decker recalled later, that "bathtub gin was somehow secretly mixed with the punch at frequent intervals and the dedication turned out to be a whale of a success. Even Mrs. Martin was feeling no pain."

Martin, as president and general manager, and Decker, as secretary-treasurer charged with selling, advertising, and service seemed to complement each other. The ambitious, exuberant young man brought ideas for new designs from the oil fields, and the experienced older man directed their conversion into products. In addition to the first commercially successful weight indicator and recorder, the company introduced gauges and recorders for rotary tables, mud pumps, and drills. Cash reserves were nearly depleted in the early days of the Great Depression, but the two men kept their company alive by discontinuing their own salaries and letting employees share jobs rather than face layoffs. Those years were used to consolidate the variety of instruments into a single package, introduced with much fanfare in 1934 as the Martin-Decker Quintuplex. (Promoter Decker, who named the new product, reported

W.R. "Frosty" Martin, left, in 1930, and E.L. "Deck" Decker in 1955.

that publicity surrounding the birth of the Dionne quintuplets that year "didn't hurt the Quintuplex.") Later in that decade, development of a small diameter, wire-reinforced hose greatly improved the high-pressure capabilities of most Martin-Decker products.

World War II development of resources increased Martin-Decker's business along with that of nearly all American industries. "Frosty" Martin, who had reached the age of seventy in 1943, was instrumental in helping the war effort through activities not associated with the company, one of which created a shipyard at Long Beach. Leaving the company operation almost entirely to Decker, he also made plans to transfer much of his stock to his heirs. Decker, however, exercised the clause in their original agreement by which neither could sell, transfer, or dispose of stock without giving the other a ten-day option to purchase it. Martin fought the move without success and, convinced that a postwar depression was imminent, he sold his interest to Decker. Although the two remained courteous after the transaction, their friendship became tense until the time of Martin's death in 1955.

Through the years the company produced new product lines and became the exclusive marketing outlet for others. After the acquisition by

For heavy duty crane work, Martin-Decker produced measuring devices such as this 200,000-pound sensater scale with a 24-inch indicator in the early 1960s.

Gardner-Denver, it continued operating as a wholly-owned subsidiary until 1970, when it became a division of the parent company. Decker remained as president and general manager for five years after the acquisition, and a new plant constructed at Santa Ana was opened in early 1968.

In 1966, Gardner-Denver expanded operations in the manufacture of pneumatic products by purchasing a plant in Green Bay, Wisconsin. Beginning with the production of a new "Distribut-Air" system for hoist operations, the plant suffered a temporary setback during a general recession in 1970 to recover and increase its line of air hoists and air motors. A new plant constructed at the city's industrial park in 1972 featured the first complete heat treat facility in northern Wisconsin.

But the company's primary growth pattern was through acquisition, and in 1967 it reached into the picturesque community of Coffeyville, Kansas, to diversify operations with purchase of a power transmission manufacturing company. In studying the feasibility of the purchase it was difficult to determine which had the more intriguing history, the Funk Manufacturing Company or the city in which it was located.

Settled near the Kansas-Missouri border on the fringe of Cherokee country, Coffeyville in the late nineteenth century was a gathering point for cattlemen, soldiers, and Indians who turned the main thoroughfare of saloons, dance halls, and gambling houses into a boisterous community nicknamed "Cow Town." Desperados murdered three town marshals there, and eight persons perished in a gun battle with the Dalton gang during a bank robbery in 1892. After the turn of the century, Coffeyville evolved through the stages of an oil and natural gas boom and a temporary spurt as a glass manufacturing center to become an attractive, peaceful city, preserving its unusual heritage only in such reminders as the Dalton Museum. Among its citizens at various times were school teacher Wendell Wilkie, baseball pitcher Walter Johnson, and the Funk twins.

Born in 1910, Joseph and Howard Funk moved with their parents to Akron, Ohio, where they were raised, educated, and introduced to the skills of flying airplanes. By 1932 they had built and flown their own two-place glider and prepared themselves for further involvement in aviation by enrolling in engine design classes at Akron University. Subsequent years found them building a powered monoplane, modifying it with a Ford engine, then creating a second model that received the blessings of the Civil Aeronautics Authority. Raising money to attempt commercial production, the brothers experimented with various designs, and in 1941 the Funk Model B-75L became competitive with other light aircraft on the market. Two other brothers, William and Ray Jensen, who were in the oil business at Coffeyville, became partners with the Funks, moving them and the company back to the city of their birth, just as World War II put the sport of private flying into limbo. When the war

Howard Funk, left, Charles Seiberling (co-founder of Goodyear Tire and Rubber Co.) and Joe Funk, right, at the unveiling and dedication of the first production Funk airplane, Akron, Ohio, 1938.

ended, however, the company resumed operations, producing 217 airplanes before a slack in private aircraft flying prompted the Funks and Jensens to phase out that business in 1948. They then incorporated the company and converted it to manufacturing a line of power unit accessories for Ford engines.

After a fire gutted the Funk Manufacturing Company plant in 1954, the group rebuilt, increased its products, and expanded four times before the merger with Gardner-Denver. With additional capital then available, plant facilities were doubled in 1968. Subsequent additions expanded operations into plants at an industrial park near McGugin Field, which in turn were enlarged several times in the 1970s. Funk mechanical and automatic transmissions, hydraulic pump drives, and planetary reducers were by then being used in construction and industrial equipment all over the world. And in a few scattered locations, some adventurous weekend pilots maintained that their Funk airplanes, with near stall-proof performance and gentle handling characteristics, offered features still unmatched in private aircraft.

The next acquisitions came in 1973, in the same year Lynn L. Leigh, a nineteen-year veteran in the oil supply business before joining Gardner-Denver in 1967, was elected president and chief operating officer, with Rieman becoming chairman. Under Leigh's leadership, the company expanded international manufacturing and marketing with acquisition of Padley & Venables, Ltd., near the steel city of Sheffield, England. The successor of a company founded by Richard Padley in 1911, and later joined by Thomas Venables in a partnership, the British corporation manufactured a wide range of equipment for pneumatic and gasoline driven hammers, including concrete breakers, asphalt cutters, special chisels, and various types of drill steel used in mining and tunneling. It had become part of a group merged with Tarmac, Ltd., which included Bedford Steels, a small Sheffield rolling mill also acquired by Gardner-Denver. Under the Gardner-Denver umbrella, the two companies were operated in tandem as a subsidiary.

Later in the year, Gardner-Denver purchased Drill Carrier Corporation of Salem, Virginia, putting it for the first time into the business of producing track-mounted, self-propelled carriers used by mining and construction industries in conjunction with pneumatic and hydraulic-operated drilling equipment.

After months of study and debate, Gardner-Denver in mid-1973 announced it would move corporate headquarters to an office building in Dallas. President Leigh explained that directors wanted to separate corporate management from manufacturing functions and gain better accessibility not as adequate in a small city — an exact parallel to the reasoning behind Cooper's move from Mt. Vernon to Houston in 1967. Leigh stressed that the move would "in no way affect manufacturing operations in Quincy," and that directors realized there was "an emotional overtone to relocating headquarters of a company for 114 years identified with Quincy." A group of stockholders was formed to oppose the move, but the board stayed with its decision. The International Division moved to Dallas first, in October 1973, and total relocation of corporate management was completed the following July.

While the move was in progress, the company again extended its oil drilling product line by acquiring Demco Corporation of Oklahoma City. Organized as the Drilling Equipment Manufacturing Company in 1945, with its name shortened later through common usage, Demco had grown to a position of leadership in manufacturing butterfly valves, ball valves, gate valves, solids-separating equipment, centrifugal pumps, waste treatment units, and expandable tools used in processing applications, as well as drilling. The company's founders, Paul Snetcher and B.C. Christensen had operated as partners until the latter's death in 1950. Snetcher continued to manage the company until he also died in 1965. C.L. Knight then became president and chief executive officer until the merger with Gardner-Denver. Most manufacturing was carried out at the Oklahoma City plant although limited valve production also was done at leased facilities in Edmonton, Alberta. Distribution was carried out through leased warehouses in the U.S. Southwest and Edmonton. The merger into Gardner-Denver was completed in March of 1975.

Four months later, Dotco Corporation of Hicksville, Ohio, was added to the growing Gardner-Denver family. The company had been founded in 1953 by Roland E. Doeden, an inventive-minded engineer who discovered the need for a small air driven motor that could power such tools as pressure-sensitive abrasive discs. As manager of a Mall Tool Company plant near Chicago, he noticed that small tools for work in confined areas had to be driven by large, awkward power units not at all compatible with the job at hand. Determined to find a better way, he launched the Doeden Tool Company at an abandoned gasoline service station in his hometown of Sherwood, Ohio, accepting job work to finance his more important venture. After designing and developing an air motor that could be held easily in the palm of his hand, Doeden introduced his new product to another Chicago firm, the Metal Removal Company, a producer of carbide burrs. Officers of that company were so elated they ordered one hundred of the air motors without bothering to ask the price. Creating the brand name of Dotco as an acronym of his company title, Doeden began marketing the product for his own distribution and as a Metal Removal Company item bearing that firm's name. Soon he was selling regularly to the automotive industry and others, to the extent that he adopted Dotco as the company name, taking advantage of its spreading brand recognition. Moving to a new plant at Hicksville, eleven miles from Sherwood, he was joined by his brother, Gerald, who handled marketing and advertising. The company grew rapidly, adding new finishing tool lines, all powered by the original air-motor. Doeden continued as chairman and chief executive officer until the July 1975 acquisition by Gardner-Denver. At that time his son, Douglas, became CEO, later leaving to begin his own business after the merger with Cooper Industries.

In 1977, Gardner-Denver purchased Advanced Controls Corporation of Irvine, California, a manufacturer of automatic drilling, routing, and inspection equipment for the printed circuit board industry. The acquisition was made to complement the Pneutronics Division's fast-selling "Wire-Wrap" machines that had reached a high level of sophistication in automatically stripping and simultaneously wrapping wire into specified patterns at high rates of speed. Advanced Controls had entered the mushrooming electronics field in 1970, when a group of investors and engineers began operations at Pico Rivera, California. Their products were designed for more reliable production of printed circuit boards, which were in great demand. Steady growth of the company brought early needs for expansion, and subsequent relocations to Anaheim in 1972, then to Santa Ana in 1974. After just five years in business, sales volume reached $5 million and the young company employed seventy-five persons. The acquisition by Gardner-Denver provided growth capital for even more rapid expansion, and in 1978 another move was made to Irvine. Advanced Controls continued to engineer and develop products based on the specialized needs of the telecommunications and com-

Hollis Engineering, producer of equipment that solders and cleans printed circuit board assemblies, was acquired by Gardner-Denver just two months before that company became part of Cooper Industries in 1979.

puter industries, often meeting individual specifications required by customers, and soon after it became a part of Cooper Industries it reached an employment figure of three hundred.

At the time Gardner-Denver was merging with Cooper Industries, it also was negotiating its own final acquisition with another electronics-oriented company, Hollis Engineering of Nashua, New Hampshire. Founded at Hollis, New Hampshire, in 1956 by Howard Wegener and Dudley Bell, it had grown from a temporary garage operation producing wave soldering equipment, to a manufacturing plant at Nashua, with Wegener as president and chief executive officer. Like the founders of Advanced Controls, Wegener and Bell organized the business to produce equipment that would bring savings to the preparation of printed circuit boards — operations for many years performed by hand. The Nashua plant was soon expanded to manufacture a wide range of electro-mechanical systems and related equipment used in the production of printed circuit boards (considered the most basic subassembly for virtually all electronic equipment) and small electronic subassemblies. The sale of spare parts also became increasingly important as the number of installed units grew.

In 1971, a new management group assumed company leadership when both Wegener and Bell retired. Christos Papoutsy, who had joined the company in 1964, became president and chief executive officer. Kenneth G. Boynton was named executive vice president. In the years that followed, the company developed new markets, particularly overseas. Sales representatives and distributors, supported by seven direct-sales/service officers, were active throughout the United States and in thirty foreign countries. Exports accounted for approximately 35 percent of sales by the mid-1970s. Papoutsy continued to head Hollis operations after the merger with Gardner-Denver, and then Cooper. Later he would become president of Cooper's consolidated electronics division.

Official acquisition of Hollis took place in February, 1979, just two months before Gardner-Denver became a part of Cooper Industries.

Two officers of Gardner-Denver moved into corporate management jobs with Cooper Industries after the merger, and each would advance to an executive vice presidential position with a reorganization in 1982. They were Donald E. Kipley, who went to Gardner-Denver with the Keller acquisition, then became vice president and general manager of the Industrial Machinery Division in 1973; and Michael J. Sebastian, who joined Gardner-Denver in 1978 as general manager of the Rotary Machinery Division after twenty-five years with FMC Corporation.

29

Adjusting for Evolution

The Gardner-Denver merger represented a new avenue of growth for Cooper Industries. Whereas previous acquisitions had been combined to create new business areas (hand tools and airmotives), Gardner-Denver was an entity in itself; the challenge was to weave it into the Cooper system, solving its previous *corporate* management problems and building on its *operational* management strengths. Cooper's high regard for the latter was reflected in the large number of operational executives retained, and later promoted within Cooper Industries. The merger was described by Cizik as a "complementary move" rather than a pure diversification, because it was an expansion of machinery manufacturing, albeit into more direct applications of energy exploration and production, and into the new field of construction. The two companies had, in fact, shared several markets, although with different products.

Cooper management, aware of some overlapping areas vulnerable to anti-trust charges, had prepared a frank presentation to the Federal Trade Commission. Senior Vice President Riedel conceded to Commission members the overlap in horsepower size of Ajax small gas compressors and those manufactured by Gardner-Denver's Industrial Machinery division at Quincy, but defended the production and marketing differences between the larger Cooper-Bessemer gas compressors and Gardner-Denver air compressors. "They are made in the same types of plants by similar types of machine tools, and to the untrained eye, they look the same," he said. "But they are different; we know you will make your independent investigation and we are confident you will find they are sold in different markets and do not compete." He pledged Cooper's total honesty and cooperation in providing further information and negotiating a settlement.

Subsequently, Cooper agreed to sell the machinery, patterns, and inventory but not plant facilities on the small natural gas compressor manufacturing operation at Quincy. (Annual sales were less than $5 million.) In addition, it was barred for ten years from acquiring any other reciprocating natural gas compressors under 1,000 horsepower. Cooper found a buyer in the Creole Engineering Company of Houston.

Reluctantly, the company also agreed to sell Rotor Tool, considered by the FTC — although not by Cooper — to represent an overlap with acquired air tool operations of Gardner-Denver. That order was carried out in January of 1981, when Cleveland-based Rotor Tool, which twenty-two years earlier had been Cooper's first acquisition since its merger with the Bessemser Gas Engine Company in 1929, was sold for $24.1 million. The buyer was R.T. Acquiring Company of San Francisco, a new organization formed to make the purchase and one in which Rotor Tool management personnel had major investments. Negotiation of the consent order with the FTC by Riedel was accomplished in a time frame which did not upset the delicate financial balance of the transaction, and the Gardner-Denver merger closed on April 30, 1979.

Cooper set about the task of integrating Gardner-Denver's centralized functional management structure into its own decentralized profit-centers system by focusing on what it determined to be soft spots in the former Gardner-Denver anatomy: overuse of centralized marketing; poor communications between operations and sales; stifling of management decision making at operational levels. All were major deviations from what Cizik considered cardinal rules of management. "You have to give operational people the tools, responsibility, and authority to do the job you demand of them," the Cooper president explained. "Each operation has to stand on its own feet in manufacturing and selling its products, with direct responsibility to corporate management for its contributions to the total financial pattern. If you fragment responsibility too much, you'll end up with more finger pointing than problems solving. But if you try to combine too much under one umbrella, such as consolidating sales into a corporate function, you end up with a lot of people who can't possibly cover such a huge, diverse marketplace, or know much about the plethora of products they're trying to sell." Cizik admitted proposed changes would not occur overnight and that care must be taken to minimize the loss of plus factors. "You can't break up a system without having something fall through the cracks," he said.

Plants with comingled manufacturing were slated for early change. Air compression production was relocated from the Expressway plant at Quincy, leaving the manufacture of mud pumps as the sole operation there. When the demand for mud pumps jumped sharply the following year, the plant had sufficient capacity to step up production accordingly. Similar streamlining gradually brought transitions affecting every area of activity except Cooper Airmotive. The most visual change from a media viewpoint was closing the former Gardner-Denver corporate office in Dallas, and assumption of these corporate functions by Cooper's staff in Houston.

To begin the evolution that would spread over the next few years, the newly structured company was molded into six operating groups and two independent divisions. Cooper Energy Services, Petroleum and Exploration, and Industrial Machinery, all serving the petroleum industry market, reported to Tom Naugle, who was promoted to the newly established corporate position of senior vice president of compressors and petroleum equipment operations. The others, Industrial Equipment, Funk Manufacturing, Mining and Construction, Consumer & Industrial Tools, and Aircraft Services, reported directly to President Cizik. As before, a high degree of flexibility was maintained, accommodating further development certain to come about as the enlarged Cooper family settled into its new corporate life. With the merger, employment doubled from thirteen thousand to slightly more than twenty-six thousand. The number of shareholders also doubled, and plant locations were increased from twenty-one to forty in the United States, and from eleven to twenty-one in other countries.

Reaching the new company milestone had particular significance for Gene Miller. At the annual meeting of stockholders, the personable chairman, whose intended visit to a friend at Mt. Vernon blossomed into an illustrious 33-year management career, announced his retirement from active employment with the company. He continued to serve as chairman of the board of directors, however, and carried out special board assignments for President Cizik.

Miller's career mirrored the company's striking transformation since the end of World War II. One of his first engineering assignments had been the design of diesel locomotive engines, an important segment that later faded into history. His election to the presidency in 1957 represented the company's transition from family management domination. He had carried forward the philosophy of changing leadership in an orderly fashion, playing the major role in working with Cizik and others who brought Cooper to its newest plateau as a premier manufacturing company. An indicator of the changes that had taken place was the $16 million in sales when Miller joined the company in 1946 as compared to the over $1 billion when he retired.

During his career, Miller had been president of the Diesel Engine Manufacturers Association, both president and chairman of the Compressed Air and Gas Institute, a member of the executive committee of the Machinery and Allied Products Institute, and a member of numerous industrial and nonprofit organization boards. He received honorary doctorates from two colleges, and was named to the Oklahoma State University Engineering Hall of Fame in 1967. A measure of his character and reputation was provided by analyst Michael J. Howard, C.P.A., C.F.A., and first vice president of Drexel Burnham Lambert, in New York City:

> I learned about E.L. Miller the hard way — trying to keep up with him: on a ten-mile walk along the Thames in 1974, when he (with me to carry his bag) brought the first word about Cooper Industries to British investors; at

a 5:00 A.M. departure from Youngstown, Ohio (after being up 'til midnight bending an elbow and discussing ways of salvaging the U.S. economy generally and its financial markets particularly) during the whirlwind tour of every major plant in the company in two and a half days; at a truck stop outside Jacksonville, Florida; where we got a few fitful hours of sleep before a breakfast meeting with members of the Jacksonville investment community. (Miller was at his best all the next day.)

A colleague of mine once said Gene (whose only two jobs ever were Colonel, U.S. Army and Cooper) had a better knowledge of the details of his company's diverse operations than any other chief executive he'd ever met. That's not a bad assessment for a corporate executive, but Gene is a whole lot more than that. I learned more about corporate strategy and personnel development from a few hours here and there with Miller, than anyone else I'd met during two degrees in economics and business, two professional certifications, and twenty years of public accounting and Wall Street experience. I also learned a great deal about human empathy and about how to live life to the hilt. I've been with Gene to shop for oriental rugs (he has both taste and a nose for value), when he browsed around a hardware store to see whether Cooper Group tools were being given adequate shelf space, and when we scrambled together around the old ships at the museum at Fisherman's Wharf in San Francisco. ("C'mon boy, let's go down into the engine room to see what they use to power this old tub.") In 1977 and 1978, when Cooper's new image was beginning to achieve recognition in the financial community, the manager of the pension fund of a large corporation (one that typifies traditional establishment-type virtues) said something I think Gene Miller would consider the best possible tribute: "Cooper proves the (American free enterprise) system still works."

After leaving active management, Miller gave more than yeoman effort to board matters, but utilized most of his considerable vigor working with a son in raising a specialized breed of Santa Gertrudis cattle on their spreads near Brenham, Texas. Deciding to renovate an old (1873) Brenham bank building into an office in the early 1980s, he became extremely interested in the project and characteristically soon became a leader in other historic preservation projects there.

Cooper's deeper penetration into energy markets came at a time when the United States was taking measures to overcome the lethargy of previous years. A five-year lease schedule for energy development on the Outer Continental Shelf and on some federal lands was issued by the Interior Department early in 1980, bringing an acceleration of drilling for gas and oil. Overall domestic energy production rose more than 4 percent, and the gradual deregulation of prices was paralleled by a steady increase in exploration. Discovery of new domestic gas resources actually outstripped production, reversing a trend of the 1970s. Despite uncertainties brought about by a war between Iran and Iraq, disputes within OPEC nations, and a worldwide recession, the year was characterized by at least limited optimism concerning energy.

Accordingly, in 1980, Cooper's expanded Energy Service product lines now used in exploration, production, transmission, distribution, and storage of oil and natural gas experienced strong demand, with new orders climbing to $1.1 billion. President Cizik was able to report that the recession was not affecting the sale of compression, drilling, mining, and electronics production equipment, nor of aircraft services. Domestic market conditions were weak for construction products such as rock drills, portable air compressors, and specialty transmissions, but they remained strong in other countries. Similarly, strong international demand for hand tools offset a weakened domestic market brought about by depressed housing and industrial production. In August of 1980, The Cooper Group family of hand tools was extended again by acquiring the Plumb line of quality striking tools from McDonough Company of Parkersburg, West Virginia. The acquisition added an eighth brand name to the company's growing "tool basket."

30

Plumb

When Jonathan Yerkes opened a blacksmith shop in the Germantown section of Philadelphia in 1856, one of the nation's earliest long-distance railroads was being constructed between that city and Pittsburgh. Among the tools sold by Yerkes to the hardware industry were the heavy sledge hammers used by Pennsylvania Railroad crews in driving "the spikes of progress" on the new line, as well as shorter railways spreading in many directions through the East. Eight years later, his shop had grown into a two-story plant producing a variety of striking tools for the hardware trade. By 1869, business had expanded further, prompting him to move into a larger plant between Church Street and the railroad in Frankfort, which also became a part of Philadelphia.

The brawny blacksmith was well known for his excellent forging and tempering ability at a time when tool making was an individual art. But he had no sales or financial interest and, in fact, did not attempt to hide an intolerance for white-collar personnel, whom he sometimes referred to as "office lice."

In the course of business, however, Yerkes grew to like a young employee of the Supplee-Biddle Hardware Company who was quite his opposite in appearance and demeanor. Perhaps it was because Fayette R. Plumb's first job with the company was greasing chains in the basement, which might have belied his reputation as a fastidious dresser whose ambitions were focused on sales and management. At the age of nineteen, he had left home in Gowanda, New York, to take a job with Supplee-Biddle in Philadelphia, having been given the opportunity through a family connection. Records are unclear as to how the friendship blossomed into a business association, but in 1870 the young hardware company employee purchased half interest in the manufacturing firm which became known as Yerkes & Plumb. During the next decade the partners did well enough to build a new plant at Bridesburg, later to be annexed by Philadelphia, selling their old quarters to the Pennsylvania Railroad for use as a freight station.

Typical of the times, the Yerkes & Plumb plant included buildings with massive floors and spacious areas for the installation of two Corliss steam engines. (It is possible, although not documented, that the engines were purchased from C. & G. Cooper & Company, leading producer of the Corliss engine when the Yerkes & Plumb buildings were constructed in 1881.) One of the engines provided power for the forge room. The other, located in a building next to the tool grinding room, was large enough to have belts driving machinery on two separate floors. In 1887, Fayette Plumb bought out his partner, who retired and moved to Florida. The Philadelphia business became Fayette R. Plumb, Ltd., producer of hammers, sledges, picks, railroad track tools, and axes of many varieties.

The following year was one of great significance for the forty-year-old owner. The plant was expanded, his ninth (and last) child was born, and teenager Harry T. Jackson started working in one of the Plumb shops. A few days after joining the company, young Jackson sat on a box for a momentary rest from his job of painting picks — just in time to be spotted by the owner, who was walking through the plant. Admonished for loafing, Jackson offered to get his lunch pail and leave if Plumb didn't think he was worth his wages. "No," Plumb replied, "just don't let it happen again." Those who came to know Jackson in the years ahead agreed that his capacity for work indicated he must have taken the boss literally. He later became factory manager and spent sixty-five years with the company before retiring in 1952.

Another incident remembered by employees reflected a feeling of good humor that later existed between the freewheeling Jackson and Plumb, known as a model of decorum and a family disciplinarian. A frequent traveller, Plumb had an arrangement with the railroad company whereby he could be picked up at the plant crossing. On one particular day he decided to take his youngest son, Billy, with him, and to save time he brought the youngster to the plant, instructing him to wait in the shipping room until it was time to leave. Jackson, who was in the shipping room stenciling the company name on boxes, spotted six-year old Billy wearing a white sailor suit, and was overcome by temptation. When it came time to board the train, Billy dutifully followed his father up the steps and down the aisle, amidst a chorus of laughter. All eyes except the father's were on the back of Billy's sailor suit, imprinted with the black stenciled words, "Manufactured by Fayette R. Plumb, Philadelphia, Pennsylvania."

The burdens of Fayette Plumb were described by a colleague as "great but self-imposed by his driving ambition, his organizing talent, and his love of salesmanship." Some of his early catalogs were so elaborate they looked like works of art. The company won international awards at more than one worlds fair, including the Centennial Exposition of 1876, and Plumb was the founding president of the American Hardware Manufacturers Association.

In 1897, the company was incorporated and the trademark changed to "FRP Anchor Brand." The product line had been broadened to include mattocks, crow bars, bush hooks, hatchets, butcher's cleavers, and such items of limited use as coopers' froes and slaters' trimmers. Another plant expansion had taken place the previous year.

The founder's second son, Fayette R. Plumb, Jr., joined the family firm in 1899 after completing his education at Harvard. Within a few years he and another new employee, Calvin C. Bascom, were given the assignment of modernizing the plant, machinery, and processes. Bascom, who had financed his education at M.I.T. by working nights as a pipe fitter, updated the steam generation and distribution, and the younger Plumb improved both operations and management procedures. When the founder died suddenly in 1905 while en route to Arizona with his daughter, Fayette Plumb, Jr., became president of the corporation. Among new employees at that time were three men destined to play key roles in the company's future: William J. Walsh, who designed and built a gas producer for the forge; Frank Campbell, who became sales manager; and Frank P. Green, a future vice president.

Sharp-edged tools in those years were formed by shaping the head from wrought iron or soft steel, welding it to a strip of hard carbon steel hammered to a cutting edge, then hardening and tempering the combined unit. Quality depended on the skills of experienced blacksmiths who eyeballed the forgings, and other employees who determined proper tempering by observing color changes. No two forgings were exactly alike in size or shape. On March 26, 1908, a group headed by Bascom forged on a steam drop hammer the first solid steel axe, revolutionizing the company's production of sharp-edged tools. (Not only was the new axe stronger, it could be ground many more times before wearing out.) The day was hailed as a manufacturing milestone, and names of all employees involved in the pioneering production were inscribed on the first axe, called the "Prima Dolabra," placed on an office wall for permanent display. To everyone's surprise, however, one-piece axes and hatchets did not capture the immediate enthusiasm of customers. Quite the opposite; old buying habits could not be overcome through personal salesmanship and ordinary advertising. A solution was found, however, when one of the young office employees spent nights at the public library researching the history of axes, from the stone age to the "new one-piece steel age," then prepared a booklet, "The Evolution of the Axe." More than one-hundred-thousand copies were distributed to wholesale and retail hardware outlets — a tremendous circulation in 1908 — and sales mushroomed. Even then, it was almost twenty years before one-piece axes were adopted by the entire industry.

The "Prima Dolabra," first solid steel axe that revolutionized Plumb's production of sharp-edged tools, was produced in 1908 and presented to the founder. Here it is held by Fayette R. Plumb II, last member of the family to be associated with the company.

Success of the new process convinced management to build an axe plant at St. Louis, investing jointly with a hardware jobber there. Selection of that city was based on the Plumb president's feeling that (1) it would surpass Chicago as a commercial center and (2) it had a good location as a gateway to the West. With the Panama Canal under construction, shipping to West Coast lumbering markets would soon be less expensive via the Mississippi River than overland. In the latter judgment, the president proved to be correct. Soon after the St. Louis plant went into operation in 1911, Plumb bought out its partner in the venture and operated it as a wholly-owned subsidiary. A complementary handle factory was started in Arkansas, but when it proved to be a management headache it was moved to the St. Louis location.

William D. Plumb, who had survived the sailor suit experience to finish school in Philadelphia and attend Harvard, joined the company in 1913 and was trained in all areas of operations. When World War I struck, both Philadelphia and St. Louis plants began the production of bayonets and bolo knives, also routing regular products to war-related markets in the United States, England, and Russia. To reestablish itself with previous customers after the armistice, the company in 1919 took the industry by surprise in announcing a million dollar advertising campaign, with full-color pages in the *Saturday Evening Post,* other national magazines, and trade journals. To help establish identity, it focused advertisements on the "red handle and the black head" of Plumb products, even managing to get trademark rights on that color combination by what Vice President Green later revealed as "proving there were fewer competitive manufacturers than there were combinations of the two primary colors." He believed the strong advertising thrust later helped the company improve its marketing position while such competitors as Maydole, Hammond, and Black "fell by the wayside and went out of business."

In 1920, Plumb built a new boiler plant and purchased the Carver File Company of Philadelphia, for the first time adding a product not described as a "striking" tool. The company urged dealers to "concentrate on one brand of tools — Plumb hammers, hatchets, files, sledges, and axes; secure the advantage of money we are spending in advertising to tell the customer to buy from *you* . . . and you'll find a better condition in your business in a mighty short time." It also promoted a "take-up screw wedge," which continued for three decades as the best method of solving loose handle problems. Purchase of controlling interest in the Kennedy-Plumb Company briefly put it into the business of making replaceable bits for oil well drilling in the mid-1920s. "Our bits practically drilled the Seminole Field in Oklahoma," one former officer recalled, but new products by competitors later made the company's bits obsolete and the effort was abandoned.

A 1929 fire destroyed one Philadelphia building storing more than five hundred thousand dry hickory handles, but favorable winds and an alert fire department saved the rest of the plant. Less than a year later, a silver lining emerged from the ashes when insurance money helped Plumb face the Great Depression. Orders for tools faded rapidly after the stock market crash, and only a few employees were kept on the payroll. In 1931, the company opened a lunch kitchen in the Pratt House (a former residential mansion purchased with land obtained in the 1881 move to James Street) to provide hot soup lunches for those on layoff.

To generate employment and sales, and with little concern for profit, the company introduced two cheap lines of axes, "Knocker Brand" at Philadelphia and "Faultless Brand" at St. Louis. A sit-down strike by United Steel Workers members was short lived during that time, when it did nothing except save money for the company. When employees returned to work without a union shop agreement, the national organization lost interest and did not return for several years.

When the outbreak of war in Europe brought a new demand for business in the late 1930s, Plumb introduced such new high-quality products as the chrome plated octagon nail hammer to revive its reputation from the "Knocker Brand" days. Again, large quantities of the company's products went to war, with only forged parachute hooks and a few other special items requiring variations from its regular lines.

The third family generation arrived on the company scene during the 1940s. Fayette R. Plumb II, son of Factory Manager William Plumb, became an employee in 1941, joined the Navy later that year, and returned in 1946. D. Rumsey Plumb, son of the president, became a management trainee in Philadelphia in 1946, then went into the field as a salesman. (William Plumb died in 1944 and Harry Jackson succeeded him as factory manager.) Other young men returning from military service also helped stimulate new investigations of operational methods and a drive for improved products. "With this infusion of new, young blood, self-satisfaction was replaced by inquiry," said Vice President Green. Steam hammers were replaced by drop hammers, air-clutch presses were purchased, and material handling was updated. By 1950, the company could barely keep pace with its orders.

Fayette Plumb II was promoted to factory manager when Jackson retired in 1952. The following year, Rumsey Plumb was elected president, with his father becoming chairman of the board. The first objectives of the new management team were to introduce improvements that would create extraordinary customer awareness and to diversify. These objectives were attained simultaneously in 1954 when the company introduced a fiberglass-reinforced handle permanently bonded to the head of a hammer, then formed the Plumb Chemical Corporation to make the new handles and produce molding compounds for the plastics industry. After a year's trial, the entire line of small tools was converted to "Permabond," design and the "take-up screw wedge" became obsolete. In 1956, a balsa core lightened the weight of the tools, and in 1957 the grips were improved by dipping them in neoprene. An engineering building opened in 1955 and was the center of more development activity.

While the trend in some areas was to broaden product lines, in others progress was measured in cutbacks. Before World War II, axes were offered in more than five hundred different types, weights, and handle lengths, dating back to the days when wood-cutting specialists demanded traditional products that varied with different sections of the country. If a timberman grew up using a twenty-eight-inch handle with a four-pound, single bit, three-point-grind axe, by God, that's what he wanted. But that era was gone, and one Plumb employee summed up a manufacturer's view of its passing in two words: "thank goodness." Lightweight axes of a more standard nature increased in popularity with the country's tremendous interest in family outdoor living and camping. But a decrease in the total demand for axes prompted Plumb to close its St. Louis manufacturing in 1959, expanding similar facilities at Philadelphia to pick up the slack.

The next major production change came in 1965, when the mandrel axe-forging method (a mandrel, or plug, was used to form the eye then forced out of the head after forging) was replaced by a two-ton hammer that punched out the eye with a single stroke. The change quadrupled man-hour production. Sales of woodchopper mauls, axes, wedges, and sledges increased when energy conscious homeowners restored the wood-burning stove to a position of heavy demand. But after years of low profits, Plumb closed its Delta File Works in 1965 and succumbed to the competition from Nicholson, with whom it someday would be associated in the Cooper "tool basket."

In 1971, Plumb's reorganized United Steel Workers struck the plant, because of an economic dispute. During the strike, Plumb Tool was sold to McDonough Company of Parkersburg, West Virginia. Rumsey Plumb retired, but maintained control of the Plumb Chemical Corporation, which was not part of the purchase by McDonough. Fayette R. Plumb II continued as a member of management.

During the next nine years, product lines were decreased and new machinery installed under the leadership of plant managers C.D. Memel and George N. AvDellas. But Plumb's products, despite their high quality, did not mesh well with McDonough's A.O. Ames Division line of lawn and gardening equipment, and profits did not meet expectations. The combination of quality recognition and opportunity for improved market penetration did, however, fit the pattern of Cooper's acquisitions. After the 1980 merger, Cooper looked to plant improvement that would assimilate Plumb into its hand tool group.

31

A Dramatic Conflict

During 1980, Cooper effected a two-for-one common stock split and achieved its ninth consecutive gain in both revenues and earnings. The continuing long-range integration of Gardner-Denver into Cooper Industries received a substantial amount of attention during the year, bringing more pruning and consolidation on several fronts.

Jumbo, self-propelled drilling machine operations were relocated from Dallas to the Salem, Virginia, track-mounted drilling equipment manufacturing plant, consolidating the production of drill carriers into one expanded facility. Capacity of petroleum drilling equipment production was increased at the Sunnyvale, Texas, plant by moving blast hole and rock drill manufacturing operations to other facilities in Dallas and Salem. Rotary screw industrial air compressor operations in Quincy, Illinois, were relocated in Sedalia, Missouri. A Mining & Construction parts distribution center was opened near the Dallas-Fort Worth airport to improve communication and service to a network of distributors, dealers, and subsidiaries supplying more than 150 countries. The company's commitment to mining and construction machinery operations acquired in the merger was underscored by an expanded manufacturing facility in Denver, for increased production of the Gardner-Denver line of pneumatic and hydraulic percussion rock drilling equipment and various drilling accessories. The expanded plant was one of the most modern in the Rocky Mountain region, which was becoming recognized as the nation's fastest growing energy and natural resource area.

Compression equipment orders of $15.5 million from ARCO Oil & Gas Company and $13 million from Mexico and Venezuela were among those building the company's backlog in energy-related products to a record level.

Cooper's progress in pulling together two manufacturing organizations of equal size at the time of merger was recognized by *The Wall Street Transcript* in its selection of President Cizik as the "Outstanding Chief Executive Officer in the Machinery Industry." (Cizik received the award again in 1981.)

Gardner-Denver Hydra-Trac™ rock drills bore blast holes for a sewer pipeline construction project near Greenville, S.C. in 1980.

Before the Gardner-Denver acquisition, Cooper's ratio of working capital requirements to sales dollar was held at a level of approximately 24¢. The merger pushed it to nearly 36¢; but the implementation of Cooper's working capital management techniques to the Gardner-Denver operations resulted in reduction of this ratio by 4.6¢ during 1980, saving more than $11 million in interest expense. Most persons, including Wall Street observers and the financial press, assumed Cooper would continue reducing that figure by settling back to digest its huge acquisition before taking another bite. Indeed, that is what President Cizik and other members of corporate management intended, but not to the extent of blinding themselves to unexpected opportunities fitting their long-range plans.

As it happened, events of late 1980 brought a sudden change in Cooper's timetable for growth, and by Thanksgiving the company was immersed in a complex struggle that startled both writers and investors. *Business Week* correctly reported the shock as occurring, "when Cooper Industries leaped in as a white knight to rescue Crouse-Hinds Company, a maker of electrical parts, from the clutches of InterNorth, Inc." Cizik defended the move from the standpoint of an electrical components company being "on our wish list for years," and the fact that answering the unexpected knock of opportunity was in the best interest of the company and its shareholders. Riedel told the *Wall Street Journal,* "We don't suffer from analysis paralysis like some companies; we grasp opportunities when they present themselves."

Those who watched the drama — and there were many — agreed it was difficult to follow the action without a program. The opening scene, in fact, seemed unrelated to the scenario, when on July 22, 1980, Ampco-Pittsburgh Corporation purchased 6.1 percent of Belden Corporation as the first step in a takeover attempt. A month later, Belden made a defensive move against Ampco-Pittsburgh by agreeing to be acquired by Crouse-Hinds Company of Syracuse, New York, for $180 million. Scarcely had that maneuver been announced, however, when on September 12, Crouse-Hinds Chairman Chris J. Witting received a telephone call from InterNorth Chairman Sam Segnar informing him that the Omaha-based pipeline company intended to acquire the Syracuse producer of electrical equipment through a tender announced that day by advertisements in the press. The unfriendly tender, vehemently opposed by Crouse-Hinds, offered forty dollars a share for Crouse-Hinds stock, with the stipulation that the price would be reduced to thirty-seven dollars if Crouse-Hinds completed its proposed acquisition of Belden. In retaliation, Belden filed a suit to enjoin InterNorth from meddling, but both that litigation and a preliminary injunction by Crouse-Hinds were denied by the courts. Meanwhile, Crouse-Hinds asked investment banker Felix Rohatyn of Lazard Freres to find an alternate merger plan that could halt the InterNorth attack. Rohatyn telephoned Bob Cizik, and in late November *Barron's* was able to report, "Cooper Industries has weighed in with a competing bid." Chris J. Witting, Crouse-Hinds chairman, told *Business Week* that Cooper "has gone to great lengths to explain themselves to us," and "we have a natural affinity for another manufacturer." He wrote Crouse-Hinds shareholders, urging them to withhold sales to InterNorth while their company worked on "a better deal."

With Ampco-Pittsburgh reduced to the supporting role of a large Belden stockholder, the main cast now read: Belden Corporation, Geneva, Illinois, a leading manufacturer of electronic and electrical wire, cable, cord, and related products; Crouse-Hinds Company of Syracuse, New York, international manufacturer of quality electrical fittings, couplings, enclosures, switches, wiring devices, switchboards, traffic controls and signals, industrial and outdoor/indoor lighting fixtures, and aviation group lighting equipment; InterNorth Corporation, Omaha, Nebraska, diversified natural gas pipeline company; and Cooper Industries, last participant to enter the stage, offering a stock exchange acquisition arrangement valued at $777 million, compared with InterNorth's cash offer of $684 million.

The plot centered on whether Cooper or InterNorth would be successful in acquiring Crouse-Hinds, which in turn was in the process of

Belden, an important supplier for the electronics industry, with products such as this molded-cable data terminal assembly, became part of a complicated series of merger negotiations that led to its becoming part of Cooper, along with Crouse-Hinds, in 1981.

purchasing Belden. A plot thickener was added when *Business Week* issued a reminder that InterNorth was a good customer of Cooper Industries and headed a consortium building the Northern Border Pipeline, which could eventually be in a position to purchase up to $175 million worth of equipment manufactured by Cooper and/or its competitors.

In December, shareholders of Belden and Crouse-Hinds completed merger of those two companies. InterNorth quickly altered its proposal to include Belden, but Crouse-Hinds announced it had accepted Cooper's proposal to exchange (1) .725 shares of Cooper common stock for each outstanding share, up to an aggregate of 7,395,000 shares of Crouse-Hinds common stock, and (2) 4.026 shares of Cooper common stock for each outstanding share of Crouse-Hinds preferred, validly tendered and not withdrawn. The offer, which was not conditioned upon any minimum number of Crouse-Hinds shares being tendered, was scheduled to expire January 22, 1981, unless extended.

The Cooper offer was sweetened to a .75 share offer on the common stock exchange when its value dropped a few weeks later on the Big Board. There was wide speculation on the reason for that drop. Some observers attributed it to investors' disapproval of the move coming on the heels of the Gardner-Denver acquisition, and others attributed it to a dilution that would follow the proposed stock swap. But the *New York Times* pointed out that stock prices of all oil services companies were depressed momentarily by rising interest rates and an announcement of large oil discoveries in the Soviet Union.

With antitrust issues in this merger unimportant, Riedel took charge of the swirl of litigation. Cooper and InterNorth filed countering federal court charges of unfair practices against each other during the fierce bidding war. InterNorth also petitioned for an investigation of Cooper's actions with the New York attorney general, but the charges were found to be "without substance." As the year ended, InterNorth improved its tender to $38.50 for each Crouse-Hinds share (it previously had established that amount only if at least two million shares were tendered) and having already extended previous deadlines, announced the offer would expire at midnight January 9, 1981. When less than 6 percent of the Crouse-Hinds shares were tendered by that time, the company withdrew, making way for a final merger of Crouse-Hinds into Cooper Industries. All litigation relating to the acquisition was dismissed, and President Segnar issued a press release stating, "InterNorth continues to hold Crouse-Hinds in high regard, but we made a firm decision about its value to us, and we did not think it would be prudent and responsible on our part to disregard that evaluation, even when the temptation to do so might be present in the heat of a contest. We congratulate Cooper Industries on the apparently successful acquisition of an excellent company."

President Cizik replied, "Naturally, we are pleased with InterNorth's decision, and we look forward to completing the merger with Crouse-Hinds on a friendly basis."

Attending the April 16 annual meeting of Crouse-Hinds shareholders, at which time the merger was accepted, Cizik told his audience, "This merger is a very significant development for Cooper. It's the kind of major diversification we've considered for many years, and now that the time has finally come, we're full of anticipation and excitement. I'm sensitive to a natural regret among many of you that this is the last meeting of Crouse-Hinds as an independent company. With time I'm hopeful you'll conclude that, while merging with Cooper Industries may not have been the best thing in the world that could have happened to Crouse-Hinds, it was at least second best. I'm too much of a realist to try to persuade you at this time that remaining independent is not the best of all possible worlds."

The merger became effective April 2, 1981, following approval of Cooper shareholders at their annual meeting in Houston.

32

Crouse-Hinds

The union of Huntington B. Crouse and Jesse L. Hinds was an improbable one. When the two New Yorkers met in the late nineteenth century, Crouse was just twenty-four, Hinds a mature fifty-one. But the age difference was dwarfed by a common interest — each had a burning desire to start his own business.

Born in Fayetteville, eight miles from Syracuse, young Huntington Crouse had worked in a jewelry store, then joined his uncle in operating two businesses, one a flour and feed mill, the other an iron foundry. Two years later, however, the uncle died and Crouse was named executor. Forced to settle the estate by selling both businesses in 1896, he was left with no job, a tidy two thousand dollars in the bank, and a strong drive for independence that was totally unchanneled. Any reasonable business would have been considered, as long as he could be owner.

Jesse Hinds, on the other hand, had a specific goal but no capital. Employment as the factory superintendent of a Syracuse manufacturer of switches, switchboards, and panelboards had convinced him the upstart energy system known as electricity — threatening to become a power contender with natural gas and steam — offered spectacular opportunities.

Brought together by another uncle of Crouse, the two men felt an immediate rapport despite their age difference, and it was not difficult for Hinds to guide the enthusiasm of his new friend toward manufacturing articles for the electrical industry. An expert mechanic, Hinds held the patent on a tubular-arm knife switch that could help them get started. Partnership papers were signed on January 18, 1897, and Crouse-Hinds Electric Company took up residency on the second floor of a Water Street building in Syracuse, agreeing to a monthly rental of $33.33 including heat and power.

Although the experience of Hinds played an important role in initial success, his young partner clearly became the management leader as the company began to grow. Great risk was involved with an industry still considered experimental. Only five years had elapsed since the first

The first home of Crouse-Hinds was on the second floor of this Water Street building in Syracuse, N.Y.

At the turn of the twentieth century, Crouse-Hinds moved into its own building in Syracuse.

transmission station began supplying direct current electricity on a commercial basis. As similar plants went into operation, the design and manufacture of sockets, switches, fuses, insulators, and other electrical needs proliferated so rapidly it was difficult to find employees who understood the business. The introduction of alternating current by George Westinghouse, even before most persons comprehended direct current, led one writer to describe the situation as "confusion worse confounded." The company for which Jesse Hinds previously had worked was among those unable to meet the challenge, and when it closed its doors the infant Crouse-Hinds organization hired its workers "as rapidly as the new business required and its finances would permit," Crouse later recalled. Among its earliest employees were Charles M. Crofoot, a shipping clerk, and Frederick F. Skeel, hired as ad manager when there was so little advertising he worked at odd jobs to keep busy. Both men eventually became commercial vice presidents, heading the New York and Chicago offices respectively. Early company plans were limited to making panelboards, switchboards, and the knife switch. But fate intervened, prompting almost immediate entry into another venture that someday would bring the company worldwide notoriety in the field of illumination.

In an isolated corner of the Crouse-Hinds floor at 500 Water Street, a budding inventor named Frank Rorabeck was putting finishing touches on a newfangled trolley car headlight he had designed. Its uniqueness was based primarily on a portability that would permit a conductor to remove it at the conclusion of a trolley run, then mount it on the opposite end of the car for the return trip. Rather than go into production himself, Rorabeck suggested that Crouse-Hinds manufacture and sell his headlight. Convinced that electric streetcars and prospective interurbans would enjoy long lives, Crouse and Hinds signed an agreement, and before the company was one year old it made its maiden voyage into diversification. The "Syracuse Changeable Electric Headlight" fell short of becoming a runaway bonanza but it did reasonably well, and three-quarters of a century after it began lighting trolley lines its descendents would be illuminating NASA launch and landing areas for space shuttle vehicles.

Products and profits grew steadily. A year after start-up, each partner was able to draw a salary of twenty-five dollars per week, and the company took over the entire floor employing a factory-engineering-sales office force of thirty-four. Two years later it celebrated the birth of a new century by moving into a four-story West Jefferson Street industrial building vacated by the previous employer of Hinds. The following year, the company hired 27-year-old Albert F. Hills, who would become the key figure in sales development for many years to come.

Although its primary products continued as before, the company added what it advertised as "special appliances of all kinds." Descriptive records were not preserved, but decades later renovation projects in Syracuse uncovered a wide variety of early appliances including time clocks bearing the Crouse-Hinds name. One of those time clocks adorns a wall in the famous Ghirardelli Square — in San Francisco.

To better prepare management for twentieth-century business, the partnership was dissolved in 1903 and replaced by a corporate structure, with Crouse as president and Hinds as vice president. The word "Electric" was dropped, making the new name simply "Crouse-Hinds Company."

That same year it was joined by William L. Hinds, a nephew of Jesse, who was just two years younger than President Crouse. Having gained experience at the Davis Sewing Machine Company in Dayton, Ohio, "Bill" Hinds was hired as assistant to Crouse, quickly assuming important management duties that would lead to the company presidency. Also hired that year was William C. Blanding, who went to work in the stockroom, later advanced to management, and served many years as company treasurer.

History repeated itself in 1906 when another noncompany inventor caught the interest of Messrs. Crouse and Hinds. Until that time, the conduit, or pipe, containing electrical conductors, had been concealed between walls. Consequently, it was designed along functional lines. When the feasibility of running conduit along exposed routes was introduced, junction boxes proved to be both unhandy and unsightly. An Albany electrical contractor, Morton Havens, Jr., anxious to maintain pride in his work, designed and built prototype fittings that met both his own high standards and those of the U.S. Patent Office. Being a contractor with no desire for manufacturing, he suggested that Crouse-Hinds, with whom he had enjoyed pleasant business relations, develop his fittings into marketable products.

Albert Hills, by then head of sales, was confident that the idea was revolutionary. President Crouse was interested, but skeptical. Accepting the proposal would entail large investment in machinery for an unproven idea he considered "gambling on a horse with no track record." Spurred by the enthusiasm of Hills, however, the horse could be counted on to make a good showing, Crouse reasoned, so he agreed to move ahead with what he labeled "a prospecting expedition in the search of pay dirt." Within months the expedition progresssed into a chain of discoveries, united into the family of "Condulet," an acronym of conduit and outlet, and "Bert" Hills would be remembered as the man most responsible for one of the premier developments in the company's history.

Coincidentally, the Condulet conduit fittings line was developed in the same year the tungsten filament incandescent lamp was introduced as a new light source, superior to the carbon lamp for ordinary purposes, and challenging the arc for outdoor illumination. In response, Crouse-

Early Crouse-Hinds management team members from left are: William L. Hinds, Albert Hills, Huntington B. Crouse, and W.C. Blanding.

Hinds tooled up to produce new reflectors and cases that became fore-runners of floodlights and searchlights.

Combined success of the Condulet line and new outdoor lights neces-sitated a succession of factory expansions into several nearby buildings all connected by tunnels, forming a maze employees referred to as "the catacombs." Realization that such an arrangement would be temporary was enhanced by annual spring flooding of Onondaga Creek, inundat-ing "the catacombs," and damaging inventories. Consequently, a 25-acre triangle of land in northern Syracuse was purchased, and in 1911 the cornerstone was laid for a building that would become the new home of Crouse-Hinds.

Helping plan the move was the last official management duty per-formed by Jesse Hinds, who retired in 1910, selling his interest in the company to Crouse. During their years together, the two men had never lost the mutual respect and warmth of friendship that prompted them to form their company. The feeling extended to other employees, also, as both men spent much of their time getting to know everyone in the plant. Nearly all employees there called Hinds by the nickname "father" and during his retirement years he spent several days at the plant whenever he was passing to or from his winter home in Florida, until his death in 1928. Not only did Crouse continue his former partner's pay during those eighteen years, he made sure it was increased to meet living costs from time to time. Often quoting Hinds in speeches, Crouse told a 1915 audience of manufacturers and jobbers, "He [Hinds] had several sayings which he seemed to keep in stock for immediate delivery, and it took me many years to appreciate some of them. I think perhaps one of his best was, 'All we have to work with is our best judgment.'"

Crouse used the statement to illustrate his own strong belief in building the integrity of an industry beset with what he considered unfair practices and lack of standards. Possessing a fiery personality and powerful voice known throughout his plant and throughout the Association of Electrical Manufacturers, he shouted the gospel of making honest policy judgments and sticking to them. In the face of strong opposition, he did more than any other person in the industry to end the accepted practice of structuring prices "like a weather vane" to give preferred buyers advantages over their competitors. His company suffered many losses of sales by holding to its standards, but Crouse was unwavering in his policy. His obvious influence, if not his byline, could be detected in sales advice appearing in a June 1914 issue of the company's employee publication, *Family Talks:*

> When a customer seems ready to ask for a price cut, a salesman should run away. If you cannot get away, turn on him and say, "Mr. Smith, I want your business and I hope I can get it, but the Crouse-Hinds Company is a one-price house and I cannot change my figure. Now don't tell me you won't give me the business unless I cut the price because that puts us both in wrong. I cannot cut my price and you, after having said it, cannot give me the business without proving yourself a liar."

Crouse justified his strict adherence to policy by showing that each time an exception is made, it will be expected the next time followed by attempts to extend it to a greater degree. "The question then arises as to how far the rubber line will stretch before it breaks," he said.

Twenty-four years after admonishing manufacturers and jobbers to set fair policies and stand by them regardless of temptations that were "numerous and attractive," he spoke again to a similar group in Chicago, assuring them that "in light of the experience I have gained (since that time), I feel sure I was more nearly right than I realized at the time." By then his standards of equal discounts to all distributors and equal prices to other purchasers had been adopted generally by the electrical industry that considered them unobtainable in 1911.

Construction of the Crouse-Hinds manufacturing facility consumed nearly two years, with completion in 1912. While construction was underway, the company also established a subsidiary in Toronto, Canada, with many of the details handled by Bill Hinds, who by then had assumed wide responsibility, reminiscent of his uncle's close association with Crouse. The Crouse-Hinds Company of Canada, Ltd., was incorporated September 23, 1911, and E.G. Mack became its first managing director.

As the Condulet family tree continued to blossom during the following years, reaching thousands of products sold throughout the world, the physical plant kept pace and grew into an industrial complex covering several acres of the triangle.

Crouse-Hinds salesmen were easily identified because each always wore high buttoned shoes, spats, a vest, and a bowler or derby hat — "trademarks" that lasted well into the 1930s. They were paid more than competitors, with the result that longevity became another distinctive feature enhancing personal customer relations.

Ideas were generated regularly for identifying possible new markets for the company's floodlights, which evolved into high-candle-power products utilizing lenses capable of focusing the beam. On one October afternoon in 1915 the company rigged a light on the roof of a building, mounting it at an angle to concentrate the beam on a large flag. That night, spectators were astonished to see what appeared to be a self-illuminated flag floating in the sky, free of all support. "The unusual spectacle created considerable comment," reported a Crouse-Hinds employee. "It leads us to believe reflectors and headlights can also be used to illuminate, by floodlighting, large advertising signs." A memo from Bert Hills to salesmen reminded them also that the company had "the most complete line of arc headlights on the market," as well as "incandescent headlights that equal anything on the market, and which in many ways are superior to the products of our competitors."

But pioneering high quality conduit fittings was producing the most far reaching effects among the company's products, even exceeding anticipated results. It put the company in a position to benefit greatly from the automobile phenomenon, followed by the age of flight and the emergence of synthetics. With an almost overwhelming demand for petroleum products, new refineries and increased drilling efforts exploded onto the industrial scene, both figuratively and literally. Improved technologies were accompanied by fire and explosion hazards. Enclosed and gasketed lighting fixtures were introduced, with early versions using Mason jars for the incandescent lamp bulb enclosure. Later, glass globes were developed to serve the purpose better. In a hazardous environment an electrical arc or spark can ignite the surrounding atmosphere; so Crouse-Hinds countered with explosion-proof Condulet conduit fittings that received immediate acceptance. By the 1920s they were being used

Several Crouse-Hinds products are represented in this photo of the early 1920s. A pioneer in the manufacture of traffic signals and trolley headlights, the company also made headlights for automobiles.

Creating new markets for its high-candle-power floodlights in the 1920s, Crouse-Hinds became a pioneer in lighting service stations and buildings for promotional purposes.

wherever there was danger from the presence of explosive vapors, gases or combustible dusts. Subsequent introduction of other products permitting the safe use of electricity in such hazardous environments as oil drilling, petroleum and petrochemical processing, mining, and pipeline pumping stations were to make the company a world leader in its field and eventually provide an advantageous link with Cooper Industries.

The same automobile industry that brought demands for Condulet products in its own huge, electrically operated factories and in associated petroleum facilities created yet another market opportunity — recognized early by Crouse-Hinds. City intersections were becoming so congested by the end of World War I that it was unfeasible and even dangerous for policemen to direct traffic. Perhaps colored lighting units of some kind would be better.

There is strong evidence, although not documented conclusively, that Crouse-Hinds lights used at trolley sidings in Syracuse inspired someone in the company to invent the traffic signal. (With several trolleys using a single set of tracks through the city, it was necessary to pass at sidings scattered along each route. Colored lights were installed as right-of-way signals at all siding locations.) Whatever the source of inspiration, the fact *is documented* that Crouse-Hinds converted those lights into traffic signals, and one of the first produced in 1921 was installed at an intersection in Houston, Texas. By the mid-1920s, plants using Crouse-Hinds Condulet conduit fittings produced automobiles equipped with Crouse-Hinds headlights; the automobiles stopped at traffic lights manufactured by Crouse-Hinds and were refuelled at service stations illuminated by Crouse-Hinds floodlights.

Not surprisingly, the company next moved into the manufacture of searchlights, airport beacons, and runway lights. Later, its Lighting Products Division added special lights for shopping centers, industrial parks and plants, apartment developments, national monuments, tennis courts, ski slopes, and sports stadiums. Descendants of the changeable headlight for trolleys had indeed come of age.

Although it was forced to tighten its economic belt during the Great Depression of the 1930s, Crouse-Hinds fared better than most companies and gained prominence as an employer and community leader in Syracuse. "My parents always advocated that I go to work for Crouse-Hinds because it was considered the prestigious place to be," recalled Jane Klausman, who joined the company as a secretary in 1941 and later rose to supervisor of administrative services of electrical construction materials. "When I told my family I got the job, you would think I had landed on Mt. Olympus." Many sons and daughters followed parents as employees, and the company felt great pride in being known as a family-oriented organization.

In 1943, Huntington Crouse died and was succeeded as president by William Hinds. By then the company was immersed in war production.

Crouse-Hinds, noted for its World War II bond rallies, also was awarded the Army-Navy "E" four times.

Despite Crouse-Hinds' diversification into such fields as airport lighting, floodlighting, and traffic signals, the continuous development of its Condulet conduit outlet fittings remained the company's chief line of manufacturing through the years.

Condulet conduit fittings were vital to accelerating production at munitions factories, oil refineries, and manufacturing plants. "Black light" signaling equipment was developed for the Navy, and portable traffic signals directed aircraft. (A Crouse-Hinds light was said to have signaled the start of the Normandy invasion.) War Bond rallies became regular events in the company parking lot, with employees spending $2.25 million on bonds during the war, a record exceeded by only one much larger corporation in central New York State. The Army-Navy "E" was awarded four times to the company's work force, and 497 employees entered the armed forces. Twelve gave their lives.

In the years following World War II, Crouse-Hinds continued expansion at the Syracuse plant. A succession of presidents into the mid-1960s included Huntington B. Crouse, Jr., Albert Hills, John R. Tuttle, and Robert J. Sloan, each of whom moved up through company management. During that time, product lines were broadened in all manufacturing areas. Crouse-Hinds-Domex was established as a Mexican affiliate in 1959, and half interest in Machne Crouse-Hinds, S.P.A., Trieste, Italy, was purchased in 1963. The use of highly flammable hydrogen as a missile propellent led to the development of the Crouse-Hinds hydrogen-safe connector in 1964, specified as a standard for the Saturn missile project and then for NASA installations around the world.

Business was growing, but not at a rate considered commensurate with projected market opportunities in a time of technological acceleration, when the company for the first time in its history reached outside its own ranks to bring in a new president and chief operating officer in 1965. He was Chris J. Witting, who had been vice president and executive assistant to the chairman then president of International Telephone and Telegraph Corporation, after serving as group vice president of the Westinghouse Electric Corporation.

A native of Cranford, New Jersey, who earned a degree from New York University's College of Business and Public Administration over a twelve-year period while working with accounting and financial firms, Chris Witting was known as a vigorous, tough executive with a strong belief in corporate involvement with educational and community endeavors. His principal objective as president was to lead Crouse-Hinds into a new era of growth through internal expansion and acquisition.

The groundwork for more rapid development of new products already had been laid when Witting arrived, through construction of a Product Development Center on a ninety-acre site the company had purchased on the outskirts of Syracuse. The Center was dedicated to the memory of former President Sloan in July of 1965. Among products introduced that year was a computerized traffic control system, "Traflo," which could be programmed to read the fluctuating pulse of traffic flow and adjust lights automatically.

Witting wasted no time in getting the acquisition program underway. In March, 1966, Crouse-Hinds purchased the Taylor Die & Tool Manufacturing Company, Ltd. of Scarborough, Ontario, and its wholly-owned London, Ontario, subsidiary. The company manufactured steel outlet boxes, industrial switches, bus ducts, industrial panels, electric panels, and circuit breakers. Six months later it acquired the Revere Electric Manufacturing Company, a Chicago manufacturer of outdoor lighting products sold in commercial markets not served by Crouse-Hinds. Among Revere's products were decorative and roadway lighting fixtures, service station lighting equipment, lighting poles, lighting brackets and associated components. The year also marked the beginning of Crouse-Hinds stock being listed on the New York Stock Exchange, and purchase of the remaining 50 percent interest in the company's Italian affiliate.

The next five years brought rapid internal growth and product expansion. A Hills Lighting Center was constructed next to the Product Development Center, providing facilities for increased outdoor lighting and newly organized solid state electronics production. More than fifty thousand separate products, eighteen thousand of them in the Condulet conduit fitting line alone, were being manufactured in domestic and foreign plants by 1971.

In March of 1972, Crouse-Hinds entered new markets through the acquisition of Midwest Electric Manufacturing Corporation of Chicago. The addition of that well-respected firm gave the company one of the most complete secondary electrical distribution lines in the industry, serving manufacturing plants, hospitals, offices and commercial buildings. The next month it bought the New England Die Casting Company of West Haven, Connecticut, supplementing production of the two Crouse-Hinds foundries in Syracuse. In 1974, further foundry capabilities were added with purchase of the Laconia Malleable Iron Company of Laconia, New Hampshire.

After considering possible avenues of new growth in the lighting business, President Witting elected to concentrate on high intensity discharge and exotic kinds of products. "These were more costly than the common fluorescent and incandescent lights, but they were tremendously energy-saving," he explained. "We decided to make our own path, rather than follow what others were doing, and lo and behold, energy became so expensive our lighting business grew by leaps and bounds, making us a major factor in the business. People were willing to burn our energy-efficient lights, even though individual fixture cost was greater."

In some instances, representatives of Crouse-Hinds worked with architects on such large projects as the Dallas-Forth Worth airport and large shopping malls, with custom lighting becoming a part of the

As a gift from Crouse-Hinds to the American people on the eve of the nation's bicentennial, the company created a unique blend of multi-colored light sources to provide four times the previous illumination of the Statue of Liberty, while using one-third less energy.

design. Full lighting systems were also installed on large campuses, a renovated Yankee Stadium, Aloha Stadium in the Hawaiian Islands, the world's largest airport in Montreal, and Houston's Memorial Drive Country Club, where a tennis lighting arrangement won the top award in National Illuminating Engineering Society competition. In preparing for the nation's bicentennial, Crouse-Hinds donated an innovative illumination system that bathed the Statue of Liberty in an array of white and colored lights from the tip of the torch to the granite pedestal. The arrangement provided four times more illumination than its predecessor, while using one-third less energy.

The Occupational Safety and Health Act (OSHA), which set rigid safety regulations in the 1970s, brought heavy ordering of products Crouse-Hinds had been developing to prevent ignition of volatile atmospheres by electric sparks. "A spark exists whenever a switch is turned, whether it's on a spacecraft at Cape Kennedy, equipment in a hospital, or the light on a miner's helmet." Witting said. "Engineering firms around the world specify our products in their plants, and in open bidding situations, the U.S. government agencies often specify 'Crouse-Hinds-type' standards." Fiber optics introduced in the 1970s created new generations of products ranging from traffic control signals to instrumentation for high energy particle accelerators.

In 1975, Chris Witting was elected chairman, continuing as chief executive officer, and Paul A. Brunner advanced from executive vice president to president. Ten years after it had launched its major growth campaign, Crouse-Hinds was ready for its largest acquisition up to that time. Arrow-Hart, Inc., a well-known manufacturer of electrical products in Hartford, Connecticut, was seeking the kind of management impetus that could move it into a more profitable position and counterbalance the cyclicality of its traditional industrial markets. Its annual sales of $90 million were approximately half those of Crouse-Hinds (whose own sales had quadrupled since 1965), and its sixteen plants — ten in the United States and six in five other countries — offered a sizeable boost to worldwide operations. Both companies agreed a merger would be highly beneficial, and on April 30, 1975, Arrow-Hart became a subsidiary of Crouse-Hinds Company.

Arrow-Hart itself had been formed by the merger of two companies dating back to the nineteenth century, then grown and developed through a series of acquisitions. Charles G. Perkins entered the switch business in 1880 and disposed of his property a few years later, but resumed it at Hartford in 1905 as the Arrow Electric Company. Gerald W. Hart, a former superintendent of the Edison Electric Light Company, converted an attic in his Kansas City home to manufacture the first satisfactory rotary snap switch for electric lights in 1890. The next year he moved the tiny company to Hartford. In 1928, the two firms merged as Arrow-Hart, and the company grew into a major manufacturer of wiring devices, motor controls, specialty switches, and enclosed switches, with five plants in Hartford and another in Danielson, Connecticut. By 1932 it had manufacturing subsidiaries in Canada and England, and had begun a marketing program leading to sales offices and warehouses across the country. Later it purchased a New Jersey subsidiary producing ceramic products (including porcelain for Arrow-Hart's own use), established a manufacturing plant in Mexico, and acquired controlling interest in a New Zealand company through its English subsidiary.

An accelerated program of acquisitions began in 1965 with purchase of a plant in Australia, and the Continental Electric Equipment Company in Ludlow, Kentucky. The latter produced a broad line of switchgears, control centers, and panelboards. Dano Electric Company of Winsted, Connecticut, manufacturer of electric coils and transformers,

T.E. Murray, Sr., founder of a company that later
became part of Arrow-Hart, was a leading inventor
of his time. In this early 1920s photograph, he is
shown with two good friends, Thomas A. Edison,
center, and Walter P. Chrysler, right.

was purchased in 1967. The following year brought the addition of
Kellek Company, Norwood, Massachusetts, producer of custom-built
control boards and a variety of switches.

In 1970, Arrow-Hart purchased Murray Manufacturing Corporation
of Jericho, New York, a leading manufacturer of circuit breakers, load
centers, and meter entrance equipment used in residential, commercial,
and institutional building construction markets, and Paul B. Murray became a member of the Arrow-Hart board. The company's founder, T.E.
Murray, Sr., was a pioneer in the electrical industry and held more than
two thousand patents, a record surpassed only by his friend, Thomas A.
Edison.

Despite problems described by *Barron's* as "inadequate cost controls at
the manufacturing level and poor product distribution," Arrow-Hart
played an important role in the progress of Crouse-Hinds. Soon after
the merger it was reorganized into four separate profit centers, and its
financial picture improved rapidly.

Crouse-Hinds provided the lighting system for Syracuse University's 50,000-seat Carrier Dome, unveiled in 1980.

In 1976, energy development continued to bring strong demands for Crouse-Hinds products. With increased oil exploration in Mexico and Canada, the International Division kept pace with its record year of 1975, and Crouse-Hinds of Canada's largest single order in history for explosion-proof switch racks came from a new refinery in that country. Other large orders were received for a wide range of products used at pumping stations, power plants, and remote-control valves along the trans-Alaskan pipeline.

Two more acquisitions were made in 1978. They were Electro of Paramount, California, manufacturer of molded rubber plugs and receptacles for sealed electrical connections under water and in adverse conditions, and Connecticut International Corporation (trade name, SEPCO) of Windsor, Connecticut, producer of visual landing aids for airport runways, including lighting isolation transformers and constant current regulators. (Crouse-Hinds Vice President Robert K. McCabe reported that Sepco representatives explained the plant was located on land leased from the government for 999 years, but, "in true Yankee spirit," they hastened to explain that 100 of those years had already been used up.)

Annual revenues maintained a steady growth, reaching $754,000,000 at the end of 1980, compared with $48,522,000 when Witting joined the company in 1965. In 1980, the company opened a highly automated ferrous foundry and machining facility in Amarillo, Texas, adding to its ability to meet expanding needs of worldwide energy and primary process markets. With no indication that InterNorth, Inc., would soon initiate an attempted takeover, Crouse-Hinds arranged for the acquisition of Belden Corporation.

Several parallels existed between histories of the two companies. As a young employee of a Chicago switchboard and supply company at the turn of the twentieth century, Joseph C. Belden had recognized the need for a high quality silk-covered magnet wire to serve the growing telephone industry. With assistance from an experienced Western Electric employee, Albert Beutler, and several investors, he formed and incorporated the Belden Manufacturing Company in 1902, at the age of twenty-six.

Working in a fifth-floor Chicago factory, lighted by kerosene lamps and reached by climbing steep stairs, employees began operations with a single order for five spools of wire, packed and boxed by the president himself. Business grew steadily in the first part of the century and the company moved twice into progressively larger rental quarters. It expanded into the manufacture of rubber insulated wire, which included the addition of its own rubber mill. It found success also with the development of an enamel insulation ("Beldenamel"), that for the first time could be used to wrap wire without becoming hard and brittle.

The first dramatic rush of business, however, was brought on by World War I and was followed by a flood of commercial orders in the postwar recovery. Operating day and night for nearly three years beginning in 1919, Belden was hard pressed to meet all of its orders. A letter from Thomas Edison, preserved in Belden archives, beseeched the company to provide "relief during this very severe shortage," promising that if it could in some way manage to accommodate the inventor's needs, he would "not forget the favor." Production at that time was facilitated greatly by construction in late 1920 of a four-story manufacturing plant on Van Buren Street.

When the postwar business balloon burst, Belden's orders dropped as suddenly as they had risen, prompting the company to launch a program of diversification into products for the automotive, electrical appliance, and radio industries. It was a propitious move. Small manufacturers of telephones who had represented Belden's principal market, went out of business or were absorbed by a new giant, AT&T, which turned to its manufacturing subsidiary, Western Electric, for its wire needs. Fortunately, new markets soon picked up the slack. Invention of the soft rubber electrical plug by research engineer Hugo Wermine (who later received the Award of the Modern Pioneer of the American Frontier of Industry for his invention) helped greatly in the recovery and expansion

Reprint of advertisement appearing in May
1928 issues of Aero Digest and Aviation

Early Belden hardware store
display.

Lindy's New Ryan Monoplane is Equipped with Belden Wire

MATERIALS were selected with the utmost care by the B. F. Mahoney Aircraft Corporation for the new monoplane recently built for the nation's air hero, Colonel Charles A. Lindbergh.

It is significant that Belden Wire is used throughout for navigation lights, landing lights, electric starter, and all other low-tension wiring on this plane, to which the eyes of the nation are turned.

Belden Manufacturing Co. 2308-B S. Western Ave. Chicago, Illinois

Specify **Belden**

Consult Belden Airplane Engineers regarding specially designed airplane harnesses—either high or low tension—radio shielded or unshielded.

After marketing almost exclusively to the telephone industry, Belden diversified in the 1920s, finding new uses for its quality wire and promoting them with advertisements such as this.

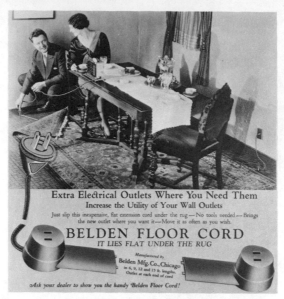

One in a series of advertisements for the Belden Floor Cord.

that came with the late 1920s. Prosperity was such, in fact, that a new plant was opened in Richmond, Indiana, in the spring of 1929. Eventually, it would become Belden's largest manufacturing facility and headquarters of the Electronic Division. President Belden told shareholders, "Your company's prospects seem brighter than for any previous year in its history."

Like others, however, the president could not predict that the year's end would begin a depression that would last a decade. Prosperity was not "just around the corner," as some politicians claimed; yet, Belden weathered the 1930s better than most. Radio and automotive markets kept it alive, and a marketing agreement with the newly organized National Automotive Parts Association (NAPA) grew into the company's principal outlet for automotive wire and cable.

Joseph Belden died in 1939 and was succeeded as president by Whipple Jacobs, who had joined the company in 1914 at a weekly salary of nine dollars. One of the new president's first responsibilities was to prepare for war production, which by 1942 represented the company's entire manufacturing effort. Belden materials were used in myriad products from walkie-talkies to submarines, tanks, and "Flying Fortresses." A single superfortress required six miles of insulated wire.

Following World War II, Belden began to establish leadership in wire and cable technology, vinyl, nylon, neoprene, and other new chemical compounds used for insulation. Charles S. Craigmile, hired as an assistant engineer in 1915, became president in 1948, beginning a sixteen-year administration marked by addition of new technologists and growth at both the Chicago and Richmond plants. His successor, Robert Hawkinson, described by Richmond *Palladium Item* business writer Rick Kennedy as "an extremely popular leader who had the reputation for being able to meet somebody at the plant one time and remember the person's name for life," led the company into a period of expansion and acquisition.

The opening of a new plant in 1966 at Franklin, North Carolina, was followed by moves into Pontotoc, Mississippi, Jena, Lousiana, Monticello, Kentucky, and Clinton and Dumas, Arkansas. Renamed "Belden Corporation" in 1967, the company purchased a Technical Research Center in Geneva, Illinois, the following year and moved toward decentralization that would accommodate its growing diversification. It acquired Complete-Reading Electric Company of Chicago in 1968 and Electric Specialty Company of South San Francisco in 1969. General Wire and Cable Company in Ontario, Canada, also was acquired in 1969, and in 1970 Belden stock was listed on the New York Stock Exchange. In 1972, the corporate office was relocated to Geneva. Acquisitions made in the late 1970s included Geneva Pacific Corporation of Glenview, Illinois, Exploration Data Consultants, Inc., of Denver, Magnum Electric Company of Erie, Michigan, and Cable Concepts Corporation of Ivyland, Pennsylvania.

Concentrating on areas of greatest profit, Belden became an important supplier for the electronics industry with products for such markets as fiber optic communications. The Chicago plant was closed in 1976, although corporate headquarters remained in the Chicago suburb of Geneva.

Just three months before it was acquired by Crouse-Hinds in December of 1980, Belden acquired MiliBride, Inc., of Williston, Vermont. It also was in the process of building a new wire and cable manufacturing plant in Tompkinsville, Kentucky, a project completed in 1982 after Belden and Crouse-Hinds joined Cooper Industries. Robert Hawkinson continued to head Belden operations until his retirement in February of 1982.

33

Unexpected
Acceleration

In his final annual report to Crouse-Hinds' shareholders, Chairman Witting summed up the accomplishments of a year that ended in a flurry of incredible experiences: "Another record performance is always satisfying, but the Crouse-Hinds' team's record performance in 1980 was forged in the face of unusual challenges — a national recession; an unsuccessful, hostile takeover attempt; our acquisition of the Belden Corporation; and an agreement and preliminary actions to merge with Cooper Industries. Against such odds, the performances of our operating units were more than just satisfying — they were commendable."

Crouse-Hinds had completed 1980 with revenues of $753,566,000, making it approximately equal in size to Cooper or Gardner-Denver before their 1979 merger. It was considered to be an extremely well-managed company that would blend into the Cooper structure without extensive realignments required in other acquisitions. Cooper had traded thirteen million of its thirty-six million shares for a company with 22 percent return on equity, only slightly less than Cooper's own 24 percent. Most important, the acquisition moved Cooper Industries into another important marketplace with highly optimistic promise of growth. "This is a true diversification, compared with what I referred to as a complementary move with Gardner-Denver," Cizik said. "In that respect, it compares to our acquisitions of Lufkin and Dallas Airmotive, except on a much larger scale, of course." The president described it as the "core of a new electrical and electronics business," hinting that it could become the base for other acquisitions in that field. "When you look ahead to the end-uses of energy in the years ahead, you realize this new business represents the highest technology area of our company," he said. "We've never before been what you could describe as a 'high tech' company." The electronics industry alone was experiencing an explosion of technology resulting in early obsolescence and short life cycles of

314

equipment requiring wire, cable, electrical shielding, and electronic devices.

Witting continued to head Crouse-Hinds operations and was elected to Cooper's board of directors (along with Senior Vice President Riedel) soon after the merger. Later in the year, he was named vice chairman of the board, remaining also at the Crouse-Hinds operational helm until mid-1982 when that responsibility was assigned to H. John Riley, Jr. A graduate of Syracuse University, Riley had joined Crouse-Hinds in 1963 and advanced through several levels of management. In late 1982, Witting retired from the company to pursue other business activities but remained on the board until the annual meeting in 1983.

However overpowering the acquisition saga may seem, it reveals only part of Cooper's 1980–81 transitional period, described in simplified language by *Fortune* magazine as "busy, busy." During the complex proceedings, Cooper also was busy negotiating the purchase of Kirsch Company in Sturgis, Michigan, manufacturer of drapery hardware, which was fighting an attempted takeover by Bliss & Laughlin Industries of Chicago.

The world's largest manufacturer of drapery hardware, Kirsch Company was described by *Financial World* "as the safe, solid blue chip of its industry." Products ranged from traditional curtain rods to a wide variety of venetian blinds, shelving systems, bath and wall accessories, housewares, and custom office furnishings. Through internal growth and acquisitions over the years, it had developed annual net sales exceeding $171 million, which were significantly larger than those of any company previously acquired by Cooper in building its hardware business. Yet, it shared the key characteristics necessary to meet established criteria for that division — an established quality brand name and market leadership, but lackluster profit performance, which was partially the result of capital investments that had hurt earnings.

Kirsch had been identified as a potential Cooper acquisition candidate in the early 1970s, as a result of normal strategic planning investigation. Cooper had approached Kirsch management in 1975, but found the company uninterested in being acquired by anyone at that time. The situation changed, however, in the spring of 1980 when Bliss & Laughlin Industries, a diversified manufacturer of steel and other products, purchased nearly 10 percent of Kirsch stock through open market transactions. Alarmed by the prospect of a hostile takeover, Kirsch contacted other companies who might have been interested in a merger, among them Cooper Industries. Meanwhile, Kirsch was able to obtain a court order temporarily restraining Bliss & Laughlin from purchasing more of its stock.

Working through an intermediary banking firm, Cooper and Kirsch executives formulated an agreement late in the year, just when the battle with InterNorth was raging. The agreement, accepted by the Kirsch Board in early December, called for Kirsch to be merged into Cooper for a price of $35.51 cash for each share of common stock, a total of approximately $102 million. Cooper's board approved the proposed transaction on December 12, 1980, the same day it approved the Crouse-Hinds plan. "If Cooper had its choice, it probably would have wanted to finish one deal and then work on the other, but the world doesn't wait for you," Dean Witter Reynolds analyst James McCann told the *Wall Street Journal*. The merger became effective April 1, 1981, following approval by shareholders of both companies. Because the Crouse-Hinds merger involved an exchange of stock, only the $102 million for Kirsch increased Cooper's debt-to-capital ratio, and that by just a few percentage points to 30 percent.

The combination of mergers prompted *Fortune* magazine to question Cizik about his rescue mission, then make the following report:

> For companies with takeover jitters, one of the most sought-after white knights is actually a corporate Texas Ranger. Pullman Kellogg turned to Houston-based Cooper Industries when it was pursued by McDermott; so did Mead, which was fighting off Occidental Petroleum, and Babcock & Wilcox in its battle with United Technologies. Says Cooper's 49-year-old chief executive, Robert Cizik, who decided not to rescue those companies, "I don't mind if people like coming to us when they're in trouble as long as it's a business we're interested in." . . . With Crouse-Hinds and Kirsch, Cooper's 1981 revenues will top $3 billion. In the past ten years, Cooper's revenues have grown eightfold and earnings have leaped twelvefold.

"Every merger we've undertaken has resulted in a mutually rewarding relationship," Cizik said, "and we have more reason than usual to assume the same outcome with Crouse-Hinds. We have as much respect for the management as for the products they've manufactured and marketed so well. We're pleased also to add Kirsch to the quality brand names comprising the consumer and industrial tools segment of our business."

34

Kirsch

In discussing the founding of a company that was to make his name known around the world, Charles W. Kirsch once told an interviewer, "If anybody ever started out with less than I did, I'd like to meet him and compare notes." Such a person would be difficult to find. In 1907, the former Wisconsin farm boy was in Three Rivers, Michigan, suddenly out of work when his employer, National Tool Company, became the victim of a severe economic depression. Forty years old, with a wife and two young sons, he found himself sitting in the family's modest home, contemplating his situation.

Since boyhood, Kirsch had enjoyed working with tools. He had even started his own machine shop while still in high school, and although the venture had died of inexperience, he later designed labor-saving machinery for paper mills and for bridge and elevator manufacturers. After joining National Tool, he continued to utilize his inventive talent, and had been working on a curtain rod when the business collapsed. One day, staring out the window of his living room, he glanced at the round, sagging curtain rod. Suddenly, he later explained, the thought came to him that a flat curtain rod would have the strength to remain rigid under a reasonable weight load. With that idea, and very little else, he set out amidst the "Panic of 1907" to form a company manufacturing a single unknown product for a market with which he had no experience. Making a successful prototype proved to be much easier than using it to get financial backing, but a bank in nearby Sturgis, Michigan, finally agreed to help, and in 1908 Kirsch Manufacturing Company was moved to that city.

The scale of early operations was reflected in the experience of a materials salesman who visited the company early one morning and found Kirsch in overalls, sweeping the floor. Not recognizing the owner, the salesman asked, "When can I see the proprietor?" Without stopping his sweeping, Kirsch answered, "At nine o'clock." Precisely at that time, the salesman returned, this time to find Kirsch in business attire, seated at a desk. "I want to see the proprietor," he said. "You're looking at him right

317

**Charles W. Kirsch, founder
of the Kirsch Manufacturing
Company.**

now," Kirsch replied. Puzzled, the salesman asked, "Didn't I see you earlier sweeping the floor?" Without changing expression, Kirsch replied, "No, that was the janitor."

Kirsch's flat, nonsagging curtain rod was popular in the small market it served. During the first year of the company's operation the product was improved even more when the inventor/owner made it adjustable, eliminating the need to customize each item. But spreading the word of his revolutionary product was a slow process. The company's lone salesman, returning from one unsuccessful trip complained that no one had ever heard of extension curtain rods, so prospective dealers wouldn't buy them.

Confident that housewives would be receptive to transforming window drapings from drab utilities to attractive features of the home, Kirsch decided to educate both dealers and the public in the art of creating beauty through decorative colors and styles. Rather than concentrate on a plain piece of hardware, he chose to emphasize what that product could do for the home. It was a promotional concept to be followed from that day forward, eventually making the Kirsch name almost a generic term in drapery hardware.

The first step in the educational plan was to convince dealers that they would make profitable sales by becoming knowledgeable in window decorating. To get that message across, Kirsch initiated publication of a manual providing them with a practical course in imaginative window

C.W. Kirsch moved his small company into this Sturgis, Michigan, factory in 1908, a year after its founding at nearby Three Rivers.

Sixteen dray-loads of more than four tons each represented a record-breaking shipment for Kirsch Manufacturing Co. on the first day of January, 1916.

decorating, and another explaining how to boost sales. At the same time, *Kirsch Drapery Review* was offered to both dealers and consumers. It was the first in a series of decorating style books that would guide homemakers in beautifying windows for decades.

In 1915, the company initiated another effort that would become an important factor in its rise to world leadership in drapery hardware. It began a program of constant national advertising, following the policy of promoting window beauty rather than the hardware it produced. When advertisements in such magazines as *Woman's Home Companion, Ladies Home Journal,* and *Good Housekeeping* included invitations to send for Kirsch style books, orders were received by the thousands. Although the advertisements described "recipes for attractive windows" and help in "planning new curtains," they did contain reminders to ask the dealer for Kirsch flat curtain rods, which made attractive window decorations possible.

For many years, Charles Kirsch continued to design the machinery to produce an increasing number of products while supplying management and promotional leadership as well. His personal enthusiasm extended to all areas of production as the plant expanded from a cluster of small shops into a factory complex. Kirsch insisted that success was attributed to a basic policy that "It is always possible to evolve a plan whereby everybody wins and no one loses . . . profit to all, loss to none." It was a statement he quoted often.

Kirsch also wrote many of the company's publications himself, and contributed articles on sales education that were said to have helped the entire industry improve its stature. When competition led to price wars, however, he steadfastly opposed what he considered "bargain counter practices" and refused to do anything that would threaten fair profits to his company or its dealers. His philosophy was an exact parallel to that of Huntington Crouse, who espoused the same message at that time in the electrical industry.

Friends of Kirsch described him as a man with a compelling concern for the welfare of others. When World War I brought a shortage in housing, Kirsch built eighty-five houses for employees and assumed financial responsibility for sales. The city of Sturgis was given first emergency priority on the Kirsch power plant. A company welfare division was organized long before the idea became a public concern. In his later years, Kirsch wrote and published a booklet entitled "What the World Needs," dedicated to "peace, harmony, and brotherly love," and containing such "Kirschograms" as, "It should be the constant endeavor of every man to so live that the world will be a little better for his having lived in it." The booklet, which went through eight printings, included a song called, "What the World Needs," with words by Kirsch and music by his wife, Flora. The song also was sold in sheet music form.

Kirsch took advantage of Hollywood's use of its window-treatment products by using this advertisement in the early 1940s.

It was suggested that Kirsch deserved co-star billing with James Stewart in the motion picture *The Jackpot.*

When the founder died in 1933, he was succeeded as president and general manager by his older son, Guy W. Kirsch, who had joined the company nine years earlier following graduation from the University of Michigan. By then, the company was distributing products through branch warehouses in the United States and through an export department serving three thousand merchants in thirty-two other countries. Its product line had grown to include several other "firsts," including adjustable draw-cord traverse rods, decorative drapery hardware, and cut-to-measure rods for bay and corner windows. Three plants covered nine acres in Sturgis, making it the largest drapery hardware plant in the world. Kirsch of Canada, operating as a manufacturing affiliate in Woodstock, Ontario, since 1921, had been expanding steadily before the Great Depression slowed activities everywhere.

Despite the most difficult time in its history, Kirsch company began its revival from depression depths by looking for new design ideas. The first to appear in 1935 was a modern version of a 300-year-old invention — the venetian blind. Evolving rapidly from wood to light-weight aluminum slats, formed to an S-shape for greater rigidity, the Kirsch "Sun-Aire" blind became another market leader until it was discontinued many years later. It revived in "miniblind" form in 1979.

The early years of World War II brought an end to most European marketing, prompting Kirsch to develop new opportunities in Latin America. Within a year its business there exceeded what it had lost in Europe, whetting the company's appetite for widening its foreign marketing position further in the postwar years. So while production activities were altered temporarily to meet the needs of 359 war contracts, Kirsch prepared also to launch an aggressive new export effort when the fighting stopped. Three years after the armistice it was shipping products to nearly every country in the world.

Experience in manufacturing glider nose sections and a variety of other aircraft components for the war effort convinced management it should consider diversification. After extensive planning a Condenser business was organized and in 1946 it began to produce a line of steel refrigeration condensers. This introduced processes and machines that were later accepted as standard throughout the industry. Six years later, facilities were added to produce aluminum fin condensers and evaporators for air conditioners. A steel finishing plant was constructed at the nearby village of White Pigeon in 1948, supplementing the Sturgis drapery hardware manufacturing facilities and providing economies through improved control of raw material processing.

President Guy Kirsch died in 1950 and was succeeded by his brother, John N. Kirsch, who had joined the company in 1923 and served in most departments. The following year he became chairman, with Phillip B. Stratton advancing from executive vice president to president. The only nonfamily member ever to hold the presidency of Kirsch, Stratton had started as an office boy in 1914 and worked at almost every job within the company, including janitor. Considered by colleagues to be the epitome of a "self-made man," Stratton had taught himself accounting, learned sales and management, led the way in creating the Canadian affiliate, played an active role in community affairs, and carefully prepared himself for company leadership.

To boost its drive toward increased foreign sales, Kirsch began the 1950s with an International Sales Conference in Paris, with distributors attending from such widely scattered locations as Peru, Scandinavia, French Indochina, and the Belgian Congo. The *New York Herald Tribune* reported:

> A medium-sized American business concern took over a small portion of Paris last week to demonstrate that the post-war world market is more accessible to private enterprise than it generally is supposed to be. . . . Building on the base of a pre-war export business, the Kirsch company has managed to work its way far enough around exchange regulations and the dollar shortage to enjoy a larger foreign market now than before the war — and without any government aid. . . . The meeting itself was an investment whose returns will be difficult to measure, but none of the company officials on hand doubted that they would be substantial in terms of good will and greater understanding of marketing problems and requirements in most of the consuming countries. On a wider scale, these are major ingredients in the world trade pattern that American aid programs have been trying to restore.

Modernization of manufacturing facilities to include new presses, more automatic equipment, and conveyor-line production methods highlighted the 1950s. Distribution branches grew from seven to twenty-four, and employment increased 60 percent to include 824 women and 941 men. Product designs were restyled regularly, and vertical traverse blinds were introduced as "combining the advantages of draperies with the wonderful control of light and air that is possible with venetian blinds." A new style of round "cafe" curtain rods also helped Kirsch maintain its claim of having "the only complete drapery hardware line." Construction of a second major plant in Sturgis was completed in June of 1956. Through a series of later expansions, "Plant 2" was to grow through the years to the point of taking over all Kirsch manufacturing operations in that city.

An interesting sidelight of the '50s was that during the Korean War, the Refrigeration Division moved even farther from the company's primary product lines to manufacture metal track bodies for U.S. army tanks.

In October of 1960, Philip Stratton was named vice chairman of the board, and John W. 'Jack' Kirsch, the son of John N. Kirsch, became president. Carrying on the family tradition of learning the business by working in most production and management areas for more than ten years, he most recently had served as executive vice president in charge of operations. Charles E. "Chuck" Kirsch, who also had worked in various departments since joining the company in 1949 but had concentrated more on marketing than operations, was elected executive vice president. He was the son of Guy Kirsch and a first cousin of the new president.

Chuck Kirsch also was named president of the company's first U.S. manufacturing subsidiary, Scotscraft, Inc., which began production of drapery hardware at Scottsville, Kentucky, early in 1961. Citizens of that community, led by an active economic development committee, had worked hard to influence Kirsch's site selection, and an $850,000 bond issue by the city financed construction of the new plant.

In 1965, Jack Kirsch became chairman of the board and Chuck Kirsch advanced to the presidency. Having continued its internal expansion of both products and facilities (including the addition of its own plastics molding operations in 1964), the company then looked toward acquisition as a further avenue of growth. Its first move in that direction came later in the year when it purchased the Ideal Manufacturing Company of Beacon Falls, Connecticut. Founded in 1946 by Stuart M. Lamb, Ideal manufactured a variety of pins and wire goods, including drapery hardware items supplied to Kirsch. Robert A. Addison, Kirsch vice president of manufacturing, was named president of the new wholly owned subsidiary with Lamb becoming vice president and general manager. To supplement the subsidiary's product lines, Kirsch later acquired Union Pin Company of Winstead, Connecticut, the world's largest producer of stainless steel common pins.

Kirsch management also looked to the future with plans for diversification into areas that could benefit most from its established marketing strengths. Discontinuing its Refrigeration Division operations, the company opted for new products more closely aligned to its primary interests. Having made that decision, it moved quickly.

Entry into the wood shelving market began in 1969, with the manufacturing and test marketing of a line called "Royal Oak." A few months later, Kirsch acquired Rockware, Inc., a Rockford, Illinois, shelving manufacturer, then expanded both operations to introduce a variety of new shelving systems (sold as kits or components) with names like Button-Ups, Cranmere, and Contempo. Although it was a highly competitive field, Kirsch combined its well-known brand name with the advantage of offering a single source for comprehensive style and price selections to quickly gain a strong position in the marketplace.

Concurrently, the company purchased Worldsbest Industries of Cudahy, Wisconsin, whose products included a varied line of laundry aids and such juvenile products as rack-type clothes dryers, portable ironing boards, and safety gates.

In what management considered the "most natural" of its diversifications, Kirsch in July of 1970 purchased Idamatic, Inc., of Irvine, California, a well-known producer of drapery and commercially quilted bedspreads, and the related Johnson Leasing Company of Sturgis. Seven months later it acquired Max Rawicz Designs of California, a design and custom bedspread business, merging it into Idamatic. The combination enabled Kirsch to offer a full price and style range of bedspreads and matching draperies through its already established nationwide network of branch offices. (Six years later it sold the bedspread segment of the business.)

Another diversification was carried out internally with the 1970 introduction of Kirsch decorative bath accessories. Beginning with a line of fifteen products ranging from shower bars to soap dishes, the company soon expanded into other items coordinated in design to provide a matching appearance.

Within a three-year period, Kirsch had diversified into four new competitive business arenas while also improving its drapery hardware lines to include new styles of decorative traverse rods — its fastest growing segment — and "Electrac" electromatic rod systems to open and close draperies with the flip of a switch, or by radio remote control. It had been listed for the first time on the New York Stock Exchange in 1969, and net sales had doubled in the past decade to $78 million in 1972.

The company's heralded advertising and sales promotion programs had entered the world of television in 1967 with regular thirty-second spots on NBC's "Today" show, then expanded to such other network favorites as "The Loretta Young Show" and "Tennessee Ernie Ford Show," and into the logical programming area known as "Daytime TV." Products were used so often on television and motion picture sets that in some instances, such as the James Stewart film, *The Jackpot*, it was suggested that Kirsch drapery hardware should get co-star billing. Permanent sales showrooms were maintained in Dallas, New York, and Chicago. National awards for catalogs and dealer publications had almost become commonplace for the company's only two directors of advertising and sales promotion — Arthur W. Evers and his successor in 1962, John J. Lichty. But the unchallenged leader in the company's parade of promotional concepts continued to be the celebrated books of window fashion suggestions, produced regularly since the first issue was created by the founder in 1915. Their success was considered nothing short of phenomenal throughout the advertising industry. Although they were sold at prices commensurate with general publications, their circulation reached more than a million a year, putting them in the top fifty magazines of any kind in the nation. They were so popular, in fact, that Lichty initiated a successful program of letting drapery hardware dealers make substantial extra profits by selling the decorating idea books. Placed in newsstands for one period of time, they sold so well that the company withdrew them to avoid getting involved in the complicated business of magazine distribution.

Diversification continued in late 1974 with a cash purchase of Vanguard Studios, Inc., a leading producer of framed art and wall accessories. The Chatsworth, California, company was best known for its framed, high quality art reproductions, but it also had a broad line of hand-painted oils, serigraphs, etchings, oriental paintings on silk, molded wall plaques, clocks, mirrors, and other accessories for both commercial and residential use. It also manufactured and distributed custom office furniture under the trade name of Alex Stuart Design. Three years after the purchase, a new combination factory, office, and showroom was constructed for Vanguard operations at Westlake, California, consolidating several facilities into one location.

The acquisition of another California company in December of 1975 enabled Kirsch to expand its window decorating line into the relatively new field of woven woods. Golden West Woven Woods, based in Santa Ana, fabricated custom shades, blinds, draperies, and folding doors from woven fabric composed of decorative yarns and wooden slats. A second plant was located in Kansas City, and a third was added in Shamokin, Pennsylvania, a year after the company was acquired by Kirsch. Kirsch of Canada also started fabrication of woven woods in 1979, and woven roll goods were shipped to customers in England, Sweden, and Italy for fabrication in those countries. In 1978, Kirsch expanded its trucking and delivery system and put into operation a nationwide toll-free telephone center to receive customer orders. A new building for the center was constructed later at Tempe, Arizona.

Despite entries into various new markets, drapery hardware sales remained prominent, fluctuating between 68 and 75 percent of the company's annual income. Styles were subject to constant change to accommodate fashion conscious homemakers, but surprisingly, the basic curtain rod still resembled the original product responsible for the company's beginning. James A. Ford, who became vice president of marketing in 1981 after heading research and development, then custom window treatment operations, recalled discussing that topic with colleagues in 1980. "For more than seventy years we made one-inch-wide flat curtain rods, while others changed dramatically," he said. "But whenever the subject arose, we shrugged and asked ourselves, 'what can you do with a plain flat curtain rod that works just fine?' Then one day someone in the group answered, 'Well, you could make it four and one half inches wide and promote the idea of having wide-shirred curtains.' You know, we did just that. We introduced the new size as our 'Continental' look, and we sold $4.5 million worth in the first year."

Among the other most popular designs of the early 1980s were the thin miniblinds which represented an updated version of the old venetian blinds, colorful vertical blinds knitted from spun-glass fabrics to re-

The Kirsch line of drapery hardware, largest in the world, was integrated into Cooper's Tools & Hardware division after the acquisition in 1981.

semble draperies, and window shades containing graphic patterns. Emphasis on energy conservation also led to the development of metalized treatment on the backs of shades, giving the effect of an extra storm window. Colors became increasingly important, so Kirsch joined a Color Marketing Group that included representatives from carpeting, paint, and other related industries. By working together, members of the group planned new color schemes that would not be in conflict for designers. "We've always been in the fashion business, not just the hardware business," said Vice President Ford.

When it became part of Cooper Industries, Kirsch was continuing to build its distribution center network, already fully computerized for coordinated sales and inventory controls. Fabrication plants were established in several strategic areas and provided rapid service on custom products such as woven wood and narrow slat venetian blind window coverings. The company held a 70 percent interest in an Italian subsidiary and 30 percent interests in Spanish and Swedish affiliates. Licensees were located in several other nations. After the acquisition, Chairman John Kirsch retired, but Charles Kirsch continued as president, and Senior Vice President Robert Addison was named general manager.

35

A Management Strategy

Having increased another 50 percent in size, Cooper Industries made a series of operational readjustments, personnel changes, and financial management revisions during 1981, some of them still reflecting the earlier acquisition of Gardner-Denver. Kirsch was easily assimilated into the Cooper system because it had a similar customer base and used many of the same manufacturing processes as the company's other tool and hardware operations, even though its products were quite unlike the others. Crouse-Hinds, on the other hand, represented an entirely new area of operations and marketing, including the Belden and Arrow-Hart product lines. Consequently, that segment of Cooper's business added a totally new dimension extending from the corporate management level throughout operations and sales.

Some of the acquisitions Kirsch had made in previous years, although contributing to its diversification then, were not substantial enough to fit the long-range development strategy of Cooper. An example was Vanguard, sold along with some of its real estate holdings soon after Kirsch joined Cooper (Alex Stuart Design, which manufactured office furniture was not included in the sale). The Vanguard sale reduced Cooper's investment base by some $2.5 million. Any lost sales and earnings were more than balanced by integration into Cooper's hardware operations, which utilized 15 percent less operating working capital per sales dollar than Kirsch at the time of acquisition. The earnings increase, coupled with tighter working capital control and a reduced investment base, provided a cash flow profile expected to make Kirsch an excellent long-term investment.

Having extended itself financially, Cooper could have been expected to ignore any immediate suggestion for further expansion. But two months after the Crouse-Hinds and Kirsch acquisitions, an almost bankrupt International Harvester Company was forced to put its Solar Division on the market. The aggressive Cooper management team recognized Solar as an extremely desirable business that could be cradled comfortably in its Energy Services arm and become very profitable.

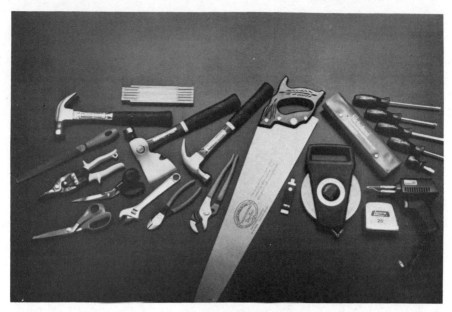

The Cooper "Tool Basket" in 1981 featured a variety of products representing seven acquisitions during the previous 14 years.

With drilling activity continuing at a high level in 1981, Cooper increased sales of Martin-Decker instrumentation for super rigs drilling beyond 30,000 feet.

A Gardner-Denver mud pump provides lubrication and flushes drillings to the surface at an oil rig in Oklahoma's Anadarko Basin in 1981.

Realizing impending difficulties, Cooper nevertheless decided to compete for Solar. Officers pushed themselves once again, putting together a complex proposal in a very short period of time, but the effort fell just short of its goal when the company came in second to Caterpillar among a host of hopeful bidders.

Despite a generally sluggish U.S. economy, Cooper's earnings and return on equity remained consistent with its goal of a minimum 20 percent annual increase. On the high side, demand for compression and drilling equipment was booming. Mexico, where oil production had increased by nearly one million barrels a day in each of the previous three years, was a particularly good market. Others were Canada, and the Alaskan North Slope, where secondary oil recovery projects were being scheduled. The company also penetrated a major new market with sale of Ajax compressors to the People's Republic of China. At the other end of the business scale, tools and hardware products suffered from America's low level of construction and turnover of homes, although the problem was offset somewhat by resulting increases in do-it-yourself homeowner activities. Steady overall earnings performance, leveling out the wide disparity among various market strengths, was interpreted as an endorsement of Cooper's diversification program. With that marketing balance strengthened considerably by acquisitions of the past two years, Cooper chose to sell its aircraft services business.

Cooper En-Tronic control system is the heart of Pump Station 9 on the Trans-Alaskan pipeline.

Cooper's 1981 annual report illustrated the company's hand tool do-it-yourself market with this photograph.

Sentimentally, the sale of Cooper Airmotive would be losing a close member of the family — one who had grown sevenfold in eleven years, helping to provide both income and protection during a period of vulnerability ("I think it helped keep us somewhat impregnable during the time we were building," Cizik said later). Realistically, the family had then achieved a sturdiness and established a heading that could be served better by selling its aircraft services to reduce debt and reinvest in its more highly proprietary manufacturing-oriented businesses.

In December of 1981, Cooper sold its aircraft services organization to an investment group that combined the operations with a smaller company, Aviation Power Supply, to form Aviall, Inc. Cooper received $151 million cash and 9 percent of Aviall's equity, with a resulting pretax gain of $52 million. The institutional investors in Aviall were led by Citicorp Venture Capital, Ltd., and included First Capital Corporation of Chicago, Inco Securities Corporation, Union Venture Corporation, Northwest Growth Fund, and Charles River Resources. Additional financing for the privately held Dallas company was provided by Drexel Burnham Lambert and a bank group led by Continental Illinois Bank and Trust Company of Chicago. Robert G. Lambert, who had headed the Cooper Airmotive group since 1973, left Cooper to become president of Aviall.

Cooper's business relationship with the Soviet Union was dealt a severe blow as the year ended, when the Federal Administration levied sanctions against involvement of American companies in the Russian Urengol (Yamal) pipeline project. The immediate effect on Cooper was to suspend negotiations for a contract that would have provided spare parts for compression equipment sold to the Soviets in the 1970s. The value of that contract would have been between $1 million and $2 million a year. When the sanctions were broadened later, the additional effect was to bar Cooper from several million dollars in sales of component parts for transmission equipment to Creusot Loire, its licensee and joint-venture partner in France. Company executives estimated its subsequent loss of contracts at more than $100 million. They questioned the effectiveness of sanctions as instruments of foreign policy, pointing to the drastic loss of United States competitiveness in a situation where products simply could be obtained by the Soviets from other nations, without preventing pipeline construction. A report to stockholders assured Cooper's stand against "transfer of pure technology to the Soviet Bloc," and its intention to "comply fully with applicable U.S. trade laws and regulations," but opposed sanctions it felt would "seriously erode the American lead in oil and gas equipment and technology," elevating foreign companies "from minor players to major competitors" in international gas compression and transmission markets. "For years we were sent chasing international business, egged on by the government as a way to restore the balance of payments," said a company spokesman.

A Crouse-Hinds heavy duty fitting is added to a switchrack assembly in 1981, providing for safe use of electricity in a hostile environment.

"Now we are told it is illegal." The sanctions were to have far deeper consequences when the nation fell into a deep economic recession in 1982.

Behind the dramatic events of 1981, however, a background of "business as usual" was punctuated by the familiar beat of expansion, consolidation, and relocation. A Juarez, Mexico, plant for assembly of specialty switches and industrial control products became operational, meeting such success that plans were started almost immediately to double its size. A new foundry for industrial electrical products was opened at Amarillo, Texas, and Crouse-Hinds aviation lighting operations were consolidated in a new facility at Windsor, Connecticut. At Springfield, Ohio, Superior added state-of-the-art machining centers and increased foundry capacity by 50 percent. A new Demco fabrication plant equipped with automated equipment to produce a wide variety of specialized oil field equipment, was nearing completion at Oklahoma City. Construction was started on a new consolidated and expanded compressor valve plant in Spartanburg, South Carolina. A new turbocharger facility was begun at Tulsa, Oklahoma, to expand servicing and overhaul capability for compression and drilling equipment. Plans were announced to transfer the Wire-Wrap product line from Grand Haven, Michigan, to the Hollis plant in Nashua, New Hampshire, where former Gardner-Denver operations producing equipment for the electronics

Special pneumatic assembly machinery designed and built by Deutsche Gardner-Denver in Germany features automatic multiple torque control and monitoring on these critical engine fasteners manufactured at a Mexican Volkswagen plant in 1981.

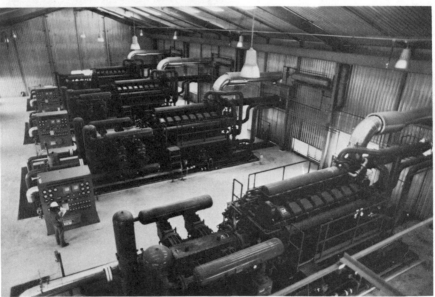

In 1981, Superior increased manufacturing capacity appreciably to produce products such as these engine-compressor packages pumping natural gas into underground storage in Texas.

industry were consolidated into a new business unit. This was called Cooper Electronics, and it included plants in Irvine, California, and Reed City, Michigan.

Press coverage in cities affected by some Cooper relocation plans provided topical insight into concerns being echoed over a wide cross section of the nation at that time. Speculation on moving Plumb tool production from Philadelphia brought immediate reaction from writer Peter H. Binzen of *The Evening Bulletin:*

> For 125 years, Plumb Tools has been making axes, hammers, hatchets, and sledges in Philadelphia. Its quality products are recognized around the world. Its 300 workers, a nearly even mix of Polish-Americans and inner-city blacks, plus a small number of newly arrived immigrants from Asia, are turning out close to 12,000 finely made tools every day. The pay is good, and the turnover is relatively low. But the factory, at 4837 James St. in the city's Bridesburg section, is old and dirty. The loading dock is inadequate. The property — wedged between Conrail freight tracks and Aramingo Ave., just off I-95 — lacks space for expansion. Cooper Industries, the Houston-based corporation that bought Plumb from another absentee owner last summer, plans production increases. The goal is 13,000 hammers, hatchets, sledges, and axes (daily) in 1982, and 15,000 in 1983. To increase Plumb's efficiency, Cooper is considering purchasing $2.5 million worth of new equipment. The question is, will this expensive new machinery be installed in the deteriorated century-old plant in Bridesburg, or will Plumb move South? ... Plumb's labor contract with Local 7411 of the United Steelworker's Union, which represents its production and maintenance workers, expires August 12.

Early in the summer of 1981, Cooper announced firm plans to gradually phase out Philadelphia operations and move them to Monroe, North Carolina, where a new 290,000-square-foot plant would eventually employ about 475 persons. Local 7411 at the Philadelphia plant overwhelmingly ratified a plant-closing agreement which extended their labor contract for an additional two years and provided substantial termination benefits to employees. The agreement called for severance pay allowances, guaranteed pension benefits, and an extension of medical insurance for terminated workers. In addition, the company pledged to assist workers in obtaining new employment when the plant closed.

When Cooper announced later in the year that air tools manufacturing would be moved from Grand Haven, Michigan, to an existing, more modern, energy and labor efficient plant in Lexington, South Carolina, the *Grand Haven Tribune* responded with an editorial:

> The other shoe fell Wednesday when Cooper Industries formally announced it would move its pneumatic tools division from Grand Haven to greener economic pastures in South Carolina. Cooper had earlier announced the move of its Wire Wrap division to New Hampshire. The dol-

lars and cents of the decision are certainly understandable from Cooper's point of view. Despite offers of wage restraint by local workers and despite a chance of earning tax incentives, Cooper to no one's surprise decided to move to a much newer facility requiring lower labor, utility, and other costs. All this, of course, is little consolation to Grand Haven, which has been learning day by day over the past few years how a recession and loss of jobs in the industrial sector stun the rest of the local economy. A move of 300 jobs from Cooper on top of the loss of AP Parts early this year and horrible conditions in Michigan's auto industry really hurts. It's no good and probably unfair and unproductive to start pointing fingers over the shrinkage of the local industrial base. The biggest adverse factors — high labor costs, aging facilities, high utility bills, exorbitant workmen's compensation rates and high tax rates — plague all of Michigan, not just the Tri-Cities. There has been one heartening development in Lansing: the state reform bill that will substantially lower the insurance rates to business and industry. We urge the local governments, local industry, and local organizations whose job is to promote this area as an industrial site to begin working together as they never have before. There must be a singleness of purpose that can only be obtained by having a single organization to promote industrial growth for the whole Tri-Cities area. The potential consequences of doing otherwise are too frightening to imagine.

In South Carolina, Lexington City Council Chairman Russell Shealy said the addition of Cooper's plant would "pick up slack from jobs we've lost." Cooper Air Tools was slated to move into a three-year-old plant abandoned by a toy manufacturing subsidiary of Colgate Palmolive when it was unable to meet the competition of another company. Lexington's work force also had been affected by layoffs of about 250 employees from a company manufacturing electric lift trucks. To counteract those losses, community leaders launched a cooperative effort to bring in new industry, stressing its favorable climate, excellent school system, availability of the labor market, and, in the case of Cooper Industries, its proximity to the company's tool distribution center at Apex, North Carolina.

Easily qualifying as the shortest and fastest relocation of the year, however, was Cooper's move of corporate headquarters from Two Houston Center, across the street to First City Tower. Carl Mueller, manager of public relations, described the August 22–23 event in an article for plant publications:

The move posed some major challenges, not only in the volume and weight of material to be moved, but in the amount of time allowed to move it. Every box and piece of furniture had to be moved over a 48-hour period so the company could resume business without interference on Monday morning. Thanks to Bobbie Smith, Cooper's manager of office services, and the cooperation of Corporate Office employees (not to mention 60 moving men), the chore was accomplished with only one casualty — a damaged typewriter. Quite an accomplishment considering that 5,000 boxes and the furniture of more than 150 employees were transported. Anytime a major corporation moves its headquarters, maintaining contact with the outside world is a primary concern. The company's telephone system was turned off at Two Houston Center at 5 p.m. Friday, and one half hour later, turned on in the new building. By 11 p.m. Sunday, the move was history. It was so complete, when employees arrived for work on Monday morning the art was on the walls and the plants were situated in their proper places.

The total 1981 revenue of $2,866,031,000 (excluding Cooper Airmotive sales of $269 million) and per-share earnings of $5.13 represented the tenth consecutive annual increase since the company's disastrous low point in 1971. However, a former Belden shareholder showed great concern over what appeared to be a loss suffered in the conversion of his stock following the Crouse-Hinds acquisition. In answer, a letter from Thomas W. Campbell, who recently had joined the company as vice president of public affairs, provided a comparison of relative values:

. . . First, the stock price. You mentioned a drop of 25 percent in the price of the stock. In that connection, I am sending you several articles that have been published recently about Cooper and its acquisitions. Whenever a company is aggressive in its internal growth plans and acquisitions, there will be those who question the decisions that are made. This, together with high prime rates and a 15 to 20 percent decline in oil services stock generally, have made themselves felt on the price of Cooper stock. However, looking to the longer term, there is no doubt in our minds that the right decisions have been made to ensure that our company and your investment enjoy steady growth. As the prime rate declines, it is apparent that more and more investors agree with us — witness the fact that the stock is recovering at this time. But let me be more specific by way of illustration. Let's assume you acquired your Belden stock in 1973, which is as far back as my available records go. The low price of Belden stock in 1973 was $15.125. For Cooper, it was $5.40 after adjustments for previous splits. At the end of August, 1980, Belden stock was priced at $32 a share. Cooper's was $47. So, while Belden stock was appreciating at a compound growth rate of 11.3 percent during this period, Cooper stock was growing at a rate of 36.2 percent, or more than three times as fast.

Second, dividends. Between 1973 and 1979, dividends on Belden stock rose from $1.20 per share per year to $1.56 per share. That is a 4.5 percent compound growth rate. During the same period, Cooper's dividends advanced from 21¢ a share to 92¢ a share — compound growth rate of 27.9 percent. Of course, you received more dollars in dividends from Belden than you would have from Cooper, but then you had more invested than a Cooper shareholder with an equal number of shares. As a result, the total yield on your investment was just under 21 percent; while the total yield to the Cooper shareholder on his investment was almost 27 percent.

Third, and I think you will agree this is the bottom line: The return on Belden's equity between January, 1973 and August of this year was 13.2 percent. Had you owned Cooper stock from the beginning (1973), the return on equity would have been 19.8 percent. Not even the money market funds have matched that.

Early in 1982, a product extension was completed when the Crouse-Hinds Lighting Productions Division acquired Pfaff & Kendall of Newark, New Jersey, in a tax-free exchange for approximately one hundred thousand shares of Cooper stock. A leading producer of spun aluminum poles for outdoor lighting and traffic signals, the family-owned company had been in business since 1902. President Henry C. Pfaff, Jr., who was making plans for retirement, championed the merger with Crouse-Hinds as a means of providing increased opportunities for the company's employees. A few months later, Cooper sold Electrical Specialty Company and Complete-Reading Electric Company to an Atlanta electrical supply company. As distribution and service units acquired in the Crouse-Hinds merger, they did not fit into Cooper's manufacturing strategies.

In other areas of Cooper operations, rearrangement and expansion of Quincy, Illinois, facilities, representing one of the most ambitious capital investments in the company's history, were completed, the new Demco fabrication plant was dedicated at Oklahoma City, construction was begun on a worldwide distribution center for Cooper Air Compressors in Memphis, Tennessee, and the Cooper Air Tools plant went on stream at Lexington, South Carolina. Product development, drawings, and inventory of Sullair Mining and Equipment Company's Garland, Texas, subsidiary were purchased by Cooper and added to its Gardner-Denver lines of machinery and oil field equipment.

In mid-1982, the company began construction of a $6.2 million administration building in Grove City, where Cooper Energy Services was consolidating all functions of its reciprocating products division. For many years the company had manufactured all its reciprocating engine-compressors in Grove City and its rotating units in Mt. Vernon. However, marketing and engineering for both had been located in the latter city. Under the new plan, marketing and engineering departments of the reciprocating products division would move to Grove City. Marketing and engineering for the rotating products division, as well as headquarters for Cooper Energy Services, would remain in Mt. Vernon.

Later in the year, Cooper purchased the U.S. lighting division of Westinghouse Electric Corporation. At the same time, Westinghouse Canada, Inc. was purchased by Crouse-Hinds Canada Ltd., a Cooper subsidiary. The two separate, but related transactions, added a broad range of commercial and industrial indoor lighting fixtures to Cooper products marketed under the Crouse-Hinds name. Acquired Westinghouse operations, previously headquartered in Vicksburg, Mississippi, and

Cambridge, Ontario, became part of Crouse-Hinds Commercial Electrical Products's lighting products division. They included manufacturing plants at El Paso, Texas, Burlington, Vermont, Granby, Quebec, and Juarez, Mexico, as well as Vicksburg and Cambridge, adding six hundred employees to the Cooper corporate family.

As its 150 anniversary year of 1983 approached, Cooper had no plan for further diversification, although President Cizik assured analysts, "We always will be ready to make some changes in our organization — to spin off those businesses that don't meet our standards, and acquire complementary businesses that do." Having followed a pattern of alternating periods of acquisition with those of adjustment, the company was unquestionably in a period of making changes to accommodate its most recent surge. Cizik likened it to an army that needed to pause after an advancement to establish its new position. "A growing company can outrun its capabilities if it isn't careful to bring up the supply lines," he said. "We have to restructure ourselves at a time like this, before we feel comfortable in moving out again."

One specific objective was to avoid over extending presidential involvement in operational matters, while maintaining the homogeneous quality of corporate management that had been built over the years. Despite its rapid growth, Cooper was determined to preserve its "operating company" philosophy, as opposed to a "holding company" style of management, with officers participating in key operating decisions, particularly those affecting long-term directions. Consequently, Cizik created an executive vice presidents (operations) level to improve day-to-day contact with top corporate officers who were assigned direct responsibilities for major operational segments. The list of corporate officers reflected that adjustment:

Robert Cizik, president and chief executive officer
Alan E. Riedel, senior vice president, administration
Dewain K. Cross, senior vice president, finance
C. Baker Cunningham, executive vice president, operations, Tools & Hardware
Robert B. Dyer, senior vice president, planning and development
Donald E. Kipley, executive vice president, operations, Drilling Equipment
H. John Riley, Jr., executive vice president, operations, Electrical and Electronic Products
Michael J. Sebastian, executive vice president, operations, Compression Machinery
Edgar A. Bircher, vice president and general counsel
Thomas W. Campbell, vice president, public affairs
D. Bradley McWilliams, vice president, taxes
Carl J. Plesnicher, Jr., vice president, employee relations
Roger A. Scott, vice president, secretary and corporation counsel
William A. Agnew, controller
Alan Hill, treasurer

From a two-man iron foundry operation on Ohio's "Western Frontier" in 1833, Cooper had grown to a multibillion dollar international manufacturing corporation employing forty thousand men and women in forty-two states and twenty-eight foreign countries. Domestic sales represented 75 percent of total income, but the company was moving aggressively into the international marketplace, with investments ranging from wholly-owned and joint-venture manufacturing plants to sales and warehouse or service facilities, and, in some instances, to agent, distributor, and licensee arrangements.

Among its major Latin American operations were plants in Mexico, Brazil, Colombia, and Venezuela, where economies were growing rapidly and commerce was moving from traditional agricultural products to manufactured goods. In Europe, Cooper conducted business through nine manufacturing and six warehousing facilities in the United Kingdom, France, West Germany, Italy, the Netherlands, and Spain. Canadian plants were located in eight cities. In the Far East, Cooper had three relatively large Australian manufacturing operations, one in New Zealand, and a joint venture in Japan. African plants were located in Nigeria, Zambia, and South Africa. Middle East sales and service centers were in Kuwait, Dubai, and Bahrain.

Reorganization of U.S. plant operations, blending new acquisitions into the existing system, brought Cooper recognition as the most efficient producer of nearly all products it manufactured. A publication of the Public Affairs Department offered a compendium of the three major business segments, Compression & Drilling Equipment, Tools & Hardware, and Electrical & Electronics Products, on the eve of the company's sesquicentennial year:

> Cooper Industries' Compression & Drilling Equipment segment is the company's largest area of business, contributing more than 50 percent of revenues and earnings. It's also Cooper Industries' oldest area of business, with some product lines traceable to the company's earliest days in the mid-nineteenth century. Through this segment, Cooper Industries serves the oil and natural gas industry as well as the mining, construction, chemical process, utility, and general industries. Cooper products can be found at virtually every phase of the oil and natural gas industries, from exploration to distribution. We manufacture Gardner-Denver portable rigs for both seismic and shallow oilfield drilling operations. In these applications, as well as medium and deep drilling, Gardner-Denver mud pumps, drawworks, swivels, and rotary tables, Demco valves, pumps, and mud handling equipment (also commonly used in petroleum production and industrial applications), and Martin-Decker driller's consoles and rig instrumentation are components commonly used on both onshore and offshore rigs. When it comes to production, transmission, storage and distribution, compression is employed in virtually every step taken to transform oil and natural gas into two of man's most important and versatile energy sources. Cooper is the only company that can supply the full range of compression horse-

A Coberra gas turbine-compressor reaches completion in 1981.

power, from 10 hp to 35,000 hp. Our Ajax and Superior compressors aid oil and gas production through gas lift, gathering, and injection techniques, as well as other enhanced recovery methods. Our larger horsepower Cooper-Bessemer engine-compressors and Coberra gas turbine-compressors are used for secondary recovery applications, reinjection of gas, and to transport oil or gas through pipelines. Our En-Tronic Controls products provide control systems for this equipment. Each of these products enjoys a reputation for quality and reliability and is reinforced by one of the strongest sales and service support organizations in the industry. Cooper compression and drilling equipment is highly regarded within the mining and construction industries as well. Gardner-Denver pneumatic and hydraulic percussion rock drilling equipment, and portable air compressors, Bedford Steels rolled steel products, and Padley and Venables drill steel, mining bits, and drilling accessories are used in the mining of hard rock minerals, quarry mining of aggregates, and the construction of highways, dams, buildings, tunnels, and other public and private projects. In addition, our Funk transmissions can be found worldwide as a major component in the drive systems of most any size equipment. Common applications are construction equipment such as cranes, motor graders, fork trucks, or road-building machines. Other applications include forest vehicles, mining machinery, fishing boats, agricultural equipment, and petroleum exploration, drilling, and recovery equipment. Finally, many of these same product names can be found in the process and general industries. Pennsylvania Process Compressors and Cooper-Bessemer motor-driven reciprocating compressors are widely used in air separation, refining, and chemical processing. Gardner-Denver industrial air compressors supply compressed air to power machines in manufacturing and assembly plants. These compressors also are incorporated in such products as water well drilling rigs, locomotive braking systems, and vacuum processes. Gardner-Denver blowers move hundreds of types of dry bulk materials through pipelines and help purify waste liquids.

With the acquisition of Crouse-Hinds, Cooper assumed a preeminent position among manufacturers of electrical and electronic products. Under the Crouse-Hinds, Belden, and Arrow-Hart product line names, Cooper serves diverse markets with literally tens of thousands of electrical products. Crouse-Hinds heavy duty plugs and receptacles, junction boxes, and explosion-proof lights are found on oil or gas drilling rigs and in paper and steel mills, chemical plants, mines, and other harsh environments. Crouse-Hinds is the name preferred by most buyers of these products. The Crouse-Hinds name can be found also on aviation ground lighting products, traffic control and signalling systems, commercial lighting fixtures, such as those used to illuminate sports stadiums, and distribution equipment. The Arrow-Hart name can be found on three basic categories of electrical equipment. More than 1,800 different Arrow-Hart wiring devices are used in various areas of construction, maintenance and original equipment manufacturing. Arrow-Hart industrial controls, such as push buttons and motor starts, are for use on computers, machine tools, heating and refrigeration equipment, and all types of packaging and processing machinery. Arrow-Hart specialty switches are sold to manufacturers of appliances, power tools, business machines, instruments, computers, and welders. Belden is the premier name in electrical and electronic wire, cable, and cord products. Belden electronic products find primary application in the computer and instrumentation manufacturing markets. Belden multi-conductor cable is the leading brand used to transmit low power, low voltage, high integrity signals in data control, signal and communications circuits. Belden coaxial cable is used in radio frequency transmission for the military. Belden flat cable and connectors are aimed at fast growth markets such as computers, instrumentation, and interconnect wiring. Belden is also the name on many more specialized electronic products such as flourocarbon cables, molded cable assemblies, fiber optic cable, and geophysical cable. Many cable television companies transmit their pictures through Belden cable. The Belden name also is found on a wide range of electrical wire and cable products. Belden ignition wire sets and battery cables are sold to the automotive aftermarket. Many Belden cords are incorporated in the products of consumer and personal care appliance manufacturers, as well as industrial and home power tools. Finally, Cooper serves the electrical and electronic markets under such trademarks as Advanced Controls, Hollis, and Gardner-Denver. Advanced Controls drilling machines are used for precision hole drilling in printed circuit boards. Hollis wave soldering and cleaning machines also are used extensively for printed circuit boards. Gardner-Denver Wire-Wrap machines and specialty tools help produce solderless electrical connections.

The Tools & Hardware segment includes eight well-known hand tool brand names, many with century-old reputations for premium quality, providing a comprehensive range of products for the professional, industrial, electronic, hobby, and do-it-yourself markets throughout the world. Cooper is the leading worldwide manufacturer of quality hand tools, the leader in the drapery hardware business, and a principal producer of industrial power tools. Crescent provides professionals, tradesmen, and homeowners with the finest in adjustable wrenches, pliers, screwdrivers, nail pullers, and awls. Our Lufkin pocket and special purpose tapes are joined by a host of other products matched to the needs of the architect, surveyor, home craftsman, and carpenter. The Nicholson product line includes files, rasps, circular saw blades, bandsaw blades, and handsaws. Weller is the world's leading supplier of professional quality soldering equipment, including the famous Weller temperature-controlled irons and soldering guns. Wiss scissors and shears are extremely popular in the garment and dressmaking field and are found in household sewing baskets everywhere. Our Boker Tree Brand knives include utility, sporting, and hunting knives, plus commemorative knives for a fast-growing collectors' market. The Xcelite name is known throughout the electronics industry for a comprehensive range of screwdrivers of various sizes and types, nutdrivers, convertible nutdriver/screwdriver sets, interchangeable blade drivers, service tools and kits, pliers and cutters, shears, snips, wire strippers, and wrenches. Finally, the list of hand tool brand names includes an extensive line of Plumb striking tools such as standard and specialty hammers, sledges, wedges, axes, and hatchets. Cooper Industries is also the manufacturer of the Kirsch line of drapery hardware and other window covering products. Kirsch is the premier brand name in the field and virtually the only name in drapery hardware recognized by consumers. More than 2,000 Kirsch items are manufactured for consumer and commercial use. Our industrial power tools and related accessories are used throughout industry in the manufacturing and assembly processes. In the United States and the rest of the Western Hemisphere, Dotco and Gardner-Denver pneumatic tools find primary application in the ground transportation and airframe manufacturing industries. In Western Europe, Deutsche Gardner-Denver pneumatic tools and automated assembly machinery are sold chiefly to the automotive industry. Cooper's line of Apex screwdriver bits and socket wrenches are used on assembly lines, particularly in power tool applications. Apex universal joints are the only ones "qualified" for use on military and commercial aircraft.

36

Sesquicentennial

In observing a 150th anniversary, it is difficult to avoid the temptation to contrive an historic benchmark as if it were a natural culmination of past events and the beginning of a specific new era. But Dr. Frederick D. Kershner, Jr., professor of American social and intellectual history at Columbia University before his retirement in 1982, defined history as "everything behind the moving hands of your clock," emphasizing that no one can really think fast enough to record the present as separate from the past.

Certainly Cooper Industries would not break its momentum in 1983, pausing to reflect on the past before accelerating into a bright new future. Yet, the sesquicentennial offered legitimate reason for comparisons — and for sponsoring a Public Broadcasting Service television documentary in which Richard Reeves toured America, asking questions about democracy that had been posed by the French nobleman Alexis de Tocqueville a century and a half earlier. The company also retained historian Kershner to select and comment on important Tocqueville observations for a book distributed in the sesquicentennial year. The book, *Tocqueville's America: The Great Quotations,* was published, along with this history, by The Ohio University Press.

Cooper was one of a handful of American companies able to trace unbroken lineage 150 years to a founder whose name it continued to bear. As with the Tocqueville television program, it was interesting to compare philosophies and events separated by such a long period of time, as a means of accessing certain basic values.

Charles Cooper, for instance, was a community leader who strongly supported programs he personally considered worthwhile. One hundred and fifty years later, the company he founded was equally concerned with what by then had become known as "corporate citizenship." With many thousands of employees and owners, however, "worthwhile" community projects could hardly be determined by a single corporate conscience. Consequently, the company had adopted a policy of reflecting individual consciences by committing most of its monetary support of nonprofit health, educational, welfare, and cultural organizations to communities where its people lived and worked. Recommendations came from staffs at its manufacturing and service facilities in response to requests received locally. To extend the philosophy of responding individually, a long-time program of matching employee gifts to colleges was expanded to include nearly all charitable organizations including health, youth, educational, cultural, arts, civic, and social groups. Moreover, volunteerism was encouraged by doubling any matching gift if the contributing employee was involved in a leadership role with the recipient organization.

Contributions in various forms could be identified throughout the company's history, of course. But greatest impetus had been evident since the establishment of the Cooper Industries Foundation in 1964. Like many other companies, Cooper had a formal procedure for studying requests for Foundation funding, and money not designated for local support — about 10 percent of the total — went into programs cutting across community, state, and regional boundaries.

"To be innovative with that small portion of the total Foundation budget, we do attempt to lead, rather than react," explained Public Affairs Vice President Campbell. "Underwriting the Tocqueville television program is an example. Here is an opportunity for us to help Americans reexamine democratic principles and how they evolved over the same period of time that our corporation has been in existence. Another example is our sponsoring a Texas Opera Theatre tour through Midwestern states, with the group performing light opera in selected cities where Cooper has plants. We also support a Lyric Theatre, Childrens Festival Theatre, the Syracuse Symphony, and others. But we are not trying to build an identity as a patron of the arts. We're after a balance of social involvement."

That balance was typified by multiyear contributions to a Grove City Community Hospital building fund, a Kenyon College recreation complex, projects at Wittenberg, Case Western Reserve, Houston, St. Thomas, Syracuse, Texas A & M, and Ohio Universities, the Dallas and Houston Museums of Fine Arts, a radio series called "Cooper Kaleidoscope," drug abuse treatment, YMCA expansion at Raleigh, and an emergency flood relief program at Port Hope, Canada. Company contributions to United Way groups totalled $446,288 in 1981, in addition to money given by individual employees. A formula based on goals, populations, and number of Cooper employees in each area assured continued feasible levels of United Way participation.

But the company viewed its primary contribution to communities as promoting the welfare of employees through safe and healthy working conditions, reasonable health, disability, pension benefits, and such voluntary programs as a stock purchase plan in which nearly half of its employees were enrolled by the beginning of the anniversary year. It also felt an obligation to bear its fair share of efforts to improve communities. "We are leaders in some communities by virtue of being the largest employer with the most resources," Campbell said. "Where we are not in that leadership position, we at least make certain we are not laggards."

Good corporate citizenship was difficult to define, and sometimes even more difficult to maintain in the eyes of the citizenry. Like all companies, Cooper exists in the real world of political and social pressures, government regulations, and employee and community needs. "If we are to live up to our primary objectives of providing employment, products, and a return to shareholders, like all companies we sometimes have to make difficult decisions," Campbell said. "No one enjoys closing a plant, laying off people, or getting rid of waste by burying or burning it some place. But what are companies to do? These are decisions that have to be made. They are dictated by economic conditions, and the quality of those decisions depends on the leadership within the company — on the attitudes of its managers and their desire to do the right thing. We give that kind of leadership, but it isn't something we flaunt. We don't believe in 'merchandising' acts of corporate citizenship through advertising. It's self defeating to brag about the good things you do, because that just diminishes them in most persons' eyes."

Some things were almost certain to be misunderstood. One seeming paradox was the continued high level of charitable contributions in times of serious recession, with employees on layoff across the country. Yet, the Foundation was funded on a long-term basis that enabled it to honor charitable commitments, regardless of economic fluctuations. The pre-anniversary year of 1982 was one of those periods when substantial Foundation pledges were met while many employees were temporarily out of work. Reconciling what might seem to be conflicting decisions in the minds of those suffering layoffs was an impossible task. But the company could not simply renege on promises in order to avoid an awkward situation. Corporate citizenship sometimes could be painful.

Looking back always compacts history into a convenient summary of selected events, usually softening periods of sacrifice in favor of emphasizing the good times. But peering into the future is like gazing at the sky; time and distance are infinite. The only certainty is that all progress will not be what Milton described as "throned on highest bliss."

At age 150, Cooper was losing much of the informality typical of its earlier years. Not everyone was happy with changes brought about by the tremendous increase in size, not so much from fear of decreased opportunities (indeed, overwhelming evidence indicated a general increase) as from an incompatibility with bigness. President Cizik was well aware of the discomfort that often comes with growth. "As I look back, I wish there were things we could have retained, but I would be unrealistic to do more than just wish, because it cannot be," he said. "A company must be prepared to adapt to new circumstances. Cooper as a $3 billion corporation operates and acts in a much different way than it did as a $60 million corporation. And there seems to be something about this particular level that requires a major structural change such as we have experienced. Changes that took place from $60 million to $800 million extended over a relatively long period of time, and people adapted almost without realizing it. But the change from $800 million to $3 billion took place in two years. It was a quantum leap, and it struck employees with sudden force, which is much more noticeable. That can be a shock to some who prefer a smaller organization. Each person has to evaluate it personally, and I can understand why some opt to drop out along the way. On the other hand, most have adjusted very well, and Cooper today is geared for a growing, dynamic corporate life. We would be uncomfortable now in anything else — just like a racehorse who has been trained to run becomes unhappy when put out to pasture."

If there was a single historic thread running through all companies that had come together as Cooper Industries, it was a periodic lapse into what Cizik termed "caretaker management," when leaders felt they had reached a level that could be maintained and enjoyed in comfort and relative prosperity. But success outside the mainstream of American commerce was not to be. Survival came from revived leadership — reminiscent of the spirit to build and grow that had motivated the Coopers, Crouse, Hinds, Gardner, Kirsch, Fithian, Nicholson, Wiss, Martin, Decker, Belden, the Funks, and others who set the corporation's evolution into motion.

Bigness was not an absolute measure of success, but some form of advancement seemed necessary. Like human beings, organizations that stopped growing altogether soon deteriorated. When complacency set in, as it often did, an unusual event or change in management was usually necessary to motivate a company's regeneration. Inertia worked both ways — when a company was on a seemingly comfortable plateau, or when it was racing toward a new height. So Cooper eventually had chosen to keep its momentum in a building pattern, diversifying to compensate for economic cycles that could be expected to occur in the future, just as they had in the past.

Its objective was to continue the kind of year-to-year financial growth that led to its seventh-place ranking on a list of twenty stocks, reported in the May 3, 1982 issue of *Fortune* as "the purest gold to investors over the past decade." The "gold," wrote author Gwen Kinkead, "is best weighed by a stock's total return, which measures both a share's appreciation in price and its dividends — in this case from the end of 1971 to the end of 1981." Cooper's average annual return in that period was 27.8 percent, compared with 8.5 percent for the total Fortune 500.

In looking beyond 1983, Cooper planned its strategy along lines of assessing critical economic, political, and industrial issues that could determine its directions. "This doesn't mean we depend on guessing what the future will hold," explained Planning and Development Senior Vice President Dyer. "We can't assume with any degree of precision what really is going to happen, but we can determine our range of possibilities in reacting to such variables as housing starts, disposable income, interest rates, and energy consumption. You look at alternatives and plan accordingly. It could be that an alternative with a low probability will come into being, or it might even be something no one anticipates at all. In either case, the whole management organization has gone through a process that improves abilities to appraise trends and make good judgments in all our major areas of operations. And if you are accustomed to doing that kind of thing, you adjust more quickly than others."

Thus, flexibility and adaptability were at the base of Cooper's corporate philosophy, as it built an organization that could gain, rather than suffer from changing conditions. "It would be ridiculous for me to say this is the company that is going to exist twenty years from now," Cizik said. "Our ability to adapt to changing economic environments offers a chance to perform better than other companies. If it were not for change, the same companies would always dominate their fields, and that has not happened in this country. Adapting to changes is what got Cooper into a position of leadership, so if history says anything to us it is that we dare not rest on our oars now that we have reached this level."

History has shown also that over long periods of time, the simple law of supply and demand overrides all complexities of government and industrial manipulation: with strong demand, production goes up; when the demand diminishes, production goes down.

In 1983, there remained those who would stake their futures on attempts to control that economic cycle. Cooper Industries elected to maintain a competitive edge by being prepared for its uncertainties.

Appendices

Cooper Industries
Chief Executive
Officers

with terms

1833-1895
Charles Cooper

1895-1912
Frank L. Fairchild

1912-1919
Charles Gray "C.G." Cooper

1919-1920
Desault B. Kirk

1920-1940
Beatty B. Williams
(also 1941-1943)

1940-1941
Charles B. Jahnke

1943-1955
Gordon Lefebvre

1955-1957
Lawrence Williams

1957-1975
Eugene L. Miller

1975-
Robert Cizik

353

Cooper Directors Since 1895 Incorporation

1895–1901	Charles Cooper, Chairman
1895–1923	Charles Gray Cooper, President
1895–1912	Frank L. Fairchild, President
1895–1920	Desault B. Kirk, President
1895–1900	A. Lincoln White
1900–1916	E. Henry Fairchild, Treasurer
1901–1906	C.M. Stamp, Superintendent
1906–1959	Beatty B. Williams, President, Chairman
1912–1958	Zenno E. Taylor, Secretary
1917–1932	Fred H. Thomas, Vice President
1919–1930	Norman L. Daney, Treasurer and Comptroller
1919–1934	Gordon S. Rentschler
1927–1956	Hewitt A. Gehres, Vice President
1929–1945	E.J. Fithian, Chairman
1929–1962	H.C. Pollock, Vice President and Assistant Secretary
1929–1930	John Speed Elliott
1931–1942	J.H. Anderson, Vice President
1932–1934	J.G. Scarff
1934–1960	F.C. Van Cleef, Van Cleef, Jordan & Wood, New York City
1935–1945	W.A. Ackermann
1935–1941	J.E. Galvin
1939–1941	C.B. Jahnke, President
1939–1945	W.C. Heath
1941–1971	Lawrence F. Williams, President, Cooper Industries
1942–1955	Gordon Lefebvre, President, Cooper Industries
1944–1964	L.L. Warriner, The Master Electric Company, Dayton

1945–1967	Charles G. Cooper, Vice President, Cooper Industries
1946–1956	C.G. Conley, Mt. Vernon Bridge Company
1946–1965	Paul A. Frank, National Rubber Machinery Company
1946–1965	Stanley E. Johnson, Sr., Vice President, Cooper Industries
1950–1965	Ralph L. Boyer, Vice President, Cooper Industries
1950–1959	W.E. Stevenson, President, Oberlin College
1956–1961	P.J. Bickel, Squire, Sanders & Dempsey, Attorneys, Cleveland
1956–1975	Edward P. Riley, Thompson Products, Cleveland
1956–	Eugene L. Miller, Chairman of the Board and Retired Chief Executive Officer, Cooper Industries
1958–1980	Leonor F. Loree II, Chase Manhattan Bank, New York City
1959–1961	H.P. Bailey, The Rotor Tool Company
1959–1967	R. Edwin Moore, Bell & Gossett Company, `Morton Grove, Illinois
1960–1966	Leslie R. Groves, Lt. General, U.S. Army (Ret.)
1961–1966	Walter K. Bailey, Warner & Swasey Company, Cleveland
1961–1965	Arthur E. Palmer, Jr., White, Weld & Company, New York City
1962–1965	Sheldon V. Clarke, Union Carbide Corporation, New York City
1964–1968	William J. Nuelle, Petrolite Corporation
1965–1971	Stanley E. Johnson, Jr., Vice President, Cooper Industries
1965–1978	Robert B. Gilmore, DeGolyer & MacNaughton
1965–1970	Thomas E. Kraner, President, Cooper Industries
1966–1972	James C. Hodge, Warner & Swasey Company, Cleveland
1968–1978	William G. Rector, Senior Vice President, Cooper Industries
1970–1976	Henry I. McGee, Jr., Chairman, Cooper Airmotive
1971–	*Robert Cizik, President and Chief Executive Officer, Cooper Industries
1971–	C. Roland Christensen, Professor, Harvard Graduate School of Business Administration

1972–1981	Robert D. McEvers, Trans Union Corporation
1975–	John D. Ong, Chairman and President, B.F. Goodrich Company
1976–1982	Joe H. Foy, Senior Partner, Bracewell & Patterson, Attorneys at Law, Houston
1978–1981	Nelson R. Henry, business consultant
1978–	John G. McElwee, Chairman of the Board and Chief Executive Officer, John Hancock Mutual Life Insurance Company
1979–1980	Harker Collins, Harker Collins & Company
1979–1983	Stanley E.G. Hillman, former trustee, Chicago, Milwaukee, St. Paul & Pacific Railroad and Retired President and Chief Operating Officer, I.C. Industries
1979–1980	Lynn L. Leigh, former president, Gardner-Denver Company
1979–1980	L. Chester May, Chicago Bank of Commerce
1979–1980	Peter G. Scotese, Spring Mills, Inc.
1980–	John P. Diescl, President, Tenneco, Inc.
1981–	Alan E. Riedel, Senior Vice President, Administration, Cooper Industries
1981–1983	Chris J. Witting, Vice Chairman of the Board, Cooper Industries
1981–	Robert W. Baldwin, Retired President, Gulf Refining and Marketing Company, a division of Gulf Oil Corporation

*Robert Cizik was elected Chairman of the Board in April 1983, following Eugene L. Miller's announcement of his retirement as Chairman at the annual shareholders' meeting. Mr. Cizik continues as President and Chief Executive Officer.

COOPER INDUSTRIES 1833–1983

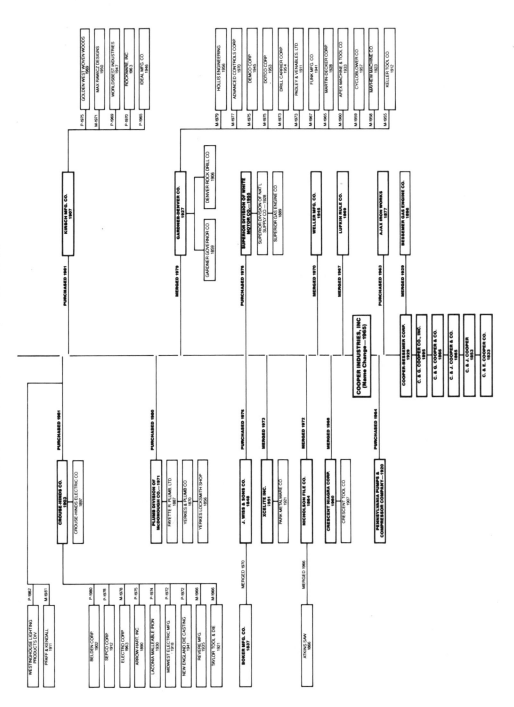

Documentation

In compiling information for an indepth history, one quickly becomes appreciative of those persons who have thought to date their material. An amazing number of documents, including catalogs, news releases, brochures, personal notes, company memoranda, and letters, contain enlightening observations, but no date. Others, particularly newspaper articles, have frequent errors, but fortunately are dated when the entire page is left intact. By cross checking these and many other sources, the researcher is able not only to piece together the true story, but also to discover how errors have been made in the past. That is part of the excitement of writing a history.

Annual reports, minutes of board meetings, and quarterly statements offered precise statistics and dates that formed the most reliable foundation for assimilating other information into a proper framework. Courthouse records, county histories, documents preserved by museums and historical societies, magazine advertisements, and company files proved invaluable in recording the early years of companies now included in Cooper Industries. Happily, many retired employees, widows, and descendants of the company leaders kept documents that provided some newly discovered facts, and substantiated others. A few of the founders and other key executives had written personal memoirs.

Dozens of persons throughout the country provided the kind of honest, often profound interviews that enabled this history to extend well beyond a recitation of data. Some men like Hewitt Gehres, who celebrated his 100th birthday in the company's sesquicentennial year, had amazing recall of names and events dating back to the early part of the century. They also could refer to newspaper stories or documents that subsequently could be located to confirm dates and details of their recollections.

Nearly all information in the Cooper history has been cross checked through two or more sources to make it as accurate as possible. Another book would be required to provide a chapter-by-chapter account of these sources. Since many are either cited in the text, or made obvious by the nature of their content, this listing refers only to statements that might require more specific documentation. Except for a few instances, it does not name persons interviewed, but many of them are listed in the Acknowledgments at the front of this book.

CHAPTER 1

America's nineteenth-century westward movement is described in the *Encyclopedia of American History,* published by Harper & Row to coincide with the nation's bicentennial in 1976. Early days of Mt. Vernon, Ohio, are recorded in *Hill's History of Knox County* and in Knox County Courthouse records. Quotations from Charles Cooper are from his memoirs. Other information on the family is recorded in letters kept by Charles G. Cooper, the late grandson of Elias Cooper. Early products are described in copies of newspaper advertisements, the first of which appeared in 1835, and in a booklet, *75 Years of Engine Building,* published in 1908. American industrialization was gleaned from the following books: *Industrialization and Economic History,* by Jonathan Hughes; *Industrial History of the United States,* by Albert S. Bolles; *The Age of Enterprise,* by Thomas Cochran and William Miller; *The Drive to Industrial Maturity,* by Harold G. Vatter; and *Essays in American Economic History,* edited by A.W. Coats and Ross M. Robertson. Alexis de Tocqueville's observations were recorded in his *De la Democratie en Amerique,* and in *American Journey,* by Richard Reeves.

CHAPTER 2

Charles Cooper's political and community involvement is recorded in *Hill's History of Knox County,* in *Past and Present of Knox County,* and in file materials of the Knox County Historical Society. Family information in documents of the late grandson of Elias Cooper includes the "Squirrel Hunter's Discharge" of Charles Gray Cooper. Corliss engine data is found in the Thomas Newcomen Library, operated by The Newcomen Society of North America, in Chester County, Pennsylvania, and a book, *Milestones in the Mighty Age of Steam.* Specifics on sales of blowing engines are in a company mimeographed publication of 1966. Traction engine information came from a booklet, *95 Years of Engine Building,* published in 1928, from early advertisements, and from personal historical records compiled by Ralph Boyer.

CHAPTER 3

Personal information about the founder was provided by letters and interviews with Charles Cooper, grandson of Elias Cooper. Specifics of company reorganization came from a copy of the incorporation papers. The profile of Frank Fairchild was drawn from interviews with his grandson, Lawrence Williams, letters from Fairchild to Cooper, and company sales reports. Entry into the gas engine business was recorded in a company booklet, *100 Years of Power,* and in newspaper clippings, with additional information obtained in an interview with Hewitt Gehres, who joined the company in 1910. Specifics on the American economy in World War I were found in the *Encyclopedia of American History,* while Cooper's involvement in the war was recorded in a company booklet, *Our Bit.* Some details of the first subsidiary were also contained in *Our Bit,* and others were obtained from Charles Cooper, who was a subsidiary engineer who compiled documents of its operations. Postwar facts were taken from the booklet, *Gas Engines, 1920,* published by the company, and from a brief history of steam power compiled by Boyer in 1957.

CHAPTER 4

Early days of the Bessemer Gas Engine Company are well chronicled in newspaper articles, personal letters, company employee publications, and in the founder's detailed memoirs kept by his son, Edwin Fithian. Interviews with his two sons-in-law, both of whom were company vice presidents, and several other retired employees were supplemented by their personal records, letters, and newspaper clippings. Information on products was taken from the following booklets: *Bessemer Gas Engine Company, Bessemer Gas Engines, Cylinders & Roller Pumping Powers, Bessemer Two Cylinders, The Bessemer Oil Engines, A Manual of Instructions, Bessemer Marine Diesel Engines, Bessemer Power Equipment for the Oil Industry and for Industrial Power Users, The Bessemer Manual of Gasoline Recovery, Bessemer Stationary Diesel Engines, The Carruthers-Fithian Clutch,* and *A Cracker Jack.* Information about the company's first gas cylinder and friction clutch was contained in Dr. Fithian's letter in answer to a customer's query, undated, but presumed to be in the early 1900s, and in the first known Carruthers-Fithian Clutch Company catalog. Dr. Fithian's career was traced in a Grove City newspaper story appearing on his eighty-fifth birthday, July 2, 1948. The history of natural gas development is contained in a manual of gasoline recovery by the compression method.

CHAPTER 5

A copy of the original Cooper-Bessemer merger agreement was made available by Edwin Fithian. Other merger information came from a certification of change of name, dated April 4, 1929, an undated newspaper account of the first Cooper-Bessemer meeting, an explanation by B.B. Williams in the *C-B News*, a May 2, 1929, letter from Vice President Thomas to customers, and a later report to directors entitled "Principles of the C-B Acquisition Program." Information on yachts powered by Bessemer diesel engines came from two booklets: *Cruising on the Seven Seas*, a series of photos and technical explanations on yachts; and *Seven Ships and Their Power Story*, a description of various kinds of vessels equipped with C-B engines. Other product information was summarized in a centennial booklet, *100 Years of Power*, published in 1933. Involvement in the production of diesel engines for locomotives was explained in interviews and excerpts from the *C-B News* and the *C-B Manifold*. Employee publications provided good sources of information about the World War II production years, and supplemented interviews. A history of the company during that time was compiled by an employee in 1950.

CHAPTER 6

Much of the post-World War II reconversion was described in newspaper interviews with B.B. Williams and in his reports to the Board of Directors. The introduction of new engines was described in a study of events and dates compiled in 1966, in a company publication, *Some Engineering Decisions*, produced in 1965, and in an article, "Generating more power from less fuel, in the April 25, 1953, issue of *Business Week*. Economic problems of the time were presented in a joint report by the U.S. Department of Economics and the Research Department of the McGraw-Hill Publishing Company. Industry information was also gleaned from several issues of *The Oil & Gas Journal*, and from *Business Week*, March 13, 1948. The details and ramifications of the Phillips Petroleum Case, as well as other controversies concerning price controls in the mid-1950s, came from a book, *The Regulation of Natural Gas*, by James W. McKie; from *Business Week*, August 21 and December 18, 1954; from *The Oil and Gas Journal*, February 13 and February 27, 1956; and from an interview with W. Timothy Dowd, executive director of the Interstate Oil Compact Commission, Oklahoma City.

CHAPTER 7

Information on Paul Harvey appeared in *Who's Who in the World*, and information on Patti Page and Tony Randall was from *Who's Who in Show Business*. Negotiations between Dresser Industries and Gardner-Denver were described by *Initiative in Energy,* by Darwin Payne. Rotor Tool information was compiled primarily from interviews, with some supplemental data from a November 1971 employee magazine, a March 1968 article in *Rotor Blade,* an undated newspaper article telling of management changes, and a July 14, 1961, *Cleveland Press* article, "Rotor Tool Thrives in Merger." Growing international plans were outlined in an April 28, 1959, issue of the *Mt. Vernon News,* reporting a talk by Charles Cooper to the Kiwanis Club. The company's ten-year objectives were specified in board minutes.

CHAPTER 8

President Kennedy's statement was taken from congressional records covering his first address to Congress after his inauguration. Some reasons for the "rash" of takeovers were discussed at length in *Business Week,* February 18, February 25, and March 11, 1961. A review of the Common Market and European Free Trade Association in the early 1960s was contained in a book, *The Common Market,* written by Stephen Holt and published in Great Britain.

CHAPTER 9

Early oil exploration was documented in the *Encyclopedia of American History* and *Energy in the U.S.* The settlement of Corry and the founding of Harmon, Gibbs and Company was described in newspaper clippings kept by the Bliss family; in several company publications (among them *Ajax Success Story,* printed on the company's 75th anniversary, and *Ajax Since 1877,* printed in 1948); and in the official centennial program of Corry, Pennsylvania, in 1961. Much of Ajax's early history, following the company's incorporation as the Ajax Iron Works in 1892, was preserved in documents and newspaper clippings kept by the Bliss and Castor families. This proved to be fortunate, because the Corry newspaper's "morgue" had been destroyed in a flood. Confirmation of some dates required a search of tombstones in the city's cemetery. The company-wide celebration of a patent victory was described in the employee publication, *Flywheel,* November 14, 1947. Product development in the 1920s was described in the November 28, 1947, *Flywheel* and in an undated magazine, *The Erie Story.* Later product information came from a variety of company publications and from a 1958 article, "Steam Engine Power," which appeared in a magazine of the plywood industry. Products for the World War II effort were described in an undated company publication, *Ajax Marine Compound Uniflow Steam Engine.* A February 24, 1950, *Flywheel* article explained the purchase of Superior engine rights and the decision to emphasize gas-oriented products.

CHAPTER 10

Gas utilization by international oil companies was researched through all 1964–65 issues of *The Oil and Gas Journal*. Management's long interest in the Pennsylvania Pump and Compressor Company was explained in a special report to the board by Ralph Boyer. Information on the International Division reorganization was found in board minutes and the 1964 annual report of Cooper-Bessemer.

CHAPTER 11

The formation of Pennsylvania Pump and Compressor Company was described in organizational meeting minutes, dated April 19, 1920. Early history came from an article, "A Visit to Easton," which appeared in the Cooper Energy Division's publication, *Manifold,* from a brief history compiled by the company in 1974, and from a 1976 special publication, *Power/Compressor.* The details of post-Depression years and of later sales comparisons were derived from a Cooper-Bessemer board document, "Proposed Acquisition No. 202," dated June 4, 1964. Interviews, newspaper articles, and records maintained at Easton provided most of the information about the company during the decade prior to its acquisition by Cooper.

CHAPTER 12

An address by President Miller to the New York Society of Security Analysts on February 11, 1966, gave reasons for changing the corporate name to Cooper Industries, Inc. News releases covered the plans and construction of facilities for offshore production operations, and an article in *Investor's Reader Magazine,* July 26, 1967, described CB/Southern expansion. Other reports of CB/Southern activities appeared in *World Oil,* May 1967; *Gas Industries,* May 1967; *Offshore,* April 1967; and *Gas Age,* April 1967. Discussion of company policies, operations, and projections, along with a recommendation of the company's stock, came from an August 7, 1967, feature article in the *Wall Street Transcript.* Business Editor Sam Weiner's discussion of Cooper's plans for future acquisitions, and his prediction of a Lufkin merger appeared in the *Houston Post* on June 2, 1967. Specific data on Lufkin operations prior to the merger came from that company's last annual report.

CHAPTER 13

Old catalogs dating back to 1885 offered a wealth of information on Lufkin products, and each contained historical company information pertinent to its time. Lufkin's early history was recorded in an undated brochure, in data compiled by the company in 1974, and in a brief sketch written by a company executive in the early part of the century. Details of the industry were outlined in the reprint of a 1916 magazine article, "Things Worth Knowing about Measuring Tapes," and in a booklet, *The Amazing Story of Measurement*. Post-World War II activities, acquisitions, and personal stories were related in great detail by former President Lewis Bernard, with supporting documentation he kept in the form of letters and newspaper clippings.

CHAPTER 14

The statement of corporate objectives and broad policy guidelines was sent by President Miller in memo form to company officers and division presidents. A January 2, 1968, news release announced Cooper's decision to abandon the proposed Waukesha merger, and other news releases described new sales and product developments. Specific examples of worldwide social unrest came from *The Americana Annual*, published by the Americana Corporation, and from *Business Week*, May 4, 1968.

CHAPTER 15

Founding of the Crescent Tool Company was traced in the company's fiftieth anniversary book, published in 1957, and in numerous earlier documents. The development of the adjustable wrench was explained in two early publications: *How to Use the Crescent Wrench and Other Tools* and *The Crescent Fact Book*. An excellent description of manufacturing was entitled, *Forgings, Machiner*. William A. Hauck, director of industrial relations, recalled employee situations in a professional magazine article, "The Pain of Labor Pains." Company policies were detailed in an employee handbook, *You and Crescent*. Interesting customer comments contained in letters kept by the company helped profile the do-it-yourself craze.

CHAPTER 16

The Coberra engine was described in news releases and employee publications. The Santa Barbara oil pollution incident was reported in *The Americana Annual* and *The Oil and Gas Journal*. Some of the specifics on Alaska's pipeline plans were taken from *The Sohioan* magazine, others from various periodicals. Mobile home statistics were listed in *The Encyclopedia of American History*.

CHAPTER 17

Because most key persons involved in Weller's history were alive at the time the book was written, nearly all information came from interviews and from material kept in their individual possessions. A brief history of the company, published in 1970, provided a good cross-check on dates and figures. In addition, Edwin Y. Thompson, an original Weller employee who became general manager of manufacturing, had put his reminiscences of the company on a tape made available to the writer.

CHAPTER 18

Cooper's rationale for moving into the aircraft service business, explained in interviews with officers, was also reported in the *Underwood, Neuhaus Report,* October 1, 1975. Statistics indicating the market growth potential of that business were taken from *The Encyclopedia of American History.* The founding of Dallas Airmotive was described in interviews with the persons involved, and also in two issues of *Cooper Aeroviews,* May 1976 and July 1976, and in *Skylights* magazine, December 1974. A Dallas Airmotive brochure gave complete data on overhauling engines, and another explained operational divisions and functions. Biographic sketches of key employees were available from company files. Financial information was detailed in an article, "Meet James Squires of Dallas Airmotive," appearing in the February 15, 1963, issue of *Finance Magazine.* Walter Heller's comparison of ecologists and economists appeared in *Energy, Economic Growth and the Environment,* published in 1971.

CHAPTER 19

Earnings' comparisons were taken from company annual reports. The government's wage and price freeze and long-range program of price controls were reported in *The Oil and Gas Journal,* May 17, June 28, August 16, November 15, and November 22, 1971. Steps taken for major changes in heavy machinery and equipment were reported in a news release, January 11, 1972. The evaluation of Nicholson File Company appeared in the seventh edition of *Case Problems in Finance,* edited by J. Keith Butters, William E. Fruhan, Jr., and Thomas R. Piper, and published in 1975 by Richard D. Irwin, Inc.

CHAPTER 20

The only known copy of a frequently quoted book, *A Treatise on Files,* published by William T. Nicholson in 1878, is owned by Mason Cocroft, who also provided numerous valuable letters and documents for use in compiling the early history of Nicholson File Company. The company's chartering appeared in a brief history published in 1972. Other information about the early years is contained in *Chain Saw Age,* May 1972, in a company booklet published in 1911, and a 1929 paper prepared by Edward Fitz, then company superintendent. Several specific episodes were presented in an early (undated) speech given by a company officer. A company book written in 1911 gave histories, descriptions, and uses of files manufactured up to that time. Catalogs through the years, beginning with the first published in 1878, contained historical data into the 1970s. Newspaper articles were also kept in family records, and made available by Paul C. Nicholson, Jr., for research on this book. Early history of E.C. Atkins and Company, later the Atkins Saw Division of Borg-Warner, was described in two issues of a booklet, *Saws and Saw Tools,* published by the company in 1888 and 1901. A 1928 speech by C.C. Pierre explained the development of hand saws. The acquisition by Borg-Warner was reported in the *Indianapolis Times,* August 19, 1952.

CHAPTER 21

"Cooper's Comeback," was reported in the December 20, 1972, issue of *Financial World.* The history of Southwest Airmotive was well chronicled in several company publications, including *A Proud History,* 1962; *Southwest Airmotive,* by Winston Castleberry (undated); *The Southwest Airmotive Story,* 1957; and in magazine articles appearing in *Rotor & Wing,* March/April 1973; and *Professional Pilot,* June 1972. The history of Executive Aircraft was traced in a 1970 article in *The Executive Flyer,* in an undated company publication, and in information sheets describing specific product developments. Material on the combined company was gleaned from brochures, interviews, news releases, and annual reports.

CHAPTER 22

Founding of Park Metalware Company is recorded in *History of Xcelite and Its Products,* printed in 1973. Major events of the company's history were compiled from catalogs, news accounts, letters, and other sources by Clarence Schwabel in the early 1970s. Product information was taken from catalogs. The *Dun & Bradstreet* report of 1940 provided financial information dating back to the company's beginning. Events of the Great Depression appeared in a special 1939 *President's Report* by F.B. Farrington. Coining of the name "nutdriver" and the introduction of that tool to the radio and electronics assembly and repair markets was described in a newspaper article dated May 28, 1972.

CHAPTER 23

The world energy crisis of 1973 was reviewed in the 1974 edition of *The Americana,* in a special report, "The Energy Squeeze," by Frederic Golden, science editor of *Time* magazine, and in *The Oil and Gas Journal* columns by London correspondent Frank Gardner. Comments by William O. Doub, commissioner of the U.S. Atomic Energy Commission, appeared in *Energy: Today's Choices, Tomorrow's Opportunities,* a report of the General Assembly of the World Future Society, published in 1973. The *Mt. Vernon News* story about Sam Trott appeared October 2, 1973. The settlement of the Alaskan pipeline dispute was reported in the October 1974 issue of *Smithsonian* magazine. An indepth study of Cooper's highly automated hand tools plant at Sumter, South Carolina, appeared in the January 28 issue of *American Metal Market* magazine. The *Barron's* report on Cooper business was printed in the December 9, 1974, issue. Historic highlights of Standard Aircraft Equipment Company were gathered from an interview with founder Louis J. Bollo and from materials in his private files. Discontinuance of CB/Southern operations was reported in the *Underwood, Neuhaus Report,* of October 1, 1975.

CHAPTER 24

Characterization of Jacob Wiss and the company he founded was drawn from the pages of several publications. Among company-published booklets were *Wiss: The Edge of Excellence since 1848; A Story of Shears and Scissors, 1848–1948;* and *The Wiss Story of Shears & Scissors.* Historical data also was contained in the articles: "Wiss Has the Edge," in a 1965 publication of the New Jersey Bell Company; "The Evolution of Shear Perfection," in *Oakite* magazine, 1962; and "The Kindest Cut of All," in a 1960 Esso magazine. A profile of personalities was printed in a brief Wiss family history. Products were described in illustrated price lists and catalogs, which also contained occasional period excerpts on company history. The company had a wealth of documents, letters, memoranda, and newspaper clippings in archives compiled in 1967 and maintained in a large safe. Basic Boker Manufacturing Company information was contained in two volumes, *Great American Story I: Boker Tree Brand Knives,* and *Great American Story II, Boker Tree Brand Knives,* published for general distribution promoting a series of products, and in a scrapbook of newspaper clippings.

CHAPTER 25

The *Gas Turbine International* magazine editorial on contracts with Russia appeared in the August 1976 issue. Coberrow contract information was in a company news release of December 9, 1976. Use of Lufkin tapes in Olympics competition was reported in the July 1976 issue of *Premium Incentive Business* magazine. President Cizik's remarks to shareholders, "The Need to Free Free Enterprise," formed the basis for an article in the October 1977 issue of *Finance* magazine. White Motor Company problems and Cooper's offer to purchase its Superior Division were covered in a June 4, 1976, *Cleveland Plain Dealer* article.

CHAPTER 26

Accounts of Patrick Shouvlin's machine shop and its growth into the Superior Gas Engine Company are chronicled in a history compiled by the White Superior Division in 1955, a booklet prepared for a company "open house" in 1972, and a 1966 booklet, *Superior Division as a Good Neighbor,* as well as newspaper clippings and several undated interoffice communiques. Information on founder Shouvlin was contained in the "History of Springfield and Clark County," published in 1922. A collection of magazine advertisements supplemented early catalogs in detailing products and operations. Packets of newspaper clippings had also been preserved as records of events by decades, covering a period from 1940 well into the 1970s. National Supply Company and its purchase of Superior were described in an undated booklet, *The Story of the National Supply Co.,* and in a mimeographed history compiled soon after the acquisition in 1928. A series of advertisements described Superior product uses in generation plants, Titan II silos, other defense systems, and early offshore drilling. White Motor Company's acquisition of Superior was reported in company press releases, in a 1956 report by economic consultants, and later in an article, "The White Story," in the winter of 1962–63 issue of *Dana Digest.* Events immediately following the acquisition were described in a 1957 issue of *Coal Age.* A 1966 *Dun's Review* report, "The Hard Drive of White Motor," provided relevant financial and product information, as did a 1967 review by Paine, Webber, Jackson & Curtis.

CHAPTER 27

President Cizik's presentation of Cooper's business philosophy was made to the Association for Corporate Growth at a September 20, 1977, meeting in Houston. Changes in government regulatory agencies were examined in *The Americana* review of energy policies during 1977, and in an October 9, 1978, *Time* magazine summary of events. Cooper's increased European activities were covered in great detail by a May 1977 *Diesel & Gas Turbine Progress Worldwide* article, written by John Moon. More supporting material on foreign markets was summarized in an article on energy that appeared in the August 1, 1977, issue of *Newsweek,* and in a speech by Senior Vice President Riedel to a group in Canada. A report on Cooper's Coberra turbine-compressors was written by Keith Fanshier in *Oil Daily,* after he attended a press conference in Mt. Vernon. The unit also was featured in a July 1977 issue of *Diesel & Gas Turbine Progress Worldwide.* President Cizik's "Silver Winner" award was announced in the March 15, 1978, *Financial World.* Cooper and Gardner-Denver negotiations were covered thoroughly in the financial press, with a particularly detailed analysis of both companies and the merger reported by James Flanigan in the July 9, 1979, issue of *Forbes.*

CHAPTER 28

Background on Robert W. Gardner was contained in several company publications and a vignette that appeared in the May 12, 1900, issue of *The Quincy Daily Herald.* The company's early history also was reviewed frequently in company publications, in an 1888 issue of *The Quincy Daily Herald,* and in an indepth article in the December 29, 1935, *Quincy Herald-Whig.* A description of the first Gardner governor was contained in an old undated document entitled "The Drama of the Steam Governor." A wide variety of specific information covering the first one hundred years of the company's history was gathered for a centennial news packet and motion picture in 1959. Excellent statements on products and policies were presented in a 1959 address by President Gifford Leece, when the company was honored by The Newcomen Society in North America at New York City. Denver Rock Drill Company early history was best described by the founder, William Leonard, who wrote company memoirs in 1919 and updated them in 1959; in an early company booklet, *Waugh Products for Contracting, Quarrying, Mining and Other Industries;* and in a collection of lengthy obituaries kept by Leonard's family. The period of growth beginning with the 1950s was described by President Leece in the transcript of a recorded interview prepared in 1972, and in the cover story of *Finance* magazine, November 15, 1960. Journalists' commentaries on company policies, finances, and acquisitions were found in *Business Week,* September 5, 1959; *Financial World,* July 23, 1969, and March 6, 1974; *Barrons,* March 9, 1970, and January 15, 1979; and *Forbes,* February 15, 1973. Files of the employee publication, *Gardner-Denver News,* provided excellent checks on dates of events and product development. Material on Martin-Decker was voluminous, and included a straightforward history written by one of the founders, Elmer Decker, in 1972. A wealth of material was also available on the Keller Tool Company, the most helpful being a financial history prepared in 1951 by Standard Research Consultants, Inc., of New York City. Complete details of the Funk airplanes and their organization were reported in a column, "Plane Portraits by Pauley," in the August 1972 issue of *The Great Lakes Flyer.* Other material on companies acquired by Gardner-Denver was gleaned from interviews, annual reports, company publications, and newspaper articles. Several boxes full of unsorted materials had been collected by Gardner-Denver in a 1972 company-wide effort to gather historical data.

CHAPTER 29

Although nearly all information on structural changes following the Gardner-Denver acquisition came from interviews with corporate officers, some was contained in a speech by President Cizik to New York financial analysts on April 25, 1980. *The Americana* of 1981 provided a review of the nation's energy programs in 1980.

CHAPTER 30

Brief histories of Plumb were compiled by Frank P. Green in the early 1960s, and Fayette R. Plumb II, in 1981. I am particularly indebted to the latter, who submitted to lengthy telephone interviews, as well as making his history available. Supplemental material was obtained from catalogs, some of which contained historical information in addition to product descriptions.

CHAPTER 31

Controversial events surrounding the battle between Cooper and InterNorth received regular coverage in the nation's press. Most pertinent to this history were those in *Business Week,* September 29, 1980, January 19 and March 9, 1981; *Fortune,* February 9, 1981; *Syracuse Herald-Journal,* November 26 and November 27, 1980; *Wall Street Journal,* November 28 and December 10, 11, 18, 23, 24, 26, and 30, 1980, and January 12, 1981; *The Houston Chronicle,* November 27, 1980, and January 10, 1981; *The Houston Post,* December 12, 1980; *The New York Times,* December 23, 1980, and January 12, 1981; *Houston Business Journal,* January 5, 1981; *Syracuse Post-Standard,* December 12, 1980; and *The Oil Daily,* December 4, 1980. Information on countering federal court charges by Cooper and InterNorth was contained in public records of the U.S. District Court Southern District of New York, dated December 29, 1980. Cooper's offer for Crouse-Hinds stock was detailed in a December 23, 1980, prospectus. Statements on the merger outcome were taken from press announcements released by both Cooper and InterNorth.

CHAPTER 32

Research on Crouse-Hinds history was facilitated greatly by the fact that one of the founders, Huntington Crouse, was a prolific writer and speaker. Early company events were traced in his frequent writings, which appeared in various forms and were often excerpted for anniversary publications. The company's business philosophy was revealed in his regular contributions to an employee publication, *Family Talks.* Successive employee publications were helpful in determining the progression of important happenings. Dates concerning the founders' participation, some of which had been reported incorrectly in noncompany publications, were verified through the writings of Crouse and a booklet distributed to guests at a twentieth anniversary party February 1, 1917. Other helpful information was gathered into a large special fiftieth anniversary issue of the company publication, *Family Circle,* dated January 1947. The story of pioneer traffic signals appeared in a 1976 book, *They Built a City,* published by the Manlius Publishing Corporation. The acquisitions following the naming of Chris Witting to the presidency in 1965 were described in annual reports, press releases, and other documents gathered by Jane Klausman for a company library. The information on acquired companies was gathered separately from documents at the various plants. The effects of the Occupational Safety and Health Act on Crouse-Hinds business were reported in *Financial World,* January 9, 1974. The *Barron's* report on Arrow-Hart and its acquisition by Crouse-Hinds appeared on June 7, 1976, and again on January 2, 1978. *Barron's* also made an extensive report on Belden, August 7, 1978, which supplemented information from that company. Belden's role in the controversy involving Cooper, InterNorth, and Crouse-Hinds was included in many of the newspaper accounts listed with documentation for Chapter 31.

CHAPTER 33

The statement by Chris Witting and revenue information of Crouse-Hinds were taken from the company's final annual report of 1980, actually printed after the agreement to merge into Cooper Industries. Media references are to *Fortune,* February 9, 1981; and *Financial World,* August 1, 1979.

CHAPTER 34

Most of the early history of Kirsch was taken from two publications, *The Story of a Great Faith and Enterprise,* published in 1932, and the golden anniversary edition of *The Kirsch Courier,* published in 1957. Other issues of *The Kirsch Courier* (an employee publication) provided reports of events from the 1940s to 1981. Product information was reported regularly for many years in *Rods & Rings,* a quarterly publication for members of the company's sales force. *What the World Needs* had eight editions, the last printed in 1933. Copies of numerous advertisements and company-published books on window treatment were made available by the company's advertising department.

CHAPTER 35

The newspaper reaction to speculation on moving Plumb from Philadelphia appeared in the March 11, 1981, issue of *The Evening Bulletin.* The editorial on Cooper's announced move of Grand Haven air tools operations to South Carolina was in the December 17, 1981, *Grand Haven Tribune.* The sale of Cooper Airmotive was detailed in the company's second quarter report of 1981. Information on other changes was taken from company press releases with policy significance added through interviews. Thomas Campbell's letter to a shareholder was dated November 9, 1981. Purchase of Pfaff & Kendall, together with a brief history of that company, was reported in the January 10, 1982, Newark, New Jersey *Sunday Star Ledger.* Information on worldwide activities was excerpted from a detailed report prepared by Senior Vice President Cross and presented in installments to the board of directors over a period of several meetings.

CHAPTER 36

The quotation from Dr. Frederick Kershner was from an article in *The Rainbow,* Spring, 1982. Examples of community involvement were contained in speeches by President Cizik and Senior Vice President Riedel, and in company news releases.

INDEX

Numbers in bold face indicate photographs.